T0245545

PRAISE FOR *Whiteout*

"Hansen, Netherland, and Herzberg's *Whiteout* is a dramatic and much-needed challenge to our outdated ways of understanding addiction. They bravely place our drug policies in the context of the devastating and universal apartheid within which we all suffer. This book will change you and change us!"

—Mindy Thompson Fullilove, author of *Main Street: How a City's Heart Connects Us All*

"*Whiteout* is the most clear-eyed and comprehensive study of America's overdose crisis to date. The authors' electric scholarship reveals how Whiteness determines the boundaries of categories we often think of as being derived scientifically and rationally. When it comes to drugs, America seems to suffer from a peculiar sort of historical amnesia. *Whiteout* shows us what we forget, what we choose to remember, and what's kept hidden."

—Zachary Siegel, writer and drug policy journalist for *Harper's Magazine,* the *New York Times Magazine,* and the *New Republic*

Whiteout

Whiteout

How Racial Capitalism Changed the
Color of Opioids in America

Helena Hansen, Jules Netherland, and David Herzberg

UNIVERSITY OF CALIFORNIA PRESS

University of California Press
Oakland, California

© 2023 by Helena Hansen, Jules Netherland, and David
Herzberg

Library of Congress Cataloging-in-Publication Data

Names: Hansen, Helena, 1969– author. | Netherland,
Julie, author. | Herzberg, David L. (David Lowell),
author.
Title: Whiteout : how racial capitalism changed the color
of opioids in America / Helena Hansen, Jules
Netherland, and David Herzberg.
Description: Oakland, California : University of
California Press, [2023] | Includes bibliographical
references and index.
Identifiers: LCCN 2022029645| ISBN 9780520384057
(cloth) | ISBN 9780520384071 (epub)
Subjects: LCSH: Opioid abuse—United States. | White
people—Substance use—United States. | Racism—
Economic aspects—United States. | Capitalism—
United States. | Pharmaceutical industry—United
States.
Classification: LCC RC568.O45 H36 2023 |
DDC 362.29/30973 23/eng/20220—dc22
LC record available at https://lccn.loc.gov/2022029645

Manufactured in the United States of America

32 31 30 29 28 27 26 25 24 23
10 9 8 7 6 5 4 3 2 1

Contents

Illustrations

Acknowledgments

This book was over a decade in the making and is the product of many conversations, insights, and suggestions from scores of our colleagues working in the fields of social science and humanities of medicine, drug policy, drug policy research, and medical research.

We'd like to collectively thank Jen Carroll, whose investment of energy and deep insight helped to move this manuscript from drafts of chapters to a coherent book, and the anonymous reviewers of the book, whose incisive comments also accelerated this process. Most especially we thank Tamie Parker Song, our gifted developmental editor, who was such a sage and guide in the last year of our work on the manuscript. Richard Deverell came through for us with expert reference editing in the final hour, and Lauren Textor brought her multiple talents to bear in creating our glossary and time line.

DAVID HERZBERG

I feel enormous gratitude to Helena and Jules for welcoming me in to this project. Working with them has been an honor, a pleasure, and revelatory in so many ways. I thank the State University of New York at Buffalo College of Arts and Sciences for their support of the project. I am also grateful for insights and support from colleagues and friends, including especially Susan Cahn, Nancy Campbell, Nan Enstad, Erin Hatton, Rebecca McCullough, Mike Rembis, and Lucas Richert. As always, Don, Vickie, Jill, Ray, Erin, Rex, Leo, and Felix bring meaning and love where it's most needed, and I'm so, so glad for that.

JULES NETHERLAND

My deepest thanks to Helena and David for one of the richest collaborations of my career. The gratitude and admiration I feel for my colleagues at the Drug Policy Alliance cannot be overstated. Not only have they shared generously of their time and insight for this book, but they helped carry me when COVID and cancer treatment were almost too much to bear. Their commitment to acting as humanely and justly as possible while always deepening their analysis of race, often in impossible circumstances, inspires me daily. A special thanks to Kassandra Frederique, Sheila Vakharia, Aliza Cohen, Melissa Moore, Lindsay LaSalle, Ingrid Walker, David Glowka, Stephanie Polito, Dionna King, Grant Smith, Artie Malkin, Laura Thomas, Michael Collins, Ethan Nadelmann, Maria McFarland Sanchez Moreno, Alex Hatcher, Jeronimo Saldana, Alexis Posey, Anna Saini, VOCAL NY, gabriel sayegh, Jessica Schafroth, members of drug user unions across the country, and my beloved members of the Compassionate Care NY campaign. My gratitude also goes to Cris Beam, Lisa Kron, and Jessie Daniels for important conversations about writing, Whiteness, and white privilege. To my love squad—Tyson Smith Ray, Victoria Albina, Nancy Netherland, Laura McTighe—thank you for your unflagging support and kindness. I will always be indebted to Ruth Finkelstein and Janet Weinberg for their kind mentorship. And to Amy Moran, my big favorite, thank you for your wisdom, your shine, and your love.

HELENA HANSEN

My thanks also to my coauthors Jules Netherland and David Herzberg, who are incomparable in their intellectual and ethical rigor. My contributions to this book would not have been possible without an amazing constellation of mentors, colleagues, friends, and family. My research coordinator Sonia Mendoza absolutely made this project, along with other research associates and interns Caroline Parker, Allyssa Rivera, Alexandrea Hatcher, Parth Patel, Nichole Roxas, and Laura Duncan. Lucy Anderton has been on this journey with me since my freshman year of high school and most recently helped us to organize and to title this book. My research mentors Mindy Fullilove, Robert Fullilove,

Margarita Alegria, Rayna Rapp, Emily Martin, Rebecca Jordan-Young, Dorothy Roberts, Philippe Bourgois, Tony George, Linda-Anne Rebhun, Carole Siegel, Steve Shoptaw, Bruce Link, and Peter Bearman have provided essential insights and inspiration. My amazing clinical mentors also provided indispensable support for this book, including Annatina Miescher, Lena Friedman, Caren Bowers, Alana Garcia, Marc Galanter, Stephen Ross, Susan Whitley, and Soteri Polydouro. I want to thank the many participants in the studies that led up to this book, many of whom became close friends and provided ongoing help with understanding and interpreting what I found. They include Cisco Villar, Ruben Lopez, Camille, Jonathan, Bob, Janet, Richard, Joe, Mitch, Michael, Rose, and so many more. My family provided unwavering support and listened to hundreds of versions of presentations based on this book: Mark, Kirin, and Ananda Turner on a daily basis, and from afar Jackie Jackson, Bill Jackson, Hattie Marie Golette, Arne Bjerring Hansen, Kari Damhaug, Sara and Martin Damhaug, Ben Hansen, Anni Kirkland, Cyrus and Annika Hansen, Jon Lund Hansen and Anne Cecily, Joyce Dixon and Al Dixon II, as well as Albert Dixon III, Cassandra James, Robert Jackson, and Debbie Jackson.

Research funding from the Robert Wood Johnson Foundation, the National Institute on Drug Abuse (NIDA), the New York State Office of Mental Health via Nathan Kline Institute, and the American Psychiatric Association's SAMHSA Minority Fellowship sustained my research for this book over the years.

I dedicate my contributions to this book to the loving memory of Mary Skinner, Robert Lopez, Arne Bjerring Hansen, Al Dixon Jr., Isaiah Berkman, Ed, and Cory.

Jim Crow/"Classic" Era

1800

1830s: Imperial Britain introduces opium smoking in China at gunpoint

1840s: Chinese immigrant laborers bring opium smoking to US

1870s: Anti-immigrant panic focused on Chinese opium dens

1898: Bayer Pharmaceuticals introduces heroin as a cough suppressant

1906: Pure Food and Drug Act

1914: Harrison Anti-Narcotic Act

1916–1970 Great Migration: Mass exodus of Black Americans from southern to northern states amid widespread lynchings and political violence

1924: Anti-Heroin Act

1929: Predecessor of College on Problems of Drug Dependence founded

1951: Boggs Act pioneers mandatory-minimum jail sentences for drug "pushers"

1952: FDA enforces prescription-only rules for barbiturates, amphetamines

Civil Rights/Reform Era

1960s: Heroin addiction wave: organized crime recruits sales force from Black/Latinx inner cities with high unemployment

1965: First clinical trial of methadone maintenance; Social Security Act creates Medicaid/Medicare

1970: Drug Abuse Control Act

1971: Nixon declares War on Drugs

1973: Bureau of Narcotics and Dangerous Drugs merges with Office of Drug Abuse Law Enforcement to form Drug Enforcement Administration

"New Jim Crow"/Neurochemistry Era

2020

1986: Anti-Drug Abuse Act mandates five-year minimum sentencing for possession of 1/100 the weight of crack compared to powder cocaine

1990: President George H. W. Bush names 1990–1999 "Decade of the Brain"

1996: Drug/alcohol dependence no longer eligible for Social Security Disability; FDA approves OxyContin for moderate to severe chronic pain; American Pain Society institutes "pain as the fifth vital sign" campaign

1997: Temporary Assistance for Needy Families places five-year limits and work requirements on welfare

2000: Drug Addiction Treatment Act (DATA) passes, permitting Schedule III drugs including buprenorphine to be prescribed for office-based addiction treatment

2004: Opioid pain relievers more commonly used nonmedically than heroin in US

2005: 91% of buprenorphine patients are white

2008: U.S. incarceration rate peaks, a tenfold increase in number incarcerated since 1980, surpassing all other countries

2010: Purdue introduces tamper-resistant time-release formulation of OxyContin

2013–2016: Fentanyl-related deaths increase by 540%; synthetic opioids surpass all other opioids causing overdose deaths

PART ONE

Technologies of Whiteness in the Clinic, the Statehouse, and the Archive

CHAPTER I

Pharmakon of Racial Poisons and Cures

(as told by Helena Hansen, psychiatrist-anthropologist)

"Why did you stop working as a journalist?" I asked. Charlie* pulled his black T-shirt over his tattooed shoulder and ran his fingers through his buzz cut. "I got fired." His eyes darkened. "I don't blame them. Toward the end I got pretty outrageous. I showed up for work totally high, so high that one day I had a needle and syringe hanging from my neck with blood running from it. I didn't even realize."

Charlie was part of a crop of educated white patients who were beginning to appear at this large New York City hospital. It was the only public hospital in the region that, at that time, offered treatment with buprenorphine, commercially known as Suboxone. Ordinarily, the hospital's clientele was Medicaid insured or uninsured, Latin American, African American, or recently migrated from China. The white patients we saw were undocumented immigrants from Poland or Russia, many of them day laborers living in Coney Island. If we saw American-born, white patients, they had been homeless for long periods of time before being sent to us for treatment by a shelter social worker or a drug court. But the patients in the new Suboxone clinic were different. The clinic was on the primary care unit, nestled in between diabetes and asthma

---

* All names of patients and opioid users in this book are pseudonyms, and key elements of their biographies are hybridized with those of other patients and opioid users in order to protect their identities, which was a condition of their consent to participation in my research. The same is true for Drs. Pine and Abrams.

specialists, and was open only one day per week. It was staffed by a vanguard crew of primary care doctors who had gotten certified to prescribe Suboxone because they were committed to bringing new technologies to indigent patients.

I first saw Charlie in 2009, but the clinic had been founded in 2005, three years after the US Food and Drug Administration (FDA) approved buprenorphine for treatment of opioid dependence, by Dr. Abrams, an internist who had made his name promoting harm reduction and HIV treatment for heroin-addicted people. Abrams had recruited Dr. Pine, a buzz-cut, muscular physician, to lead the Suboxone clinic. He looked like a Marine but spent his free time volunteering in homeless shelters. Pine gave his personal cell phone number to all patients who were starting Suboxone and encouraged them to call with questions about how to dose themselves in the first twenty-four hours of treatment. He welcomed everyone but did not expect to see so many patients come in from the suburbs. These new patients commuted to our clinic because they would not, or could not, pay the $1,000 fee charged by private doctors near their homes for an initial Suboxone prescription.

None of the staff had predicted that their Suboxone clinic, the first of its kind in a public New York City hospital, would draw patients from affluent suburbs in Long Island, Staten Island, and New Jersey. Although many of these new patients were on Medicaid, and some were uninsured, a good number had attended college and had worked as professionals before their opioid use got in the way. Charlie was an example. His father paid the rent on his studio apartment in the fashionable East Village neighborhood of Manhattan, but he was on food stamps and on Medicaid, having exhausted his unemployment benefits.

Charlie's sojourn to our public clinic was one sign of a massive shift in American imagination surrounding addiction.† The ascendant "brain disease" model of addiction afforded opioid- and heroin-dependent middle-class white Americans an escape valve from the racialized moral blame that has historically been attached to narcotics in the US. The language used to describe addiction changed in accord with this shift to locating problem drug use in biological causes—in neuroreceptor dysregulation or genetics—and away from locating it in the character flaws

---

† Throughout the book we use the colloquial term *addiction* and the more neutral term *problem substance use* in order to distinguish everyday understandings from the clinically diagnostic terms *substance use disorder* and *opioid use disorder* in order to highlight how biomedical practitioners and pharmaceutical manufacturers use clinical language to shift the definition of problem drug use toward that of a biological disease.

of the individual, or in social influences on the person. Increasingly, clinical journals and later the popular press replaced the terms *addiction* and *substance abuse* with the diagnostic terms *substance use disorder* and more specifically *opioid use disorder.*

The logic of the brain disease model not only opened the door to biomedical treatment for addiction but also made the idea of technological fixes for the addictiveness of new formulations of opioids plausible; opioid manufacturers tapped into its ethos in their claims of safety and the aggressive marketing of technologically enhanced opioid pain relievers to insured, largely white Americans. Then, in response to the overdose crisis, the brain disease model led to pharmaceuticals as the primary response to problem drug use such as opioid use disorder. It led to federal promotion of buprenorphine maintenance as a rational, modern, science-based approach to addiction under the rubric of "medication-assisted treatment," or MAT, increasingly referred to as "medication for opioid use disorder," or MOUD. Buprenorphine's advocates hailed it as a neuroscience-based, radical new policy innovation. But in fact, methadone maintenance for opioid addiction had been available, primarily for poorer Black and Brown people, since the late 1960s. What was new was the effort to, quite literally, whitewash addiction and addiction treatment—to replace the stigma and aggressive policing of methadone with the cleaner, medicalized empathy of buprenorphine. Yet even this effort was not new. It drew on a century-old system of narcotic segregation in the US, in which some drugs become illegal through association with nonwhite users, and other drugs are legal and are deemed "medicines" reserved for white and middle-class consumers: in short, a system in which the Whiteness‡ of certain drugs medicalizes them.

In this book, we examine this unspoken but determinative Whiteness of opioids, to make the ways that Whiteness works in drug policy and treatment visible. Here, *whiteout* refers to the use of white imagery to hide or cover the inner workings of segregation in drug policies and health care industries. It also refers to the need to bring Whiteness out of the silence and shadows of drug policy and health care so that it can be seen—so that its harms to white people *and* people of color can be collectively addressed.

‡ Throughout this book, we capitalize *Whiteness* in order to bring attention to it as a system that undergirds the phenomena we describe, as opposed to racial identity as signaled by *white*, which we do not capitalize.

The buprenorphine clinic of this New York City hospital was a theater in which the contradictions and ironies of this system came into view. Like Charlie, the buprenorphine clinic patients were not only more likely than traditional public addiction clinic patients to be white but also more likely to be young and physically healthy. Many had never before needed health care and were not used to the routines of a large public hospital. Jennie, a thin blonde woman who arrived at monthly appointments in form-fitting gym clothes, commuted almost two hours from her house at the far end of Long Island. The staff chuckled when they saw her name on the appointment list. "Oh, it's Jennie. We can take the other patients first." She never arrived at her appointed time, but when she did arrive, she pulled her car into the taxi stand at the hospital entrance and called the clinic staff from her cell phone. "I'm right downstairs and there's nowhere to park. Could you just bring down my script?" None of the staff ever brought down her prescription. She always ended up parking at a meter on the crowded city streets nestled between high-rise buildings, but not before calling from downstairs. The clinic manager had her own theory as to why. "She thinks we are dealers. In Long Island, the dealer hand-delivers the goods to you in a strip mall lot."

Jennie took her prescribed Suboxone tablets in her own way. Monday through Thursday, before leaving for her office job, she took them at breakfast, as her doctor instructed. But on Friday she would sometimes skip her dose so that she could "feel something" when she celebrated Saturday and Sunday with OxyContin from a dealer. She was honest with her doctor about it. Her doctor kept prescribing Suboxone, reasoning that at least Monday through Thursday, Suboxone kept her safe from overdose and arrest. This fit the rationale behind Suboxone treatment: reduce the harms of illegal opioid use by prescribing safer, medical opioids to prevent opioid withdrawal symptoms and reduce the patient's use of dangerous street drugs.

Even those most committed to the logic of Suboxone treatment can have a hard time freeing themselves entirely from older conceptions of addiction. Jennie's doctor, for example, was still worried about her patients' decision-making. She carefully screened all of her patients for signs that they were getting pleasure from Suboxone, and she lowered the dose if they were. She reminded patients to take Suboxone every day at the same time, "like a vitamin," and lectured them on the difference between a medication—designed to prevent withdrawal symptoms—and a drug that was used for pleasure. Perhaps she worried about the most common critique of medications for opioid use disorder—that maintaining patients on Suboxone, itself an opioid, was just substituting one addiction for another. Her worry revealed that, while more medicalized than the prior century of American responses to drug epidemics, buprenorphine and other medications for opioid use disorder had not completely displaced older ideas that narcotics users needed to be disciplined.

The Suboxone clinic was only two floors below the methadone clinic, in the same hospital, but it rarely got referrals from, or made referrals to, the methadone clinic. The methadone clinic ran as it had run for decades: serving primarily African American and Latinx people from the South Bronx and Lower East Side of Manhattan, along with a handful of middle-aged, homeless white patients. Patients lined up in one of two shifts—at 7 a.m. or at 3 p.m.—in front of a medication window where a nurse watched them drink methadone from a cup and checked their mouths to ensure that they were not "cheeking" the medication for resale on the streets. After the line thinned and the medication window closed, patients gathered in group therapy rooms. The methadone clinic ethos was communal; it lacked the trappings of patient privacy.

I knew that private-office buprenorphine represented an important new development as an alternative to methadone clinics. When I was in medical school, my professors had run an early clinical trial of buprenorphine for opioid addiction; this was in the late 1990s, before it was approved by the FDA for addiction treatment and received the commercial name of Suboxone. These professors were excited by buprenorphine's promise to "change the culture of medicine": to have addiction finally recognized as a chronic, physiological disease, similar to diabetes, asthma, or hypertension and treated in the same way—with long-term medications—and in the same places, primary care clinics. They were eager to find alternatives to methadone. Methadone clinics were so stigmatized that they were often located a bus or train ride away from their parent hospital, in run-down neighborhoods whose residents were not organized enough to protest them. Methadone clinics were regulated by the Drug Enforcement Administration (DEA), required daily observed dosing, and had such restrictive hours that at times patients had to choose between methadone and a job. Affluent white patients usually refused to be seen at a methadone clinic, and most poor, rural, white patients lived hundreds of miles from one.

. . .

The golf resort's largest lecture hall was filled to capacity with addiction specialists attending the annual meeting of the College on Problems of

Drug Dependence (CPDD). The much-anticipated panel addressed the question of how to reduce the risk of overdose from prescription opioids. The second speaker was from Purdue Pharmaceuticals, manufacturer of OxyContin. He presented protocols for physicians to screen patients for risk of prescription opioid misuse, and graphs showing that use of the protocols led physicians to select patients for opioid pain relief who had lower rates of overdose.

The next speaker was slated to speak about the effectiveness of naloxone opioid reversal kits in reducing overdose. But he went off script. Turning to the speaker from Purdue, he leaned into the microphone and said in a sharp tone not often heard at this otherwise dry, scientific meeting: "Before I speak, I want to point out what you are doing for Purdue. You are putting blame for overdose on the patients, and on prescribing physicians. Overdose is *not* due to inadequate patient screening. It's due to the false claims and marketing of your company."

After a moment of silence, audience members stood up one by one to clap. After a few minutes, most of the room stood in a standing ovation. This was an awkward moment in the history of the CPDD, the oldest and largest organization focused on the science of substance use disorders in the US. Founded in 1929 by the National Academy of Sciences, from the beginning it faced questions about responsible clinical use of narcotics and narcotic drug development in an era of federal prohibitionist policies that limited physicians' use of narcotics. An exclusive organization to which new members had to be invited, the CPDD showcased pharmacological science and clinical trials; its members were leading researchers and authorities on state-of-the-art treatment. After World War II, its members thrived on federal funding for laboratory science in the Cold War race for modernity. CPDD, originally called the Committee on Drug Addiction, had ties to the pharmaceutical industry. It secured corporate funding for early animal and human testing of synthetic opioids and fed data on promising compounds back to manufacturers,[1] and its corporate sponsorship dated back to the 1950s.[2] By the time of my attendance at their annual conference, the CPDD had pharmaceutical executives on its board and hosted "Friends of NIDA" (National Institute on Drug Abuse), a group of industry donors to addictions research.

The panelist I had just witnessed pointed out one way that research could be reframed in the interest of pharmaceutical manufacturers. The connection that the panelist did not make, but that I came to make in studying how opioids became white, was that ideas about who is "at risk" for addiction and overdose from prescribed opioids were the key not only to pharmaceutical company strategy but also to the demographics of overdose. While the Purdue Pharmaceuticals researcher at this conference encouraged physicians to begin screening their patients for risk of addiction, his company had in fact employed many screens in their marketing since OxyContin's 1996 FDA approval for pain. These screens involved the geographic targeting of white neighborhoods and coded drug representative language about prescribing to "trustworthy" and "legitimate" patients among American physicians who had been shown to attribute lower addiction risk to white patients and to attribute higher tolerance for pain, and thus less need of pain relief, to Black patients.[3] The success of blockbuster drugs such as OxyContin and analogous new opioids such as Opana and Roxicodone, followed by the success of blockbuster formulations of buprenorphine such as Suboxone for treatment of opioid dependence, hinged on appealing to longstanding race-based popular, professional, and political conflations of biology with morality, as well as to race-based distinctions between the need for medical treatment versus punishment.

When I started observing the buprenorphine clinic of my hospital, I did not know that I was seeing a pharmaceutical response to what the national press called the "new face of addiction." I did not know that the opioid buprenorphine, sold as Suboxone, was especially designed and marketed as a white treatment for dependence on another white drug, OxyContin. OxyContin's manufacturer finessed traditional federal restrictions on opioids; its marketing targeted suburban and rural primary care physicians—those with a white patient population—leading them to prescribe it for an unprecedented range of conditions beyond the severe postsurgical and cancer pain to which opioids had long been restricted. The manufacturer promoted new indications for OxyContin including lower back pain, contributing to a tripling of prescription opioid sales within the first decade after OxyContin's FDA approval as a less addictive opioid formulation appropriate for "moderate pain."[4]

It turns out that racial patterns of access to opioid pain relievers, and to pharmaceutical treatments for addiction to them, are not unintentionally caused health disparities. Rather, they are produced by intentional racialization, not only of drug policy, but of the drugs themselves.

I could not have predicted then how interesting OxyContin and Suboxone would become from the standpoint of drug development, drug policy, and race—*that chemically and symbolically forged within the American cultural politics of narcotics, OxyContin and Suboxone were encoded from their inception with white racial identities, designed to confer Whiteness on those who took them.*

It happened that the Suboxone clinic that I studied opened on the heels of New York's heroin chic of the 1990s, involving young affluent whites, including fashion models such as Kate Moss. Columbian drug cartels had begun marketing cheap, snortable heroin to the white American middle class; they sent high-purity heroin to local distributors in major US cities such as New York, knowing that this would lower the cost of Colombian heroin below that of competing cartels in the Middle East and Asia, and that the high purity of Colombian heroin would enable heroin snorting among middle-class users, who saw injection as highly stigmatized but had long sniffed powder cocaine. This strategy followed Colombian cartels' successful marketing of crack cocaine to poor US Black and Latinx people; the cartels later diversified their markets by planting poppies in order to produce heroin.[5] US authorities had responded to the cartels' successful ethnic marketing of crack with racially disparate sentencing through the 1986 Federal Anti-Drug Abuse Act, which mandated five-year mandatory-minimum sentencing for crack possession, with only one-one-hundredth the weight of crack (seen as a Black drug) compared to powder cocaine (seen as a white drug) needed to trigger sentencing. It is an example of drug policies based on racial imagery (reflected in policy makers' references to inner-city crack-addicted "superpredators") that exacerbate racial inequalities through disparate law enforcement and sentencing, but without naming race—an example of the institutional "color-blind ideology" described by Michelle Alexander.[6] This disparity foreshadowed later law enforcement distinctions between nonmedical prescription opioids and heroin.

I learned of Suboxone during the late 1990s' rise of prescription opioid use in the suburbs, when opioids began their ascent to the most prescribed drug class in the US.[7] By 2010, opioids were second only to marijuana as the most common recreational drug among high school seniors.[8] All this was happening in the midst of a national move toward stop-and-frisk and sting operations in Black and Latinx city neighborhoods that led drug charges to drive unprecedented incarceration rates, peaking in 2008, and putting the US prison population well above all other countries in the world in terms of both percentage of population and raw numbers.[9]

White opioid use and pharmaceutical addiction treatment grew in the midst of an intensified inner-city drug war. To make sense of this pattern, I observed dozens of drug policy and addiction science meetings, observed interactions in clinics over four years, and interviewed over two hundred addiction scientists, treatment advocates, pharma executives, policy makers, administrators, prescribers, and patients. In the process, I discovered an unrecognized form of ethnic marketing that, because it targets white people, works by *not* marking itself as racial. The story was invisible by design. Only through sustained participant observation and interviews with key participants have I been able to unravel the threads.

Intrigued by the aspirations of my medical school professors to redefine addiction as a chronic medical illness, I started my study with Suboxone. It is easiest to see its racial identity by comparing it to its predecessor, methadone, the only other opioid that can legally be used to treat opioid dependence in the US. The first nationally representative study to compare buprenorphine patients to methadone patients by race and class found that in 2005, three years after FDA approval of office-based buprenorphine, 91 percent of buprenorphine patients were white, over half had attended college, and over half were employed at treatment initiation, compared with methadone patients, 53 percent of whom were white, 29 percent of whom were employed, and 19 percent of whom had attended college.[10] By 2019, another national study found that among patients with opioid use disorder, whites were still three to four times as likely as Blacks to receive buprenorphine, and the vast majority of those receiving buprenorphine (at a cost starting at $300 per month) paid for it with cash or with private insurance rather than Medicaid or Medicare.[11]

What we did not know from these trends was *how* they had occurred: How had the two pharmaceuticals, methadone and buprenorphine, been *racialized*? By what process had they gained their racial identities?

For that story, I went back to 1965. Race riots had burned through Harlem, Philadelphia, and Watts, Los Angeles. The unemployment rate for Blacks was twice that of whites.[12] The Mafia had years before gained control of Asian heroin imports and had recruited a sales force from Black and Latinx inner cities.[13] Also in that year, Rockefeller University diabetes researcher Vincent Dole, who conceptualized heroin addiction as opiate receptor deficiency, analogous to insulin deficiency in diabetes, published findings from the first clinical trial of methadone maintenance with his coinvestigators Marie Nyswander and Mary Jeanne Kreek.[14] The study's subjects were African American heroin-injecting men from Harlem, and its outcomes of decreased criminal activity and increased employment at six months brought it national attention. By

1970, news of methadone as a pharmacological solution to urban heroin reached President Nixon, who appointed pioneering psychiatrist and methadone advocate Jerome Jaffe as the nation's first drug czar. Nixon targeted inner-city Black and Latinx people, as well as returning Vietnam veterans, with methadone, the major weapon in his War on Drugs.[15] To prevent diversion and street sale of methadone, the DEA regulated methadone clinics, requiring daily observed dosing and regular urine testing. Because of community resistance, the clinics were located in marginal neighborhoods in the city, remote from other medical services.[16]

What I noticed in reading about the architects of 1970s methadone policy was their prevailing concern in that period with containing unruly Black populations. Methadone was a Big Government intervention in the midst of racial unrest, of white flight from "urban crime," in the era of the War on Poverty. Beny Primm, a prominent African American physician who founded the first methadone programs in New York City's Black neighborhoods of Harlem and Bedford-Stuyvesant Brooklyn in the 1970s, told me that methadone was met by suspicion in Black communities given its connection to crime control: "The Democratic party had pretty much decided that [Mayor John Lindsay] was going to be their [presidential] candidate. . . . One of the shortcomings of his mayoralty reign was that he hadn't done very well for the addict population, neither in Harlem nor Brooklyn nor elsewhere, and it was kind of taking over the city, and crime was rampant. . . . I had gotten caught up in the street thinking about methadone, that, as it were, white people [were] further enslaving Black people who were on drugs, and I was part of that whole cabal."

Despite this resistance, early methadone scientists successfully lobbied for methadone to become the standard of medical care in largely Black and Latinx urban neighborhoods. In the late 1960s and early 1970s, they used the language of neuroscience to argue for pharmaceutical treatment of addiction as a biological rather than a social problem. As Mary Jean Kreek, who coauthored one of the first papers on methadone maintenance with Vincent Dole and Marie Nyswander in 1966, recalled in her Rockefeller University lab during our 2011 interview: "We therefore set the hypothesis that opiate addiction, and I've extended that to all addictions, are not criminal behaviors, nor are they weak personalities. They are diseases of the brain with behavioral manifestations that include drug hunger, drug craving, drug seeking, and drug self-administration." The tension between the explicitly racial politics around 1970s inner-city heroin and the universal, deracialized language of neuroscience gave methadone the ambivalent, quasi-medicalized, and still marginal position that it holds in clinical care today.

Fast forward to October 8, 2002. A new kind of opiate problem had developed following Purdue Pharma's aggressive marketing of OxyContin as a minimally addictive pain reliever. Most of these newly addicted people were white and many of them middle to upper income. The FDA had just approved the synthetic opioid buprenorphine for maintenance treatment of dependence on opioids such as OxyContin in certified doctor's offices. Like methadone, it blocked opiate receptors in the brains of addicted patients, but unlike methadone, it could be prescribed monthly for use at home. This was the first time since the 1920s that generalist doctors were permitted to use opioids to treat opiate addiction.

The manufacturers of buprenorphine, and the architects of opioid treatment policy almost thirty years after methadone, working in a period of health care privatization and of rapid growth in psychotropic pharmaceutical markets, had to distinguish buprenorphine, symbolically and spatially, from racially burdened methadone. Buprenorphine, pharmacologically in the same drug class as methadone, had to be whitened. That is, manufacturers had to craft the social identity of buprenorphine to contrast with that of methadone in terms of race and class; to associate buprenorphine in the popular and clinical imagination with white, middle-class—and therefore *legitimately* ill, treatment-adherent, and noncriminal—consumers. In this book, we argue that they actively achieved this Whiteness of buprenorphine with specific social technologies.

. . .

This book examines Whiteness in US society as an ideological system, rather than a biological trait or as something an individual possesses. It tracks the way that ideas about Whiteness operate through opioids in contemporary biotechnologies, consumer markets, and drug policies. This is a story I have been following for two decades—while training in addiction medicine; practicing addiction medicine; and observing and interviewing the scientists, policy makers, and company executives that disseminate new opioids, as well as the people to whom they are marketed. I tracked these actors as they moved between clinics, laboratories, policy committees, homes, homeless shelters, social service agencies, and courtrooms. Over time, I assembled a fieldwork team that did observations in clinics and pharmacies and scoured the archives for pharmaceutical ads and for legal records of lawsuits against manufacturers. Our team of undergraduate and graduate students of anthropology, public health, and social work research (Alyssa Rivera, Parth Patel, Caroline Parker, Sonia Mendoza, and Alexandrea Hatcher) was multiracial and made up of astute analysts of race.

To write this book, I joined forces with sociologist Jules Netherland at the Drug Policy Alliance, with whom I have had a decade-long writing partnership on the Whiteness we saw evolving in opioid policy and media coverage. Together we looked at Whiteness and opioids from many angles: as it manifests in community clinics, scientific meetings, sessions of Congress, and national news. Jules and I then reached out to David Herzberg, whose work on the history of pharmaceutical Whiteness we had been citing. David was the linchpin of thought-provoking conferences and journal issues on the history of drug policy, drug marketing, gender, and race that had profoundly shaped our thinking.

The story of Whiteness through opioids has become personal. Many of my heroes—Black, white, Latinx, and otherwise—have died of overdose and of many other drug-related causes along the road to my writing this book. The deceased include members and relatives of a video therapy group in the New York City public addiction clinic in which I volunteered for ten years. Walter, an Afro-Caribbean war veteran who had put his life on the line for his country many times, told us on video that he'd twice escaped death after serving in Iraq: once when driving under the influence led him to roll his car over the side of a bridge, and once in a drug-induced attempt to hang himself before his dog pulled him down from a tree. In his second year of sobriety, when Walter had embraced his will to live and had reunited with his daughters, he was diagnosed with a form of cancer that was likely caused by his drug use.

Rob was the beloved brother of Ruben, a Puerto Rican cab driver who became an outsider artist as a result of our clinic's art therapy group. Our video group camera crew filmed Ruben reuniting with his brother Rob after decades of estrangement. One week later, Rob was beaten to death outside of a bar in drug trade–related retaliation.

The list of video group members and of drug casualties goes on: Black, white, Chinese, and Mexican American, some educated, more of them working class, a large number referred to us by the homeless shelter next door to the clinic.

At least one member of our video group was acutely aware of her own Whiteness and her affluence. Julia, of quick wit and Marilyn Monroe upsweep, had actually worked in Hollywood as a producer before coming to New York for a mental health break. The granddaughter of a food industry mogul, she felt survivor guilt when video group members talked of serving time for drug charges and seeing roommates murdered in their homeless shelters. She paid their legal bills and overdue rent; she brought enormous platters of food to our video shoots as she nibbled quietly on salad. A short-statured woman standing under four feet tall, she had grown up among wealthy white people who put a premium on thinness. She was terrified of becoming fat on top of being short. For years she struggled with using stimulants to keep thin, even though they gave her high blood pressure. Ultimately, she convinced a private psychiatrist on the wealthy Upper East Side of Manhattan to prescribe her stimulants for an adult ADHD diagnosis.

A month later she was found in the back of a taxicab, slumped over from a massive stroke. Julia was a casualty of the double-edged "privilege" of access to narcotics in the private, legal, yet treacherous white pharmaceutical market. At her memorial in the clinic, we screened a short film that we had made from the rare footage that, without her noticing, we got of her during shoots where she always worked behind the camera. There was not a dry eye among the fifty-plus current and former drug users in the room, who reminded each other that Julia had, in the end, gotten her wish: to die "young and beautiful." And I wondered what would have happened if her upscale psychiatrist had helped her to see how much she meant to us, and to see that she did not need a prescription, or to be thin.

There are other ways that drugs and race are personal for me. I grew up in a middle-class Black household in the 1970s and 1980s, first in Oakland, California, and later in Berkeley near the university campus. Race and drugs hovered beneath the surface of our family dynamics and of local politics. I saw the vestiges of the hippie movement when some of my white classmates' parents smoked marijuana in public. In high school, the parents of white students encouraged them to try marijuana and other drugs as a route to self-discovery.

At home with my single mother, my maternal grandparents, and my younger brother, we knew that only white people could do such things. My mother was the embodiment of Black middle-class respectability; she insisted on clean, ironed clothing that fully covered the body. She spoke with perfect grammar and was nauseated by the smell of marijuana and other drugs. She studied child psychology and eventually took a job in the county's child protective services, where she saw hundreds of poor Black and Latinx children sent to foster care when their mothers tested positive for drugs, against her professional advice. Over and over again she told judges that child attachment theory directed them to give extended families, if not birth parents, the financial and social support they needed to keep custody. But instead, the institutional incentives of the foster care system were to take children away from mothers of color and to pay foster parents—most often white people living in rural or suburban white areas—to care for them. Although she was a psychologist, my mother did not see child removal as the result of parents' psychological problems. She saw the need for socioeconomic stabilization of Black and Brown families and neighborhoods that had been decimated by the outsourcing of members to jails and prisons on drug-related charges. As if that decimation were not enough, my mother observed, drug and sex traffickers preyed on Black and Latinx foster children who had no kin to protect them as they aged out of the foster system. These children did not have the institutional shield of Whiteness in agencies charged with determining their "appropriate" care.

And then, there was the matter of my uncles. My mother's brothers all came of age in the 1960s, a turbulent time for young Black men in Oakland. My uncles found themselves in the middle of Black Power and civil rights movements, and also in new drug markets targeting unemployed Black youth, followed by the launch of the War on Drugs. My grandparents and I knew that at any moment a police cruiser could pull up in front of our house, looking for my uncles James, Bubsie, or Billy. More than once my grandparents got late-night calls from the precinct where my uncles were jailed on drug charges. And Bubsie, who succumbed to psychosis during drug-induced confrontations with police, died in the state mental hospital to which he was mandated after biting off someone's earlobe.

My coming of age was marked by race and by drugs. I was the product of my mother's short-lived marriage to a Norwegian man who returned to Norway without her after two years as a UC Berkeley student at the end of the 1960s. Although I knew that the one-drop rule, written into US law a century ago and still an American cultural practice, defined me as Black, I was also aware from an early age that Whiteness is relative. My mother lied about our address to get me into the predominantly white "high-performing" public primary schools outside of our residential district. I saw my teachers bristle when my dark-skinned mother attended parent-teacher night, a dark fleck against a sea of white parents. My teachers relaxed around my less threatening light-brown freckled face and the perfect grammar that my mother taught me. I learned to weave my way in and out of places that were too white for my mother and to participate in white conversations, playing up my ties to Norway with the white girls who studied magazine photos of royal European families at recess.

Through high school, I covered myself in loose clothing and rejected cigarettes, alcohol, and drugs, in fear that I'd be mistaken for the drug- and sex-crazed mulatta whore of American movies. In my mind, my abstinent image, along with the grammar of my speech, provided a measure of Whiteness that could protect me against racial violence. I had learned what a liability drugs were if you were Black; I knew that drugs could blacken you if you were not fully white but that if you were white, drugs were the marker and the benefit of your Whiteness.

Decades later, after I'd finished medical school and a psychiatry residency and was a research fellow, I was at dinner with my advisers and passed on wine as I usually do. We had been discussing the abstinence required by twelve-step programs, and one of them turned to me, saying, "I notice that you never have wine!" I suddenly realized that they thought I was in recovery myself. How ironic, I thought, that for me to have a place in the white world of health research, in their minds and in my actions, I had to be in recovery. And at the same time, being in recovery was a reflection of my blackness: in the minds of my advisers, being not-quite-white gave me the potential for uncontrollable substance use.

Writing this book forced me to articulate something that I had not talked about before: my own Whiteness. When I show up to the clinic or the classroom as a doctor, rather than a patient, I am stepping into a white role. The confidence with which I sign my name on a prescription, or call an insurance administrator to debate denial of coverage for my patient, or submit a manuscript to a health research journal—these are white actions taken from a white position in the social hierarchy. When I stop at a motel while driving across country and my husband asks me to check us in, knowing the legacy of racial terror that for over two centuries prevented Black men from traveling freely through white spaces, I tap into a form of Whiteness that is closed to my husband.

And then there are moments when I see how Whiteness skips over some white people. For instance, along with everyone in my clinic's video therapy group, I adopted Tim as one of my own. Rail thin with a tooth- less smile, having spent decades on the streets, Tim did marvelous pho- tography, but he barely spoke. Over time, with gentle nudging, we dis- covered that his singular passion was the music of David Bowie. It was the music he had heard as a teenager in the 1970s when his stepfather turned him out and he had to find his way around the world from rural

Pennsylvania. At a karaoke party to celebrate recovery, we conspired to dress Tim up as David Bowie, replete with a full face of glam rock glitter makeup, a red wig, and a space suit. Strumming his air guitar and crooning "Ground control to Major Tom," Tim *was* David Bowie.

Months later I invited him to speak to my class of college students about recovery. He started by saying, "I came here because of Dr. Hansen. But I don't have anything to say." I showed the video of Tim as David Bowie, and Tim described his journey from sleeping in the Pennsylvania woods, to hanging out on the city park benches where police officers kicked him in the mouth, to starring in Bowie's "Space Oddity." All the while, he apologized for speaking instead of me, since I was the professor. And I understood that in the United States, where race is intertwined with class, there are times that I am whiter than some white people.

Whiteness, as a system, does not include all white people, and this is by design. Travis Linnemann, a sociologist who studied the white people in rural America who were caught up with crystal methamphetamine in the 1990s, explained this when we met at a drug policy conference. At the time, he was teaching at Eastern Kentucky University and documenting how poor white Appalachians were incarcerated, and their children put into foster care, at ever higher rates even after the "kinder, gentler" national drug policies that followed media coverage of opioids in suburban white America. Travis had interviewed policy makers and analyzed media coverage of drug use in the predominantly white, rural states of Kentucky and West Virginia, finding that the way they described poor whites who used drugs—in terms of cultural depravity, laziness, inclination to have too many children, and violence—was similar to the ways Black and Brown people were described in parts of the country that were less white. The racial images deployed in drug policy are about justifying inequality, Travis said. In places where poor whites are the "other," poor whites play honorary Blacks in our national theater of drugs and blame.

The mark of Whiteness as a system, rather than a quality of individuals, is that those who inhabit a white position do not dictate the form their Whiteness will take. White doctors who want to prescribe medications for Black patients but cannot, because Black patients do not have the right health insurance, and white pharmaceutical executives who use stereotypes of middle-class white consumers as at lower risk of addiction to get around regulators, do not choose the terms of Whiteness. I do not control the forces shaping my Whiteness relative to my mother and my husband when I use it to get an education or reserve a motel room. Whiteness, as an overarching mechanism that preserves the American hierarchy, sweeps individuals up in its path: participation often feels mandatory and is often unconscious. Only through sustained and collective action can white people, and people of color, push back against the Whiteness that overdetermines our health care system, our drug policies, our overdose deaths, and our social order.

. . .

Thirty invited researchers arranged themselves at the National Institutes of Health (NIH), in the personal conference room of its director, Francis Collins. I was seated to Collins's far left. A panel of four social scientists presented national data on opioid overdoses and their correlates. Pausing on a graph of mortality by race, one of them commented, "Whites are just not making progress. This is very disturbing." As she listed other variables that predicted white mortality, such as being out of the workforce, never having been married, having children out of wedlock, and lacking a sense of social connection, her co-presenter chimed in: "It's not just current wages. It is . . . not knowing your kids, the decline in standard of living from one generation to the next." A participant asked why whites were disproportionately dying prematurely under those conditions, given that Black and Latinx people had also experienced the decline in US manufacturing jobs. In response, the last panelist stumbled over his words, and landed on religion. Blacks had churches, he reasoned, and that might be protective against overdose.

Barely able to contain myself, I raised my hand. "I suggest we need a more nuanced understanding of how racism works," I proffered:

> It's not that religion is protective, it's that Black life expectancy has been a decade lower for half a century. The classic quote from the 1990s is that a Black man in Harlem has lower life expectancy than a man in Bangladesh. What we see in unemployed whites now happened to Blacks forty years ago. Postwar gains in working-class standards of living were lost decades earlier among Blacks, who were last hired and first fired in manufacturing, excluded from segregated unions. What about heroin injection–related HIV epidemics and drug war policies driving mass incarceration that wiped out a generation of Black and Latinx people over the past three decades? What about the current statistic that Black men are now experiencing the fastest increase in opioid overdoses? What kinds of data do we need to explain this?

I was met with silence. The "deaths of despair" discourse that the panel employed was geared to whites, not Blacks, and could not absorb the realities of the earlier, Black epidemic of heroin that had been represented in 1970s US media as a crisis of crime, rather than a crisis of public health. The concept of "deaths of despair" was spearheaded by Princeton economists Anne Case and Angus Deaton, who published a widely cited article just before the 2016 presidential election reporting that the life expectancy of US whites had fallen by five years over the past two decades, while the life expectancy of every other ethnic/racial group—except Native Americans—had risen. They found that the primary cause of premature white death was drug overdose, followed by cirrhosis of the liver and suicide, and they pointed to chronic unemployment among blue-collar whites in the Rust Belt of former manufacturing and mining towns across the midwestern US as a cause.[17] Their contention that community-wide unemployment led to disintegration of social networks and thus to opioid use and overdose was supported by sociological studies finding community-level correlations of high overdose rates with low levels of social connectedness.[18] This argument made sense to me, having witnessed so many people come to my hospital for addiction treatment who had long been unemployed, disconnected from the formal economy and from sober people. But their humanizing, socioeconomic argument contrasted with demonizing media images of addiction prior to the opioid crisis: of criminal, menacing "junkies" of 1960s-'70s Black and Latinx inner cities that had fed white anxiety and flight from cities to the suburbs, and of violent drug-dealing "superpredators" and oversexed "crackheads" in those same neighborhoods from the 1980s-'90s that had led to mandatory-minimum drug sentencing and the acceleration of racially targeted mass incarceration.[19] The major distinction of the opioid crisis from prior narcotic epidemics was the perceived Whiteness of contemporary opioid use.

The deaths-of-despair socioeconomic explanation for the (white) opioid crisis peacefully coexisted at this NIH meeting with what might have been a competing frame: that of neuroreceptor-level biological vulnerability. NIH director Francis Collins convened our meeting by reviewing the priority that the NIH gave technological breakthroughs such as injectable buprenorphine, now formulated as six-month-release probuphine, which had emerged from an NIH collaboration with a private biotech firm. He cited the President's Opioid Commission Report of November 2017, which advised that "the NIH begin work immediately with the pharmaceutical industry to develop novel technologies."[20] His agency fostered public-private partnerships and met with pharmaceutical industry leaders to define scientific opportunities. The main goal, from Collins's point of view, was to "enhance the range of medical options to treat addiction and prevent overdose," and our job at this meeting was to help develop "precision medicine" by finding the "psychosocial components to improve the effectiveness of MAT (Medication Assisted Treatment) [and] predict which individuals will respond."[21]

Yet the apparent contrast between the deaths-of-despair explanation for the opioid crisis and the brain disease explanation for opioid deaths belied that the two operated with parallel ideologies of Whiteness. On one hand, in addition to gesturing toward a nostalgia for an American industrial past in which the white working class shared the fruits of the racial hierarchy with white elites, the fact that "deaths of despair" were visible among white but not Black opioid users signaled that despair was a racially coded way of humanizing addiction, of placing blame for addiction outside of the affected individual. As we detail in this book, the racial coding of despair is apparent in the ways people with opioid use disorder are represented in the media and in historical and geographical comparisons of drug policies by race and class.

On the other hand, the very idea of individual biological vulnerability to substance use disorders is racialized, implicitly, in brain disease models of addiction. Locating addiction in molecular interactions in the brain abstracts it from the social identity, neighborhood conditions, institutional resources, and regional drug policies of the affected person. Then, in the US, the abstract, universal, standard human of clinical studies has been imagined to be the proverbial "70 kg white male."[22] White men have long been the normative patients, the unmarked humans, and other humans (such as nonwhite people, women, or nonbinary people) have had marked status as variants in the symbolic hierarchy. As we detail in this book, the chronic brain disease model of addiction widely adopted by researchers and federal agencies, including the NIH, in the 1990s and 2000s was pivotal in changing the racial associations that government regulators and clinical practitioners made with consumers of opioids, with their risks of addiction, and with their medical need for treatment as opposed to legal intervention. Whiteness is the key to decoding shifts in drug regulation, drug policy, and clinical standards of addiction treatment at the turn of the twenty-first century.

CHAPTER 2

How to See Whiteness

(as told by all three authors)

The story of the racial encoding of new opioids offers the key to a number of puzzles in turn-of-the-twenty-first-century America:

> Why did the life expectancy of white US residents decline in the two decades leading up to COVID while it rose among almost every other racial group? The most common cause of white excess mortality was drug overdose, but why should white Americans overdose more often than others?

> Why, in those two decades, did the federal government's primary response to opioid overdose come to be private office prescription of another opioid?

> How did white women become the majority of new heroin users in that time period, given that they made up a small fraction of illicit opioid users throughout the twentieth century?

> Why, given that no drug has been more criminalized or more demonized in the American imagination than heroin, are Republicans and Democrats now both supporting diversion of heroin users from incarceration to treatment?

> Why, with these bipartisan calls for treatment, do drug-related arrests and police violence persist in poor, in Black, and in Brown communities?

> And how, during what some had pronounced a "postracial" Obama era (2008–16), did we develop a white crisis in the first place?

These contradictions are not as easy to explain as you might expect. That is because they are produced by political-economic logics and by societal systems that are hard to see using everyday, commonsense understandings of racial identity or personal choice. For explanation, you need conceptual tools that account for phenomena that, on the surface, do not make sense. In this chapter, we three authors of this book collectively detour from our personal accounts of the Whiteness of opioid policy and treatment in order to provide such conceptual tools.

Here is the Big Picture: in this new millennium, 200 years after the emergence of the European industrial revolution, and 150 years after emancipation of Black Americans from slavery, opioids show us how racial capitalism plays out in contemporary biomedicine. Pharmaceutical, biotechnology, and health care industries together make up the largest sector of the US economy.[1] These industries, like many others, require expandable consumer markets with the resources to pay for new products, extraction of labor and raw materials from people and places without the resources to resist, and evasion of responsibility for the collateral damage from this extraction and consumption in order maximize returns to investors. While a century ago such markets revolved around coal, sugar, and cotton, in this era extraction and consumption increasingly revolve around molecular technologies that regulate bodies and brains—creating, as sociologist of bioscience Nikolas Rose put it, a "politics of life itself."[2]

A host of historians, sociologists, and anthropologists in the field of science and technology studies have described this global commodification of bioactive molecules through genetic, microbiological, and neuroscientific industries. They use terms that capture this industrial biotechnologization, accelerated by the Human Genome Project during the Decade of the Brain (1990–2000), such as *biocapital, biovalue, biopolitics, bioprospecting, biocolonialism, the pharmaceutical self, biosociality,* and *biological citizenship*.[3] Yet as some point out, given that human sustenance has always required plants and animals, "The bio-economy is one of the oldest sectors known to humanity."[4] What is new is not the economic importance of biology but rather the ways that multinational corporations have created societal demand for technological control of bodies. At the same time, the global economy is transforming from one of tangible commodity production and material labor to one based on intangible abstractions such as asset accumulation, financialization, market exchange, and the intellectual property of biotechnological industries. Leading scholars of race have uncovered the ways that the race of formerly enslaved and colonized people is both defined by, and generates profit for, biotechnology and health care industries, which often explain racial differences in disease, behaviors, pharmaceutical response, brain development, and beyond in terms of inherent biological differences, notably genetics.[5]

In our era, however, Whiteness must also be explained in relation to this biocapital. How do the ascending pharmaceutical, biotechnological, and clinical care industries capitalize on concepts of white biological purity, self-control, and morality that are centuries in the making, and, in the process, how do they update, alter, and conceal Whiteness as an ideological system? While studies of race in economic exploitation usually focus on the domination of the colonized—those not considered white—Whiteness itself, as an organizing principle of domination, is often taken for granted. This is especially true in science and technology studies. This is because Whiteness derives power from its silence and invisibility. If the presumed Whiteness of the imagined American patient, consumer, and citizen-voter is not made explicit, the assumption that white Americans are the only Americans that matter will continue unchecked, and policies, health, and social service systems will develop with white Americans as primary beneficiaries in ways that are difficult to detect and challenge. Within a system of Whiteness, "human biology" and "normal psychology" are presumed to be white, pathology and deviation are implicitly not-white, and the idea of racial improvement through eugenics has been a racial theme in popular culture and policy of nineteenth- and twentieth-century America.[6] Advertising executives visually project phenotypic and cultural Whiteness as an ideal against which aspirational Latinx and Black consumers measure their likeness.[7] In mainstream Euro-American images of science and scientists, Whiteness (and maleness) are equated with technological progress and intellectual genius. Euro-American corporate domination increasingly involves the biological extraction of clonable cells, transplantable organs, genetic materials, and clinical trial participation of populations in the Global South, as well as in the "fourth world" of Black and Brown US inner cities.[8] All of these things occur without being named or spoken; they are naturalized features of the global scientific landscape.

UNDERSTANDING WHITENESS AND RACIAL CAPITALISM IN MEDICINE

Our story of how the US opioid crisis came to be seen as white illustrates two concepts: (1) *technologies of Whiteness*, an analytic approach that we developed on the basis of prior studies of the invention of white race in America, as well as studies of social and institutional techniques for sorting people by race; and (2) *racial capitalism*, the ways that racial hierarchies are integral to capitalist production, consumption, and wealth accumulation, as conceptualized a century ago by Black scholars such as W. E. B. Du Bois and C. L. R. James, then later systematized by political historian Cedric Robinson. Racial capitalism is foundational to the US economy, and its effects are especially pernicious in drug policy and health care. Racial capitalism is the ideology that makes the privatization, commodification, and racial segregation of health care in the US seem natural; it defines alternative systems such as universal health care, or public health as a collective good, as radical or foreign to US policy. The failure to invest in public health infrastructure, as produced by racial capitalism, is largely responsible for the fact that the US spends the most per capita on health care of any nation in the world but has the worst health outcomes of any industrialized nation.[9]

Racial capitalism is potent precisely because it is difficult to see; it is ingrained in the cultural logics of everyday life in America. For example, US popular culture takes for granted that there should be two health care systems: on one hand, a privatized, biotechnology-laden system that advertises its services to affluent white markets and participates in national contests for rankings that attract the best consumers (such as US News and World Report contests for "Best Hospital" and "Best Physicians"); and on the other hand, an underfunded and less quality-controlled system for poor, Black and Brown people that can't retain licensed professionals, that has long waiting lists for care, and that focuses on state-mandated emergency rooms and services in jails, prisons, and immigrant detention facilities. For those growing up with such a racial capitalist logic, the idea of a national health system in which all are served by the same practitioners seems alien and undesirable even if it were politically achievable. This logic applies across sectors: a parallel division exists in the US educational divide between aggressively marketed private schools and underfunded, understaffed public schools, with little popular imagination or motivation for a national educational system that would more evenly distribute tax-based payments—another manifestation of racial capitalism.[10] In this book, we tease apart the cultural logics and institutional causes of the "white" opioid crisis in order to show how our taken-for-granted ideas about race, drugs, and health have become so lethal.

As a first step in this analysis, we draw on ideas from critical race theory (CRT) and Whiteness studies, as well as theories of racial capitalism. On the one hand, these concepts help to make visible the unacknowledged racial dynamics driving the science, regulation, clinical use, and public perception of opioids. On the other hand, their application to the opioid crisis leads us to two insights that extend beyond opioids to update these theories. First, biotechnology and pharmaceuticals are now major sites of racial capitalist production. Therefore, in addition to attending to race-based extraction of labor, an analysis of racial capitalism must attend to new forms of biologization and technologization of race that play into biomedical device and product development, marketing, and consumption. Second, racial capitalism kills white people. The racial imagery used in consumer and labor markets is deployed for the profit of elite executives and shareholders, not in the service of white people as a group. Therefore, racial justice in our economic system is not only in the interest of Black and Brown people but in the interest of the whole society.

Critical Race Theory

In order to dismantle racial capitalism, we call on the analytic tools of CRT, a field initiated by civil rights legal scholars and activists in the 1970s. It was originally used in landmark court cases on discrimination in employment and education, as well as court cases on the unequal racial impact of punitive drug laws and laws designed to protect women from domestic violence.[11] CRT was quickly embraced by social scientists and humanities scholars to examine social structures and institutions that enact white power over people of color, including in education, the workplace, social welfare, and health care.[12]

Core insights from CRT include:

1. Race is not biologically determined; rather, it is a social invention designed to uphold power relations of exploitation and oppression that began in the colonial era and have persisted through industrial and postindustrial eras.

2. Race is a core organizing principle in the US and other colonized and colonizing countries, as expressed in their institutions and policies.

3. As a result, racial inequalities are structurally enforced by institutional practices and public policies that are based on implicit, unstated racial convention—by mundane, everyday interactions with social systems that foster racial inequality—rather than by

the psychological racism of individuals. For example, "merit"-based guidelines for college admissions involving standardized test scores appear color blind if the fact of racially segregated, neighborhood-based school systems with unequal funding for college preparatory programs, including standardized test preparation, is overlooked.

4. CRT therefore calls for analysis of institutions and policies of racial oppression to make these hidden mechanisms visible.

What makes CRT "critical" is that it does not accept at face value that the systems regulating society work in the way that they claim—that they are impartial, or color blind—rather, CRT looks for racially stratifying mechanisms of apparently neutral institutions that are, by design, hidden. They therefore require excavation and a reading of systemic patterns against state and industry claims of race neutrality. Since conventionally collected data on educational, legal, and health systems are constructed in the interests of the white power structure, those data often omit or hide the very dynamics that critical race theorists seek to excavate. Alternative sources of data, including case studies and narratives from the point of view of oppressed people, are therefore essential sources of knowledge for CRT. By fostering a critical consciousness of racial inequalities as created by social systems, CRT strives through political organizing to enable race-conscious change in the institutions that regulate social life, rather than to change inequalities by changing the attitudes of individuals.

Whiteness Studies

One of the tenets of CRT is to "center the margins": that is, to amplify the voices and experiences of people of color who are systematically excluded from positions of power. However, this leaves less examined questions about how white identity is used to systemically consolidate power. Whiteness studies therefore emerged to complement CRT by foregrounding the mechanisms of white identity, white power, and their expression in policies and institutions. Pioneering Black scholars of race from earlier in the twentieth century, including W.E.B. Du Bois and James Baldwin, described the ways that American institutions protected the interests of white people, often without their conscious consideration, since white people took their own power for granted. Many decades later, in the 1980s, the field of Whiteness studies began to take on its current form, prompted by the "canon wars" that emerged from the backlash against efforts to make more multicultural the required content of American education, which had long been composed almost exclusively of white authors. These struggles over race and representation led not only to increased attention to the contributions of scholars of color but also to critical study of the origins of white identity and power.

One foundational insight from Whiteness studies is that white racial identity is a recent cultural invention, developed over the seventeenth, eighteenth, and nineteenth centuries by ruling colonists and industrialists who offered white European indentured servants race-based privileges to prevent them from politically organizing with people of color. Historians and social scholars have examined this evolution of Whiteness in the twentieth century.[13] Whiteness, like other racial categories, is socially constructed and actively maintained through social boundaries—for example, those defining who is white and is not white—and these boundaries shift with time and place.[14] For example, starting in the 1930s Irish and southern European Catholics and Jewish eastern European migrants gained much of the Whiteness formerly solely associated with Anglo-Saxon Protestants when they were included in labor organizing, segregated housing, and New Deal policies.[15]

Class intersects differently with white race than with Black race. As Du Bois first argued, and David Roediger documented historically, from the founding of the United States, laboring white people reaped a psychological wage from their status relative to Black people; they were admitted to white public spaces and were afforded the vote; they were granted access to better-funded schools, the ability to get loans, and the opportunity to buy houses and equipment in ways that were closed to Black people.[16] This helped to make up for their low monetary wages in an industrializing country that was moving away from Black slave labor toward white immigrant labor. From the beginning, then, the peculiar racial capitalism in the US allowed people of European descent partial, but tangible, access to Whiteness, while simultaneously strengthening white, property-owning elites' hold on political and economic power.

And Whiteness itself was codified into law as something of monetary and political value. As Cheryl Harris points out, for a century after the abolition of Black slavery, American law recognized the right of white people to use, enjoy, and exclude others from Whiteness by partaking of privileges that were available only to white people and to sue for damages if someone wrongfully stained their reputation by challenging the purity of their European heritage. The very idea of a white American people, as an amalgam of various European groups, depended on its counterpoint in Black people. The contrast between the absolute subordinate status of Black people and the only partial subordination of laboring white people to their employers also enhanced white workers' experience of themselves as independent, full citizens.[17] If we take seriously Harris's contention that Whiteness is property, we can see Whiteness as interchangeable to some degree with monetary capital and with other forms of cultural (e.g., educational) and social (e.g., political) capital. Whiteness functions as a form of symbolic capital, if we apply sociologist Pierre Bourdieu's framework.[18] Whiteness has been cultivated and preserved through American property law and economic practice for over two centuries as the currency of racial capitalism.

Whiteness as capital also helps to explain why white people with stable, well-paid blue-collar jobs identify themselves as middle class, and explains why blue-collar Black workers are less likely to have the job stability and higher income that come with unionization or guild membership given the long history of their racial exclusion from unions and guilds.[19] Whiteness as capital explains why white high school dropouts are wealthier, on average, than Black or Latinx college graduates.[20] The very definition of class differs by white and Black, with the highest-income and most educated Black Americans identifying themselves as "middle class,"[21] in a gesture toward the impossibility of truly entering the American elite class without the capital of Whiteness.

Another foundational insight is that institutions designed to protect white privilege do not require their beneficiaries to understand or acknowledge their race privilege. Many white Americans take for granted their access to education, to well-paid work, and to respectful treatment by public officials; these seem to happen naturally, and it may not occur to them that people of color experience a different everyday reality. When white Americans achieve upward mobility, that mobility appears to be the result of hard work and merit; the fact that systemic inequalities prevent people of color from advancing is hidden from white Americans by virtue of segregated neighborhoods and workplaces that prevent them from closely observing the daily realities of their counterparts of color. The seeming invisibility of Whiteness is one of its central mechanisms because it allows those within the category "white" to think of themselves as simply human, individual, and without race, while others are racialized.[22] The fact that white people have dominated the US since the country's founding has also meant that they have shaped the population's view of reality through everything from laws, to media, to political discourse. This shaping of how we frame our grasp of the social world is referred to by Joe Feagin as the "white racial frame."[23] Philosopher Charles W. Mills refers to an "epistemology of ignorance," in which white people cannot understand the world they themselves have helped to construct.[24] Sociologist Jennifer Mueller refers to the everyday mechanisms of "white ignorance" that prevent whites from seeing racial inequality because they are steeped in rhetorics of color blindness.[25] This prevents white Americans from examining racist institutional practices while priming them for alternate explanations for the distribution of wealth and power, such as individual merit and procedural color blindness—explanations that imply that the people of color who are left behind are culturally or biologically deficient.

And yet, not all people with white social identities partake of the fruits of Whiteness to the same degree. Although, as we detail in chapter 5, the manufacturers of OxyContin and similar opioids took advantage of early market opportunities among rural working-class white patients who had workers' compensation or veterans' benefits, subsequent policy responses to the "white" opioid crisis revealed where the working class fell short on the spectrum of stratified Whiteness. As we detail in chapter 6, the medicalization and decriminalization of "opioid use disorder" have focused on middle-class and affluent white people with access to private doctors for buprenorphine treatment and with political access to district attorneys in higher-income neighborhoods who divert them from sentencing for drug violation and toward treatment. Working-class white people are dying at the highest rates—the fallout from a betrayal: from the failure of drug companies to deliver on promised protections of Whiteness and from the incomplete protections of Whiteness that follow from the capitalist imperatives of racial capital. As we outline in chapter 5, the media's preoccupation, in the 1990s to early 2000s, with rural methamphetamine use as "hillbilly cocaine" fell away to be replaced by a preoccupation with emerging rural opioid use as "hillbilly heroin." The attendant stereotypes of cultural depravity that justified punitive policing of working-class white people and a lack of economic or political incentives to provide them with addiction treatment revealed their partial status in relation to gradations of Whiteness.

Whiteness is a core element of transactional biocapitalism; there is no principle of fidelity between white capitalists and white consumers or workers. Whiteness does not emerge from an actual caring community of people who share European physiognomy or culture. People who do not serve the imperatives of capitalist elites to consolidate their earnings or power will be dropped like a hot potato; within this imperative, people with white social identities, like others, are disposable. Furthermore, while all people categorized as white have at some point been a part of this agenda of Whiteness, they benefit only when their interests align with those of racial capital. The more privileged white people are, the more they align with capitalism based on Whiteness.

In our critique of Whiteness, therefore, we are not criticizing white communities. We are criticizing an abuse of the idea of white communities—the attempt to camouflage something as soulless and violent as racial capitalism under the mantle of community tradition and culture. Our critique is far more concerned about the future of poor white people, and also of middle-class white people, than racial capitalism is concerned about them. We reject the artifice of a race war. While the avatars of Whiteness pretend that CRT is opposed to authentic community, in reality it enables whites to create authentic community against the destruction and polarization of racial capital. And those who partake in the power and profit of racial capitalism trade authentic community for momentary personal gains that are ultimately destructive to all.

Whiteness shapes housing, education, politics, law, social science research methods, and indeed our (mis)understandings of society.[26] Yet Whiteness is not a static, unchangeable, easily definable entity; it requires direct study in context.[27] Despite almost two decades of research in the field of Whiteness studies, relatively little literature explores the myriad connections between Whiteness and health in the US.[28]

For those seeking a critical understanding of the "white" opioid crisis that began in the late 1990s, Whiteness studies offers useful tools for disentangling the systemic, institutional, and policy-related forces that contributed to the perception of opioid use as a public health crisis, and to the sea change in drug policy that followed. For instance, Whiteness studies would predict that in the US we would find the following:

1. Whiteness is a category of exclusion and therefore requires cultural and political maintenance of its boundaries.[29] For instance, in the early twentieth-century US, many states did not legally define a person as white if they had, depending on the state, one-eighth to one-thirty-second Black ancestry (the "one-drop rule," otherwise known as hypodescent laws). This social process of racial boundary maintenance continues in American

medicine. In US medical research, racial categories based on social identity do not align well with geographic ancestry; people from mixed-ancestry regions such as Latin America are often treated as a single race, "Hispanic/Latino," and non-Latinos with mixed African and European ancestry are counted as Black.[30] At the same time, the health consequences (for example, diabetes) of race-based public policies that prevent people with indigenous or African ancestry from accessing fresh food and safe, walkable environments are attributed to their genetic predisposition without investigation of how "race *becomes* biology" through toxic racial segregation.[31]

2. The white race is unmarked: as the assumed norm in the US, it is rarely explicitly named, either in public policies or in the media. White dominance rests on its own denial—by not naming the white race and therefore upholding the illusion of race neutrality—creating what sociologist Eduardo Bonilla-Silva terms "racism without racists."[32] In media stories, white protagonists are usually referred to in terms of nonracial markers. For example, those named "American" are usually white, as are those named by social role or stage of life ("thirty-one-year-old mother," "police officer"). When ethnicity or race is mentioned in such stories, it is of protagonists of color ("Puerto Rican student" or "Black shop owner"). Even in media coverage of the "white" opioid crisis that started in the late 1990s, news stories about the opioid crisis rarely explicitly used the word *white*. Rather, they used coded language such as *suburban* or *the new face of addiction*.[33]

3. Whiteness is defined by its "other." White and Black or other are interdependent. For instance, punitive American drug policy aimed at Black and Brown people has long had a mutually defining twin of legal narcotics for white people who have access to personal doctors, starting with morphine for middle-class Victorian housewives, then moving to post–World War II barbiturates, stimulant diet pills, Valium, otherwise known as (white) suburban "mothers' little helper,"[34] and now back to prescription opioids.

4. Whiteness costs white people. Here it is paramount to distinguish Whiteness from white people. This book takes aim at Whiteness, a system of racial sorting and control that operates beyond the actions of any one white person, a system that brings benefits and

also costs to people who are socially identified as white. Indeed, as we described above, white people with different class statuses, geographic locations, genders, and ability/disability partake quite differently in Whiteness. All have access to Whiteness to some extent and may benefit from it, but to varying degrees, and some bear the costs associated with Whiteness more heavily than others. The moral and health costs of the extreme inequality created by Whiteness are substantial for white people, and white people will ultimately benefit from its deconstruction and replacement with a more equitable system.

James Baldwin wrote forcefully about the moral corruption of Whiteness that was violently enforced: "this cowardice, this necessity of justifying a totally false identity and of justifying what must be called a genocidal history. . . . In this debasement and definition of Black people, [white people] debased and defamed themselves."[35] In the area of opioids, the violence has circled back to exclusive white consumers. Not only do white middle-class consumers pay inflated prices for patented prescription opioids, but they also pay with their lives for lethal substances to which they have privileged access. And America's racialized systemic underinvestment in public health and overinvestment in law enforcement means that poor whites often do not have access to needed services and are caught up in the criminal legal system originally designed to police Black and Brown communities. Racial capitalists pragmatically manipulate the vestiges of race power among white consumers for the benefit of elite investors, rather than for the benefit of white people as a whole.

In this book, we analyze the contemporary white opioid crisis in terms of what we call "technologies of Whiteness": that is, social technologies such as policy and industry strategies to maintain racial boundaries around biomedical uses of opioids. Our use of the term *technologies* to refer to racializing policies, regulations, and marketing strategies is, in part, inspired by philosopher-historian Michel Foucault, who theorized that in modern societies the population is controlled by institutions such as clinics, hospitals, courts, prisons, and schools that discipline individual minds and bodies. They control populations not only through direct surveillance, punishment, and reward but also by entraining individuals with habits of thought and speech that lead them to discipline themselves out of a sense of duty to maximize their own personal health and character.[36] In the case of the opioid crisis, a large cast of characters acted out of a sense of duty and social responsibility—from prescribing doctors, policy makers, and neuroscientists to regulatory officials. But they acted within institutional structures such as selective marketing and prescribing guidelines for opioids that stem from implicit assumptions that white patients are less susceptible to addiction than people of color and that white patients who use opioids compulsively do so because of universal biological factors rather than their flawed character. These techniques of marketing and prescribing created the racialized patterns of opioid use that we see today.

For the term *technologies*, we are equally indebted to Foucault's predecessors, including early twentieth-century anthropologist Marcel Mauss, who theorized cultural variation in the ways people physically navigate daily life with the term *techniques of the body*.[37] Examining the range of techniques for managing opioid-dependent bodies leads us to see the contrast of methadone given in public clinics under the watch of a nurse who immediately inspects the mouths of patients to ensure they have swallowed, with prescribed buprenorphine that middle-class private patients place under their own tongues each morning before leaving home for work. Both involve medications for opioid use disorder, but the techniques for their bodily management diverge by race and class, because in contemporary US society the boundaries of race and class are culturally enforced through segregated institutions—drug treatment in jail, prison, or methadone clinics for Black and Brown low-income patients, and drug treatment by prescription from private doctors for white middle-class patients.

Nineteenth-century philosopher Friedrich Nietzsche wrote of "moral technologies" to describe the Christian ethical systems that compelled believers to submit themselves to unequal relations of power, as pious slaves or servants, and to obey righteous masters.[38] Like Nietzsche's moral technologies, the technologies of Whiteness that we describe here are moral systems that create racially distinct subject positions such as those of unruly, noncompliant methadone patients, or upwardly striving, pharmaceutically enhanced buprenorphine consumers. Both methadone and buprenorphine maintenance are based on the idea that addicted people are incomplete, whether they are considered to be deficient in character, criminal personalities in need of surveillance by methadone clinics, or biologically deficient sufferers of "chronic relapsing brain disease" in need of buprenorphine prescriptions to maintain their productivity as professionals. Both forms of addiction management offer prosthesis, enabling addicted people to compensate for their internal deficiencies—compelling them, by an implicit Christian morality of grace through submission to a higher power, to use medications to bolster the weakened self.

The terms *technique* and *technology* help us to see how pharmaceutical companies, federal and state governments, and clinical researchers produce the patterns that we call "racial disparities in substance use and addiction treatment" and to see how institutional practices work in concert to shape the possibilities of patients and consumers in their everyday lives.

RACIAL CAPITAL AS PRODUCED BY TECHNOLOGIES OF WHITENESS

The ways that the pharmaceutical industry, clinicians, government drug regulators, and popular media draw on (often unspoken) ideas about Whiteness in order to define diagnoses, treatments, consumers, and boundaries between legal and illegal practices and between worthy and unworthy citizens also illuminate the inner workings of American racial capital. Capital accumulation was, and continues to be, enabled by race-based hierarchies that justify extracted labor, the differential value of workers, and racially stratified citizenship with different claims to rights, protection, and benefits from the state (or, increasingly, from multinational corporations). Social theorists use the concept of racial capitalism to analyze racial styles of thought in popular and political culture that legitimize social oppressions through mass incarceration, forced geographical displacement, and extreme inequalities in wealth, and to illuminate the ways race produces social separateness and the denial of citizenship of "othered" groups that these oppressions require.[39] For our purposes, an understanding of how Whiteness shores up boundaries between legal and illegal consumption and trade, the ways it stratifies markets and segregates institutions of social control, is critical for an analysis of opioids in relation to capital.

In this book, we outline four technologies of Whiteness that enable racial capital in drug industries: addiction neuroscience, new biotechnologies, drug regulation, and pharmaceutical marketing. The racial symbolism of these technologies is least visible at the molecular level of neuroscience and pharmaceutical development and is more apparent in drug control policies, in corporate marketing, and in popular media. All are driven by hidden racial coding from two sources. The first is a partnership of pragmatic pharmaceutical executives with lawmakers who are conscious of the racial symbolism of opioids and eager to use product association with the white race to deregulate opioid pain relievers and disseminate treatments for opioid addiction. The second is the unconscious collusion of addiction scientists eager to biologize and therefore decriminalize and democratize addiction treatment, while failing to recognize the white racial coding of their brain disease concept. Inherent in the effort of pharmaceutical manufacturers, policy makers, and neuroscientists alike to distinguish licit from illicit drugs is an unspoken racial symbolism of white biology and Black crime.

Technology 1: Addiction Neuroscience

Addiction neuroscience has generated Whiteness in three key ways, starting in the 1990s. First, its reliance on brain imagery has created a racially unmarked, biological, and hence medicalized image, first of the patient being treated for pain, and later of the addicted patient, as implicitly white. Second, addiction neuroscience has largely erased the role of environmental factors or discussions of social and structural causes of problem drug use, leaving in their place an individualized and molecular-level explanation for addiction. Third, addiction neuroscience has been used to create a medicalized tier of drug policy designed for white drug users, while Black and Latinx drug users continue to have low levels of access to health care and high levels of exposure to law enforcement and punitive drug policy.

Let's place buprenorphine development against the backdrop of what President George H. W. Bush declared the Decade of the Brain (1990–2000) (figure 1). This was an era in which the US National Institute on Drug Abuse (NIDA) was directed to look for neuromolecular bases for addiction, in anticipation of breakthroughs from the Human Genome Project and subsequent growth in biotechnology industries.

In 1997, Alan Leshner, then-director of NIDA, published a landmark article entitled "Addiction Is a Brain Disease, and It Matters," stating, "That addiction is tied to changes in brain structure and function is what makes it, fundamentally, a brain disease,"[40] and arguing that treatment must compensate for or reverse changes in the brain. Leshner went on to lobby to rebrand addiction as "chronic relapsing brain disease." His ambition was shared by other leading NIDA researchers who coauthored a widely cited article published in JAMA in 2000, entitled "Drug Dependence: A Chronic Medical Illness."[41] In it, they argued that narcotics dependence was comparable to diabetes, hypertension,

FIGURE I. On July 17, 1990, President George H. W. Bush signed into law House Joint Resolution 174 declaring the 1990s to be the "Decade of the Brain" and issued a proclamation calling attention to the importance of brain research for, among other things, "our war on drugs." Presidential Proclamation 6158, July 17, 1990. Source: Library of Congress, Project on the Decade of the Brain.

and asthma in terms of heritability, treatment adherence, and relapse rates and as such should be treated as a chronic medical disease.

Brain imaging of addicted people featured in neuroscience journals during the Decade of the Brain (figure 2) took the human subject and his or her trappings of gender, race, and class out of the picture, and, in fact, took the offending organ (the brain) out of its body altogether, symbolically conveying an unmarked universality of addiction physiology. (The president's proclamation of the Decade of the Brain begins, "The human brain, a 3-pound mass of interwoven nerve cells that controls our activity, is one of the most magnificent and mysterious wonders of creation.")[42] Neuroscientists further reduced the cause of addiction to molecules binding to neuroreceptors: the ultimate disembodiment of addiction. Neuroscientific models of addiction, and in particular brain scan images of addiction, omitted racial identity: expunging the racial identity of the addict, they left a racially unmarked and thus implicitly white social figure. Through these tendencies, neuroscientific images operated as technologies of Whiteness. The covert whitening at

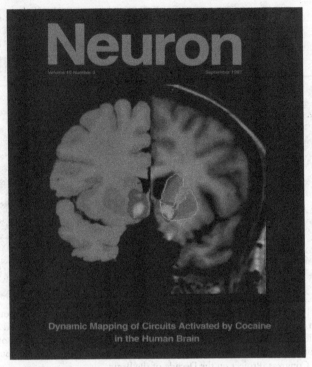

FIGURE 2. Functional MRI of brain circuitry activated by
cocaine, cover illustration for a neurology research journal in
1997. Source: *Neuron* 19, no. 3 (September 1997).

play in addiction neuroscience was analogous to the way in which the
iconic Framingham study of predominantly white study participants
became the reference point for clinical researchers of heart disease, how
spirometer lung function measures of white populations were distinguished from spirometer measures of Blacks, with white measures serving as the norm for lung function, and, in general, how twentieth-
century research on "universal" human biology was long based on a
standard 70 kg white male subject.[43]

The scientists involved in the movement to define addiction as a brain
disease had a social justice intent: they wanted to destigmatize addiction
by demonstrating it to be a legitimate, biological condition, not a problem of morality or choice. What they did not anticipate was that scientific universalism, because it implied a standard white male subject,
would help open white markets to new opioids. Neither did they anticipate that the unequal ways that biotechnologies were disseminated in

the US would enhance the social stratification of addiction. The apparent "universality" of this molecular model implied an assumed white norm; it took a problem long associated with Black and Latinx crime and gave it a new implicit association with whites (as standard humans). This process ended up excluding social conditions. The scientists involved wanted to counteract a drug war mentality by erasing the social context of drug use. Yet they paradoxically set the stage for renewed racial stratification of opioids. While their efforts represented an improvement on punitive drug policies, their insistence on decontextualizing addiction neuroscience, according to an ethic of color blindness, prevented them from addressing the racial stereotypes and structural inequalities underlying access to treatment as opposed to incarceration. This result shows the flexibility of unrecognized Whiteness to adapt and persist, undermining even well-intended efforts promote justice.

Technology 2: New Biotechnologies

Neuroscientists unwittingly aided corporate strategies that capitalized on this erasure of the social. Building on a neuroscientific ideology of technological solutions to addiction, in 1996 Purdue Pharmaceuticals got Food and Drug Administration (FDA) approval for OxyContin as a "minimally addictive opioid pain reliever" suitable for chronic management of moderate pain. This was based on its patented sustained-release capsule technology, which in theory lowered the reward for users by preventing an initial rush. The manufacturer influenced the national Joint Commission on Accreditation of Healthcare Organizations to call for pain to be aggressively monitored and treated as the "5th vital sign,"[44] while drug reps advised new opioid prescribers to direct Oxy-Contin to "trustworthy" patients, in a national workforce of physicians that had been shown more likely to prescribe pain relievers to white patients and to suspect nonwhite patients of drug abuse.[45]

Of course, what the model of addiction-proof biotechnology left out was the social context of drug use. OxyContin users interested in a rush quickly learned to crush and snort or inject the oxycodone in each capsule.

After steep increases in opioid misuse and overdose, public pressure mounted for intervention. In August of 2010, just as the original patent on OxyContin ran out, Purdue Pharmaceuticals introduced its tamper-resistant time-release formulation, embedding oxycodone into polymers that converted tablets into "gummies" should users attempt to crush and dissolve them.[46] By keeping prices high through new patents, and representing OxyContin as technologically sealed off from misuse, the manufacturer kept OxyContin symbolically a step ahead of urban, non-white street markets.

Another biotechnology developed specifically in response to the white suburban and rural prescription opioid epidemic was buprenorphine itself, most often combined with opioid reversal agent naloxone and branded Suboxone. Reckitt Benckiser Pharmaceuticals promoted this combination as a "smart drug": although buprenorphine was an abusable opioid, the naloxone with which buprenorphine was combined caused withdrawal symptoms if injected, but not if dissolved under the tongue as prescribed, since naloxone could not be absorbed sublingually. Buprenorphine also posed a lower risk of overdose death than other opioids because it did not suppress breathing as much.

The manufacturer also benefited from a "public-private partnership" in which the state channeled taxpayer funds to new, privately manufactured technologies designed to meet the challenge of what was widely understood as a white problem. In the 1990s, NIDA subsidized Suboxone's manufacturer with $23 million to test it for use in addiction treatment and sharply distinguished it from methadone, lobbying Congress and the Drug Enforcement Administration (DEA) to lower the abuse potential rating of buprenorphine/Suboxone from Narcotics Schedule II, where OxyContin and methadone fall, to Schedule III, along with codeine cough syrup.[47] This made it possible to prescribe Suboxone in private doctors' offices. In addition, Reckitt-Benckiser, the holder of the patent to buprenorphine, lobbied Congress to get buprenorphine included under an orphan drug clause designed to promote pharma development (such as malaria drugs) for unprofitable diseases in low-income countries. Patent law gives the corporate holder of the formula for a new medication or other technology exclusive rights to manufacture and profit from the new technology for twenty years after the technology's patent registration. Medications can take up to ten years to get FDA approval for use in humans, because manufacturers are required to test the medication in extensive clinical trials, which then significantly shorten the period of time for which the patent holder has exclusive manufacture rights. In the case of buprenorphine, Congress designated it an orphan drug based on the manufacturer's argument that addiction was an unprofitable condition for which to produce treatments. This doubled Reckitt-Benckiser's period of exclusive manufacture, and therefore of unilateral power to set prices, by giving the company a patent extension through 2009 on a drug it had initially developed in the late 1960s.[48]

As we will elaborate in more detail in chapters 5 and 6, in a race- and class-stratified health care system such as that in the US, where access to generalist doctors is often limited to those who can pay, patented, expensive technologies for private office delivery in themselves encode white race and middle class.

Technology 3: Regulation

OxyContin and similar newly approved opioids such as Opana and Roxicodone quickly made their way to illegal markets for nonmedical sale and use. Their chemical effects, including their ability to cause overdose, were similar to those of illegal opioids like heroin, but their legal manufacture and the legal elements of the supply chain leading up to their illegal sale, as well as the white identity of the neighborhoods in which they were marketed and ultimately used, led to a law enforcement response that starkly contrasted with enforcement of heroin laws in Black and Brown neighborhoods. Although by 2004 opioid pain relievers were more commonly used nonmedically than heroin in the US, the arrest rate for illegal possession of opioids was one-fourth that for possession of heroin. The number of arrests for illegal sale of prescription drugs was less than one-fifth that of the number of arrests for selling heroin.[49] Not coincidentally, the "nonmedical use" of pain relievers was twice as high among whites as Blacks at that time,[50] while rates of heroin use among Blacks and non-Hispanic whites were similar.[51]

Since suburban and rural white opioid users were not politically popular targets for drug law enforcement, the DEA and other regulators instead focused surveillance and enforcement on prescription opioid prescribers and pharmacists, the majority of whom were located in white suburban or rural areas. One sign of this was the spread of prescription drug monitoring programs, eventually enacted in all fifty states, half of which mandated prescriber participation with threats of loss of physician license and prosecution.[52] At the same time, in 2000 the US Congress relaxed restrictions on buprenorphine by passing the Drug Addiction Treatment Act (DATA 2000), which enabled any certified physician to prescribe buprenorphine for opioid use disorder in the privacy of his or her own office.

In congressional debates leading to passage of DATA 2000, there was a clear emphasis on a "new kind of drug user," one who was young, suburban, "not hardcore," and, implicitly, white. Alan Leschner, then-director of NIDA, stressed that buprenorphine was uniquely appropriate for a new kind of opioid user—as opposed to methadone, "which tends to concentrate in urban areas, [and] is a poor fit for the suburban spread of narcotic addiction."[53] Then–Health and Human Services director Donna Shalala noted that buprenorphine, as an alternative to methadone, would serve "a new kind of addict," "including citizens who would not normally be associated with the term addiction."[54] With this euphemistic language, in which "suburban" and "new kind of addict" referred to middle-class whites, DATA 2000 passed Congress and reversed eighty years of federal prohibition against private physician opioid maintenance for opioid dependence. DATA 2000 made no mention of the restrictive methadone system, which stayed intact for a darker and poorer clientele, and did nothing to alter the drug laws that mandated inner-city heroin users to prison, but it did create a new treatment track for those with the resources to use it.

To give additional assurance to the DEA that buprenorphine wouldn't spill over into illicit markets, buprenorphine's manufacturer, along with the federal Substance Abuse and Mental Health Services Administration, developed an eight-hour certification course that was required for doctors to prescribe buprenorphine, the first and only prescription drug in the US to come with such a requirement.

Public clinic doctors told me in interviews that the certification requirement was a major barrier to making buprenorphine available to low-income people, as public clinics did not provide time or incentives to pursue certification, while prescribers in the private sector could charge fees of up to $1,000 for an initial visit for buprenorphine induction.[55] The shortage of public sector prescribers, along with the cost of buprenorphine, long kept buprenorphine primarily in the private sector.

Technology 4: Ethnic Marketing and Media

Citing recent industry-sponsored guidelines based on deeply flawed or, in some cases, misrepresented studies, Purdue (and later other opioid manufacturers) argued that the risk of addiction when opioids were used to treat "legitimate" pain was miniscule. Even though such claims were still controversial in the 1990s, Purdue was able to win FDA approval of OxyContin for moderate pain, cracking open an opioid market that had previously been restricted to those with severe acute pain—such as postsurgical or end-stage cancer pain—to a new, much larger market of patients with chronic pain, such as lower back pain.[56] The company hired almost seven hundred drug representatives who canvassed a call list of nearly one hundred thousand physicians, mostly generalists in suburban, small town, and rural areas,[57] serving patients that the public and the DEA would not think of as at high risk of addiction and diversion of prescribed narcotics. Purdue's strategy was successful: it led to a tenfold increase in prescription of OxyContin for non-cancer-related pain nationally from 1997 to 2001, with the disproportionate uptake of OxyContin by prescribers in white suburban, small town, and rural areas of states like Maine, West Virginia, Kentucky, and Virginia.[58] This positive association between opioid prescribing rates and percentage of white residents endured as Purdue's competitors jumped into and helped radically expand the newly opened market, extending and worsening the opioid crisis through 2015 and beyond.[59]

In a newspaper content analysis that our research team completed on one hundred articles reporting on opioids selected randomly from major national newspapers in 2001 and 2011, we found that, in contrast to Black and Latinx drug users, who were portrayed in the media as criminals, suburbanites addicted to OxyContin were portrayed sympathetically in the media as victims of overprescription or as people struggling with physical or existential pain (figure 3).[60]

Ironically, Purdue's technological response to the first wave of white prescription opioid overdose deaths, their tamper-resistant formulations of oxycodone, combined with new prescription drug monitoring programs, led many of these opioid users to look for heroin when prescribed oxycodone became hard to get and to use. One consequence of this was a whitening of the media coverage of heroin users who had long been portrayed as Black and Latinx (figures 4 and 5). The fact that many of the media images and humanizing stories of white middle-class people representing the "new face of heroin addiction" were of women—often described as mothers, teachers, or college students who began their opioid use with prescribed painkillers—helped to convey that they were blameless and vulnerable. It also reflected the reality of a large percentage of female opioid users, given that women are more likely to seek medical attention for pain.[61]

The targeted intervention for these new heroin users, buprenorphine (Suboxone), was marketed to middle-class, insured patients over the

I was a painkiller addict

After being prescribed powerful opiate drugs to manage chronic pain, I gradually descended into full-blown dependency. Here is my story

FIGURE 3. The "new face of opioid addiction": Cathryn. Source: Cathryn Kemp, "I Was a Painkiller Addict," *The Guardian*, September 9, 2012, www.theguardian.com /lifeandstyle/2012/sep/09/i-was-a-painkiller-addict. Photo credit: Frank Baron for *The Guardian*.

internet. Manufacturer-sponsored, web-based public service announcements, such as those of naabt.org (National Association of Advocates of Buprenorphine Treatment), featured images of white professionals and business owners on buprenorphine maintenance (figure 6).

The same website featured a link to a buprenorphine prescriber locator service created by the federal Substance Abuse and Mental Health Services Administration; browsers entered their zip code under a tab (next to an image of a blond man in a collared business shirt) labeled "Patients: Find a Buprenorphine Provider" to generate a list of certified prescribers, most of them in private practice. These strategies created an exclusive, yet lucrative segment of the market for Suboxone, making it a blockbuster drug at $1.4 billion a year in US sales by 2012,[62] second only to OxyContin, whose US sales exceeded $3 billion by 2009.[63]

Hooked: A teacher's addiction and the new face of heroin

For years, Michelle lived a double life – a teacher and mother, she was also a heroin addict willing to risk everything for the drug.

FIGURE 4. The "new face of heroin addiction": Michelle. Source: Linda Carroll, "Hooked: A Teacher's Addiction and the New Face of Heroin," *Today*, April 8, 2014, www.today.com/health/hooked-teacher-s-addiction-new-face-heroin-t74881.

The new face of heroin addiction

By Deseret News | Feb 19, 2015, 7:00am MST
Kelsey Dallas and Sandy Balazic, For the Deseret News

f 𝕏 ⤴ SHARE

FIGURE 5. The "new face of heroin addiction": Blake. Source: Kelsey Dallas and Sandy Balazic, "The New Face of Heroin Addiction," *Deseret News*, February 19, 2015, www.deseret.com/2015/2/19/20558592/the-new-face-of-heroin-addiction. Photo credit: Dominick DiFurio.

FIGURE 6. Manufacturer-sponsored buprenorphine website. Source: National Alliance of Advocates for Buprenorphine Treatment, accessed January 14, 2021. https://naabt .org.

DISRUPTING THE CYCLE OF WHITE OPIOIDS

This racial segmentation of drug markets into licit and illicit, white and Black, clinical and recreational, encouraged a continuous stream of new technologies targeting the white middle class. This is an old cycle, started by Bayer Pharmaceutical's own heroin, marketed in 1898 as a miracle cough medicine for the white doctor-visiting classes (figure 7).

We might use the case of white opioids to update Cedric Robinson's insights about the role of race in capitalism. Worldwide, health care and biotechnology make up one of the largest economic sectors, at $11.9 trillion in annual sales.[64] Our biomedical economy depends not only on cheap labor but also on consumption of high-cost pharmaceuticals driven by increasing numbers of medical diagnoses. Opioids create physiological dependence, often calling for escalating doses over time to ward off withdrawal symptoms, and thus a population of people diagnosed with opioid use disorder who are then prescribed maintenance opioids for that dependence, driving a closed feedback loop of biocapital. Add this to a neurosci-

FIGURE 7. Ad for Bayer's Heroin, 1898.

entific cultural logic that (1) propagates the image of the universal brain with a hidden, implicit white racial identity, thereby (2) erasing social environment as a factor in drug use, and (3) leading to further translation of neuroscience into racialized biotechnologies, while (4) using neuroscientific claims to bolster racialized marketing of these new biotechnologies.

While Robinson's historical account of racial capital focused on the ways nonwhites provided expendable labor for colonial ventures initiated in Europe and operating in Africa, the Americas, and Asia, opioids today show that Whiteness fuels biotechnology development, global marketing, and consumption. As the pharmaceutical industry executives we have interviewed explained, white upper- and middle-class markets drive demand for newly patented drugs, as affluent white consumers use their social and economic capital to access "cutting-edge technology," thereby lending their symbolic capital as elites to the technology so that it is seen as a desirable consumer item. Then, closer to the end of a drug's patent life, when the shortfalls and side effects of the drug become apparent, drug manufacturers seek to patent new formulations while marketing the original formulation to nonwhite, publicly insured patients in order to extend sales of the drug just before the patent expiration.

The US Centers for Disease Control reported that by 2016, Black men were the group with the largest increase in overdose rates,[65] likely related to their disproportionate incarceration on drug charges. Upon

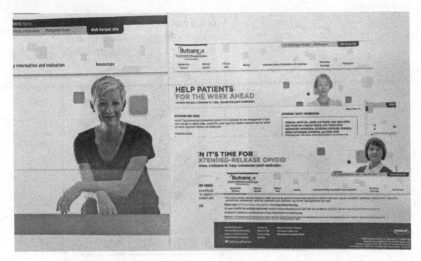

FIGURE 8. 2000s promotionals for Butran, Purdue's buprenorphine patch, on desk of author. Photo credit: Helena Hansen.

release, their physiological tolerance to opioids is low because they have not had access to opioids while incarcerated, yet they are at high risk for relapse and are exposed to ultrapotent illicit opioids such as fentanyl in illegal markets. Because of this overdose risk, drug manufacturers are now marketing older formulations of buprenorphine and especially the long-acting injectable opioid reversal agent naltrexone to incarcerated populations via criminal justice administrators. At the same time, federal funds such as National Institutes of Health public-private partnership grants are subsidizing drug manufacturers to develop newly patented formulations of opioids for pain and for addiction that will be available to privately insured patients.

Even Purdue Pharmaceuticals, manufacturer of OxyContin, the product that initiated the current opioid crisis, capitalized on this cycle: Purdue owns the patent for buprenorphine skin patches (Butran), which were originally FDA approved for pain, but as a member of Purdue's board informed us, the company sought FDA approval for their use to treat opioid use disorder. As reflected in the images of white, professionally dressed (and female) patients in Purdue's advertisements (figure 8), the targeted market for Butran is the white middle class, in a race- and class-segregated health care system. These deliberate strategies are imperatives of racial capitalism: pharmaceutical industry profits hinge on accurate racial readings of segments of consumers who are predisposed to buy their products, have the means to buy them (whether with private income or public subsidy), and provide the easiest paths around regulations that could otherwise retard or restrict their sales.

Racially segregated drug policies and lucrative narcotic marketing can be sustained only if there is a separate route to categorize and discipline drug use among whites—and that route must appear, at least on its face, to be race neutral. Racialized drug policies and marketing have costs that are borne by whites, who pay inflated prices and sometimes pay with their lives. The ambiguity of the Greek word *pharmakon*—its dual identity as medicine and poison—is exploited in this white "war on drugs that wasn't," in which unprecedented profits are made in the liminal space between licit and illicit sales—a space that is protected by its symbolic Whiteness.

THREE TALES OF ONE OPIOID CRISIS

To tell the story of race in the US opioid crisis, we have woven together one story from three starting points. Helena Hansen, an addiction psychiatrist and cultural anthropologist, documents institutional actors in the story of the opioid crisis and policy responses, drawing from a decade of firsthand observation in the field of addiction psychiatry, having treated patients with buprenorphine and methadone in the public clinics of New York City while interviewing patients and practitioners of addiction medicine throughout the city. She observed and interviewed addiction researchers and clinical administrators who strove to establish office-based buprenorphine as the standard of care across the US, and observed and interviewed policy makers and pharmaceutical executives as they debated treatment protocols, target clientele, and reimbursements. She was assisted in collecting data by a cohort of graduate students who have published their analyses in a range of journals.[*] Her

* This ethnographic research team included Sonia Mendoza, Alyssa Rivera, Alexandrea Hatcher, and Caroline Parker. Their published work from the project includes C. Parker and H. Hansen, "How Opioids Became 'Safe': Pharmaceutical Splitting and the Racial Politics of Opioid Safety," *Biosocieties*, June 14, 2021, 1–24, https://doi.org/10.1057 /s41292-021-00230-y; S. Mendoza, A. Rivera, and H. Hansen, "Re-racialization of Addiction and the Re-distribution of Blame in the White Opioid Epidemic," *Medical Anthropology Quarterly* 33, no. 2 (2018): 242–62; A. Hatcher and H. Hansen, "At the Expense of a Life: Race, Class, and the Meaning of Buprenorphine in Pharmaceuticalized 'Care,'" *Substance Use and Misuse* 53, no. 2 (2018): 301–10; S. Mendoza, A. Rivera, and H. Hansen, "The Prescription Opioid 'Crisis' among Middle Class White Americans," *Transcultural Psychiatry* 53, no. 4 (2016): 465–87.

findings are foreshadowed in chapter 1 and are developed through the second half of the book in the form of biographies of three opioids that have taken center stage in the white opioid crisis: OxyContin, buprenorphine, and heroin. These opioid biographies were coauthored by Jules Netherland and David Herzberg, who imbued them with political and historical analysis.

In the third chapter, policy advocate Jules Netherland charts the logic of targeted drug policies designed for white middle-class Americans, as these have unfolded in the racially selective decriminalization of narcotics. She begins by comparing her firsthand observations of the white middle-class mothers of severely ill children who lobbied for legalization of medical marijuana with national campaigns for medical treatment of opioid use disorder. As she shows, the newly white middle-class identity of opioid use disorder forced an unprecedented reversal of the drug war logic from punitive to clinical approaches to problem drug use—at least in selected, white middle-class spaces. Jules then cowrites the second half of the book with Helena Hansen and David Herzberg to shine a light on the policies shaping the racial identity of OxyContin, buprenorphine, and heroin.

In the third chapter, historian David Herzberg shows that technologies of Whiteness have been shaping American experiences with drugs since the nineteenth-century days of "Demon Rum." Indeed, he argues, Whiteness was baked in from the beginning of distinctions between medicine and drugs, therapy and addiction. Malleable but persistent technologies of Whiteness helped enable—and even encourage—the seemingly contradictory flourishing of a thriving industry of habit-forming medications accessible to whites with easy access to prescribers, alongside increasingly punitive narcotics laws that created and governed dangerously unregulated prohibition markets preferentially available to groups racialized as nonwhite. Herzberg cowrites the remaining chapters of the book with Helena Hansen and Jules Netherland to historicize OxyContin, buprenorphine, and heroin as products of the racial politics of their time.

Chapter 5 provides a racial biography of OxyContin, the most recent addition to a string of legal narcotics developed for a white clientele in the twentieth century. A child of NIDA's Decade of the Brain, OxyContin played to the neuroscientific aspirations of drug regulators who, in their hope for magic bullets in the form of new molecular safeguards from opioid addiction, failed to question the social conditions of OxyContin's use. Regulators' belief in OxyContin as a "minimally addictive" opioid was further reinforced by the racial and class identity of the pre-sumed consumer: white, with a regular doctor, and therefore middle class. The aggressive marketing undertaken by OxyContin's manufac-turer in primarily white areas of states like Maine, Kentucky, West Vir-ginia, Florida, Virginia, and Ohio, as well as the policies enacted by fed-eral and state governments after they could no longer ignore the white death toll following accelerated opioid prescription on the heels of that targeted marketing, were the direct result of OxyContin's racial identity.

The ascendance of buprenorphine, commercially distributed as Sub-oxone, as the federal government's primary response to the opioid over-dose deaths fueled by OxyContin marketing is traced in chapter 6. Within two years of the FDA's approval of OxyContin for "moderate pain," the US Congress debated the optimal response to opioid use among "suburban youth not appropriate for methadone." Reversing eight decades of prohibition on private office treatment of opioid addic-tion with opioids, they created a new regulatory structure for a priva-tized system of opioid maintenance with a legal status and racial iden-tity distinct from that of methadone. Only by uncovering the segregationist logic of opioid maintenance treatment from the origins of methadone, President Nixon's first weapon in the war on drugs in Black and Latinx city neighborhoods, through the divergent origin of Subox-one in the profitable frontier of white middle America can one under-stand how two molecules with similar pharmacological action—metha-done and buprenorphine—came to have such distinct social identities and legal infrastructures.

Heroin's racial darkening through the twentieth century, and its eventual recapture of its white identity, is chronicled in chapter 7. When the contemporary opioid crisis led drug regulators to restrict OxyCon-tin and other extended-release opioid pain relievers through prescrip-tion drug monitoring programs and tamper-resistant formulations, white opioid-dependent consumers turned to heroin. For the first time in a century, a majority of new heroin users were women, given that women disproportionately see doctors and therefore were prescribed OxyContin and other opioids for pain. The result was a return to white women as the primary clientele for heroin, an echo of the late nine-teenth century when the doctor-visiting class of women were the most likely Americans to experience opioid addiction.

The book's conclusion looks internationally and forward to alterna-tive policies and health practices that do not reproduce the toxic racial structures of the opioid crisis. Chapter 8 reflects on the dangers of our national obsession with biomedicalization as an answer to addiction, as a distraction from the social and economic crisis that is manifest in white opioids. It also examines the history of selective decriminalization in US drug policy and what this history predicts about the "kinder, gentler drug war" being declared in suburban white America and its renewed racial divergence from punitive interventions in Black and brown American cities. The chapter ends with policy and practice recommendations for a more critically informed and public health–oriented approach to addictive drugs that explicitly addresses the racial capitalist drivers of "deaths of despair."

CHAPTER 3

Good Samaritans in the War on Drugs That Wasn't

(as told by Jules Netherland, policy analyst)

I couldn't believe what I was seeing. In June of 2011, flanked by white parents from Long Island, conservative Republican senator and Health Committee chair Kemp Hannon led a press conference about the passage of New York's Good Samaritan 911 Law. The law, which provides limited immunity from prosecution to those calling 911 for help during a drug overdose, was one of the first of its kind in the country. Good Samaritan laws were born out of the bifurcated approach to drug policy in the US. On the one hand, an overdose is treated as a medical emergency, and of course calling 911 can prevent the tragic loss of life. On the other hand, drug use and possession are treated as crimes, so people who use drugs or even those who happen to be in proximity of an overdose are afraid of calling 911 because they know they will likely face arrest.[1] Even though I closely followed the campaign to pass the law, I still couldn't believe I was watching conservative Republicans, who had long opposed almost every progressive drug policy proposal put forward in New York, embracing a bill that essentially carved out a space where people who were using drugs didn't need to fear prosecution. Even more inconceivably to me, this bill had been sponsored by senate Republicans and lauded by conservative senate leader Dean Skelos. Using talking points that could have been scripted by progressive drug policy reformists, Hannon explained in a press release: "If someone is witnessing a drug or alcohol overdose, their first reaction should be to get help, not worrying about personal ramifications. This bill would help alleviate some of the concern about charges an individual may face for illicit activity and provide quicker and more effective medical responses."[2]

What strange new world have I entered, I wondered, where Republican senators are leading the fight for more progressive drug policy reform and talking about medical, instead of punitive, responses to drug use? And what about these new allies—white suburban parents? What brought them to a fight traditionally framed around racial justice and criminal justice reform, particularly when many of these same players had been the architects of punitive drug laws? How did it seem suddenly that the rubric around drug use had flipped, so that compassion and care were priorities to provide to people who used drugs? And how much did racial dynamics influence this abrupt policy shift?

My education and my work have provided me with lots of opportunities to reflect on Whiteness and white privilege, and yet I find myself uncomfortable writing about it, particularly from a personal perspective. On the one hand, it saddens me that this exercise of trying to uncover how prioritization of Whiteness dehumanizes others is even necessary. On the other hand, tracing how my understanding of Whiteness developed might provide a way for white readers to better process their own Whiteness and the arguments about systemic racism that we make in this book. I would not be honest if I failed to admit that writing about Whiteness as a white person feels fraught. I do not want to center my story, and yet I understand that failing to talk about Whiteness—my own—reinscribes the privilege of silence and unexamined Whiteness. I also understand that many readers have no interest in yet another account of how a white person awakens to systems of white supremacy. For those readers, I suggest skipping ahead to the next section.

Too often, I think, well-meaning white people, like me, stay quiet because we fear getting it wrong. I have come to understand that, while Whiteness operates on the interpersonal level in ways that are harmful, it also operates on the structural and systemic level in ways that are both destructive and often insidious. White supremacy is so woven into the fabric of US society that it is hard for white people—for me—to see all the ways it operates, particularly because it is invisible by design. As a white person working in drug policy, I've found that I have to constantly interrogate (gratefully with the help of others) the ways I am either actively challenging racist practices or inadvertently reinforcing them. As scholar and activist Mariame Kaba explains: "When we set about transforming society, we must remember that we ourselves will also need to be transformed. . . . We are deeply entangled in the systems we are organizing to change. . . . We have all so thoroughly internalized these logics of oppression that if oppression were to end tomorrow, we would be likely to reproduce previous structures."[3] I believe that I have a responsibility to see and reveal Whiteness—however entrenched and elusive it may be, and however imperfectly I may do so.

When the Good Samaritan Law passed, and I saw the expected narrative around people who use drugs upended when it came to white, more affluent people, I was working as an organizer and lobbyist at the Drug Policy Alliance (DPA), and I had been working on drug policy reform and research for almost a decade. Those years had led me through many examinations of Whiteness and how it operates, especially related to people who were marginalized. The DPA is a national organization that works to end the war on drugs and policies that punish people who use drugs and instead to promote drug policies that focus on health and human rights. I discovered drug policy work in the early 1990s, through HIV activism, while working at the Gay and Lesbian Advocates and Defender's AIDS Law Project. At that time, the demographics of the people we served were changing, from predominantly gay men to people who inject drugs. What compelled me about the work was that both groups, who seemed to have little in common, were highly stigmatized and considered "throwaway" people to most of society.

As a gender-nonconforming, queer person coming of age in the 1970s and '80s, I knew a little about what it felt like to be at the margins and to have people hate you because of who you are, how you look, or how you choose to live your life. Perhaps it was this core sense of not belonging that led me to find and adopt spiritual communities in college that practiced radical acceptance—we are all welcome, particularly the "least among us"—and focused on righting social injustices. It wasn't perhaps the expected course at the time—to come out as a lesbian and then convert to Catholicism—but as the child of two social workers, I had always understood that I had been afforded privileges that others had not, through no merit of my own. I didn't then fully understand the systems at work that made unearned advantage automatically accrue to my Whiteness, but I did feel deeply that it was unfair that I had so much when others had so little.

Inhabiting both intellectually elitist and leftist progressive worlds, I have learned that talking about spirituality and religious beliefs is unpopular, and yet the ways in which I have come to understand and grapple with my own Whiteness—as well as my commitment to changing drug policy to recognize people's humanity—are rooted in my faith. Having been raised agnostic with a healthy distrust of organized religion, I continued, nonetheless, to be preoccupied by this question of how we could treat some people as disposable and dispensable, especially as I fell in with a radical wing of the Catholic Church that had grown out of the Catholic Worker Movement and the sanctuary movement in which certain congregations were welcoming into their churches and protecting political refugees from Central America. Teaching informed by liberation theology was calling on people of faith to ally with the most disadvantaged and stigmatized, and in my practice that meant working to provide food for Philadelphia's unhoused. In this living, working faith, people were not just espousing spiritual beliefs but also putting them into practice and treating people who were unhoused with love and respect grounded in the spiritual belief of the intrinsic humanity of each person. This radical acceptance of all people, most especially those considered "outcasts" by others, resonated deeply with me.

Doing street outreach to feed the homeless, I quickly became friends with a wide array of people, including people who used drugs. I soon learned that people who used drugs, far from being the dangerous, unpredictable, morally bankrupt people I had been taught they would be by a culture that too often equates drug use, criminality, and moral failing, were like the rest of us—beautiful, complex, imperfect humans. This, of course, was consistent with my deeply held spiritual beliefs that we are all equally beloved creatures of God and that any system of "othering," anything that dehumanizes another, is an anathema.

By the time I graduated from college in 1989, I had a deeper understanding of the systems of privilege that propped up not just my advantage but the advantage of white people in general. I was firmly cemented in my commitment to embracing a practice of radical acceptance and inclusivity—helping to build a world where even "the least of these" would be imbued with full dignity and worth. And I felt a desire to use my privilege in the service of others, so immediately after college, I spent a year living and working with Franciscan monks in a soup kitchen in inner-city Philadelphia. We lived in community with the people we served; they were our neighbors and friends. We ate together, worked together, and worshipped together. This was during the end of the crack era and well before there were any viable treatments for HIV/AIDS. While part of this community, I saw heart-wrenching pain and suffering. But I noticed that most of that harm was not because of crack itself but because of the policies, structures, and stigma that kept people living in poverty and prevented them from getting the help and support they needed.

The neighborhood in which I lived and worked was at the intersection of three communities: one predominantly Black, one predominantly Latinx, and one predominantly white—all low income. A yearlong witness as a white person living and working in a stigmatized community offered some insight but was clearly far different from the experience of those who made their homes there. Though people of all races and ethnicities gathered at the soup kitchen, the neighborhoods were largely segregated. While there were certainly profound differences in how groups were treated within society, by the police, for example, features of poverty and the perceived dangerousness of the neighborhood affected the entire community. I remember how the sanitation department refused to come into the neighborhood, claiming it was too risky; how potholes the size of shopping carts remained unfilled; and how when we took our soup kitchen guests to the hospital for care, they were treated with utter disdain and often turned away altogether. I learned how, although Whiteness conferred some advantages, those advantages had limitations for poor people who were white, particularly those who used drugs. Poverty and drug-related stigma seemed to override some of the benefits of Whiteness. I saw again and again the casual cruelty with which people who used crack were treated, and I also saw the transformative power of kindness and acceptance. Nonetheless, it quickly became clear that the bowls of soup and compassion we served twice daily, as critical as they were, were never going to get at the root of the suffering I saw that year.

My exposure to critical race theory in school was in some ways concretized by my being immersed in a low-income community of color, and I had a growing awareness about structural racism and the ways in which my own white privilege had advantaged me. I understood early on that my status as an upper-middle-class white person came to me through absolutely no effort of my own and that my advantages rested on the disadvantaging of others. And yet everywhere I turn, white supremacist logic works to reinforce the notion that my status is built on my own merit and hard work. Indeed, one of the privileges of Whiteness is the ability to be oblivious about one's one race, to not have to think every minute of every day about what it means to be white, to live in a world designed to recognize and benefit you, that all the while tells you that you have earned and deserved what you have.

As imperceptible as Whiteness can be for a white person, sometimes it becomes so blatant it is hard to ignore. Working as I was with people who used drugs and people living with HIV/AIDS, I was both fascinated and outraged to witness the racial politics of the Ryan White Care Act of 1990. I clearly remember how the US government ignored HIV/AIDS as scores of gay men and people who injected drugs died, and I had complicated feelings about the narrative of an "innocent white victim" being used to garner resources.[4] In the case of the Ryan White Care Act, the face of a young white boy with hemophilia who got HIV through a blood transfusion was used by Congress to help authorize funds for community AIDS prevention and care. On the one hand, I was relieved to see funds finally being appropriated for HIV/AIDS, and I knew this victory represented the hard work of activists who had been fighting for such a win for years. But I also felt a mix of both anger and grief that the suffering of those who were not white or not perceived as "innocent" had been largely ignored.

The counterpoint of this was evident on a daily basis in my community. Charlene was soft-spoken and gentle, with an easy smile, and we soon became friends. During the day, she hung out around the soup kitchen and was always willing to lend a hand. She had started using crack when she left an abusive relationship and ended up unhoused, living on the streets, doing the best she could to get by and working nights trading sex for drugs. She was HIV positive, smoked crack, sometimes injected heroin, and had been in and out of jail for an array of charges related to drug use and sex work. I had taken her to the emergency room one time when she was sick, and the doctors there treated her with such disdain that she vowed never to go back. One warm summer night, I saw her crying softly in a doorway; she had developed an abscess on her leg so severe it was becoming gangrenous. I begged her to go back to the ER, but she refused. I never saw her again. Why weren't Charlene's pain and the roadblocks that she faced— so much of these beyond her control—enough to motivate change? Was it because she was Black, because she used a substance we deemed illegal, because she engaged in sex work? None of that, of course, negated her sweetness, her deep caring for others, or her humanity. Why did it take a white face to prompt compassion? Of course, these are rhetorical questions—ones I would ask myself again a few decades later when the powerful political trope of an innocent white victim reemerged in my own drug policy work.

The question of what motivates policy change is one that has continued to fascinate me throughout my career. As someone trained as a researcher who has long straddled the divide between research and policy, I am interested in unearthing the reasons why policy makers so often reject what works: why US policies often fly in the face of what we know to be effective. What was true of early HIV policy is true of much of US drug policy: we know what works and are largely happy to ignore it.

If science and evidence about effectiveness are not driving US drug policies, what is? It didn't take me long working in the policy arena to learn that myriad forces are at work: the influence of lobbying groups, the concerns of powerful constituents, hot issues in the media, concerns about reelection, a policy maker's personal experience. In the case of drug policy, though, perhaps no force has been as powerful as that of racial politics and racial capital.

In this chapter, I want to show how the Whiteness of the current opioid problem ran headlong into the anti-Black racism that drove, and continues to drive, US drug policy—creating a paradox for policy makers. For the last fifty years, under the war on drugs declared by Nixon, policy makers have invested heavily in the association between Black and Brown communities and illicit drug use and have used the threat of drugs to ramp up fears about Black and Brown people and to craft increasingly punitive policies that have been effective tools of racial targeting and control. The well-documented result is the overpolicing of communities of color and the mass criminalization of Black and Brown people. However, when white people started to become the face of the opioid problem, policy makers (predominantly white themselves) suddenly found themselves with a dilemma on their hands. The punitive approach upon which many policy makers had built their careers was unpalatable to their white, more affluent constituents, many of whom were experiencing opioid problems in their own families. But if the drug war apparatus isn't acceptable for white people, it starts to be revealed for what it truly is: a thin guise for tactics and policies intended to control Black and Brown people and communities. Moreover, Whiteness, particularly the trope of the innocent white victim, turns out to be a powerful lever for policy change—but what kind?

Below I offer my account of the ways I have observed Whiteness being wielded to protect white drug users—sometimes successfully and sometimes not—from a massive drug war apparatus designed to criminalize Black and Brown people. This isn't a linear narrative but a nuanced and complicated story about how policies that seem race neutral on their face can create devastating racial disparities. These policy decisions also direct investments, create stigmas, and enshrine practices that ultimately have left this country ill equipped to deal effectively and humanely with drug problems in any community—white, Black, or Brown.

A LEGACY OF RACIST DRUG POLICIES

The association of illicit drugs with people of color to justify prohibition stretches back more than a century, but the modern war on drugs was declared by Richard Nixon in 1971. On June 17 of that year, Nixon stood next to his newly appointed drug czar (a high-level official designated to coordinate the nation's response to drugs) and declared drug abuse "public enemy number one." Drawing on the language of war, he went on: "In order to fight and defeat this enemy, it is necessary to wage a new, all-out offensive."[5] One of Nixon's advisers at the time, John Ehrlichman, has since made clear that at its roots the drug war was a tool for targeting Black people and antiwar protesters:

> The Nixon campaign in 1968, and the Nixon White House after that, had two enemies: the antiwar left and Black people. You understand what I'm saying? We knew we couldn't make it illegal to be either against the war or Black, but by getting the public to associate the hippies with marijuana and Blacks with heroin, and then criminalizing both heavily, we could disrupt those communities. We could arrest their leaders, raid their homes, break up their meetings, and vilify them night after night on the evening news. Did we know we were lying about the drugs? Of course we did.[6]

Nixon, however, was not alone. In the decades that followed, many politicians on both sides of the aisle and at both the state and federal levels built careers on "getting tough on crime" with drug offenses at the center. In 1973, New York governor Rockefeller created some of the most punishing drug laws in the country, instituting harsh mandatory prison terms for possession or sale of relatively small amounts of drugs and restricting the ability of judges to use their discretion to reduce sentences. Although the laws were ostensibly intended to target high-level sellers, most people incarcerated under them were convicted of low-level, nonviolent, first-time offenses. New York's Rockefeller Drug Laws became the national policy model for the drug war: throughout the 1970s other states followed and enacted their own versions of the Rockefeller Drug Laws, as did Congress in the 1980s. Interestingly, in 1977, New York exempted marijuana from the Rockefeller Drug Laws, decriminalizing the possession of small amounts. In a foreshadowing of Whiteness propelling other drug policy changes, the decriminalization of marijuana in New York was led, in part, by white suburban parents concerned that their children could be saddled with criminal records or have their lives derailed. A key legislator advocating for that bill, Richard Gottfried, at the time one of the youngest members of the state assembly, recalled that one of the most active prodecriminalization groups in 1977 was the state's Parent Teacher Association. He noted: "They were in my office every day, working the halls. Their motivation was that it was a lot of their kids who were getting arrested. It was very much a middle class and even suburban issue."[7] This exemption on behalf of white youth ultimately did little to protect urban youth of color from marijuana-related arrests, despite data showing that young white people used marijuana at higher rates than Black or Latinx young people.

Nor did the white exceptionalism of marijuana decriminalization in New York and other states do much to slow the pace of increasingly harsh drug laws throughout the US, which often passed with wide bipartisan support. Concern around not compromising the futures of kids in the suburbs did not translate to concern for other communities. Under Reagan and Clinton, incarceration rates soared as the war on drugs expanded. The number of people behind bars for nonviolent drug law offenses increased from fifty thousand in 1980 to over four hundred thousand by 1997.[8] Throughout the 1980s, in a trend buttressed by media portrayals of "crack addicts," problematic drug use became ever more affiliated with Black and Brown urban communities in the public's and policy makers' eyes.[9] And as we noted earlier, in 1986 the Anti-Drug Abuse Act helped enshrine this association in law by creating a disparity between federal penalties for crack cocaine and powder cocaine offenses, imposing the same penalties for the possession of an amount of crack cocaine as for one hundred times the same amount of powder cocaine, despite the two compounds being the same chemically. Though race was not mentioned, it soon became clear that this disparity was racist in both its intent and its effect.[10]

US drug laws did not stop at mass incarceration; they also contributed to the militarization of the police. By the end of George W. Bush's term, about forty thousand paramilitary-style SWAT raids were carried out on Americans every year—mostly for nonviolent drug law offenses, often misdemeanors.[11] Penalties for drug offenses were built into housing, child welfare, immigration, education, public benefits, and employment systems, compounding the harm and exacerbating racial disparities and bolstering a system of racial capitalism.[12]

By 2013, more than 2.3 million people were behind bars in the US. Drug offenses accounted for two-thirds of the rise in the federal inmate population and more than half of the rise in state prisoners between 1985 and 2000. Currently more than half of young Black men in large cities in the US are under the control of the criminal justice system, [13] and middle-aged Black men are more likely to have been in prison than in college or the military.[14] Although Black Americans are no more likely than whites to use illicit drugs, they are six to ten times more likely to be incarcerated for drug offenses.[15] Loïc Wacquant, Carl Hart, and others make the case that the criminal justice system, driven in large part by the war on drugs, is, in effect, a new state-sponsored racial caste system.[16]

MEDICALIZATION AS A WAY OUT?

I was well aware of drug policy's racist legacy when I went to work as a research coordinator on some National Institute on Drug Abuse–funded studies in 2000. The research team, including addiction medicine doctors and public health experts, was exploring the idea of medicalizing addiction—although they didn't use that term—which is the idea that addiction should be treated as a medical disorder. Their research was focused on getting substance use treatment integrated into regular medical practice, such as primary care and hospitals. At the time, those of us invested in medicalizing addiction thought it would be a way to destigmatize it—as neuroscientists believed—and to get people the care they needed. We were working in a low-income part of Boston with many unhoused people; we saw people struggling just to make it through each day. I was moved by this group of doctors who had committed their careers to helping and who clearly saw the failure of the criminal legal system as a solution to drug problems.

In the early 2000s, when I relocated from Boston to New York, I continued working on medical models of addiction through a federally funded multisite evaluation looking at the integration of buprenorphine into HIV care settings. HIV settings had been prioritized because buprenorphine was thought to help people living with HIV who were also dependent on injection heroin. I was excited to work on the study because I believed that, when DATA 2000 passed—the Drug Addiction Treatment Act, which made it possible for doctors to prescribe buprenorphine—it had the potential to change drug treatment and drug policy forever. I frankly couldn't believe that, after more than seventy years, legislation that overturned the restrictions of the Harrison Act on private office treatment of opiate addiction had passed, and had done so with relatively little fanfare. The restrictions had been in place since the early 1920s, when the US Supreme Court affirmed that the 1914 Harrison Anti-Narcotic Act prohibited the office-based prescribing of narcotics for the long-term treatment of addiction, a restriction that persisted when the Harrison Act was replaced by the Controlled Substances Act in 1970. DATA 2000 cut a gaping hole through this prohibition by allowing physicians to do precisely that. While I felt this new legislation was incredibly promising, its limitations soon became clear.

While working on the study, I went back to graduate school and decided to use the data from the study of buprenorphine in HIV clinics for my dissertation. The study had a large quantitative section looking at drug use, health, and quality-of-life outcomes, comparing people on buprenorphine versus methadone, which remained highly stigmatized despite its effectiveness. Would buprenorphine help destigmatize addiction even in the highly stigmatized and marginalized population of opioid-dependent people? How did they experience it in comparison to methadone, which had also been heralded as a medical treatment but which had quickly become mired in stigma and viewed as a kind of substitute drug? There was also a big process evaluation looking at how the HIV clinics were integrating these services into the health care system, involving qualitative interviews with providers and patients about their experiences. In conducting these interviews with patients, I began to get interested in how people taking buprenorphine were understanding it themselves. The question that came up for me was: Would a medication like buprenorphine, delivered in a medical setting by doctors, finally be what it took to medicalize addiction? And would people who took buprenorphine see their drug use as a medical problem? There was rhetoric about how buprenorphine was going to destigmatize addiction and make it possible to treat addiction in any physician's office. The providers I was working with on the study believed that the way Prozac had mainstreamed treatment for depression, buprenorphine could be the tool for mainstreaming addiction treatment. I was interested in how people on the ground were experiencing this supposed transformation, especially poor people who inject drugs in Federally Qualified Health Center settings.

It soon became clear to me that medicalization had its limits and that the white privilege and racism that built US drug laws were baked into the medical system as well. While the patients in the study benefited from buprenorphine, they found it hard to escape the stigma that seemed to adhere to their heroin use and race. As chapter 6 outlines, buprenorphine has thus far failed to either protect Black and Brown people from racist drug laws or to create broad access for them to be treated medically, but it has created a safe space for many white people to be treated, especially those of higher socioeconomic class with private insurance.

IN THE POLICY TRENCHES

Disillusioned by research and increasingly wary of the medical model, I took a career turn away from public health research and began working on policy change directly, taking on a new role as a policy advocate within the research institution where I had studied buprenorphine. The more I saw how research wasn't driving policy, the more I wanted to be working directly on advocating for policy reforms. This meant learning how the New York State Legislature functioned (or didn't) and working directly with legislators, their staff, and other activists to get bills passed.

Thoroughly convinced that punitive approaches did not work, I had the good fortune to begin working on a campaign to roll back the Rockefeller Drug Laws, whose mandatory minimums for low-level drug offenses were driving mass incarceration in New York. Since these were some of the first and harshest laws in the modern drug war, activists like me knew that reforming the Rockefeller Laws could carry huge symbolic weight for changing drug laws across the country. The battle was waged by a broad coalition of progressive groups and largely led by people of color who had seen their families and communities decimated by mandatory-minimum sentencing and a "lock 'em up and throw away the key" approach to drug policy. While the campaign worked hard to destigmatize addiction and drew on the public health and medical models I had been studying, the heart of the campaign was a call for racial justice and an acknowledgment that the war on drugs was a failure on its own terms. Backed by a large grassroots movement, the Rockefeller reforms were led by Democrats in Albany and managed to pass only because of a particular constellation of political forces in which the Democrats briefly gained control of the senate, the assembly, and the governor's office. Even that was remarkable, given how important Democrats had been in building and sustaining the hypercarceral phase of the war on drugs. In 2009, when the reforms passed, the criminalization of drugs still had broad bipartisan support; the reforms were less a repudiation of the war on drugs than an acknowledgment that perhaps they had gone too far.

But just two years later, some of the same Republican senators who had fought vociferously against Rockefeller reform were supporting the 911 Good Samaritan bill that decriminalized drug use, albeit in a small and limited way. What accounted for this change of heart? When Senator Hannon stood beside white families to promote a new approach to drug policy, he was bucking a long history throughout which illicit drug use had been associated with people of color and used to justify punitive strategies that resulted in the mass incarceration of Black and Brown people. But this change of heart did not extend equally to everyone affected by the drug war.

Some of these questions about how racial politics play out in policy making started to become clearer for me when I switched jobs and began working on drug policy full time. In 2012, a job opened up in the DPA, and I was lucky enough to land a position working in their New York policy office. The DPA's mission is to end the war on drugs, and it seemed like the perfect place for me to see what I could do in an advocacy organization to try to have a broader impact.

The first campaign I worked on for DPA was trying to pass medical marijuana legislation in New York, and it was an eye-opening opportunity, not only to learn about grassroots advocacy and the byzantine mores of a state legislature, but also to gain insight into the subtle ways in which Whiteness can move and shape policy. When I started the campaign, I didn't know, or frankly care, much about medical marijuana. But I did know that marijuana prohibition was responsible for tens of thousands of arrests each year. In fact, other colleagues at the DPA were working on a campaign to decriminalize possession of small amounts of marijuana "in public view."

When New York passed the Rockefeller Drug Laws in 1973, marijuana was included as one of the drugs requiring mandatory-minimum sentencing. But as noted above, white parents were successful in decriminalizing possession of small amounts of marijuana in 1977, largely sparked to action by the impact that harsh sentencing for low-level marijuana possession was having on young people who were perceived to be heading for college and to have their whole lives ahead of them; for these young adults, getting arrested and having their future prospects dimmed wasn't part of the acceptable narrative.

For several years following marijuana decriminalization, very few people were arrested. However, under mayors Giuliani and Bloomberg, law enforcement practices changed to focus on so-called broken-windows policing that involved hundreds of thousands of stop-and-frisk interactions in communities of color, especially targeting young people. This resulted in a sharp rise in marijuana possession arrests, because even though marijuana possession had been decriminalized, the law contained a loophole: it was still illegal to burn marijuana in public or to possess it in public view. In the course of a stop-and-frisk, police routinely instructed people to empty their pockets, and when they followed instructions and revealed marijuana, the police charged them for having marijuana "in public view."

Police used this loophole as well as the alleged odor of marijuana (used to criminalize people for smoking in public, even if there was no evidence, since no proof of odor was required) to charge hundreds of thousands of New Yorkers with low-level marijuana possession charges. Between 1996 and 2016, the NYPD arrested seven hundred thousand people for low-level marijuana possession, 85 percent of whom were Black and Latinx and a large portion of whom were twenty-five years old or younger.[17] The NYPD used the alleged odor of marijuana as the probable cause to stop cars as well and would arrest everyone in the car if a small amount of marijuana was found on a single person. Though this was supposedly a "race-neutral" policy, Black people were almost four times as likely to be arrested on marijuana charges, even though all racial groups used marijuana at roughly the same rates.[18] One analysis found that in the New York City borough of Manhattan Black people were arrested at fifteen times the rate of white people.[19]

Under the leadership of the DPA and VOCAL NY (a grassroots membership group of low-income people affected by HIV, the drug war, incarceration, and homelessness), the campaign fighting back against marijuana arrests had become one of the leading racial justice issues confronting legislators in Albany. By the time the DPA took up the campaign to legalize medical marijuana in New York in 2012, the focus of marijuana reform was ending racist arrests for marijuana possession.

Unlike marijuana decriminalization, which had been a hot topic for a number of years, New York's medical marijuana bill had been languishing since being introduced in 1997, just after the country's first medical marijuana bill passed in California. To pass the bill, we knew we needed support from every corner of the state. Before the legal marijuana industry was off the ground, few people other than patients were lobbying for the bill. My colleagues and I traversed the state of New York building a grassroots movement of patients. Along the way, I met

Carla, a working-class woman who had survived four bouts of cancer; Shonda, who had lived with HIV for decades and suffered from pain and nausea; and Amy and Emily, suburban moms from upstate New York who purchased marijuana illegally to treat symptoms of their MS. VOCAL was an active part of the campaign, helping across the board but especially giving voice to people living with HIV. I grew to love these and dozens of other people I met during that work, and every day I was more and more outraged that they had to choose between using a medicine that could help alleviate their suffering and breaking the law.

I also saw the power of personal stories to move policy in a way that data could not and the power of Whiteness to move policy in a way that calls for racial justice did not. About a year into the campaign, the landscape shifted radically because nationally known physician Sanjay Gupta aired a special about a young, white girl named Charlotte who received marijuana for seizure disorder. All of a sudden, suburban white moms started contacting us, wanting to get involved because they believed, rightly so, that medical marijuana could help their children suffering from seizure disorders. Suddenly we were talking about giving marijuana to kids—a strategy that had been unthinkable months before. Unlike our VOCAL allies, who had spent years developing tactics and relationships to be seen and heard and successful in Albany, most of these parents were relative newcomers. Many of them had never been politically active before and were surprised to learn just how challenging political advocacy can be.

But just as with Ryan White, the response of legislators to innocent white kids was transformative. Building on the years and years of painstaking organizing by other kinds of patients and VOCAL, the entry of these suburban moms and their children changed the debate and what was possible for medical marijuana legislation. As an advocate and a sociologist, I couldn't help but notice a through line of racial politics in policy change and who matters in these debates, from Ryan White, to the kids with seizure disorders, to "those poor people who got addicted to opioids because of their doctors." The stories of children with seizure disorders were heartbreaking and compelling, and their parents were fierce and determined advocates, and we all should be grateful for their work. We lost three kids during that campaign while trying to get them medical marijuana that might have saved their lives. I remember weeping on the train from New York City up to Albany along the frozen Hudson River, thinking about the four-year old child who had died the evening before while waiting to see if medical marijuana might have helped her. Like me, the leaders of VOCAL were equally moved and again and again provided these new parent advocates with the space and access they needed to be effective. Yet the stories of cancer patients, people living with multiple sclerosis, and folks with other chronic pain conditions were also heartbreaking and compelling—and, apparently to policy makers, were nevertheless not as powerful as the story of an innocent (white) child. While glad that we were finally getting some traction, I was also deeply troubled that "white innocence" seemed to be what legislators and the media found most moving.

We had built a movement involving thousands of patients across New York, many of them quite sick, who dragged themselves to Albany every week for months to lobby legislators. In wheelchairs, in walkers, dealing with issues of child care, in snowstorms, they came. Megan, who suffered from fibromyalgia, would carpool with Kevin, who had autism. The rowdy women from the MS organization in Syracuse would caravan down with the cancer survivors from Rochester. Busloads of people with HIV/AIDS and people who used drugs would join us from New York City. And dozens of parents, most of whom had never been politically engaged, brought their children or, when they were too sick to travel, pictures of them to show recalcitrant legislators. When they wouldn't meet with us in Albany, we found them in their home districts as we crisscrossed the state with our message. We had little in common other than a commitment to pass the bill and the deep bonds that come from shared suffering and fighting for a common goal. We held press conferences, we handed out flyers, we wrote op-eds, we staged rallies, and we marched in local parades. And again and again, we descended on the capitol in Albany and made legislators face those living with HIV/AIDS, cancer, and MS, as well as parents whose kids had intractable epilepsy, and explain why these people could not access a potentially life-saving medicine. Those fighting for marijuana decriminalization often joined our press conferences and rallies, helping us turn out huge crowds to support the bill.

One by one we changed legislators' minds, until we finally had enough clout and votes to pass the bill in the Republican-controlled senate. But the then-head of the senate refused to bring the bill to the floor for a vote, even though it was poised to pass in both the assembly and the senate. In fact, he refused to even meet with a patient. After months of trying to get a meeting with him, we found a way into his office. A constituent of his who had a very sick child had a connection to his secretary. Finally he took the meeting, and hearing the story of this one child with epilepsy, he softened and allowed the vote. But our troubles didn't end there. New York governor Cuomo said he would not sign the bill unless it was narrowed considerably. We had to make very hard decisions to get it passed. For example, the original bill included a list of medical conditions that would make one eligible for medical marijuana. While we had proposed a long list that reflected the many conditions that patients who were part of the campaign were grappling with and for which medical marijuana held great promise, in the end, the version of the bill that passed included only a handful of qualifying conditions. Nor was that list based on research, but rather on what groups had managed to gain a legislator's ear.

Once again, I learned the lesson of how interest driven and arbitrary policy can be. Hours before the legislative session was about to end, the governor's office called to offer a backchannel ultimatum: we will give you a limited, gutted bill or nothing. We stood outside the governor's office reading the names and towns of literally thousands of patients and their loved ones from across New York who had signed petitions in favor of the bill. Boxes and boxes filled with stacks of signatures, representing hours spent at train stations, canvassing neighborhoods, speaking to community groups, and holding house parties. Our advocacy crew of about thirty people, including patients in dire need of this treatment, all approached the secretary outside of the governor's office, piling her desk with stacks of petitions and begging for a meeting. Many of us cried. To have come this far only to learn that we had to choose between no bill or a bill that would leave many of us behind was devastating. We were exhausted and frustrated.

Finally, the governor's office conceded to a meeting, but they would allow only five of our group in the meeting. The small group of patients, led by Alice, a wheelchair-bound breast cancer survivor and an activist who had cut her teeth fighting for people living with HIV/AIDS, emerged from the meeting only fifteen minutes later to report that the governor's staff refused to move on key issues. They gave us one hour to decide—should we accept a bill that benefited some, especially the children with epilepsy, or should we reject the bill and wait another year to try again? We gathered our motley crew and ushered them into the back room of the statehouse cafeteria to discuss it.

We had tried to make key decisions collectively, and, while we were there debating the pros and cons, Annabelle's daughter Olivia started having a seizure, her small body growing stiff in her wheelchair. When the medics had come and gone, and Annabelle had excused herself to get Olivia home, the debate was over. Everyone agreed—we should take the narrow bill that at least would help some of the kids. People like Megan and Kevin, who had traveled more than three hours each way to get to Albany week after week, and had suffered for years with ailments that they believed medical marijuana could help, put their own interests aside to help the kids. The specter of suffering white children moved activists and legislators alike. In two years, we had passed a major piece of legislation, however flawed—one that had been widely opposed by Republican legislators when we started and had been stalled for almost twenty years. Meanwhile, the efforts to decriminalize marijuana and help tens of thousands, primarily Black and Latino young men, continued to falter, not passing until 2019.

Little did I know that, five years after I helped to get the medical marijuana bill approved, I would be diagnosed with stage III breast cancer and qualify for my own medical marijuana card. Suddenly, I was one of thousands of New Yorkers struggling to use an inadequate and prohibitively expensive program. The bill we passed was rife with problems due to the limitations that the governor had imposed, problems that exacerbated racial disparities. To participate in the original program you must have one of a few select qualifying medical conditions, and a medical provider has to complete a certification process. Certified providers are hard to find and can charge a lot, some requiring frequent recertifications for a hefty fee. Just as for buprenorphine, a lot of doctors don't want medical marijuana certification because they are concerned that their practices will be overrun by "drug seekers." And many doctors working in busy, low-income clinics do not have the time for the required training. Patients have to apply to the state for a license that allows them to go to a dispensary, and these dispensaries are limited in number and often require sick people to travel long distances to get medicine. Concerned about diversion and driven by stigma, the governor didn't want people to have access to the marijuana flower or to be smoking marijuana, so only tinctures, oils for vaping, pills, and edibles are available, and each producer is allowed only five to six strains.

The result has been limited, processed products that are expensive, and none of them covered by insurance. The market is not that big because limited numbers of people qualify, which also drives up prices. Low-income patients who manage to navigate the program's hurdles often end up being faced with the gut-wrenching choice of using their limited income to pay out of pocket for medical marijuana or being able to afford rent and food. As with buprenorphine, we have ended up with a certification system that is expensive and therefore largely limited to people with money and more likely to benefit affluent white communities than low-income communities of color. It remains cheaper and easier for many patients to go to the illicit market. The risk is not only criminal justice involvement but also contaminated products. For someone like me, with a compromised immune system and cancer medications on board, the risk of the illicit market is too great. Fortunately, the program is finally being reformed.

MEDICAL MODELS AND RACIAL DISPARITIES

Through my work on medical marijuana and buprenorphine, it has become increasingly clear to me that medical models by and large lead to racial disparities. In a recent *New England Journal of Medicine* article on structural racism, the authors note:

> In its 2003 report *Unequal Treatment: Confronting Racial and Ethnic Disparities in Health Care*, the Institute of Medicine reviewed more than 100 studies and concluded that bias, prejudice, and stereotyping contributed to widespread differences in health care by race and ethnicity. That call to action went largely unheeded. Fifteen years later, the 2018 National Healthcare Quality and Disparities Report documented that Black, American Indian and Alaska Native, and Native Hawaiian and Pacific Islander patients continued to receive poorer care than White patients on 40% of the quality measures included, with little to no improvement from decades past. Regardless of intent, actions by parties ranging from medical schools to providers, insurers, health systems, legislators, and employers have ensured that racially segregated Black communities have limited and substandard care.[20]

The structural barriers built into the US health care system, coupled with racialized and stigmatized attitudes about drugs, make it hard to conceive of a medical model that does not replicate racial disparities. In the case of medical marijuana in New York, we had always hoped to go back and expand access, believing that, if more people could participate, it would drive down the prices and bring in more low-income people of color. We went back the year after the bill was passed and asked legislators to expand the program to include patients with chronic pain. But they had moved on and told us point blank that they were done with medical marijuana.

Legislators were onto another problem—the rising rate of overdose deaths now devastating white suburban and rural districts across New York that had never thought about drugs as their problem. With increasing pressure from their predominantly white constituents—the same force that had moved the Good Samaritan legislation a few years earlier—they were searching for ways to stop the wave of deaths. Around the same time, studies came out showing lower rates of opioid overdose in states with medical marijuana, likely because some people with chronic pain were able to manage their conditions with marijuana instead of opioids. We went back to the legislature and argued that expanding access to medical marijuana might help reduce overdose deaths—an argument that was much more persuasive to representatives from suburban white districts than our earlier argument to expand access to medical marijuana on its own merits. While that amendment didn't pass in the legislature, later that year medical marijuana for chronic pain was legalized by a change in regulation.

Once again, I saw how the appeal to the concerns of their white constituents was seemingly more persuasive to many policy makers than, in this case, making sure that low-income communities of color could access needed medication. I felt that I was witnessing firsthand some of the myriad ways in which white lives are more highly valued than Black lives. Mariame Kaba, a sociologist and activist working to end racial violence and dismantle the prison industrial complex, explains that the devaluing of Black life, rooted in slavery, means that "'Innately inferior' bodies can be debased, punished, and killed without consequence. . . . Black people are never 'innocent.'"[21]

LEVERAGING WHITENESS FOR POLICY CHANGE

The concern for white opioid users that fueled the passage of the Good Samaritan Law and led to the expansion of the medical marijuana program signaled a growing shift in the racial politics of drug policy—one rooted in the reality that white suburban youth were dying at alarming rates from drug overdoses. While thrilled to see good policies move forward, I and my drug reform colleagues found particularly frustrating the attention being given to a problem that had long affected communities of color but had been ignored in the halls of power. Decades of pushing for more health-oriented approaches and for a softening of punitive policies (which had failed by any measure) had gone largely unheeded when drug use was viewed as a predominantly Black and Brown problem. But in October of 2015, in a front-page headline, the *New York Times* noted, "White Families Seek a Gentler War on Drugs."[22]

Fresh off my experience in seeing the power of white suburban families to help pass medical marijuana legislation that had languished for years, I found it increasingly clear that we were entering an era where the perceived complexion of the heroin crisis was driving a new set of policy responses—ones focused on helping instead of punishing, humanizing instead of stigmatizing, and investing instead of divesting in communities. Still, questions remained. Could we leverage this moment to move drug policy toward an approach rooted in public health and compassion? How much transformation was possible? How would race and racism shape this new policy landscape? Would reforms equally help white communities and communities of color? Or would some people get left behind, as they had in our fight for medical marijuana? Was the concern for white drug users powerful enough and were policy makers willing to dismantle the massive drug war apparatus they had built over fifty years now that the public perceived white people to be in its crosshairs?

The shift in the racial politics of drug policy did not begin in 2011 with the passage of the Good Samaritan Law. In fact, there has always been a symbiotic relationship between drug policies for whites and those for people of color. The drug war has always relied on a reciprocal relationship between the criminalization of Blackness and the decriminalization of Whiteness.[23] And we have always created a space for white drug use that is comparatively safer and less punitive than that for drug use in communities of color.[24] Although the long history of racializing accounts of drugs and drug use continues today, their racial coding is subtler than in the past.

As the problem of white opioid users has continued to grow throughout the 2000s, along with increasing media attention to the "new face of addiction," we have also seen a new openness to more progressive drug policy responses, though the change in rhetoric does not always result in a substantive change in policy. In addition to Good Samaritan Laws, we have seen a proliferation of more treatment and harm reduction–oriented policies—policies long sought but not passed when drug users were depicted as people of color.

For example, government programs to expand the use of naloxone increased exponentially in the 2010s. Naloxone is a medication that, when administered during an opioid overdose, can reverse its effects. Naloxone was first patented in 1961 but was not widely used until the 1990s, when it was first distributed by underground networks of people connected to syringe exchange and harm reduction programs.[25] As the opioid crisis grew and spread to white suburban communities, naloxone also spread. According to the CDC, the first program to encourage take-home naloxone began in 1996. By 2014, that number had grown to 644 programs reporting more than twenty-six thousand overdose reversals.[26] In 2001, New Mexico became the first state to enact legislation to increase access to naloxone. As of 2021, all fifty states and D.C. had passed laws to increase access to naloxone.[27] The majority of these laws were passed within the last five years to respond to the growing overdose problem. One study looking at naloxone administration in forty-two states found that the odds of naloxone administration were highest in suburban and rural areas.[28]

Perhaps even more surprising are the hundreds of law enforcement agencies now asking their officers to carry and use naloxone.[29] Police officers, whose previous purview had been to lock up those using drugs, are now being asked to save their lives. However, the legacy of law enforcement's hostility toward people who use drugs persists. There is also evidence to suggest that, even though police are being asked to carry and use naloxone, their negative attitudes toward people who use drugs remain,[30] and drug arrests continue at an alarming rate. According to estimated crime statistics released by the FBI, there were 1,654,282 arrests for drugs in 2018, a number that has increased every year since 2015.[31]

Progressive legislative changes, even in Republican-dominated states, were driven, in part, by outbreaks of HIV caused by the use of injection opioids in white rural and suburban communities. For example, nearly two hundred people in rural Scott County, Indiana (96.7 percent white), became infected with HIV primarily as a result of injecting Opana, a powerful prescription opioid, using unsterile needles. At the height of the outbreak, twenty people a week were being diagnosed with HIV. Finally, in 2016, a reluctant then-governor Mike Pence agreed to allow limited syringe exchange programs, saying: "I will tell you, I do not support needle exchange as antidrug policy, but this is a public health emergency."[32] Importantly, this was not a full-hearted embrace of syringe exchange or harm reduction but a very limited and reluctant action taken under extreme pressure from public health groups. It was nonetheless unprecedented in that state. Also unprecedented was the $30 million appropriation in 2021 from Congress as part of a coronavirus relief package (the American Rescue Plan Act) for syringe services programs and other harm reduction programs to help sustain operations during the pandemic and economic downturn. This marked the first time in history that Congress had appropriated dedicated federal funding for such programs.[33]

The irony here is that the historical reluctance among "small government" conservatives to invest in a public health infrastructure and the assumption that their constituents didn't need those services meant that many of those communities now faced problems that they had neither the treatment nor the harm reduction services to address. Racial capitalism, spiritually bankrupt as it is, turns out to be a currency that harms poor whites as well as people of color. The racial coding of drug problems led to disinvestment in the very systems and supports that would have helped low-income white communities. As one advocate explained to me: "Part of why New York State is so ill equipped to deal with the heroin crisis is because for all the years that New York City elected officials were calling for treatment and infrastructure to deal with substance use issues, central and western New York elected officials [from mainly white districts] didn't want those things. So they don't have any of these things because they did not believe substance use was a problem for their communities because of Whiteness." Methadone and harm reduction services have been largely sited in urban Black and Brown communities in New York, leaving more suburban and rural communities without these resources when they needed them.[34] The perception that drug use was a problem of communities of color meant that when the white opioid problem emerged, many politicians were left scrambling for some way to answer the concerns of their white constituents and turned to strategies that advocates had been tirelessly pushing for years with limited success.

For example, in 2021 New York City launched the nation's first supervised consumption spaces, also known as overdose prevention centers. Supervised consumption sites (SCSs) are places where people who use drugs can legally inject or consume drugs under supervision. SCSs have been used and evaluated across Canada, Australia, and Europe for decades, and they are proven to reduce overdose and public disorder. But until very recently, such programs were considered too controversial to seriously consider in the US, despite the work of advocates to promote them for more than a decade. Finally in 2016, the mayor of the small, predominantly white city of Ithaca, New York, which had experienced a number of overdose deaths, began to publicly advocate for SCSs. Bolstered by the national organizing by drug policy reformers, soon newspapers all over the country were talking about SCSs as a reasonable response to the growing problem of drug overdose. For example, the mayor of Seattle came out in favor of launching one in that city, and Philadelphia was ready to move forward with a program before it became mired in legal battles and local politics. The once-taboo topic was even heralded by the editorial board of the mainstream newspaper *USA Today* as a promising intervention that should be tried in the US.[35] Such support among policy makers and the media for a heretofore controversial intervention had been inconceivable before, when drug use was framed as a problem of Black and Brown communities.

Another innovation to curb the abuse of prescription opioids since the problem has affected white communities has been DEA's National Prescription Drug Take-Back programs, which allow individuals to dispose of unused prescription medications. Partnering with local law enforcement agencies, the DEA program collected two million pounds (1,018 tons) of prescription medications in four years.[36] In 2010, Congress passed the Secure and Responsible Drug Disposal Act of 2010, amending the Controlled Substances Act to allow the DEA to develop permanent, ongoing, and responsible methods for medication disposal. Prior to the passage of the act, there were no legal means for transferring possession of controlled-substance medications from prescription holders to other individuals for disposal.[37] This strategy is notable for its focus on upstream causes of use and its offer of a kind of amnesty to individual users, even though the act explicitly acknowledges the death and crime associated with the misuse of prescription medications. That the DEA is now involved in trying to help people who use (prescription) drugs is a radical departure for an agency that has spent tens of millions of dollars pursuing the drug war in communities of color.

Treatment, which has long been underfunded, is also beginning to receive more resources that appear to be largely benefiting white opioid users. Treatment admissions for opioids are increasing, especially for whites, constituting a larger and larger proportion of those receiving publicly funded treatment slots. According to a survey of publicly funded treatment programs, between 1994 and 2014 the proportion of whites among heroin admissions increased 84 percent.[38] Among private insurers, spending on substance use treatment per enrollee almost doubled between 2001 and 2009. Moreover, the percentage of the population using any medications for substance use disorder (like methadone and buprenorphine) more than tripled during the same period.[39] In New York, the legislature passed bills covering medication-assisted treatment (MAT) for private insurance and Medicaid patients, but within twenty-four hours Governor Cuomo signed into law the one for private insurance and vetoed the one for Medicaid patients—basically making a determination that the people who are Medicaid patients (more likely to be low income and people of color) were not as worthy of lifesaving treatment. A bill covering MAT for incarcerated people, who are disproportionately people of color, didn't even make it out of the legislature that year.

At the federal level over the past few years, there has also been a steady increase in funding for prevention and treatment, while funding for law enforcement and interdiction has remained level. President Trump's FY 2017 budget, for example, included $1 billion in new mandatory funding over two years to expand access to treatment specifically for opioid use disorder, including $50 million for medications, such as buprenorphine. Unfortunately, it appears that this investment in treatment will not benefit all communities equally. One study found that the number of publicly owned drug treatment facilities declined between 2002 and 2010 by 17.2 percent, whereas the number of private for-profit facilities grew 19.1 percent. Counties with high percentages of Black residents were more likely than counties with less than the mean percentage of Black residents to be served by public facilities and were thus disproportionately affected by the overall decline in public facilities.[40] Propped up by Whiteness, racial capitalism operates in ways that perpetuate racial disparities.

Even as my colleagues and I saw a burgeoning interest in harm reduction, treatment, and less punitive drug policies, it didn't take us long to understand that the gentler war on drugs was not a gentler war for everyone. Many of the policies, particularly those rooted in harm reduction, have not come to fruition nor been widely adopted, and even as some punitive policies have been rolled back, most notably with a measure to decriminalize the possession of all drugs that passed in Oregon in 2020, the vast majority of the drug war infrastructure remains intact. And the impulse to advance punitive policies, including ones that harm white people, remains. For example, Tennessee's Fetal Assault Law and North Carolina's House Bill 918 both sought to impose severe civil penalties (up to and including accelerated termination of parental rights) for perinatal substance use. It appears that support from conservative Republicans for less punitive approaches was rooted, not in a deep understanding of the racism and inhumanity inherent in the failed drug war, but in the concern from constituents in their mostly white districts about alarming rates of overdose and addiction. Nor was this a case of "rising tides lifting all boats." It soon became clear that the limits of progress would be largely bounded by race and class.

THE LIMITS OF WHITENESS

In 2016, a team of my colleagues, all of whom were young African Americans, met with a Republican state senator from a predominantly white district to discuss legislation to reduce overdose deaths across the state. He leaned back in his seat and starting walking through his legislative drug policy plan. Bill after bill was about treatment and harm reduction. They sat in stunned silence knowing that this legislator had previously been a champion for increasing penalties and punitive responses to drug use. They felt as if they had entered another dimension—one in which a conservative, white Republican legislator had adopted the talking points of progressive drug policy reformers. According to my colleague, a young Black woman who had been working to end marijuana arrests in communities of color for years:

> This guy was saying things like, we can't arrest our way out of the problem, people need more treatment options, and on and on. I was sitting in the room with three Black staff and our White lobbyist. We are all in the twilight zone, but we agree, this is great. Our lobbyist's mouth is on the floor because he's never heard a senate Republican talk this way. But then there came a point where the senator wanted to send a message. . . . The guy leaned into me and said, "But I want you to know there's one thing we'll never agree on. I'm never going to stop introducing those drug-induced homicide laws. And you can keep memo-ing [writing memos of opposition] them all you want, but I need to get *those* people out of my community; those people are poisoning our kids, and we need to hold them accountable." And suddenly I am reminded that they don't give a shit about us [Black people]. And it is back to the reality that these policies are not for us; they can't be for us because that's not how this is done. . . . That phrase "Those people are poisoning our kids" is important because between the "our" and "kids" is a bracketed "white." "Those people" means Black.

Drug-induced homicide laws, to which the legislator referred, are laws that allow district attorneys to prosecute someone who sells drugs that result in an overdose for homicide. These laws are directly from the old drug war playbook, relying on two false assumptions: one, that you can draw a bright line between people who use and people who sell drugs, and two, that tough penalties like this will somehow be an effective deterrent. In fact, many drug-induced homicide cases involve friends or family members who happened to share drugs that resulted in an overdose.[41] A preliminary analysis of the limited data available on drug-induced homicides found that prosecutions are more likely to be brought when the person who died is white, and that people of color receive median sentences that are three years longer than whites'.[42] Even as the rhetoric has shifted to excuse and empathize with people who use drugs (driven by narratives of white drug users), the instinct to rely on punitive responses and established dividing lines that are racially coded remains. In this case, the underlying assumption driving this legislator's policy positions is that Black and Brown drug dealers are infiltrating white communities and deserve to be tried for homicide because of it, despite data showing otherwise.

The distinction between drug users (who are perceived as white and needing our help) and drug sellers (who are perceived as Black and Latinx and deserving punishment) is a racially coded dividing line in drug policy. Of course, these stereotypes have been proven false by data showing that whites are more likely to deal drugs, although Black people are much more likely to be arrested for sales, and arrests of Black people for nonviolent drug crimes continue to soar.[43]

The ways in which sympathetic responses toward perceived white users continue to coexist with punitive responses toward Black and Brown communities were evident in the New York State Legislature session of 2017. That year, drug policy advocates worked on two main sets of issues: promoting treatment and harm reduction responses to the opioid crisis; and a bill that would have sealed the records of those arrested on low-level marijuana charges, allowing them to essentially clear their records. These two issues had different racial frames and different outcomes.

The marijuana record-sealing bill was an explicit attempt to redress the racism of New York's drug policies by allowing the tens of thousands arrested for misdemeanor low-level marijuana possession because of the "public view" loophole described above to clear their records—records that have lifelong consequences, such as blocking individuals from stable housing, student loans for higher education, and certain professional licenses; making it hard to get a job, affecting child custody; and leading to deportation for immigrants. As one Albany operative working that session noted: "Sealing marijuana records is a test of the proposition that they [white legislators] acknowledge the damage of the war on drugs in communities of color. That would be an acknowledgment of the repression and ill effects of a bad law on communities of color, and it's the most benign law on the book in terms of its impact on criminal records. The busts were illegal; shouldn't we at least seal these ones?"

At the same time that the marijuana record-sealing bill was being lobbied, legislators were also grappling with the escalating opioid problem. In some ways 2017 became a test case for looking at how the success of drug policy proposals aimed at helping white communities compares to that of drug policy proposals aimed at redressing the harms of racist policies of the past. While the legislature held meetings for a bipartisan task force on opioids and a host of bills addressing the opioid crisis passed, the marijuana record-sealing bill was not even brought up for a vote in the Republican-controlled state senate. The issue that would have attempted to redress one part of the harms of draconian drug policy in communities of color couldn't get a hearing, while policy proposals aimed at addressing the drug problems of people perceived to be white sailed through. Whiteness, it seemed, might be helpful in moving forward policy proposals that were perceived to help whites, but the understanding policy makers seemed to have that white drug users should be helped, not punished, was not extended to Black and Brown marijuana users who were saddled with devastating arrest records on the basis of largely bogus arrests.

It was hard to celebrate the much-needed wins addressing opioids, knowing that those victories were possible not only because of the years of tireless and exhausting activism but also because opioids were perceived as a white problem. Meanwhile, attempts to repair the damage racist drug policies had done to hundreds of thousands of young Black and Brown people hit a dead end, and overdose deaths continued to rage, as they had for decades, in communities of color, like the Bronx, where I live. These kinds of bifurcated policy responses are possible, in part, because of the racial identities of different drugs. With opioids coded as white, some possibility of progress, especially for people who used drugs, existed. But there was no relief for the hundreds of thousands of marijuana users perceived to be Black and Brown urban dwellers.

It was not until marijuana was fully legalized in New York in 2021 that legislators finally redressed some of the harms of marijuana arrests. Through the indefatigable work of advocates, who refused to compromise on the racial equity provisions in the bill, New York's marijuana legalization bill includes automatically expunging criminal records for marijuana arrests (including possession and sales), immediately releasing any incarcerated people for offenses that are no longer a crime, prohibiting probation and parole officers from using marijuana as a violation, removing the odor of marijuana as a justification for stops and searches, earmarking 40 percent of the tax revenue from sales for reinvestment into communities most harmed by the drug war, and creating intentional pathways for those harmed by marijuana prohibition to participate in and profit from the legal market.

THE COLOR OF ADVOCACY: "CONSTITUENTS WHO MATTER"

When a social issue is coded as white, several factors seem to influence policy responses to it. The biases toward policies that benefit whites are built into the system. US elected leaders are predominantly white, and therefore steeped in the white privilege and the white supremacist values that surround them. According to Pew Research Center, as of 2021, at the federal level there are only three Black senators and no Black governors.[44] Another analysis noted that in 2017, the American public was 39 percent people of color but that only 10 percent of politicians were people of color—and mostly male.[45] Moreover, elected officials tend to be considerably wealthier than the general public. For example, the median net worth of members of the 116th Congress was over $1 million, versus a median net worth of $121,760 for Americans overall.[46]

Earlier drug policy reform efforts, such as repeal of New York's Rockefeller Drug Laws, reduction of the crack and powdered-cocaine sentencing disparities, and marijuana reform, were seen as affecting primarily communities of color, and the advocacy efforts were typically led by people of color arguing that these policies had led to gross racial disparities. Generally speaking, Black and Latinx legislators, along with progressive whites, led these efforts. In contrast, current policy discussions about opioids are being advanced by many of the same advocacy organizations but are also dominated by conservative, white legislators—often the same legislators or legislators from the same districts that were responsible for imposing punitive drug policies in the first place and that, in many cases, continue to promote such policies.

Until recently, getting conservative, white legislators to care about progressive drug policy was an uphill battle. Efforts to promote harm reduction strategies or public health interventions were met with moralism about people who used drugs, undergirded by assumptions that those people were largely Black, Latinx, and/or poor, despite data showing similar rates of use across race and ethnicity. For example, at the federal level, conservatives fought repeatedly against allowing federal funds to be used for syringe exchange programs, despite overwhelming evidence that these programs prevented the spread of blood-borne diseases, like HIV and hepatitis C, and had a host of other public health benefits. Similarly, early efforts to get naloxone (a medication that reverses the effects of opioid overdoses) were treated with boredom at best and outright opposition at worst. A reformer working on Capitol Hill told me about his early efforts to get traction on a bill to address opioid overdoses:

> I started making the rounds on the Hill and talking about the picture nationally, explaining that it was impacting urban communities but increasingly impacting rural communities, and I would highlight Appalachian and the southern states affected. Most of the time I would see their eyes glaze over. I got the attitude that these aren't the people we care about. They were seen as predominantly poor people or perhaps working-class blue-collar folks. People who were "addicts." . . . I did more than one hundred visits to get support for the bill, offices from districts across the country. Across the board, there was a lack of interest in the issue during the first years I did this.

After months of work, this activist had a number of cosponsors on the bill, and with one exception they were all Democrats. However, as the opioid crisis started to reach suburban communities a few years later, the same advocate saw a change in the kind of support the bill received. He noted that white constituents with influence had started to lobby about overdose: "You saw more and more organizing on the part of parents, typically White suburban parents. . . . Slowly but surely, we got more buy-in from both sides of the aisle. It began to be framed as health issue directly as a result of it being framed as affecting 'constituents who matter.' . . . Now it's people who are cutting checks for the reelection campaign or the influential business owner who holds a fundraiser in my district."

The phrase "constituents who matter" calls forth the need for a movement like Black Lives Matter. The implicit assumption manifest in this organizing work of white parents is that the lives of their children matter, and of course they do. Indeed, it is when white lives are affected (particularly affluent white lives) that we see policy makers scrambling to make a difference. But as with so many social issues, calls to address the problem of white lives or even "all lives" too often leave behind poor people and people of color.

White suburban constituents have a particular pull in policy arenas because they are often financially well off, connected, empowered, and able to make life easy or difficult for policy makers. A DPA staffer with years of experience lobbying in D.C. told me: "Because it's those constituents, who are economically advantaged, politically active, and in some respects have more access to members of Congress, they're getting heard. That it's these constituencies along with the emerging consensus that it is a disease or a health condition—those two things are combining to result in this more compassion-based approach." As I saw with the Ryan White Care Act and the New York medical marijuana campaign, few things are as powerful politically as white parents fighting for medical access on behalf of their sick kids.

Predominantly white recovery groups, like Fed Up, began having a real presence in Washington, as did the increasingly influential coalition Alcohol Policy Forum. Scores of mostly white advocates began lobbying legislators, putting a "human face" on the crisis and reminding legislators that their constituents cared about this issue and were paying attention to what their representatives in D.C. were doing about it. In addition, according to the experts with whom I spoke, more and more legislators had a personal connection to the issues—a son, a sister, or a friend who had lost a loved one to overdose.

The same D.C.-based DPA staffer told me: "They [white legislators] now know people directly affected by opioid use. It's not like the quote unquote bad guys or an inner-city problem. . . . They were very used to othering drug use and drug users. That's a thing that only bad people do and certain communities do. It's a moral failing. It's harder to think that when it's your best friend's son or your own children."

I understand the sense of urgency and sympathy that comes from having a personal connection to an issue. I've known four people who have died from opioid overdoses in the past year alone. I did not know them well, but I felt their loss and saw the impact of their deaths on the drawn faces of their friends. Though I was already committed to changing our disastrous drug laws, their deaths compelled me to work harder. I think of the contributions they made to our work in the short time I knew them, I remember the laughter, irreverence, righteous anger, and creativity they brought, and I am staggered by what the absence of their ideas, energy, and love means, not just to me, but to all the people who were touched by their lives. The numbers are stunning and sometimes numbing. In 2020, more than ninety thousand people died from an overdose, each one someone's son or daughter, friend, partner, companion—each one a beautiful manifestation of divinity lost.

Of course, more and more people have a personal connection to the issue; more and more people are trying to come to terms with senseless, unnecessary loss. And for many, overdose deaths are nothing new. I remember working with a colleague who had spent twenty years as a medical doctor in the predominantly Black and Latinx Bronx yelling in frustration, "Our sons and daughters have been dying from overdose for decades and no one cared!" One of the tragedies of Whiteness and racial segregation in the US is the failure of many white people to either know or care about the suffering in Black and Brown communities. Drug use, so often coded as Black and steeped in stigma, created a drug-using "other" who could be punished or ignored until the problem became so pronounced, familiar, and personal in white communities, it demanded their attention.

As lobbying by white constituents picked up, the frame of the issue also changed. Suddenly, 'addicts" were no longer the stigmatized "other"; rather, they were friends and neighbors with a medical condition worthy of help and support. Advocates explain that, as we saw with the media portrayals, policy makers are now seeing people who use drugs as sympathetic individuals who became addicted through no fault of their own, people struggling with an illness that our society has a responsibility to treat and cure. It is not surprising that many of these white advocates rely on the medical and brain disease model, seeking to remove their kids' drug problems from the criminal legal arena and to render them blameless. Unfortunately, as noted above, too often this reliance on medical solutions only further exacerbates racial disparities.

A New York lobbyist who has been working on drug policy reform for over twenty years told me: "In a few short years, conservative legislators' attitudes toward drug users went from 'Lock them up and throw away the key' to 'We can't arrest our way out of the problem.' The only thing that had changed was the complexion of the epidemic." When the drug problem is perceived as Black and Brown, punishment is the answer. But when affluent white lives are on the line, we see a sharp pivot from a criminal justice approach toward a public health one. It's hard to explain the intense array of emotions that bearing witness to this kind of shift evokes. Watching years of advocacy go largely ignored, screaming into an abyss that people are dying, that lives could be saved—and then to suddenly have those screams heeded, but only because now white people with power are being affected. It is a stark example—as if we needed another—that white lives are more highly valued than Black and Brown lives. Rather than feeling elated that our policy proposals were finally getting attention, I have often felt sick, full of anger and grief. I couldn't—and can't—stop thinking about and mourning the literally hundreds of thousands of lives—mostly Black and Brown—that have been destroyed by US drug laws and the pleas of those mothers and fathers that went unheard or, worse, were heard and disregarded by a system of white supremacy that values some lives more than others. And while I understand intellectually how Whiteness operates systemically to elevate some lives above others, on an emotional level I feel the same visceral outrage and sadness I felt when Ryan White's death was leveraged to move HIV policy, while my friend Charlene from the soup kitchen in Philly couldn't even access decent medical care for a life-threatening abscess because she was poor and Black and a drug user.

PUBLIC HEALTH EMERGENCIES ARE FOR WHITE PEOPLE

Some white legislators (both liberal and conservative) seem willfully ignorant of the hypocrisy and racism inherent in this "new" approach to drugs and are treating the opioid problem as entirely novel. There is a disconnect for them between the punitive and racist drug war and the current approach. Indeed, white legislators, along with some legislators of color, were active participants in building the war on drugs. In the current era, they often stay silent on criminal justice reform of drug laws even as they advocate for medicalized approaches to the opioid epidemic in white communities.

About his conversations with white legislators, one advocate told me: "There is some recognition that we got it wrong and that we went too far in the 1980s. But on the conservative side, they don't see what happened as a race issue. Even people who are quote unquote 'very good' on criminal justice reform, they don't really see that there was sort of a policy of racism that led to the situation."

As advocates, we long for white legislators to repent or at least acknowledge the racism at play, but that seldom if ever happens in my experience. However, legislators of color, at least in some jurisdictions, are making the connections and seeing the disparate treatment. An activist of color who worked closely with Black legislators in New York had this to say: "There is an outrage among the Black and Puerto Rican Caucus that the epidemic which existed in their communities for decades and was seen only as a criminal justice issue has now become a public health issue. They more than anyone else feel the outrage that goes with the circumstances on the ground being exactly the same, yet we are treating it completely differently." The frustration of Black and Brown policy makers is well founded and shared by many in the policy arena. They have seen their communities devastated by overpolicing, mass incarceration, and all of the collateral consequences that come from drug arrests. As their communities confronted crack and heroin use, they were met, not with compassion or services, but with an increasingly draconian set of policies. When the perceived complexion of the problem shifted, so did much of the political rhetoric. And while some Black leaders supported punitive drug policies, they also called for more services, drug treatment, and investment in communities of color.[47] Many are understandably outraged. New York Assembly member Diane Richardson drove this home when she rose to speak in favor of allocating money for opioid treatment but decried the hypocrisy of our racialized drug policies:

> There are racial disparities here. When there was a drug issue in the African American community, we were prosecuted. We were put in jail. Children were put in foster care. Families were ripped apart. It was treated as a criminal justice issue. We had Rockefeller Drug Laws. Our jails were filled with men and women who looked just like me. . . . But now we have an opiate issue. It has affected another demographic. And now it is a health issue? . . . So what is missing from this package is a restorative justice package for all those individuals who were jailed, and for all those families who ripped apart, and for the individuals who have criminal records because they had addiction issues.[48]

My colleagues and I shared this outrage. Not only was the hypocrisy palpable, we had seen firsthand the destruction of the war on drugs among our friends, families, and communities. We knew how a drug charge, for example, could destroy someone's chances for public housing, public benefits, employment, and immigration. We saw how the overpolicing of low-income communities of color centered on the pretext of drug law enforcement had devastated entire neighborhoods, too often ending in police violence and killings. So many of these drug policies had been supported by the very politicians who now wanted to approach addiction, not as a crime, but as a medical problem. We saw the hypocrisy; we knew it was driven by racism; it was enraging. And yet, these newly sympathetic legislators also held the key to the change that was and remains so desperately needed.

Advocates are faced with a dilemma. Do they leverage the Whiteness of the current moment? A white advocate committed to racial justice explained the dilemma: "It's very uncomfortable to recognize that we are making positive strides in drug policy reform because White people started using heroin. If it weren't for the fact White people started using and overdosing and having issues, we'd still be in the same mess. And that's a real tragedy. You have to be honest and realize this is why we are where we are. And we can never forget what went on in the past and what still goes on in so many communities."

Forgetting the past is not just a path of political expediency. It is a path that ignores the harms done while very likely perpetuating them. The hard choices of the New York medical marijuana campaign haunt me. We stood on the shoulders and the work of VOCAL members to pass the bill, a bill that ultimately left most of the VOCAL members behind. Moreover, in the years we worked to pass the medical marijuana bill, the issue of young people of color being arrested for marijuana possession was also on the table, but it was the story of young white kids with medical needs that prevailed. Was it right to take the gutted medical marijuana bill that primarily benefited the white advocates who had helped bring it over the finish line, while leaving behind many of those from the Black and Brown communities that had been targeted for decades by racist marijuana enforcement and who had fought for the passage of a more inclusive bill for years? In that case, our political work did forget the past, and in doing so we let Whiteness drive an important but ultimately problematic victory.

It's worth noting that many of these politically expedient victories driven by Whiteness also leave behind poor people of all races, including poor whites. In the case of the medical marijuana campaign, we made the decision we did, in part, because we were placed in an almost impossible situation by a powerful and deeply entrenched system of white supremacy—one that forced a false choice between helping some people or helping no one. Advocates face these kinds of choices all the time. We live and work within the confines of a white supremacist system that is designed to resist real change, so we often accept incremental changes that leave these systems of oppression intact and, too often, perpetuate racial inequity. As a white person, I know that it is easy for me to "not see" the ways in which my choices—both personally and professionally—perpetuate racism. It is also true that much of the white privilege and racism I do see, I have little power on my own to ameliorate, though I have a responsibility and a desire to try.

Much of the racism inherent in the US political system is blatant but nonetheless seemingly intractable. I deeply appreciate and respect the hard work of chipping away at the political system to wrest from its racist roots whatever incremental change we can. But my truth is that that kind of work—the constant choosing between what you know to be right, visionary, and transformative and what is possible—sickened me both physically and emotionally. I used to joke that every time I went to lobby in Albany, a little piece of my soul died. After three years of getting progressively sicker, I took a different job within DPA that did not involve direct lobbying. Fortuitously this change also coincided with my deepening conviction that my job as an advocate is to get out of the way and to let those who do not share my Whiteness and its limitations—those who are more directly affected by our proposed policy changes—drive policy decisions.

The sudden Whiteness of drug policy reform efforts, then, has put long-term anti–drug war lobbyists in an ethical and pragmatic bind. They are forced to make choices about adopting "race-neutral" rhetoric that, in the end, may bolster the racism that has anchored American drug policy for the past century. One lobbyist noted how "forgetting" the racist history of the drug war can happen in the context of advocacy: "When you do that white campaign, you are in some ways denying the racist history. It's a very tricky dilemma. Because when the white parents go in, they don't get into a discussion about how racist the drug war has been. . . . How do we in good conscience not have that discussion with the member even though we know it's going to hurt us in getting the result we are trying to accomplish? You know without any doubt what the best advocacy plan is to accomplish the goal at hand, but does that win the day?" In the advocacy circles in which I travel, there are critical and important discussions about what "wins the day," who wins the day, and how. Campaigns to reform drug laws that do not center people of color and those most harmed by the war on drugs are inherently problematic and ultimately, I believe, ineffective. Whiteness may indeed propel policy change, but that doesn't mean it propels good policy.

OF RISING TIDES: THE FALLACY
OF "RACE-NEUTRAL" POLICY

The conventional wisdom is that a rising tide lifts all boats. When this is applied to drug policy, some might think that the shift to more empathy for drug users, because overdose is perceived as affecting white communities now, is a good thing for all. But does a rising tide lift all boats, or just the white ones?

In fact, we have learned—as we did in the case of medical marijuana in New York and as we will see in detail in the coming chapters with buprenorphine—that race-neutral drug policies tend to benefit whites while leaving people of color behind. Good Samaritan laws are race-neutral on their face, but communities of color, with long histories of being overpoliced and facing police violence, are understandably more distrustful of calling the police even with the protections afforded under the law, and immigrants are afraid to call the police because they don't want to risk getting deported.

Similarly, many are skeptical about if and how increased funding allocations for treatment or harm reduction will benefit communities of color. An experienced advocate in D.C. noted: "A danger is that because it's perceived as a white issue it's those communities that are going to benefit the most from these changes in policy. Where I see that being most applicable is in terms of who gets the grants, who gets the funding, and also the types of programs that are offered." Because the system in which we work is itself based in structural racism, all too often these structures—like the allocation of grant funding or attempts to redirect policing—benefit white communities while leaving communities of color behind. We can imagine, for example, that a white person who overdoses in a suburban community could call 911 without fearing that the call would result in violence. She might be revived with naloxone, taken to the local hospital, assessed, and connected to a buprenorphine prescriber in her community. She might then treat her addiction with a few visits to her doctor and in the privacy of her own home. With the recent increase in federal funding for harm reduction, she might even be referred to a syringe exchange program so that she could keep herself safe should she continue to inject drugs.

A Black drug user, in contrast, might be understandably fearful of calling 911 in the case of overdose, thinking about how drugs have been used as a pretext for police violence and killing in cases ranging from George Floyd to Philando Castile. If she survived the overdose and/or the interaction with police, she too might be revived with naloxone and treated in an emergency room, but her chances of receiving buprenorphine would be slim. She would be much more likely to be arrested or to receive methadone, which is disproportionately prescribed to people of color compared to buprenorphine. This would mean she had to show up daily at the clinic, pay for and coordinate that travel, wait in line, and likely receive mandatory counseling and urine drug tests. She would also have to confront the stigma associated with methadone, to explain to her family and her employer why she needed to take time off from work and her parenting responsibilities to travel daily to the clinic. And if she did have a recurrence of use, she could face being kicked out of the program, being cut off from support services, and being the target of a child custody investigation.

Increasingly I understand that, because the very institutions upon which they rely to implement policies are racist, there is simply no way race-neutral policies can benefit all groups equally. According to an advocate in California who spent years in the trenches working on HIV and drug issues: "The structures that we are relying on to implement them [race-neutral policies] are all institutionally racist structures. Left to its own devices, all of government bureaucracy, capitalism, law enforcement, will work to uphold White supremacy. . . . We are relying on long histories and structures that are primarily there to protect White capital and White economic power and White privilege." This realization along with emerging leadership by women of color in the drug reform movement is leading to a shift. Two of the most prominent drug advocacy organizations—the Drug Policy Alliance and the Harm Reduction Coalition—are now led by women of color. The drug reform movement is increasingly building important alliances with movements to end anti-Black racism and centering the suffering and harm the drug war has caused in communities of color. There is a deliberate effort to stop the "forgetting" and to insist on racial justice. As one advocate put it: "You can leverage the situation [concern about whites], but you cannot forget how we arrived at this moment, and you cannot erase the policies of the past or the individuals who have been impacted. There needs to be a broader conversation about whether you want to call it damages or compensation or reinvestment . . . about how these communities were destroyed and what do we owe these communities now that we recognize that those policies were a disaster."

Indeed, groups like the DPA and the National Harm Reduction Coalition are increasingly focused on explicitly antiracist policies and on working to redress the racial inequities created by the war on drugs. For instance, the DPA, which long worked on marijuana legalization, has focused its efforts on ensuring that legalization initiatives include provisions for criminal record expungement, creating pathways for those who worked in the illicit economy to work in and have ownership stakes in the legal industry, and directing revenue from sales to those communities most devastated by the prohibition of marijuana in the first place. In 2021, New York at long last passed a law to broadly legalize marijuana, a piece of legislation that has some of the strongest provisions to redress the harms of racist marijuana enforcement in the country, including priority licensing for people directly affected by the drug war. There is also growing interest in promoting racial impact statements, which require legislators to study how proposed legislation would affect racial disparities. And such advocacy organizations are more and more partnering with groups, like the Movement for Black Lives, to address issues such as police violence and murders, many of which are entangled in the war on drugs. In short, they reject "race-neutral" policies in favor of policies that explicitly redress racial disparities.

CODA

It seems I was naive to hope that the press conference with Senator Hannon standing side by side with white parents calling for harm reduction approaches and the *New York Times* article about white parents pushing for a gentler war on drugs would help undermine the racial disparities wrought by US drug policies and bring the drug war to a close. Instead, they have done quite the opposite. The gentler drug war has reinforced racial boundaries, carving out a safer space for white drug use while leaving the cruel criminal system for Black and Brown drug use largely intact. And yet I find myself more optimistic about the possibility for meaningful change than before as I witness the organizing happening in communities of color and what I hope is the growing awareness of white Americans of just how broken our systems are. I choose to believe that the outrage over the loss of life from police killings and skyrocketing rates of overdose, especially in the context of COVID, is beginning to awaken among those of us who are white a deeper understanding about both the sanctity and interconnectedness of all our lives.

CHAPTER 4

"Mother's Little Helpers": White Narcotics in the Medicine Cabinet

(as told by David Herzberg, historian)

When I first began reading about the opioid crisis in the early 2000s, it was with a profound sense of déjà vu. This is an occupational hazard for historians, of course, but this was a particularly bad case. You see, I had just spent years researching and writing a book on the history of popular psychiatric medicines like Prozac, and as part of that work I had read literally hundreds of magazine articles published during a panic over Valium addiction in the 1960s and 1970s. The weird thing was, if you switched out the name of the drug, those Valium stories from half a century ago read exactly like the ones I was now reading about OxyContin. They had the same setting, the same characters, the same plotline, and the same moral.

See for yourself:

1978: "The smartly dressed woman driving a sleek, late model car could be the envy of her neighbors. She has a loving husband, bright children, a beautiful home in the suburbs, and apparently no cares in the world. Except one. This woman is a junkie. She is not the kind of junkie one thinks of in terms of long-haired 'hippies,' counter-culture street people, pushers, and illicit drugs. She is dependent on legal drugs, the kind prescribed for her by a physician."[1]

1979: "The only thing that Carol, an attractive thirty-year-old stewardess for an international airline, clearly recalls about the night she was wheeled into the emergency room of St. Vincent's Hospital in the Greenwich Village section of New York City is the ambulance attendant asking a doctor—almost casually—'We've got another pillhead here. Are you going to pump her out?'"[2]

2008: "The first time Lauren, a suburban teenager in Connecticut, took a prescription pain killer, she says she was sick with strep throat during her freshman year in college and grabbed a Percocet from her parents' medicine cabinet. She never dreamed where that one pill would take her."[3]

2009: "The girl grew up in western Suffolk County, in a town where, she said, 'everything is perfect,' with white picket fences and two cars in each driveway; for her birthday last October, she received a black Jeep, and she went to a wealthy, high-performing public school. . . . Her first drive in her new black Jeep was to a heroin dealer. 'I come from a good family. . . . When you think of a heroin addict, you don't think of me.'"[4]

The stories were written decades apart but shared the same basic template of innocence defiled, titillating readers with the implicitly sexualized degradation of young, affluent white women.

The stories also shared a moral template. Even after they had become addicted, drug users were not portrayed as immoral or as vicious "fiends" to be feared. Instead, they retained their innocence even as they were victimized by political forces beyond their control. Again, see for yourself:

1979: "Karen is in her middle 20s, the wife of a rising corporation executive and the mother of two small children. Although she has many of life's advantages, she feels dull and unproductive in contrast to the vital, active life her husband leads. She becomes ever more unhappy, nervous, and depressed, and finally turns to her family physician for help. He prescribes a minor tranquilizer. The drug makes her feel better—for a time. As her husband's success grows, she is called upon increasingly to help him socialize with clients, and the pressures upon her worsen. Her doctor allows her to take more tranquilizers."[5]

2016: "Mary Kathryn Mullins . . . was prescribed OxyContin for pain in her back after a car crash. . . . 'They wrote her pain pills, and she just got hooked,' said her mother. . . . As her addiction worsened, she went to dozens of doctors, visiting pain clinics that churned out illegal prescriptions by the hundreds and pharmacies that dispensed doses by the millions. . . . As the fatalities mounted—hydrocodone and oxycodone overdose deaths increased 67 percent in West Virginia between 2007 and 2012—the drug shippers' CEOs collected salaries and bonuses in the tens of millions of dollars. Their companies made billions."[6]

Both articles are ostensibly about addiction, but they are also muckraking exposés of injustice and at least implicit calls for reform. In the 1960s and 1970s, it was the medical system's deadly support for sexist constraints on "housewives"; in the 2000s, it was profiteering pharmaceutical companies and the credulous or unscrupulous physicians who enabled them.

But the aspect of the articles that really grabbed me—that convinced me that it was time to go back to the archives—was their shared conviction that white, middle-class addiction to pharmaceuticals was a new phenomenon.

> 1967: An old and shrinking population of "urban, poor, colored" narcotic addicts has recently given way to "millions" of "White and affluent" Americans who "can't sleep, wake up or feel comfortable without drugs" and are using prescriptions as an escape hatch. "Serious drug problems" have escaped from the "slums" and are now "sweep[ing] through White America: Junction City, Kans.; Pagedale, Mo.; Woodford, Va.; Plymouth, Mich.—places with apple pie smells and wind-snapped flags."[7]

> 1971: Richard Nixon: "We used to say [that addiction] is a ghetto problem or it is a black problem . . . but today it has moved from the ghetto to the suburbs, from the poor to the upper middle class [because there is] 'a pill for every problem.'"[8]

> 2008: Though overall heroin use has remained relatively stable nationwide, numerous police agencies across the country say the drug, once the scourge of poor inner cities, has in the last several years attracted a new generation of users who are largely young, middle-class and living in rural and suburban areas. At least part of that resurgence, police say, is a side effect of the explosion in prescription drug abuse.[9]

> 2017: Johnson, a former police chief, said the opioid scourge has introduced a new kind of addict: those who became hooked after receiving a prescription for pain. "Now we're dealing with the 28-year-old mother who used to jog 5 miles a morning who sprained her knee, or the coal miner in Appalachia who hurt his back," Johnson said.[10]

Why was history repeating itself in this way, and why did no one seem to notice the repetition? On the contrary: novelty was crucial to the stories.

It didn't take long to realize that this repetition was bigger than I'd thought. The Valium and OxyContin episodes were not America's only instances of widespread addiction to pharmaceuticals. Far from it. It seemed that almost every era had its prescription drug crisis—even eras before there were such things as "prescription drugs." Since at least the late nineteenth century, widespread use of and addiction to pharmaceuticals have been consistent features of white, middle-class American life. Indeed, I realized as I began to dig deeper, in most eras this type of drug use had dwarfed "street" use of illicit drugs like heroin and cocaine.

National media had not ignored this type of addiction as I had assumed it must have, given its disappearance from popular memory.

Instead, I found, the media had covered it almost obsessively—but always describing it as a new and unprecedented phenomenon. Journalists and drug experts announced episodic panic after episodic panic like the proverbial goldfish discovering the castle in each swing around the fishbowl. In an eerie mirror inverse of Jules's story about politicians suddenly discovering heroin overdoses once they appeared among middle-class white constituents, each discovery was also an act of forgetting.

Remembering forgotten things is what historians do. So I started to wonder. Why had addiction to pharmaceuticals been so widespread, for so long? And, given its obvious prevalence, what could explain the long-standing assumption that addiction was an affair of the "ghetto" rather than of the white middle classes—a belief so at odds with reality that it survived only because the last crisis was forgotten every time a new one was "discovered"?

REMEMBERING WHITENESS

Actually, telling the story this way isn't entirely honest. I was not a disinterested bystander engaging with the world through the lens of intellectual curiosity. I was an active participant in the story. For example, I was a white person writing about drugs. White people writing about drugs have been, and continue to be, the most important group dragooning drugs into reinforcing the broader machinery of Whiteness. Is what I write different?

I'm not sure. It's not always easy for white people to see (or accept) the ways we reinforce racial hierarchies. Maybe readers should know something about me so they can place me, not as an omniscient author above the fray, but as someone with a particular relationship to Whiteness, drugs, and addiction. I feel uncomfortable about this for lots of reasons. Historians almost never introduce ourselves into the stories we tell. I'm not very interesting. Public exposure is frightening. But in this book, we are trying to decode how Whiteness works, and one way it works is white scholars like me speaking as if we represent universal expert knowledge rather than a particular viewpoint. So here goes.

Like other white people, my life has been profoundly shaped by racial privileges. In fact, I have had well more than my share. The nearly all-white small town public high school I went to in Vermont was a "feeder" for the Ivy League, helping a high-performing but otherwise unexceptional student get into Harvard. My application to graduate school, and my applications for jobs as a professor, were evaluated by nearly all-white departments whose similar experiences helped them understand and appreciate my ideas and intellectual goals. My education was made possible by financial support from professional parents and by white-person real estate "luck," most importantly when my family bought an abandoned house in a soon-to-gentrify neighborhood in Madison, Wisconsin, where I went to graduate school.

I knew I had not personally earned and did not distinctively deserve my many privileges, but I attributed this to social class, not race. Whiteness was a blind spot. Nothing in my top-notch education made the slightest effort to rectify that. Even in graduate school, my mostly all-white seminars analyzed race in sophisticated and revelatory ways but rarely if ever examined Whiteness—certainly not our own. We unthinkingly assumed ourselves to be outside or above the story, looking down into it. Studying race meant studying nonwhite people. Studying white people was simply studying "people" (or "Americans"). So when I decided to write a cultural history of psychiatric medications like Valium and Prozac, I did not at first notice the single most interesting fact about my topic: that the intense popular fascination with these drugs was almost entirely a white phenomenon. I wouldn't be analyzing how "Americans" grappled with the idea of what (white) psychiatrist Peter Kramer famously called "cosmetic psychopharmacology." Whether I recognized it or not, I would be researching white Americans talking to each other about what cosmetic psychopharmacology meant for them. The key question I did not know to ask was, why were these drugs such a compelling topic for white people—like me?

This picture of an unconsciously white scholar is accurate but incomplete. I also had experiences that worked against the unthinking confidence that Whiteness provides. As Helena explained, Whiteness is a system, not a type of person, and it serves its own masters; the privileges of Whiteness can weaken or at least change when one falls out of alignment with those larger purposes. For example, in the 1970s I lived in Little Rock, Arkansas. As a noisy, energetic Jew in a recently desegregated public elementary school that still stopped regularly for (Christian) prayer time, I was disciplined brutally and often got terrible grades. (At some point, maybe it was later when I was a teenager, my parents explicitly warned me not to get too comfortable being white—when push came to shove the real white people would not consider me one of them. I didn't understand, but it stuck with me.) In high school, in Vermont, I was a "nerd," mocked and bullied by peers who, in retrospect, probably thought I was gay. At Harvard I felt so out of place that I dropped out after the first year.

One of these misaligning experiences places me more directly as a participant in the story of this book. Living in New York City after graduating college in the early 1990s, I was one of those young white people who became addicted to the purer heroin available in major urban areas at that time. When I moved to Wisconsin for graduate school, a new friend, a Black man, explained that Madison was no place for "junkies"—it was too small a town, I wouldn't always be able to buy heroin there. He pointed me to a place I'd never heard of, a methadone clinic. It was probably the most consequential kindness anyone has ever done for me. I enrolled in the clinic and, many days, went directly from that decidedly desegregated space to those all-white seminars. In the early 2000s, long since "graduated" from the clinic but still in graduate school, I felt a similar disjuncture traveling between campus and the county welfare department as the cash-poor primary caregiver of my two young sons.

I never stopped being a white guy through these experiences. There were hard times, but I could not help but notice (and be grateful for) the protections that Whiteness afforded me. I seemed to get only approval and respect from people who might have looked differently on an "addict," a single parent, or a welfare recipient who had been a person of color (and/or a woman). The system of Whiteness equipped them with the tools necessary to recognize that I was trying, and even though I was not succeeding, they wanted to support me. This was as true at the welfare office as it was at the grocery store with children in tow.

This is one reason I feel awkward disclosing these stories. I am afraid that some people may give me a kind of credibility I do not deserve, or will think I am trying to claim that credibility. Throughout these experiences I still had the privileges of Whiteness. I relied on them, and in times of need I did my best to maximize them. Moreover, it has been more than twenty-five years since I had the slightest interest in using opioids, and I have been a well-paid professor for nearly twenty years. In other words, I don't have any special insight into the experiences of drug use and addiction and their hardships today. I do know, intimately, that people who use drugs are just people, who use drugs, and I know that they (we?) make decisions, have cares, and deserve meaningful lives just like everyone else. But there are lots of ways to know these things.

None of these misaligning experiences closed my Whiteness blind spot. That came, slowly, incompletely, and with difficulty, through friendships and collaborations with Black and Brown people. I guess it's not surprising. Maybe there are some geniuses who can accurately imagine something that they are entirely inside of. That's not me. Everything I ever learned about Whiteness I learned by reading or listening to a person of color. I have benefited from the generosity of Black and Brown colleagues who helped bring me along, outside the narrow confines of all-white academic spaces. My being part of this book is a prime example. It's still very much a work in progress.

I was still in the early stages of this learning process when I encountered those unreflectively white media stories about OxyContin in 2007. I knew those stories. I had read countless versions of them for my just-finished book on psychiatric medicines. Heck, I had almost written those stories in that first book. I knew from personal experience that the relentless forgetting those stories displayed served a purpose, linked to the similarly relentless project of maintaining the power and invisibility of Whiteness in America. I decided that maybe, in my own small way, I could use my position as a historian to push back against the massive project of forgetting. I headed for the archives.

The more I researched, the more drugs lost the distinctiveness I had assumed they must have, and the more they began to look like the rest of American history. The magic of brain chemistry receded ever further, never disappearing entirely but increasingly replaced in explanatory power by the alchemy of race, intersecting dynamically with political battles over commerce and the regulatory state. The story of drugs was disorientingly similar to the rest of American life. What I came to call "white markets" for addictive pharmaceuticals were the troubled, segregated postwar suburbs of American medical history—a protected yet also dangerous white world of drug sales, drug use, and drug policies with very different priorities than the punitive prohibition visited on the racialized prohibition markets on the other side of the tracks.

We know a lot about the damage inflicted on poor and minority communities due to a punitive "drug war" that reinforced America's racial and gender hierarchies. But what about white people, and ideas about Whiteness? How did they influence the landscape of American drug markets and drug policies? In some ways, access to pharmaceutical white markets designed just for them has been a significant privilege for white Americans—unlike racialized minorities, they have gotten legal, safer access to desirable products to ease suffering or pursue pleasure. Yet as white Americans discovered with alarming regularity, safer did not necessarily mean safe. The belief that white people were less vulnerable weakened the case for robust consumer protections in white markets, leaving white Americans exposed to addiction risks. The twenty-first-century opioid crisis was just the latest, acute manifestation of a chronic problem. In this chapter I chart the overall contours of this problem over the past 150 years, explaining how America's experiences with drugs have been shaped by the project of maintaining Whiteness.

Before doing that, I should say one last thing about how I am a participant, not just a chronicler, in this story. As a historian of addictive pharmaceuticals, I have served as a paid expert witness for the plaintiffs in the opioid litigation. I know that this litigation, and the expert witnesses who participate in it, provoke mixed feelings in at least some drug policy circles. I have done my best to be historically accurate, that is, to explain that corporate profit seeking, not drugs or the people who use them, caused the twenty-first-century opioid crisis.

ADDICTION AND JIM CROW'S AMERICA: BUILDING THE RACIALIZED DRUG/MEDICINE DIVIDE

1866: "There is something in the very character of those vast Asiatic populations, with their corrupt and effeminate manners, and their decided tastes for negative enjoyments and a dreamy and contemplative life, which seems to draw them peculiarly toward the stimulus supplied by opium."[11]

1878: "The [morphine] habit, far from being a vice, is actually a disease, produced not through the culpability of its victims, but in consequence of their physical and mental ailments, and chiefly through the instrumentality of their physicians."[12]

1914: "Most of the attacks upon White women of the South are the direct result of a cocaine-crazed Negro brain."[13]

Historians categorize ourselves, in part, by which time period we study. On the basis of my first book, I was a "postwar" historian, one who focused on the US after the end of World War II. But as I chased precedents for the twenty-first-century opioid crisis I kept having to go farther back, deeper into American history, until I reached an era where the most fundamental elements of modern American racial capitalism were built. The half century after the Civil War was defined by two major projects: first, reconfiguring the nation's racial hierarchies after the end of slavery and amid a massive wave of "new" immigrants from southern and eastern Europe; and second, building a modern capitalist economy driven by the twin engines of urbanization and industrialization. It is not surprising that these two society-altering projects became intimately intertwined, building what turned out to be an incredibly sturdy version of racial capitalism that has been unequally meting out benefits and harms for more than a century. Drugs and addiction are one location where this disparate justice has been most acutely felt.

Excluding alcohol (which would require its own whole chapter), the first time an "addiction crisis" struck America came not long after the Civil War. From a modern-day vantage point, one can see the crisis coming from a mile away. Technological advances such as the isolation of morphine from opium, the introduction of the hypodermic syringe, and the mass-manufacturing capacities of industrialization brought newly potent drugs to inexperienced consumers. Meanwhile, the regulation of markets lagged behind the technology-driven boom: inexperienced consumers had little help or protection from social authorities. *Caveat emptor* ("Let the buyer beware") was woefully insufficient to the new situation and its risks, but it still ruled the day. The result was a sharp, unprecedented spike in a kind of compulsive, harmful use of opioids (and cocaine) that would later be called addiction.[14]

The largest group of people experiencing harms from this form of opioid use were white, native born, middle-aged (twenty-five to forty-five years old), and economically stable. They were equally distributed in rural and urban areas. They were also, by a two-to-one ratio, women. Perhaps the most accurate way to describe this demographic would be to call them the "doctor-visiting classes." This is particularly apt because physicians' prescriptions were the single largest path through which the nineteenth-century opioid boom flowed. This was no cute, old-timey public health crisis. As best as historians can estimate, this period saw America's highest per capita rate of opioid addiction, eclipsed only recently, more than a century later, by the twenty-first-century opioid crisis.[15]

Interestingly, this reckless morphine fad in American medicine occurred at the same time that white cultural crusaders were stirring a panic over a different opioid: smoking opium. Opium smoking had been encouraged in China at gunpoint in the 1830s by an imperial Britain eager to profit from importing the drug there.[16] Chinese immigrant laborers brought the practice to the United States in the 1840s, where anti-immigrant whites sensationalized "opium dens" as one among many examples of "Oriental" depravity. By the 1870s, anti-Chinese activists had raised a cultural panic about pretty, innocent white "girls" seduced into sexual slavery by leering "den" proprietors.[17] The *New York Times*, for example, reported in 1873 that "a large number of young White girls residing in their neighborhood are rapidly becoming addicted to the same vice. They live with the Chinese when they can find no other home, for although people of their own race close their doors against them, they are always welcome at the firesides of those to whom they sell their souls for the sustenance of their bodies."[18] Such views were shared among medical experts as well: "Wherever the Chinese go," the *Journal of the American Medical Association* (*JAMA*) observed in 1908, "the curse of opium smoking goes with them. It is a phase of the 'yellow peril' that we may have to meet nearer our homes than we have anticipated."[19]

These denunciations, however, did little to stop physicians and their patients from eagerly embracing morphine—a more potent and, especially when injected, more dangerous form of the same drug. Few white observers drew any connections between opium smoking, a practice long associated with the Chinese and usually linked to their racial qualities as "Orientals," and use of medicinal morphine. True, there were initially no legal distinctions between the two, but the racial logic was strong enough to deter comparisons, enabling enthusiastic use of morphine for long enough for it to become widespread, entrenched, and deadly.

By the 1870s the extent of addiction had become apparent, and reformers organized to do something about it. Their efforts were deeply marked by their racist unwillingness to see links between opium smoking and morphine prescribing. Whereas the Chinese smoked opium because of their innate racial depravity, whites used morphine for the opposite reason: "A higher degree of civilization, bringing with it increased mental development among all classes ... seems to have caused the habitual use of narcotics ... to have become alarmingly common," observed the popular book *Drugs That Enslave*.[20] But highly evolved mental capacities did not entirely explain the epidemic of addiction. For that, observers focused on broad social failures that victimized otherwise decent people. As the *New York Times* put it in 1877 (a mere four years after its scalding report on "Chinese in New York"):

Opium habituates are not rendered such voluntarily, but contract the habit in spite of their intelligence, their desire, and their will, simply because, in the great majority of cases, opium has been prescribed by professional authority for some ill, and its use continued indefinitely by the patient, who, unwarned and unaware of the danger, sees only the apparent benefit . . . until at last . . . he discovers the awful truth that he has become a victim . . . To no class of unfortunates should our floodgates of pity, sympathy, and commiseration be wider opened than to the victims of opium. It is not a vice which afflicts them, but a disease.[21]

The *Catholic World* reported on the phenomenon in similar terms in 1881:

A quarter of a century ago an opium eater ... was a rarity; today opium-eaters are counted by the thousand. .... [It is] an aristocratic vice and prevails more extensively among the wealthy and educated classes than among those of inferior social position. ... The careless manner in which physicians prescribe opiates, and the prevailing custom among druggists of duplicating prescriptions, are prolific sources of the evil. The physician prescribes morphia for a patient suffering from some painful disease, and relief is obtained. ... He goes back to the drug-store and has the medicine renewed without the physician's advice or direction. ... Finally he ascertains that his health is being injured, or is otherwise warned of the danger, and attempts to give up its use. ... With a firm determination to free himself he discontinues use. Now his sufferings begin and steadily increase until they become unbearable. ... That human nature is not often equal to so extraordinary a self-denial affords little cause for astonishment. At length he surrenders.[22]

The centrality of race to authorities' understandings of addiction had an important impact on how they responded to the problem. Most importantly, because Chinese opium smoking was cast as a racial threat—part of the "Yellow Peril"—it seemed logical to borrow policy tools from the era's other great political reforms: the ones developed to protect native-born, white Protestant America from racial threats, through Jim Crow racial segregation, immigration restriction, and eventually eugenics. This borrowing exemplified how the twin projects of reaffirming racial hierarchies and building a modern market economy intertwined to produce an implicitly and explicitly racial capitalism. It is useful to see how this worked in some detail, because this is the basic architecture we still live in, 150 years later, producing such seemingly bizarre outcomes as the continual, stubborn forgetting of white market addiction. (For those looking for more detail, I tell this story at greater length in the first three chapters of *White Market Drugs*.)

Even though more people were addicted to medicinal opiates than to smoking opium in the late nineteenth century, it was smoking opium that authorities targeted first. Beginning in the 1870s and 1880s, they prohibited opium "dens" (although not the drug itself) at the municipal and state levels, often through criminal statutes. The first national smoking opium law, passed as a supplement to the 1881 treaty excluding Chinese immigration, forbade Chinese nationals—but not US citizens—from importing smoking opium into the United States.[23] Such laws reached the national level in 1909 with an outright ban on the importation of smoking opium.[24]

Unsurprisingly, over the next decades many opium smokers switched to less stigmatized, less illegal, and—not least—less conspicuous drugs such as morphine and especially Bayer's Heroin after it was introduced in 1898. As a result, "gray" markets for these drugs soon cropped up, as disreputable doctors and druggists sold without pretense of treating an illness, and street "peddlers" sold in defiance of pharmacy licensing laws.[25] In the next decades authorities responded by criminalizing sales or possession of opioids without a physician's prescription. This new approach reached the federal level in 1914 with the Harrison Anti-Narcotic Act, which formalized the distinction between medical and nonmedical sales and created a dedicated federal agency to police and punish transgressors.[26]

The distinction established by the law between "medical" and "nonmedical" was ostensibly designed to capture differences in the source, the use, and, especially, the consequences of drug use. In practice, however, like many of the era's other major reforms, it was better at dividing drug users along lines of race, class, and gender—especially because access to a physician (the only source of medical, i.e., legal, drugs) was unequally available along just such lines.

In essence, the new laws segregated American drug markets. Sales to the "doctor-visiting classes" remained legal, while sales to everyone else were criminalized. Poorer and racialized Americans had the same needs and desires for drugs as people categorized as white, but they did not have the same access to legal, regulated markets. Their informal market purchases and use were by definition "vicious" (i.e., related to vice).[27] Because of the difficult circumstances in which they purchased and used drugs (due to both punitive prohibition and urban poverty), informal market consumers were more at risk of drug-related harms like addiction. In a diabolical self-fulfilling prophecy, this then "proved" that they were too defective to use drugs safely, as white market consumers supposedly did. Drug addiction became a racial spectacle, luridly detailing the many defects and threats of America's racialized communities: opium smoking and Chinese immigrants; cocaine and African Americans; heroin among the poor whites and immigrants' children who made up the urban "dangerous classes"; and so on.

The segregative aspects of the new drug policy worked. Criminalizing informal drug markets created whole new classes of criminals, available for spectacular arrests and sensationalist reporting. All this made "non-medical" drug use more visible than ever, just in time to join other supposed threats to traditional white dominance in a changing nation.

Sexuality was central to this way of "using" drugs for political purposes. White women were considered especially vulnerable to the temptations of drugs and were thus portrayed as vulnerable to predatory nonwhite men eager to addict them and thus trap them in sexual slavery. White women, of course, were the linchpin of Whiteness: they were the only ones capable of assuring the social reproduction of the race. (As an early twenty-first-century white American politician said, "We can't restore our civilization with somebody else's babies.")[28] This existential threat justified political "reforms" to increase the state's power to police, control, and punish those categorized as nonwhite, and also to govern white women's sexuality, all supposedly in the service of "protecting" white women. One physician summed up the logic with brutal efficiency: police departments should be issued more powerful firearms because "the cocaine n-- is sure hard to kill."[29]

Spectacular punitive policing did not eliminate or even reduce nonmedical drug use. In the wake of the Harrison Act, what I call "prohibition markets" thrived, more dangerous than ever thanks to the perverse incentives of illegal commerce. It is probably better to stop even thinking that drug prohibition was the true goal. Rather, the goal was to neutralize a threat to Whiteness.

Meanwhile, white market opiate use was quickly becoming *less* visible, more hidden. This was in part because, while white authorities were building the state infrastructure to police and punish "junkies," they built a different set of policies to regulate white markets to protect consumers. Physicians and pharmacists began to be more cautious so as to limit unnecessary exposure to the risk of addiction; the total volume of medicinal opiate sales dropped significantly. New laws such as the Pure Food and Drug Act of 1906 required narcotic ingredients to be truthfully listed on drug labels. Evidence suggests that medical care led to fewer new cases of addiction starting perhaps as early as the 1890s and certainly by the 1930s.[30]

These consumer protections were accompanied by efforts to care for the large generation of white market consumers who had already become addicted. There is little evidence that these consumers stopped using opioids in large numbers. Instead, strongly motivated by the intensifying stigma of addiction, they went into hiding. Unlike less privileged groups, who had few options but to turn to unregulated prohibition markets for smuggled opioids, many people able to claim a status as "patients" were able to still purchase in medical markets. This was technically illegal, but thanks to regulatory loopholes and rudimentary surveillance, physicians were commonly able to provide morphine for a few favored patients with addiction. When these informal arrangements were interrupted for some reason—a physician's death, for example—people with "medical" addiction were often provided quiet (if ineffective) treatment instead of sensationalized arrests and prison.[31]

Thanks to these practices, opioid white markets shrank significantly, exposing fewer consumers to addiction risks, without creating a secondary crisis since people already addicted did not have to switch to prohibition markets. This success was remarkable. Markets for addictive products are legendarily resilient (i.e., demand is "inelastic") and difficult to rein in. In this case, the genie went back in the bottle thanks to a simple, pragmatic collection of policies: strong regulation of large-market suppliers (doctors, pharmacists, drug companies) to prevent them from inflating fads for dangerous drugs, and health care (including provision of drugs) rather than punishment for consumers who became harmed despite those protections.[32]

The success of this approach makes it only more tragic that it was so restrictively applied (another pattern that persists to this day, as Jules noted in chapter 3). Just as reformers had resisted recognizing the links between smoking opium and medicinal opium, they now resisted making the reverse association: policies that worked for white markets, they believed, were not applicable to the "vicious" consumers in informal markets. Indeed, success in white markets only confirmed that medicinal drug users were special: in keeping with their privileged racial and class status, they were presumed innocent, free of desire to use drugs, and eager to pursue socially laudable goals if allowed to. The success of white market consumer protection policies became ongoing evidence of white peoples' fine qualities, rather than evidence in favor of the policies themselves. Meanwhile, the failure of punitive policies to reduce "vicious" addiction became proof of the innate inferiority of poorer and racially suspect groups.

By the 1920s, then, American drug markets had evolved into a recognizably modern form of racial capitalism. Markets were segregated along lines of race and class, justified in part through appeals to gender and sexuality. Different policies governed different sectors of the market. Privileged white market consumers enjoyed relatively safe access to desirable goods, and quiet, private care when they were harmed despite protections. Marginalized prohibition market consumers, meanwhile, bought dangerous goods and were made into very public spectacles and punished if they became addicted or otherwise harmed.

The inevitable results of this disparate setup then became "proof" of the underlying principles and served as an ongoing engine for educating Americans about the meaning and importance of racial categories. Racial capitalism does more than unequally distribute benefits and harms, opportunities and obstacles. It also (mis)educates us about race by producing racially disparate outcomes. In the case of drugs, Americans are encouraged to see problem drug use in Black and Brown communities as a manifestation of the deficiencies of those communities. Problem drug use among white communities, on the other hand, is always exceptional and must be explained by some external injustice that should be fixed. One set of drug problems calls for crackdowns on drug consumers; the other calls for additional protection and support. In this way not only are drugs neither unique nor magical (or demonic); they are potent instantiations of American racial capitalism.

RACIALIZING ADDICTION

By the 1920s, a grand social experiment in drug policy had been performed in America—but the experimenters badly misunderstood the results. Facing addiction as a social problem, reformers had instituted two very different kinds of policies to reduce it in two different communities. When addiction among America's "best" men and women seemed to disappear following those reforms, experts did not credit consumer protections and harm reduction tactics. Instead, they credited the victory to Whiteness: white market consumers, searching for health rather than pleasure, had simply quit using opioids once the dangers had been explained to them. "The social and personal urge to cure," the nation's foremost addiction expert hypothesized in 1928, had "successfully eliminated many of the more normal."[33] Addiction among the "dangerous classes," however, did not decline. Rather than taking this as evidence that punitive policies had failed, experts instead decided that these less favored social groups were simply immoral or constitutionally defective. Essentially, addiction researchers projected their social prejudices onto a complex situation, adding their intellectual gravitas to the social hierarchies that, conveniently, underpinned their own privilege.

On the basis of these self-serving but erroneous conclusions, experts narrowed their thinking about addiction. Previously, there had been multiple models for addiction. Those applied to the doctor-visiting

classes had not been stigmatizing and in some ways had even been laudatory: addiction was one of the nervous disorders to which the nation's
"best" men and women were prone by virtue of their highly refined
intelligence and sensibilities. In this nineteenth-century model addiction
was not a vice but a tragic, horrifying illness that struck innocent people
who resisted it with all of their might. That this resistance was almost
always futile showed the power of the illness, not the weakness of the
victims. This power was emblemized by the belief that the symptoms of
withdrawal were so severe that they could be fatal. Hopes for cures
surfaced regularly; this was a time of striking medical advances in many
fields, and many believed that addiction, too, would soon yield to therapeutic wisdom.[34]

Once "medical addiction" had become invisible as a social phenomenon in the twentieth century, such relatively humane models of addiction disappeared. That left the other stories about addiction—those
linked to the nation's "vicious" racialized communities—as the exclusive template. A new generation of addiction experts turned to studying
the nonmedical heroin users who came to be known as "junkies," and
saw in their failure to quit not a sign of the habit's strength but of
addicted people's moral failings. The apparent disappearance of "medical addicts" only seemed to reinforce the point. Experts thus incorporated into the concept of addiction a host of morally questionable
behaviors associated with the street-hustling culture that heroin users
were forced to adopt to maintain their supply of the drug amid a tight-
ening net of criminal policing.[35] Treatment took a back seat to punishment, and efforts to study addiction gave way to a fruitless quest to find
a nonaddictive narcotic—a way to stop addiction that would not depend
on salvaging "addicts."[36]

In the early twentieth century, white authorities saw this street-
hustling "junkie" culture as characteristic of neighborhoods where "dysgenic" white immigrants from southern and eastern Europe were segregated. As the Great Migration unfolded over the next half century,
experts increasingly associated addiction with the African Americans
who were sequentially segregated into those same neighborhoods. (These
neighborhoods were also defined by their easy access to large ports and
well-developed informal economies, making them ideal for smuggling.)
Indeed, by midcentury, it had become difficult for white Americans to
purchase heroin in prohibition markets, which had become carefully hidden and protected from (white) authorities.[37] Thus race, as well as "hustling," came to be a de facto element of medical theories about addiction.

A SECOND PHARMACEUTICAL CRISIS:
UPPERS AND DOWNERS

1947: "Among some drug manufacturers, the incentive to push sales mountainously high is great, since the profit is large. . . . You have only to go to your physician and complain of insomnia or "nerves" to secure a prescription. If he is careless or overworked he may not even warn you that you are playing with a subtle fire."[38]

1965: "A blonde girl in Capri pants was lying on the filth-strewn floor. She could not have been more than fourteen years old. Her eyes were blank and her fingers clawed at the figures in the design of the linoleum . . . Just eight months before, I learned, the girl had been a normal, healthy high-school freshman from a good family—until a schoolmate introduced her to drugs. Now she began to tremble violently where she lay in a pool of her own sweat and vomit. She had been taking pills that police call 'whites, bennies.' . . . These are nice, respectable diet and wake-up pills. . . . Their use has spread like wildfire in less than a decade. . . . It seems inconceivable to many Americans that the colorful little pills in the family medicine chest that help them go to sleep or stay awake can be a national menace."[39]

The structures of racial capitalism built in response to America's first encounter with widespread opioid addiction persisted well into the twentieth century. For racialized drug consumers, this meant stigmatization, punitive policing, and intergenerational community harm. It shaped white drug consumers' experiences too.

On the one hand, it exposed them to new risks. The presumption that "medical" drug manufacturers, sellers, and consumers were all earnestly pursuing health reduced the urgency of market regulations. Why bring government intrusion into markets where all participants are guided by good intentions? This misunderstanding of drug markets and drug risks enabled a new and even larger wave of addiction to pharmaceuticals in the mid-twentieth century.

On the other hand, white market consumers also benefited. They got privileged access to drugs that, however dangerous, were still safer than those sold in prohibition markets. And if they were harmed by their drug use, the assumption that they were innocent victims of broader social and political forces gave them access to a wider and more effective range of political responses.

The new addiction crisis, in other words, replayed the old one. The drugs were different, however: instead of opioids and cocaine, they were barbiturate sedatives and amphetamine stimulants.

Barbiturate sedatives were first introduced in 1903 and were being used by millions of Americans by the late 1920s. In the 1930s they were joined by amphetamine stimulants, and both were being used by tens of millions of people by the end of World War II. Overdose deaths from barbiturates alone reached an approximate height of nearly 7 per 100,000 population in 1953—not in the top ten causes of death that year, but getting close (the tenth leading cause of death, tuberculosis, killed 12.4 per 100,000).[40] The numbers grew even larger with the introduction of a new class of enormously popular sedatives, the so-called minor tranquilizers Miltown (1955), Librium (1960), and Valium (1963), as well as new forms of amphetamine.[41]

The Whiteness of these drugs was a key factor that enabled the crisis to grow so large, for so long. First, these were new drugs that did not have the associations with racialized minorities that had stigmatized opiates and cocaine. Instead, they were used overwhelmingly by whites with privileged access to the medical system, for types of suffering understood as connected to their racial and social status. As one prominent observer noted, "Neurotic anxiety is especially a middle-class phenomenon in our culture."[42] Other racial groups, with their supposedly less complex psyches, simply felt fear: "Puerto Rican and Mexican immigrants will have their innings with anxiety later," Newsweek reported, presumably when they had had more time to evolve.[43] Race, not medicine, governed the line separating the medical condition of "anxiety" from the ordinary human state of "fear." This racial association with Whiteness cemented the drugs' status as medicines, meaning that, unlike drugs, they were supposed to be used very widely. Markets for barbiturates, amphetamines, and tranquilizers were designed not to inhibit use but to enable it.[44]

The second factor came into play once the drugs were in very wide use and problems with addiction and overdose became apparent. The people suffering from these problems did not fit the model of addiction that experts had built around street-hustling "junkies." Nor did they present a racialized threat to the perpetuation of American Whiteness. As a social problem, therefore, pill addiction was of relatively little interest to the racist moral crusaders whose political muscle had helped Harrison Act reformers overcome the resistance of pharmaceutical industry lobbying. Without their help, it took reformers decades to prod federal authorities to act, and even then, new regulations were far weaker than the ones that had reined in white market opioids. It was not until the mid-1940s that the Food and Drug Administration gave itself the power to enforce a prescription-only rule for barbiturates and amphetamines, and it was not until 1952 that Congress officially ratified that power. Even under this rule the biggest market providers, drug companies and physicians, faced no restrictions whatsoever. End consumers, too, were legally innocent: nonprescription sale, not purchase or possession, was the only crime.[45]

Once again, racial capitalism in drugs turned out to make everyone pay, even the people it was designed to benefit. White Americans in the 1950s and 1960s faced heightened risks of addiction because of—not in spite of—their privileged access to the medical system.

The costs of racial capitalism were not borne equally. Whiteness came with protections that limited the harms, or at least prevented them from spiraling into a self-reinforcing avalanche of catastrophes. Despite much hand-wringing and even occasional panics over barbiturate and amphetamine addiction, for example, no one ever raised the possibility of punishing white market consumers, even as Congress in the 1950s lengthened prison sentences and at least technically allowed the death sentence for "street" drug crimes. Barbiturate and amphetamine users may not have received effective treatment, but they did at least receive sympathy and care. Take, for example, how the popular woman's magazine *Collier's* described what it considered to be a typical case of barbiturate addiction in 1946: "A woman, a fine cultured person, worrying about her soldier sons, found herself lying awake. A doctor gave her a prescription for sleeping tablets, and she, without consulting him, had this prescription refilled repeatedly. She became an addict innocently, by taking a few tablets at night because she wanted to sleep. She ended up in a hospital . . . [having] lost 40 pounds, and [unable to] recognize friends or relatives."[46] Such sympathy did not prevent overdose deaths from reaching crisis levels—but at least it did not make things worse, unlike the punitive policing and punishment inflicted upon racialized drug users and their communities.

Also as in the nineteenth-century morphine crisis, people addicted to pills were usually portrayed as innocent victims of broad social forces, in this case a profit-hungry drug-industrial complex that included pharmaceutical companies, physicians, and pharmacists. A congressional witness at a 1953 hearing on juvenile delinquency captured the logic well in his report on an investigation in his home state:

> There were approximately 250 boys and girls in the Oklahoma City metropolitan area who were using the drugs at the time the investigation started. . . . We found that most of our boys and girls before our committee did not come from the wrong side of the track, they came from the better class of people. In fact, their mothers were heads of leagues and associations, and their

fathers sometimes were professional men or businessmen; in any event the
white-collar classes. . . . We blame the druggist [pharmacist]. We blame the
good druggist who is honest. They are so anxious to make a sale, they believe
anything. . . . The manufacturers of these "bennies" make them for a fraction of a cent apiece. They sell them out to anybody that wants to buy them.
They think more of the dollar than the youth of America.[47]

In other words, the white market addiction crisis became an opportunity for political reforms to benefit, not punish, white drug consumers.
But it would not be an easy or swift campaign. In the business-friendly
America of the 1950s, protecting white consumers' right of access to
needed drugs mattered more than building new state capacity to regulate commercial activity. (Antidrug crusaders had better luck passing
some of America's harshest punitive laws for heroin "pushers" in 1951
and 1955.)[48]

Stronger consumer protection tools did not emerge until civil rights
activists in the 1950s and 1960s challenged the racist undergirding of
America's divided drug policies. The loosening of rigid racial hierarchies
undermined segregated drug markets and their policing in multiple
ways. In the 1960s, for example, white youth began to cross racial
boundaries to purchase heroin in urban markets that had been largely
unavailable to them.[49] Authorities, once again reminded that addiction
happened in white communities, slowly began to rebuild older, more
expansive concepts of addiction that had room for addiction to
tranquilizers and amphetamines among people who did not resemble
"junkies."[50]

The result was a contested, and painfully limited, rebirth of belief in
addiction as an illness rather than as a racialized moral failing. In the
1960s state and federal governments invested in a range of treatment
modalities including methadone maintenance, self-help groups modeled
on Alcoholics Anonymous, and therapeutic communities promising
complete "rehabilitation." These new modalities still preserved mechanisms of moral blame and punishment. As noted in chapter 1, for example, methadone maintenance was tightly policed and implemented as a
crime reduction policy for Black and Brown heroin users. Therapeutic
communities often assumed that addiction was caused by deep-seated
personality problems that predated drug use.[51] Nonetheless, together
the treatments provided new ways to accommodate the reality of widespread addiction among people categorized as white.

The new, frank acknowledgment of white, middle-class addiction in
the 1960s and 1970s also made pharmaceutical markets an attractive

target for an emerging "third-wave" consumer movement. This movement forged powerful political coalitions by exposing corporate wrongdoing and consumer tragedies and then pushing to fix them by expanding state regulation of commerce.[52] Pharmaceutical sedatives and stimulants, with their eye-popping overdose rates, were ready-made for such tactics, and they featured prominently when President Kennedy launched a federal reform campaign in 1963.

The campaign bore fruit fairly quickly, as a series of new laws culminated in the 1970 Comprehensive Drug Abuse Prevention and Control Act. The centerpiece of the law was the "Schedule of Controlled Substances," which divided drugs into five categories based on their therapeutic value and potential for "abuse" (i.e., nonmedical·use). Schedule I drugs such as heroin were completely prohibited as having no medical value and high addiction risk. Schedule II drugs were the most tightly regulated legal drugs, deemed to have "high potential for abuse" but also "a currently accepted medical use in the United States or a currently accepted medical use with severe restrictions." Morphine and oxycodone, for example, were placed in this category. Schedules III, IV, and V contained drugs deemed to have higher and higher ratios of medical value to "abuse" risk and consequently faced lighter regulatory controls. The law created a closed system, in which everyone involved in commerce in controlled substances (e.g., manufacturers, distributors, prescribers, and pharmacies) was required to register with federal authorities, to restrict sales to other registrants except for prescription sales to consumers, to keep records of all sales for authorities to inspect, and to ensure that all sales were for "legitimate medical purposes."[53] All drugs were ultimately policed by the same entity, a new Drug Enforcement Administration, which would have significant regulatory powers over the drug industry and physicians as well as pharmacists and end consumers.

This was a complex law with many parts, and its nature changed significantly in the decade after it was passed. At the beginning, it recreated the two-part policy mixture that had been so successful in resolving the nineteenth-century white market morphine crisis: robust consumer protections that constrained the profit seeking of corporate drug sellers, combined with robust availability of health care for consumers harmed despite the protections, including, this time, formally legalized provision of drugs to addicted consumers (methadone maintenance).[54]

The combination worked. We often think of the 1970s as an era of widespread drug use and addiction, but the decade actually saw sharp declines in white market addiction and overdose. Amphetamine sales dropped from four billion pills in 1969 to four hundred million in 1972; sedative prescriptions declined by 50 percent. Because the drugs remained widely available (even to people with addiction—maintenance was not illegal, particularly for tranquilizers), and because of large investments in addiction treatment, overdose deaths dropped steeply as well.[55]

Of course, this was just the white market half of a complex law that also relied on prohibition and punishment to govern informal markets and the Black and Brown communities into which police had segregated them. These informal markets did not see a similar decline in use or deaths. Consumer protection and harm reduction were what drug policy looked like when drug users were understood to be white. Despite the changes brought by civil rights activism, Whiteness remained central—both in allowing the crisis to grow and in implementing a successful response to it. In the heyday of the civil rights movement, some of these humane and relatively effective policies were also extended to nonwhite prohibition market consumers. But this extension was limited and short-lived. As the forces of racial backlash gathered in the later 1970s and after, the Controlled Substances Act too easily became a vehicle for a renewed, and even more intensely harmful, "war against drugs."

OPIOIDS—AMERICA'S THIRD PHARMACEUTICAL ADDICTION CRISIS

The twenty-first century's opioid crisis is America's third pharmaceutical addiction crisis, and it provides tragic evidence of how difficult it was to maintain even the tenuous racial achievements of the civil rights era. OxyContin did not come out of nowhere; the ground had to be well prepared for it. In this case, that preparation involved a political backlash that reestablished stark racial hierarchies that had been weakened by civil rights activism. American city centers, already damaged by deindustrialization and "white flight" (i.e., government-directed capital flight, of both the financial and the political variety), faced a new round of economic hardship during the recession of the 1970s and the conservative policies of the 1980s. In this context inexpensive "crack" or smokable cocaine began to be sold largely in urban prohibition markets, resulting in a damaging crisis of addiction among communities already suffering from economic and political deprivation. Conservatives eager to "toughen" American drug laws relentlessly hyped crack addiction as a national threat symbolizing the dangers of African

Americans themselves, thus giving new force to older racial conceptions of addiction.[56]

These highly racialized conceptions of addiction enabled pharmaceutical companies to portray a new generation of their products as nonaddictive, since their users tended to be white and respectable. Just as opioids and cocaine had given way to barbiturates and amphetamines, now barbiturates and amphetamines gave way to a new generation of very similar drugs such as Xanax and Klonopin (benzodiazepine tranquilizers) and Adderall (amphetamine for ADHD), again advertised as safe tools designed for problems characterized as common among white people.

Even more significantly, opioids like OxyContin and its eventual competitors were among those revolutionary new products claimed to safely care for suffering whites. This was accomplished partly through a multilevel campaign to encourage physicians and patients to take chronic pain seriously, and to define taking pain seriously as providing opioids to treat it, and partly through claims that technological advances had made addiction less likely. Making those two strategies possible was demographics: in the harsh new racial divides of the 1980s and 1990s, when concepts of addiction had again become highly racialized, access to drugs like OxyContin was sharply unequal by race (and by class). In other words, once again, addiction was difficult to recognize because the people experiencing it did not *look* like "junkies," and the sellers did not *look* like "dealers" (in part because they refused to sell to the Black and Brown people who "looked like junkies"). The same cultural logic protected so-called pill mills that existed to sell prescriptions for addiction pharmaceuticals but that were careful to limit their clients to the white and respectable.[57]

HISTORY LESSONS

From a historical perspective, both pharmaceutical and drug war policies should be understood as different elements of a single overarching system for unequally governing drugs. The vast disparities between prohibition market drug use and white market drug use are a *consequence,* not a *cause,* of the divided drug policies. And as recurring crises of addiction to pharmaceuticals make clear, the system favors those able to claim an identity as white but it exposes everyone, including whites, to unnecessary drug risks. Consumer protections have been too weak in regulating legal commerce, allowing a series of marketing-driven fads for addictive pharmaceuticals that, like similar fads for other drugs (including, for example, estrogen replacement therapy, statins, and antidepressants), have had devastating consequences for the public health. Meanwhile, drug war policy has been too strong, destructively policing and punishing communities already suffering from a long series of external shocks, from "white flight" to urban renewal and deindustrialization, all while failing to effectively regulate prohibition markets to protect consumers from the dangers of drugs themselves.

In both cases, Whiteness has warped thinking about what should be the obvious goals of drug policy: enabling people to access the benefits of psychoactive drugs while minimizing the risks they face in doing so. Racial thinking holds that drug war and pharmaceutical policies deal with populations so fundamentally different as to require entirely different strategies. It has become relatively common to recognize how racist ideas about Black and Brown people contribute to this misconception; in this book we call for a similar awareness about the contributions of racist ideas about Whiteness. Only by shedding the mystification of Whiteness can we recognize that the drug war and pharmaceutical policy are connected elements of a single, unequal system for providing and regulating psychoactive drugs. Both should be evaluated by the same measure: their ability to secure safe access to highly prized and beneficial, but very dangerous, consumer goods.

To succeed by this commonsense measure, the divided halves of American drug policy need each other. What works in one area should be at least considered in the other. Yet this simply has not happened. Skepticism about the intentions of drug sellers, for example, is a staple of drug war policy, but it is too rarely or too weakly applied in pharmaceutical policy—even though Whiteness-enabled corporate misdeeds, not "drugs," are the real drivers of white market crises. Meanwhile, providing the benefits of psychoactive drugs safely is the raison d'être of white markets, but the notion that drugs could possibly have benefits for consumers is nearly absent in "drug war" policy—few "serious" people prioritize the safe provision of drugs to the racialized communities targeted by drug wars.

The hidden-in-plain-sight history of white drug use is like a laboratory whose experiments we have chosen to forget, repeatedly: knowledge, experience, wisdom sacrificed on the altar of Whiteness.

PART TWO

Three Opioids

Racial Biographies

CHAPTER 5

OxyContin's Racial Precision

In 1997, a year after the Food and Drug Administration (FDA) approved OxyContin as a "minimally addictive" pain reliever suitable for moderate pain, Richard Sackler, founder of OxyContin's manufacturer Purdue Pharmaceuticals, asked Purdue's head of sales and marketing, Michael Friedman, why experts believed oxycodone, the active ingredient in OxyContin, to be weaker than morphine. Dr. Friedman responded:

> We are well aware of the view held by many physicians that oxycodone is weaker than morphine. . . . This 'personality' of oxycodone is an integral part of the personality of OxyContin. . . . [We] do not want to say OxyContin is as "powerful" as morphine. Words such as "powerful" may make some people think that the drug is dangerous and should be reserved for more severe pain. This could have a negative effect in the much larger non cancer pain market. . . . Marketing is not only about what you are, but it's about what you are not. We have had success beyond our expectations that is in part due to the unique personality of OxyContin.

"Excellent points," wrote Sackler.[1]

This email, subpoenaed for a class action lawsuit against the Sackler family that privately owns Purdue Pharmaceuticals, holds a key to understanding how OxyContin became one of the most profitable prescription drugs of the century. The ways that its manufacturer crafted the "personality" of OxyContin, tapping into neuroscientific logics of safety ("weaker than morphine") and into economic logics of consumer segments (the "much larger non cancer pain market") are now known.

What is not widely known is the way the manufacturer tapped into racial logics. How did the imagined race of the patient, and of the medication itself, set the stage for OxyContin to transform opioid prescribing and regulation across the US?

The commercial success of OxyContin, and of similar extended-release opioids such as Opana, Roxicodone, and Embeda was enabled by racially coded neuroscience that lent credibility to manufacturers' claims of safety. Understanding how OxyContin helped launch a white opioid crisis requires analysis of the narratives and imagery of scientific reports; it requires reading against the grain of universal, "color-blind" laboratory findings. OxyContin's meteoric rise was also enabled by the racial politics of pain as an indicator of legitimate need in the 1980s–90s era of privatized health care, a deregulated pharmaceutical industry, and retraction of government benefits. Against a century of prohibitionist policies in US narcotic policy, and of scientific skepticism toward opioids as dangerous drugs, the ways that OxyContin infiltrated general doctor's offices, medicine cabinets, and daily realities across the country require explanation. As with most things in America, a deeper explanation leads us to Whiteness.

When the Sackler family's Purdue Pharmaceuticals reached an initial agreement to settle class action lawsuits for $4.5 billion in 2021, angry and grieving white Americans spoke out about the injustice of the Sacklers being able to keep their fortune and have immunity from future claims. As one mother of a son who died of overdose told reporters, "I would love to make [the Sacklers] watch a video of him going through withdrawals, the pain, the vomiting, him begging us to kill him." Another mother of an athlete who died at twenty-one after being prescribed Oxy-Contin for knee surgery echoed the sentiment: "I would have loved a moment in front of the Sacklers to show them pictures of my son as this beautiful boy and this happy, athletic, strong person that they decimated."[2] Commenting on the size of a settlement that paled in comparison with the half-million lives lost and the estimated $2.5 trillion that the opioid overdose crisis cost the US through the criminal legal system, health and social services, and the lost productivity from lost lives,[3] as well as the over $10 billion in wealth retained by the Sackler family, a grieving father added, "You don't take the architects of the opioid crisis and give them a sweetheart deal. . . . Where is the deterrent?"[4] An artist and opioid activist in recovery from OxyContin dependence added, "I've never seen any such abuse of justice. . . . It's shocking. It's really shocking. I've been deeply depressed and horrified."[5]

OxyContin has come to stand for the extremes of corporate greed in the US health care system—for the harm to "all Americans" that occurs when profit overshadows the public interest. Yet media coverage of legal efforts to get reparations for communities hurt by the company focuses on the lies told by executives, rather than questioning whether the pharmaceutical industry overall is structured to contribute to the common good. It implies a social contract in which the pharmaceutical industry has a right to reap the rewards from technological innovation, as long as it safeguards consumers. Purdue's breach of this contract raised unsettling questions: Who is the "public" in public interest, and who is the "consumer" that the industry will safeguard? Although the public outcry about the death toll from OxyContin appeared to apply to all Americans, a careful rereading of the rise and fall of OxyContin reveals the fault lines of racial capitalism in biomedicine.

Purdue Pharmaceuticals' betrayal turns out not to be about the betrayal of all consumers; rather, it is about the breach of an implicit promise to uphold a safe, affluent white zone of clinical narcotic consumption, segregated from illegalized and hazardous racially "other" street markets. Safety and Whiteness are intertwined in US drug and consumer protection laws, and Purdue's breach was of the guarantees of a segregated drug market. Purdue's marketers designed and executed their plans under the cover of Whiteness—the presumed safety of white clinics and white narcotics consumers—and this allowed Purdue to complete what some refer to as the "great heist" of the twenty-first century.

A full accounting of this strategy requires tracking the convergence of two, mutually reinforcing ideological trends, drawing on historical analysis contributed by David Herzberg, as well as analysis of scientific and popular media by Helena Hansen, Jules Netherland, and members of our research team, particularly Caroline Parker. The first part of the story involves a political discourse about the nature of pain and the degree to which sufferers deserve clinical relief and social accommodations for pain. A closer look reveals how pain has been a racialized phenomenon throughout American history. Showing racial inequalities in clinical treatment for pain, and in political support for disability benefits, David Herzberg relates a history of pain interpreted as legitimate among white people but interpreted as illegitimate among people of color, and he recounts the use of OxyContin to resolve the contradictions created by racial ideologies of pain.

The second part of the story is the covert but actively cultivated Whiteness of the subjects of neuroscience research and psychoactive drug development. For this side of the story, we analyze court documents from class action lawsuits against opioid manufacturers, drug advertisements, and clinical research reports, using insights from social scholars of science and technology. This analysis led us to look at Whiteness in opioid neuroscience and clinical trials as a "ghost variable" that worked behind the scenes to shape the language, concepts, and audiences for new opioid technologies. This "ghost variable" of Whiteness enabled Purdue Pharmaceuticals to associate OxyContin with consumer markets, and with clinical syndromes that they invented for marketing purposes, that justified their aggressive marketing of OxyContin's safety.

. . .

From Helena Hansen's field notes, October 2015:

I got off the commuter train at Stamford, Connecticut, and walked the platform into a maze of glass and steel high-rises. After a wrong turn, I made my way to an unassuming doorway that, I discovered, was minutes from the train station. "Purdue Pharmaceuticals" was only visible once I entered and handed my ID to the guard. The understatedness of the building surprised me—its simple white walls and glass doors, its nondescript brown-paneled elevators. I would not have guessed that I'd entered the headquarters of one of the most profitable pharmaceutical companies in the world.

I met Purdue's research leadership team in a conference room equipped with an oval table, high-back swivel chairs, and a large flatscreen on the wall. After I introduced myself as an opioid researcher, the team presented PowerPoint slides of their new public education campaign against the overuse of medication, which provided alternative pain management strategies to minimize medication use, including meditation and biofeedback. Each team member described their career path, as starting in community health programs and public health research before landing at Purdue. They saw Purdue as a powerful seat from which to act in the public interest. I was reminded that they were the new generation of Purdue researchers; their job was to monitor public opinion and to respond to epidemiological trends two decades after their forebears first developed and marketed OxyContin. Although trained in institutional health promotion—government regulation and consumer protections—their current work for Purdue involved encouraging individuals to take care of themselves by consuming the best technologies. Their public education materials were reminiscent of the pharmaceutical ads that followed the 1997 US legalization of direct-to-consumer advertising, with images of trim blonde women and clean-shaven men in sky-blue shirts and khaki pants, running through green fields with golden retrievers, liberated from physical and mental disability.

Like the original late-1990s ad campaigns for OxyContin, Purdue's second generation of pain management materials conveyed that middle-class Americans could free themselves from pain by using individually tailored, scientific "precision medicine." Also like the earlier OxyContin ads, the materials marshaled symbolic connections among Whiteness, safety, and liberation from physical limitation in order to build public confidence in Purdue's technological advancements. As it turns out, the basis for this public confidence—the cultural association of white subjects with scientific advancement—is the key to understanding OxyContin's success in the pharmaceutical market, as well as the Whiteness of the public health crisis of overdoses that followed. The manufacturer's promotion of new opioid technologies as safe for legitimate, implicitly white consumers selectively opened the floodgates to opioid supplies in white communities across America, both to those for whom they were prescribed and to an even larger population of those for whom they were not prescribed.

The first step to tracking the symbolic connections that pharmaceutical manufacturers forged between the safety and the Whiteness of OxyContin is to uncover the hidden racial logics of opioids in biomedical research. Here we conceptualize Whiteness as a "ghost variable" that operates in the science of pain and of addiction in two senses: (1) as an invisible, default assumed norm, Whiteness codes research on "universal human neurobiology" as research on the white subject; and (2) at the same time, Whiteness drives privileged access to health care in the US, funneling whites into pharmaceutical markets distinct from illegal drug markets for people of color and leading to racially patterned decreases in life expectancy. By emphasizing *Whiteness,* rather than race, as the ghost variable, we highlight the privileged place of Whiteness—as both a default "universal" subject category and a driver of privileged access— in ushering its bearers into one system of narcotic distribution that is geared toward biomedical individual consumption, while people of color are ushered into another system of narcotic criminalization and control. As we now know, and as we spoke about at length in the first chapters, many white people have died as a result of their "privilege" in the pharmaceutical market—a decriminalized, protected zone of opioid use—reflecting their access to doctors and prescriptions, and the higher prescription rate of pain medications for white than for Black patients.[6]

During the second decade of the US opioid crisis, starting in 2010, when Purdue introduced the nonmedical pain management guides for prescribers and patients cited above in response to widespread concern about opioid overdoses, Purdue developed and marketed "tamper-resistant" and "abuse-deterrent" formulations of oxycodone. These included OxyNEO, Targiniq ER, and Hysingla ER, which rapidly replaced original OxyContin in the massive market that the original OxyContin had created, along with "abuse-deterrent" opioid formulations from other manufacturers, including Pfizer, Janssen, Inspirion, and Collegium Pharmaceuticals (Embeda, Troxyca ER, NUCYNTA, Morphabond, Xtampza ER). "Tamper-resistant" formulations were those with delivery devices that made the medications difficult to use other than as directed, such as those with additives designed to deter injection, inhalation, or large-volume ingestion by forming polymer "gummies" that were impossible to inject or that slowed gut absorption of the active ingredient. "Abuse-deterrent" formulations produced unpleasant effects in users who used the medication other than as directed: they irritated nasal passages if sniffed, or put those who attempted to inject them into opioid withdrawal.[7] The FDA blocked generic manufacture of OxyContin, and Purdue stopped making its original OxyContin by 2011.

Purdue was following a corporate logic based on the fact that patents safeguard the intellectual property rights of the company holding the patent for a set period of time: other companies cannot manufacture the medication or device to which the original patent holder has exclusive rights until the patent expires. In the case of OxyContin, Purdue's patent was set to expire by 2013, so introducing alternative formulations with new patents just before that date positioned Purdue to keep exclusive rights to manufacture them. The transition from original OxyContin to "tamper-resistant" and "abuse-deterrent" formulations of OxyContin enabled the Sackler family to continue earning revenue despite public outcry against an explosion of overdose deaths: they earned over $13 billion from one of the best-selling pharmaceuticals in recent history.[8]

The steady stream of new "tamper-resistant" formulations of opioids, together with prescription drug monitoring programs mandating physicians and pharmacists to check a state database before prescribing narcotics for a patient, led an entire generation of people dependent on opioids to turn to heroin when manufactured opioids became hard to get.[9] Ironically, state and federal government initiatives to limit access to prescription opioids helped invigorate the illegal heroin and synthetic opioid trade in predominantly white suburbs, towns, and rural areas that had not previously been the focus of international narcotraffic, changing the crisis of prescription opioid overdose into a crisis of heroin, and eventually of fentanyl and other illegally manufactured synthetic opioids.[10] And the starting point for this storm of illicit opioids was a form of deliberate, if not explicit, ethnic marketing, targeting whites, that drew on deep-seated cultural aspirations to technologically precise "magic bullets" that would distinguish between innocent (implicitly white) suffering patients on one hand and manipulative (implicitly Black) addicts on the other.

As anthropologist Emily Martin wrote, drawing on her study of "pharmaceutical persons" in American pharmaceutical marketing, both marketers and consumers imbue newly patented medications with social identities, identities that are transmitted to the person ingesting medications. At the same time, marketers and consumers also speak of new medications as precise machines that can be designed and calibrated to have specific effects on the consumer, in the vein of a high-performance vehicle or machine.[11] And as anthropologist Anita Hardon shows in her international study of the symbolism of commercialized chemicals, including the skin-lightening products that are widely sold in Asia and Africa, the white identities of pharmaceuticals are both literally and figuratively transmitted to consumers and create "toxic Whiteness" by reinforcing racist hierarchies while exposing users to physiological side effects.[12] In the case of OxyContin, the manufacturer cultivated its social identity as white from its inception, often with additional markers of deservedness and blamelessness—elderly, female, or a veteran of the armed forces—as reflected in their ads. In addition, they claimed that the scientific precision of the new opioids lay in their ability to selectively relieve legitimate pain without causing addiction—in persons who were not predisposed to addiction: implicitly, whites.

In the second decade after OxyContin's FDA approval, a series of lawsuits against Purdue Pharmaceuticals and other manufacturers of similar long-acting opioid pain relievers led courts to mandate manufacturers to release their corporate marketing records to the public. These records revealed a promotional narrative that combined American cultural logics of better living and safety through technology with implicitly racialized distinctions between legitimate and illegitimate consumers. The narrative propagated an image of addiction-resistant white patients whose moderate pain-related disability could be remedied with long term pharmaceutical prosthesis. Influential neuroscientists then propagated the image of a universal brain that erased the social environment as a factor in pain control and in drug use. Yet the "universal" biological determinants of pain and addiction paradoxically helped pharmaceutical manufacturers to translate neuroscientific findings into biotechnologies that were racially coded as white.

BUILDING ON A RACIAL SCIENCE OF PAIN

The 1990s, the "Decade of the Brain," was a time of opportunity for brain scientists of both pain and addiction. US federal support for their research was deliberately linked to aspirations for growth in pharmaceutical industries, falling on the heels of the Human Genome Project and its promise to generate commercial opportunities through public-private partnerships. "Lifestyle drugs" that enhanced mood or social functioning were especially lucrative in the 1990s, following the "Prozac revolution" of psychotropic drugs that were presented as targeted "clean" drugs, free of the side effects caused by the indiscriminate neuroreceptor activation of earlier antidepressant and antianxiety medications.[13] In this ethos, Purdue Pharmaceuticals, already a powerful company privately owned by the Sacklers, a family of physicians that for decades had sold dependency-forming, antianxiety drugs such as Valium and long-acting opioids such as long-acting morphine MS Contin using innovative direct-to-prescriber marketing techniques, was well positioned to unveil OxyContin as a targeted "smart drug."[14] Through a patented sustained-release capsule technology, they claimed, Oxy-Contin converted a classical opioid, oxycodone, into a nonaddictive yet potent pain reliever by delivering small amounts of active medication over a long period of time rather than the large amount that produced a euphoric "rush" leading to dependency and craving.

Opioids have been known for thousands of years as potentially addictive. Oxycodone had been synthesized in 1916 and had been established as equivalent to morphine in addiction risk. How then did Purdue manage to repackage this old, addictive drug as nonaddictive? It did so by taking advantage of a small number of radical pain treatment specialists who had been challenging long-standing beliefs about the dangers of opioid therapy. Kathleen Foley and Russell Portenoy, for example, had published an influential 1989 article arguing that pain patients almost never became addicted to their opioids, while J. David Haddox theorized that when pain patients seemed addicted, they were actually experiencing "pseudoaddiction," a sign that they were not receiving enough opioids to manage their pain. Purdue (and later its competitors too) invested heavily in these radical pain advocates, promoting their idea that addiction risks were "vanishingly small" in legitimate pain patients. That way, they didn't have to prove that oxycodone was less addictive than morphine—both drugs were indeed addictive, but only when used by people other than pain patients.[15] Of course, this distinction relied heavily on the well-documented racial inequalities of pain care: people acknowledged by physicians as legitimate pain patients were overwhelmingly white.[16] Claiming that they were relatively immune from deviant drug desires borrowed from many long-nurtured assumptions about Whiteness (responsibility, hard work, health seeking, etc.).

Once OxyContin was approved, Purdue and its competitors invested heavily in hospital regulators and a wide range of professional medical and health care organizations to market the very idea of pain as a core indicator of quality of care and a medical specialty. This included the campaign to recognize pain as a "fifth vital sign"—as a fundamental aspect of patient care that required close monitoring, documentation, and treatment, akin to temperature, heart rate, respiratory rate, and blood pressure. While pharmaceutical manufacturers were not the only or even the first sector to advocate for more proactive treatment of pain—American nurses were vocal in calling attention to the need for pain management[17]—Purdue and its competitors took advantage of a well-timed opportunity for "unbranded advertising," which means advertising the need to treat a condition in order to create demand for a treatment product. These efforts were so successful that by 2001 the national organization that regulates hospitals—the Joint Commission on Accreditation of Healthcare Organizations—used pain monitoring and treatment as a central criterion for hospitals to maintain their accreditation and therefore their ability to bill for services.[18]

OxyContin marketing capitalized on a concept of pain in the US that had already been racialized for centuries. The deep history of pain and race dates to the transatlantic slave trade, during which white slaveholders justified Black enslavement on the basis of their assumed biological difference from whites, especially Black people's supposed higher tolerance for pain. These ideas about pain tolerance as one element of biological differences among races persist today: US physicians and medical students justify lower prescription rates of pain medication among Black patients by claiming their higher pain tolerance.[19] As Keith Wailoo outlines in *Pain: A Political History,* a racialized discourse of pain and related disability has permeated American policies surrounding social welfare and disability benefits for the past century. The veracity of claims to be in pain, and the deservedness of recipients of government relief for disability from pain, have been the subject of vigorous political struggles from the post–World War II era of veterans' benefits, to the 1954 addition of disability payments to the US Social Security program, to the 1965 passage of the Social Security Act and its creation of national health insurance through Medicaid and Medicare, to the 1980s restriction of disability payments under President Ronald Reagan, and these struggles have continued in contemporary welfare and health reforms.[20]

A throughline of these struggles has been racialized imagery of welfare and disability payment fraud: of the alleged existence of Black and Latinx "welfare queens" who live lavish lifestyles by receiving public benefits registered to multiple names and to their many children, as well as those feigning disability in order to cash in on government payments. In the 1980s–90s crack cocaine era, the popular media portrayed inner-city Black and Latinx people as using disability and welfare benefits to buy drugs. In response, policy makers severely restricted eligibility for disability payments and placed five-year term limits for welfare, driving many former recipients more deeply into poverty and making families dependent on members who could "perform" severe disability in order to qualify for benefits to survive.[21] Images of the government-dependent Black or Latinx, addicted disability and welfare cheat are thus the symbolic and political alter ego of the deserving white pain patient. Such images have also inserted themselves squarely in biomedical research and discourse, albeit thinly veiled with the appearance of scientific objectivity and universalism.

DEREGULATING PAIN: VICTORIES OVER BIG GOVERNMENT

OxyContin was not the pharmaceutical industry's first attempt to create a blockbuster opioid. In fact, it was merely the latest in a long line of would-be miracle opioids stretching back to 1898, when heroin itself had been introduced by Bayer (the details of heroin's origins to follow in chapter 6). In between heroin and OxyContin were a parade of drugs that most people have never heard of: Pantopon, Dilaudid, Demerol, Talwin, and more. In fact, one of these forgotten drugs was none other than oxycodone, the active ingredient of OxyContin. Why are these drugs not famous—or infamous—blockbusters? The answer is that, for most of the twentieth century, federal authorities stood as pharmaceutical watchdogs, swatting back companies' attempts to launch new miracle opioids. After all, American drug wars gave the government powerful tools to regulate narcotics like opioids. And Harry J. Anslinger, the canny head of the Federal Bureau of Narcotics from 1930 to 1962, seemed to relish using them all to force the pharmaceutical industry to heel when it came to new opioids.

Anslinger was a ferocious antinarcotic true believer. On the one hand, he was openly racist in denouncing Black and Brown drug consumers and the foreign powers that supposedly supplied them. On the other hand, he was also a confirmed skeptic about the pharmaceutical industry, physicians, and pharmacists who was bullishly determined to prevent them from profiting off new drug sales booms. The FDA could only look on in envy as Anslinger wielded powers they did not have. He collaborated with the nation's leading addiction pharmacologists to prove the addictiveness of each new would-be miracle opioid and used his Bureau's robust police powers to constrain opioid marketing and force opioid commerce into what was essentially a command economy where profit played relatively little role.[22]

How, then, did OxyContin slip past the watchdogs in the 1990s? It did so under the white racial cover of the pain advocacy movement. Pain had been a focus of medical and public concern—and of political battles—in America since the end of World War II.[23] During this period, traditional racist assumptions were increasingly embedded in medical and cultural concepts of pain. The prejudices could be quite bald: white Americans believed, quite simply, that racial minorities experienced pain less intensely if at all. White physicians were no exception; the false wisdom of racialized pain was taught in medical schools as well.[24] Thus a seemingly race-neutral or universal discourse about pain was, ideologically and in practice, understood to be about white people.

Whiteness was thus a crucial backstage factor in the processes that elevated a small, radical, and industry-funded group of pro-opioid medical pain reformers into prominence and that established their once-radical ideas as the new consensus standard of care for pain. Starting in the 1970s, one wing of the pain advocacy movement had begun to argue that Anslinger-style opioid controls had gone too far—that fear of addiction was depriving people dying of cancer of badly needed pain relief. An even smaller group of pain specialists were willing to go one step further and argue that opioids should be used for a much wider range of pain, including not just acute and end-of-life pain but chronic pain. To support this position, they rejected old studies from the early twentieth century and pointed to more recent and, they argued, definitive studies showing that addiction was extremely rare among pain patients treated with opioids.[25]

Later, in the aftermath of the opioid crisis, researchers returned to these supposedly definitive studies and found serious flaws. One of the most cited "studies" turned out to be no study at all, just a five-sentence 1980 letter to the editor of the *New England Journal of Medicine* noting that hospitalized patients given opioids did not appear to become addicted. Even if this side observation, with no controls, no exclusion of patients who died, or even a definition of key terms such as *addiction*, was taken as definitive, the results bore no relevance to the question of whether chronic pain patients taking opioids home with them were protected from addiction.[26] Another key study published in 1981 by leading opioid advocate (and recipient of much pharmaceutical industry funding) Kathleen Foley was similarly bewildering in that two of the seventeen chronic pain patients actually did become addicted, but Foley dismissed this worrisome number because those patients had prior history of what she called "drug abuse behavior."[27]

Most critics of the improbable elevation of these weak studies into pro-opioid gospel have focused on the money flowing from Purdue and other opioid manufacturers to "key opinion leaders" like Foley. But while money can accomplish a lot, it does not fully explain the exceptionalism of OxyContin. Opioids have been known and feared for their power to addict since ancient times; claiming that suddenly, magically, addiction was no longer a concern—and basing it on such flimsy evidence—was quite a departure. Yet many thoughtful, dedicated health care workers accepted this unlikely new argument, even many who were not on Purdue's payroll. Why?

This is where the invisible backstage work of Whiteness was crucial. It was possible to believe that pain patients were virtually immune from addiction because pain patients were implicitly (and often explicitly) white, and, by the end of the 1980s "crack" cocaine scare, addiction's cultural association with racial "others" was reinforced—as was all the visible social machinery of addiction, from informal markets located in Black and Latinx neighborhoods to jails and prisons filled with people of color there on drug charges. Health-seeking pain patients simply did not qualify as "addiction risks." White health care workers, like many white Americans, were already predisposed to believe that white pain patients were unlikely to become addicted; the industry-funded research coming from Foley and others validated existing beliefs. The path to becoming undisputed medical gospel was certainly greased with torrents of pharmaceutical industry dollars—but that grease only worked because the path had already been prepared by an ideology of legitimate white pain.

Once the new ideas about opioids and chronic pain had become the medical standard of care, embraced by medical specialty organizations such as the American Academy of Pain Medicine and the American Geriatrics Society (themselves flush with industry cash) and state medical boards (e.g., the similarly industry-funded Federation of State Medical Boards), getting by the federal watchdogs was a much easier proposition.[28] The FDA and the Drug Enforcement Administration (DEA) do not dictate medical practice; rather, their job is to enforce medical standards of care that are established within the profession of medicine. With opioids approved for chronic pain care by the relevant specialty organizations, approval by the FDA and DEA was a fait accompli. When the FDA approved OxyContin, for example, it accepted Purdue's claim that "iatrogenic [i.e., medically caused] 'addiction' to opioids legitimately used in the treatment of pain is very rare" and, at the same time, that physical dependence, tolerance, and "preoccupation with achieving adequate pain relief"—elements of "pseudoaddiction" (a syndrome invented by opioid manufacturers, as explained below) rather than true addiction—were all normal, because these ideas had already been endorsed by a range of (industry-funded) medical institutions.[29] Tellingly, the FDA also required language asserting that oxycodone had "an abuse liability similar to morphine" and required precautions similar to morphine's. For most of the twentieth century, this would have been enough to quash any hope of "blockbuster" sales: medical standards for morphine use were quite restrictive. But by the 1990s, medical ideas had changed, thanks to the alchemy of Whiteness powered by industry cash.

It is important to recognize one other way that Whiteness influenced this crucial moment in opioid history. While it is true that the FDA and DEA exist primarily to enforce rather than to create medical standards of care, these agencies have not always been as deferential to the pharmaceutical industry as they were in approving OxyContin. This, too, has a racial component. The FDA's wariness to challenge Purdue was not an isolated event; federal regulators of all sorts had been disempowered in relation to industry since the "Reagan Revolution" of the 1980s. President Reagan had promised to shrink "big government" by scaling back regulatory restraints and unleashing the power of the private sector to solve problems, and while it was slow going, his administration did make significant progress in forcing regulatory agencies like the

FDA to be more cooperative and less combative with the industries they oversaw.

This claim—that the federal government was not helping Americans but rather preventing them from enjoying the fruits of private-sector innovation—was itself highly racialized. The civil rights movement had successfully bent federal power, especially regulatory oversight, to limit some elements of white privilege in America and to redress some aspects of systematic injustice faced by people of color. To the whites referred to as the "Silent Majority" by early conservative president Richard Nixon, this reorientation of government was not a step toward justice but rather a sign that the liberal state had abandoned them and their interests.

In this sense, antigovernment political rhetoric was itself a racial argument opposing civil rights and social welfare. As Keith Wailoo has shown, this had a quite specific meaning in the ongoing political battles over pain. Liberals had long favored government support for chronic pain sufferers in the form of disability payments, while conservatives had worried that this would foster dependence or "learned helplessness." Unleashing the private sector—in this case, the opioid industry—was an unequal compromise: pain sufferers would receive support, but they would receive it through the retraction of government—through an unleashing of the private sector—rather than through traditional social welfare programs.[30]

Social class was also implicated in this antigovernment compromise of private-sector medication for the pain of Americans who were facing unstable employment because of outsourcing of mining, manufacturing, and other core industries in "Rust Belt" America. In addition to well-insured suburban white patients with private doctors, rural and small-town white communities with workers in fields such as mining and construction who had high rates of job-related injury, especially West Virginia and Kentucky, were early targets for OxyContin marketers.[31] This was for good reason: by 2009, more dollars were paid by workers' compensation for OxyContin than for any other drug, and the narcotic cost per claim doubled from 2001 to 2009.[32] Even before widespread media coverage of the suburban "new face of addiction," the early reports of nonmedical OxyContin use and overdose framed them as blue-collar problems in white rural areas of the states first saturated with OxyContin: Kentucky, West Virginia, Virginia, Maine, Pennsylvania, and Massachusetts. These reports named OxyContin "hillbilly heroin" and engaged bigoted satires of isolated "hill country people" of the Appalachian Mountains who had "relapsed into illiteracy and witchcraft." Such satires ignored the long-standing exploitation of these people by mining and timbering industries, the flight of capital from the region, and the region's exclusion from the governor's economic development investments. The earliest newspaper reports of nonmedical OxyContin use, in the late 1990s to early 2000s, linked it to rural white poverty and crime, as in the *Boston Herald*'s claim that OxyContin was "fueling a crime wave around the country, particularly in poor areas where it is dubbed 'Hillbilly Heroin.'"[33] In fact, property crime rates had gone down nationally and were lowest the states with the highest per capita OxyContin use.[34]

Far from the sympathetic portrayals of suburban housewives and college students who were victims of opioid overprescribing or of peer pressure, media reports portrayed white working-class people's use of opioids as part of their "culture of poverty" involving crime, welfare dependence, and out-of-wedlock births, in terms that were not so different from media portrayals of Black and Latinx people who used drugs. Arrest rates and foster care placement went up in working-class white communities that already been subject to the ravages of crystal methamphetamine and the accompanying negative press and incarceration that came with it.[35] As we detail in chapter 6, white working-class communities were exposed to the harms of illegal, often contaminated heroin supplies early on, leading to the "second wave" of the overdose epidemic in which heroin outpaced prescription opioids as the leading cause of death. This second wave started when law enforcement restricted opioid distribution by pharmacists and prescribers, with the result that desperate, opioid-dependent people got priced out of prescription opioid markets and turned to lower-cost heroin.[36] Life expectancy decline due to overdose was highest in the working-class white population and became the focus of a national discourse of "deaths of despair," to which we return in chapter 8.[37] In short, the provisional and partial benefits of Whiteness to blue-collar workers were obvious as they served as canaries in the coal mine of the aggressive opioid marketing that capitalized on growing US socioeconomic inequality.

WHITENESS AS "GHOST VARIABLE"

Decoding the symbolic associations among the social identity of OxyContin, its technological safeguards, drug regulation, addiction risk assessment, and the legitimacy of pain is easier if Whiteness is tracked as an unseen "ghost variable": a systemic element that explains both how prescription opioid use came to be seen as white and how it produced a lived reality of white deaths, even as drug deaths are now on the rise across most racial groups. The idea of race as something that can inhere in the very architecture of scientific technologies, in the drug development strategies of pharmacogenomics and personalized medicine, or in epidemiologists' attribution of racial differences in obesity, heart disease, and diabetes to biological-genetic heredity has given rise to a swath of studies that trace the institutional and seemingly nonracial mechanisms that reproduce white privilege in the medical sciences.[38]

In order to track how technologies of race and infrastructures of racialization operate in the US opioid market, and more specifically, how "color-blind" institutional and pharmaceutical racism led to premature overdose death among whites, it is necessary to account for the invisibility of Whiteness as the assumed norm.[39] How have opioids developed white identities without this Whiteness ever being explicit?

To attempt to answer this, we draw on Daniels and Schultz's observation that "a defining feature of whiteness . . . is the absence or unmarked invisibility of 'white' as a racial category."[40] To begin to understand how opioids came to have white identities, then, requires that we begin to search for its traces, which means looking in places where Whiteness is not obviously apparent.

Neuroscience is a site of race-making where racial and scientific ideas about the safety of OxyContin converged as a cultural and political "accomplishment."[41] We analyze the universalizing scientific contexts of pain and addiction in order to make race-making visible where it is, by design, invisible. Here we more closely examine the ways that neuroscience itself acts as a technology of Whiteness: in propagating the image of the universal brain, in erasing the social environment as a factor in drug use, in translating neuroscientific findings into implicitly racialized biotechnologies, and in using neuroscientific claims in ethnic marketing of these new biotechnologies.

The Universal (White) Brain

As outlined in chapter 2, neuroscientists increasingly rely on brain imagery, which has created a racially unmarked, biologized image of the "addict" that, because it is divorced from historically racialized images of drug users as people of color, and then universalized to represent the average human, is implicitly white in the US, where the average or norm is assumed to be white. Neuroscientists thus follow a pattern established in many other medical fields, including cardiovascular research and pulmonary research, in which clinical reference ranges for "normal" and for "universal" human biology implicitly assume a standard 70 kg white male subject.[42]

In the case of addiction science, this covert whitening involves relocating addiction from social environment or personality to the brain. As addiction researcher Herbert Kleber, who, during his time as deputy director of the Office of National Drug Policy, helped to legalize office-based buprenorphine treatment (now the most widely used pharmaceutical for treatment of opioid dependence), told us in an interview: "Addiction is a biologic disorder. Once you've been taking drugs for a period of time, your brain has changed. . . . If you don't address the biological factors, relapse is going to be very, very high."

In 2015, Nora Volkow, the director of the National Institute on Drug Abuse and a prominent neuroscientist who pioneered the use of PET scans in addiction research, revised her articulation of the brain disease model by noting that this brain disease also undermines the capacity for free will: "Because of drug use, a person's brain is no longer able to produce something needed for our functioning and that healthy people take for granted, free will. . . . We can do much to reduce the shame and the stigma of drug addiction, once medical professionals, and we as a society, understand that addiction is not just 'a disease of the brain,' but one in which the circuits that enable us to exert free will no longer function as they should."[43]

This deployment of the "chronic relapsing brain disease" model to destigmatize addiction, hoped to render those who suffer from it blameless because they are unable to exercise their own free will, contrasts sharply with several earlier images and depictions of nonwhite drug users, which have often invoked moral or cultural depravity and have in turn called for more punitive responses. For example, the turn-of-the-century media portrayals of Chinese opium dens (figure 9), "cocaine crazed negroes" (figure 10), and Mexican "marijuana madness" (figure 11) built support for the passage of heroin and marijuana control acts of the early twentieth century.[44] In stark contrast to these explicitly racialized images, and their associated punitive responses, the apparent "universality" of addiction as a brain disease, and its implicit, invisible

FIGURE 9. Cover of a dime novel, ca. 1900, portraying a Chinese opium den. Stanford University Libraries, RBC ZZ1-24, http://suloas.stanford.edu/swprd_dp/pnsubs.show_page?pid=127_13_F_F.jpg.

encoding as white, imply blamelessness: those with the brain disease of addiction biologically cannot control themselves, and thanks to neuroscientific breakthroughs, treatment, rather than punishment, is the logical response.

This white, medicalized space of addiction as a brain disease is not a new development; it builds upon a century of a two-tiered system of US drug policy, in which illegal drugs have been symbolically linked to people of color, while a separate sphere of legal, prescribed narcotic use has been reserved for white middle-class consumers with private doctors.

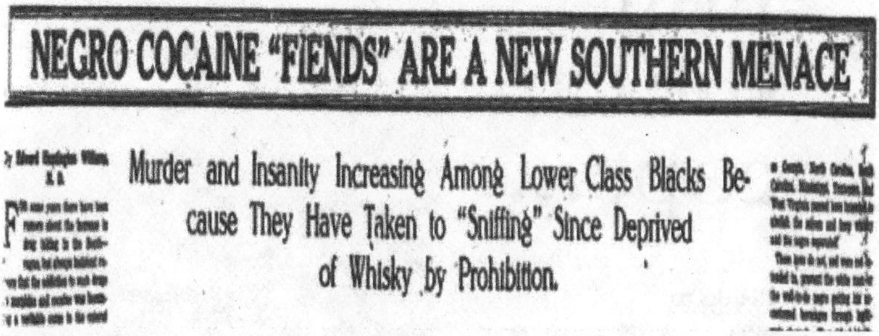

NEGRO COCAINE "FIENDS" ARE A NEW SOUTHERN MENACE

Murder and Insanity Increasing Among Lower Class Blacks Because They Have Taken to "Sniffing" Since Deprived of Whisky by Prohibition.

FIGURE 10. A 1914 newspaper article warning against cocaine-crazed southern Negroes. Edward Huntington Williams, "Negro Cocaine 'Fiends' Are a New Southern Menace," *New York Times*, February 8, 1914, SM12.

FIGURE 11. A 1940 cartoon portraying a Mexican marijuana smoker. Source: *Vidette Messenger* (Valparaiso, Indiana), July 19, 1940.

This legal narcotic market has been long been normalized, with 1940s–60s pharmaceutical advertisements depicting white, middle-class women in need of narcotic prescriptions for anxiety related to everything from rearing overactive children (figure 12) to menopause (figure 13). And it has been no less lethal for its legality and normality, with middle-class

now
she can
cope...

thanks to

Butisol SODIUM®
(SODIUM BUTABARBITAL)

"daytime sedative" for
everyday situational stress

When stress is situational—environmental pressure,
worry over illness—the treatment often calls for an
anxiety-allaying agent which has a prompt and
predictable calming action and is remarkably well
tolerated. BUTISOL SODIUM (sodium butabarbital)
meets this therapeutic need.
After 30 years of clinical use ... still a first choice
among many physicians for dependability and
economy in mild to moderate anxiety.
Contraindications: Porphyria or sensitivity to
barbiturates.
Precautions: Exercise caution in moderate to severe
hepatic disease. Elderly or debilitated patients may
react with marked excitement or depression.
Adverse Reactions: Drowsiness at daytime sedative
dose levels, skin rashes, "hangover" and systemic
disturbances are seldom seen.
Warning: May be habit forming.
Usual Adult Dosage: As a daytime sedative,
15 mg. (¼ gr.) to 30 mg. (½ gr.) t.i.d. or q.i.d.
Available for daytime sedation: Tablets, 15 mg. (¼ gr.),
30 mg. (½ gr.); Elixir, 30 mg. per 5 cc. (alcohol 7%.)
BUTICAPS® (Capsules BUTISOL SODIUM (sodium butabarbital))
15 mg. (¼ gr.), 30 mg. (½ gr.).

[McNEIL]
McNeil Laboratories, Inc., Fort Washington, Pa.

FIGURE 12. A 1960s ad for Butisol, a barbiturate. Source:
Journal of the American Medical Association 207, no. 6 (1969):
1206.

Americans overdosing on barbiturates and benzodiazepines at high rates
in the 1940s–60s that resembled those of opioid overdose fifty years
later.[45]

The Erasure of Social Environment

Despite neuroscientists' good intentions of destigmatizing addiction by
locating the cause of addiction in the brain, the neuroscientific model
has also had the effect of hiding from view the political and commercial
contexts that drive drug addiction. This erasure of social drivers
of addiction is visible in how neuroscientists envisage solutions for

FIGURE 13. A 1950s ad for Milprem, the sedative meprobamate.
Source: Wallace Laboratories, Cranbury, NJ, exact date
unknown.

managing addiction. Although environmental forces are sometimes invoked in the neuroscientific literature, they are often of interest primarily for the biochemical processes they engender. For example, Nora Volkow and Ting-Kai Li, exploring what they call the "neural consequences of environmental risk," write:

> Low socioeconomic class and poor parental support are two other factors [along with drug availability] that are consistently associated with a propensity to self-administer drugs, and stress might be a common feature of these environmental factors. . . . [There] is evidence that corticotropin-releasing factor (CRF) might play a linking role through its effects on the mesocorticolimbic dopamine system and the hypothalamic pituitary-adrenal axis. . . .

If we understand the neurobiological consequences underlying the adverse environmental factors that increase the risk for drug use and addiction, we will be able to develop interventions to counteract these changes.[46]

Though environmental influences are acknowledged here, it is striking how they are understood primarily in terms of how the stress they induce affects the brain—or, more specifically, the dopamine system of molecules that send signals in the brain. The authors go on to suggest that the future addiction interventions may include medications that work in concert with behavioral therapies to mitigate the impact of stress.[47] Clearly absent from this view of addiction, however, is the social context of drug use and the possibility of intervening with regard to root causes of addiction, such as unemployment, violence, and institutional racism.

Neuroscientific studies of addiction tend to construe the role of environmental influences narrowly without explaining social factors or the reasons for variation in prevalence of drug use by population.[48] Even in studies of neuroplasticity, the focus is on how drugs themselves reshape the individual brain, rather than on the role played by social environmental factors. These explanations of behavior are consistent with our cultural focus on the individual and interiority.[49] The apparent biomolecular "universality" of addiction hides its social and political dimensions.[50] Nancy Campbell has described the chronic relapsing brain disease model of addiction as an "ideological code" that erases the "differential histories and cultural geographies within which their subjects encounter drugs."[51] The success of the chronic relapsing brain disease model as an ideological code has meant that social issues, such as the lack of economic opportunities beyond the drug trade in poor neighborhoods, or, in the case of OxyContin, targeted and aggressive drug marketing, have received little attention in US policy. This leaves addiction researchers little capacity to look at systemic issues that might be driving opioid use.

The brain disease model of addiction, as an alternative to equally individual-level explanations for drug use such as criminality, led to racially selective, rather than global, changes in drug policy. By erasing the social context of drug use in the arena of newly patented biotechnologies to which white Americans have privileged access, it built upon a preexisting two-tiered system for managing narcotic use in the United States: a clinical tier of legally protected, medicalized use for middle-class whites with access to prescribing doctors, and a criminalized tier for low-income people of color, who have long been the target of prohibitionist law enforcement.[52]

Neuroscience in the Marketing of White Drugs

While the neuroscientists who constructed the supposedly color-blind brain disease concept of addiction believed themselves to be developing universal biological models, their work supported more deliberately racial strategies of the pharmaceutical industry. The active ingredient in OxyContin was oxycodone, which was first synthesized in Germany in 1916 and has been available in the United States since 1939. The single feature differentiating OxyContin from oxycodone (making it a new drug requiring approval from the Food and Drug Administration) was OxyContin's "controlled-release" capsule, introduced in the mid-1990s and supposedly limiting its addictive potential. As outlined in chapter 1, this allowed Purdue to pursue an enormous new market of those with moderate pain, where opioids had previously been restricted to use for severe pain such as postsurgical or cancer pain.

To access this much larger market of patients with moderate, chronic pain, Purdue spent hundreds of millions of dollars on pharmaceutical marketing, including $200 million spent on marketing and promoting OxyContin in 2001 alone and $18 million worth of advertising in major medical journals between 1996 and 2002.[53] Purdue also directed massive funds to "front groups," third-party organizations disguised as "unbiased" sources of cutting-edge medical research and information, spending over $4.15 million between January 2012 and March 2017 on twelve different organizations that were examined by the US Senate committee.[54] Across US states, Purdue hired thousands of drug representatives who visited prescribers more than 150,000 times in Massachusetts between 2007 and 2017, 229,011 times in Virginia between 2006 and 2017, and 300,000 times in Tennessee between May 7, 2007, and December 2017.[55] As we detail later in this chapter, although Purdue pioneered the 1990s opening of new, less regulated opioid markets, many other opioid manufacturers, from Teva and Endo to Janssen, quickly joined in and even exceeded Purdue in funding such third-party organizations, gaining an even larger market share for new opioids.

In a clear enactment of racial capitalism, the promotional strategies of Purdue and other opioid manufacturers were not geographically even; rather, they were significantly more commonly deployed in nonurban and white counties.[56] Opioid marketers covered predominantly white suburban areas with privately insured people who had access to primary care doctors for treatment of chronic, moderate pain, as well as predominantly white rural areas and small towns with manual labor industries offering workers' compensation as detailed above.[57] Targeting these areas also helped marketers evade the gaze of regulators such as the DEA, which was preoccupied with interdiction and surveillance in the predominantly Black and Latinx urban neighborhoods that had long been targeted by drug war policies. Meanwhile, across counties, the more money invested in opioid marketing per capita, the higher the subsequent overdose mortality rate.[58]

Because the social context of drug use was omitted from the universal biological model of addiction, regulators failed to predict that users would crush and snort or inject the contents of OxyContin capsules, which are more potent than morphine. And so the invisibility of social contexts of opioids, brought about by their neuroscientific, molecular ethos, in turn dramatically changed the racial landscape of drugs and drug policy in America.

MAKING OPIOIDS WHITE

Building on the anthropological argument that pharmaceuticals have social lives—that they acquire meanings as they enter into social circulation and find social, cultural, and psychological uses—as well as the observation that pharmaceutical marketers consciously design campaigns to give drugs distinct personalities, we see evidence that Purdue and other opioid manufacturers transformed the social identity of opioids over the last three decades.[59] They shifted the public image of opioids from that of highly addictive drugs suitable only for cancer and severe, acute forms of pain to that of safe medications suitable for the long-term treatment of chronic pain. Our content analysis of industry-sponsored medical education programs, and of corporate strategy made public through opioid litigation, revealed that opioid marketers radically transformed the image of their product through a strategy that anthropologist Caroline Parker calls "pharmaceutical splitting."[60] This refers to an act of subdividing a drug's target disorder or population, thereby attaching a different drug personality or public persona in relation to each disorder or population. Pharmaceutical splitting produced a circuitous logic whereby legitimate patients suffering from chronic pain could never, by definition, be addicted. A key aspect of this logical loop was that the pain patients who could not be addicted were white, because opioid manufacturers represented legitimate pain sufferers as white, and those who accessed prescriptions for chronic pain were disproportionately white. Racial stereotypes safeguarded white patients from suspicion of addiction, further reinforcing the white demographics of patients considered to have legitimate clinical need for pain relief.

Social analysts have long observed that pharmaceutical marketers link drugs with attractive states of mind: for example, psychiatric medications, whose ads are filled with images of happiness, creativity, or sexual fulfillment.[61] Drugs' personalities may also be shaped through their association with particular populations of consumers, such as Valium for anxious middle-class white mothers in need of relaxation, or Viagra for heterosexual couples who want to reinvigorate their sex lives, or Haldol for angry, psychotic African American men whose physicians are eager to sedate them.[62]

The opposite process—that of "distancing" or strategically disassociating a drug from a disorder or population—is another well-documented method by which pharmaceutical marketers seek to alter their drugs' personalities. In her research on Viagra, for example, Emily Wentzell describes how Pfizer deliberately represented Viagra as a "medical" treatment to enhance the intimacy of troubled heterosexual couples, and avoided association with gay male sex, which was deemed an illegitimate, "recreational" use of the drug.[63] This enabled Pfizer to retarget their drug to the larger, less politically risky heterosexual market. Similarly, Nathan Greenslit has shown how Pfizer "reinscribed" an antidepressant (fluoxetine, commercially known as Prozac) into a treatment for premenstrual disorders by changing its name (to Sarafem) and color (to pink and violet from green and yellow), thereby distancing the drug from its prior association with the more stigmatized psychiatric disorder of clinical depression and opening the larger market of menstruating women.[64]

The concept of "pharmaceutical splitting" is useful for understanding the transformation that Purdue achieved with OxyContin, from a strong, dangerous opioid capable of causing addiction and overdose, to a slow-acting, safe medication free of addictive potential.[65] Pharmaceutical splitting involves the act of pulling apart a drug's target disorder and population into fundamentally different types. Purdue discursively separated opioid consumers into two publics, "patients" and "abusers," and separated escalating OxyContin use into two disorders, "true addiction" and "pseudoaddiction," in order to characterize opioids as safe for chronic moderate pain.

From the 1990s onwards, Purdue achieved pharmaceutical splitting by investing unprecedented amounts in a multifaceted marketing campaign that included not only advertising and branding but also sponsoring scientific researchers, professional societies, and patient advocacy groups and ghostwriting research articles for clinical journals. Between 1996 and 2001, the company spent half a billion US dollars on pharmaceutical "detailing"—the practice of dispatching sales representatives to visit individual doctors and medical staff in their offices to promote Purdue products.[66] Other opioid manufacturers employed similar strategies: Janssen, Cephalon, Endo, and Actavis (along with Purdue) collectively spent $168 million on detailing branded opioids to doctors in 2014, a figure that included $34 million by Janssen, $13 million by Cephalon, $10 million by Endo, $2 million by Actavis, and $108 million by Purdue.[67] Opioid manufacturers also made financial contributions to medical education and training programs. Purdue alone funded over two thousand pain-related continuing medical education programs and dozens of national pain management training conferences.[68] Pharmaceutical companies also elected to work with individual academic scientists whose research favored their products—"thought leaders" who received financial support to attend conferences and present their findings across the United States.[69] Opioid manufacturers made financial donations to various professional societies and patient advocacy organizations, including the American Pain Foundation (APF), the American Academy of Pain Medicine (AAPA), the American Pain Society (APA), and the American Osteopathic Association (AOA), all of which led campaigns advocating to increase access to opioid pain relievers.[70] Purdue alone spent over $4.15 million between January 2012 and March 2017 on twelve different advocacy and professional organizations.[71] Opioid manufacturers engaged in ghostwriting research articles favorable to their products—enlisting well-known scientists who had little to do with research design or implementation to lend their names as authors of scientific publications—thereby lending industry-sponsored research a veneer of independence.[72] They also engaged in ghost management of research by overseeing clinical trials and closely managing the publication of scientific findings without disclosing their role in those publications.[73] These strategies for shaping the social identity or personality of opioids worked in concert to achieve three types of pharmaceutical "splitting."

Splitting Moderate Pain from Severe and Cancer Pain

As illustrated in the email to Purdue founder Richard Sackler quoted at the beginning of this chapter, which warned against making people think that OxyContin was "powerful" because it could have "a negative effect in the much larger non cancer pain market," Purdue strategically distanced OxyContin from older opioids commonly used for treating cancer-related pain. The most significant of these was morphine, widely used since the 1820s as a first-line drug for severe acute pain. Although race was not explicitly mentioned in this strategy, note that medication for moderate pain and primary care doctors as the source of pain medication are themselves raced. The company would have been aware that clinicians disproportionately prescribed pain relievers to whites and thought of nonwhite patients as at higher risk of addiction than white patients, while white Americans had greater access to primary care doctors. This was reflected in the image of white primary care patients receiving OxyContin as featured in direct-to-prescriber and direct-to-consumer ads (as illustrated below).

Pharmaceutical representatives specifically targeted primary care clinics and practitioners in rural areas who had little prior experience prescribing opioids, had little contact with specialists, and therefore were the least likely to question the company's claims of low risk.[74] This led to the most rapid uptake of OxyContin in predominantly white areas such as Maine, Kentucky, West Virginia, and southwestern Virginia.[75]

Splitting "Trustworthy" Patients from Opioid "Abusers"

When conceiving of their target market, opioid manufacturers determined that their most lucrative avenue was to prioritize consumers who were insured through either private commercial or public insurance plans. To reach them through prescribing physicians who were anxious about the addiction and overdose risks of opioids, pharmaceutical marketers split patient populations into "trustworthy patients" and opioid "abusers." Marketers presented these patient populations as easy to distinguish—in part, through implicit demographic coding including race. They reframed the problem for prescribers from one of choosing safe medications to one of choosing patients for whom opioids could safely be used for moderate pain long term. This enhanced sales by dramatically expanding the number of patients treated with opioids and the duration of treatment.

FIGURE 14. Late 1990s OxyContin promotionals on desk of author. Photo credit: Helena Hansen.

As evidenced in our analysis of branded advertising materials, the trustworthy patient was constructed on the basis of two social figures, both of which hold considerable public trust in America. The first was the (white) American grandparent, a class of people culturally considered as highly unlikely to abuse drugs. Throughout the 1990s and 2000s, Purdue circulated hundreds of thousands of pamphlets to medical prescribers with descriptions and photographs of target patients. One widely circulated pamphlet presented an image of a patient called Pam, who was elderly, white, and suffering from chronic back pain due to osteoarthritis. Nonincidentally, Pam was also insured through Medicare (figure 14). The targeting of older patients insured through Medicare was referred to in Purdue's internal documents as its "geriatric strategy."[76] To support this "geriatric strategy," Purdue trained its sales reps to emphasize the "trustworthiness" of elderly patients in their conversations with clinicians.[77] This would often involve sharing staged photographs and profiles of white elderly patients.

Images of elderly white patients suffering from osteoarthritis soon populated the pages of medical journals. In 2012, for example, Purdue ran a series of advertisements for OxyContin in medical journals. These "pain vignettes" were case studies featuring older patients with pain conditions persisting over several months. One ad described a "54-year-old writer with osteoarthritis of the hands" and implied that OxyContin would help the writer work more effectively.[78] Other opioid manufacturers developed ads that used similar emotive imagery: smiling white grandparents, who, thanks to opioid pain relievers, were now able to play with their grandchildren free from the affliction and hindrance of chronic pain. An OxyContin advertisement featured in the *Journal of the American Medical Association* in 2002 showed an older white man and a young white boy fishing, with the prominent headline, "There can be life with relief"[79] (see figure 14).

A second social figure that became a face of the trustworthy patient was the wounded veteran, whose sacrificial injuries conferred a heightened moral need for pain medication and who, noncoincidentally, enjoyed subsidized access to opioids through US veterans' insurance plans. Over the course of the late 1990s and 2000s, images of wounded white veterans suffering with chronic pain cropped up in the pages of medical journals, just as sales reps flocked in their hundreds to veterans' clinics and hospitals, where they had been especially trained to talk to prescribers about their clienteles' trustworthiness, injuries, and insurance coverage.[80]

In 2009, Purdue sponsored a book entitled *Exit Wounds: A Survival Guide to Pain Management for Returning Veterans and Their Families*. Though the book was presented as the personal story of a wounded (white) veteran, Derek McGinnis, the author was actually employed by the American Pain Foundation, an organization that received millions of dollars from Purdue[81] (figure 15). In this "self-help" guide for managing injury-related pain, McGinnis tells the story of how opioid pain medications helped to turn his life around, emphasizing the benefits of opioid pain medications throughout: "The pain-relieving properties of opioids are unsurpassed. . . . Yet, despite their great benefits, opioids are underused. For a number of reasons, healthcare providers may be afraid to prescribe them, and patients may be afraid to take them. At the core of this wariness is the fear of addiction, so I want to tackle this issue head-on. . . . Long experience with opioids *shows that people who are not predisposed to addiction* [emphasis ours] are unlikely to become addicted to opioid pain medications."[82] Inhering within this injured veteran's firsthand assurance that opioids are safe is a second and equally important message: that opioids are safe for most (reliable, implicitly white) patients but not for all (risky, implicitly nonwhite) people.

By 2001, five years after Purdue launched OxyContin, questions were being raised about the risk of addiction and overdose that came

 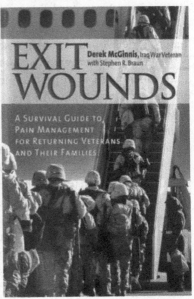

FIGURE 15. *(Left)* Purdue Pharma–sponsored veteran Derek McGinnis. Photo credit: Bart Ah You/Modesto Bee/MCT/Sipa 2008. *(Right)* Cover of Derek McGinnis's book *Exit Wounds.* Source: Derek McGinnis, *Exit Wounds: A Survival Guide to Pain Management for Returning Veterans and Their Families*, with Stephen R. Braun (Tampa, FL: Waterford Press, 2009).

with taking opioid medications. Purdue's founder, Richard Sackler, had a strategy: "We have to hammer on the abusers in every way possible," Sackler wrote in an email in February 2001. "They are the culprits and the problem. They are reckless criminals."[83]

Consider, for example, testimony from the American Pain Foundation, an organization that received major funding from Purdue. After claiming it was a myth that opioid pain medications were dangerous, the patient advocacy organization went on to argue that when taken as prescribed, under the direction of a physician for pain relief, opioids were safe and effective, and only rarely led to addiction.[84] Good use is medical use, so the story goes. Addiction, where it occurs, happens when opioids get into the "illegal hands" of "drug abusers." Pitting the illegitimate opioid abuser against the legitimate opioid patient starts to make possible the conception of drug addiction as a problem located in the consumer, in the "illegal and dangerous use of this medication by drug abusers," rather than in the drugs themselves. While these materials did not show visual images of "drug abusers" or use explicitly racial descriptors, the preponderant images of drug abusers in American popular culture and media over the preceding decades had been of people of color.

Similar messages were circulated to prescribers. For example, a Purdue-sponsored prescribing guide distributed to hundreds of thousands of clinicians in the United States, entitled *Providing Relief, Preventing Abuse: A Reference Guide to Controlled Substance Prescribing Practices,* claimed that addiction "is not caused by drugs." Instead, it assured doctors that addiction was the result of opioids getting to the wrong category of patients: "It is triggered in a susceptible individual by exposure to drugs, most commonly through *abuse* [emphasis ours]."[85]

By the early 2000s a novel category of people had emerged in the pharmaceutical advertising materials: "persons with addictive disease." Thus a widely circulated 2007 patient guide sponsored by Cephalon and Purdue and Teva, entitled *"Treatment Options: A Guide for People Living with Pain,* told patients that "people with the disease of addiction may abuse their medications, engaging in unacceptable behaviors like increasing the dose without permission or obtaining the opioid from multiple sources, among other things."[86] In what becomes a circular kind of logic, addiction is constructed as a *result* of this underlying pathology. In a notable departure from the more widely used nomenclature within clinical medicine of "people with substance use disorders" or "people with opioid use disorders"—terms that foreground *use* of a substance—the category of "person with the disease of addiction" erases that drug consumption, leaving behind only a diseased person and individualized pathology. The same patient guide continues: "Opioids get into the hands of *drug dealers* and *persons with an addictive disease* as a result of pharmacy theft, forged prescriptions, Internet sales, and even from other people with pain. . . . Adding to the problem is the increase in *abuse* of prescription drugs in the U.S. Persons with addictive disease . . . have obtained and *misused* these drugs. Others have taken them *illegally* through pharmacy thefts or under false pretenses in order to sell them 'on the street' for profit." This strategy of splitting opioid consumers into two opposing categories led to a selective, rather than global, sense of opioid safety. By harnessing preexisting social differentiations and cultural imagery, the portrayals of these two opioid publics reinforced hierarchies of blame as they were selectively drawn on to explain opioid overdose.

This bifurcation of opioid consumers was not confined to industry-sponsored patient and prescriber guides, however. Similar practices of splitting were also occurring in the scientific literature. By the early 2000s, scientists' statements about how opioids ought to be prescribed had undergone a shift. Scientists were no longer asking whether opioids were safe in a global sense. Instead, the question now turned to whom opioids were safe for, with considerations of opioid safety increasingly focused on characteristics of the patient. Increasingly, scientists came to use patients' "vulnerability to addiction" or "history of abuse" to explain opioid safety.[87]

Consider, for example, the following consensus statement presenting guidelines for the use of opioids in chronic pain treatment, published in the prestigious *Journal of Pain*. Two of the authors (Dr. Portenoy and Dr. Fine) were prominent paid "key opinion leaders" for multiple opioid manufacturers, including Purdue. The statement asserted a "legitimate medical need for opioids in *some* [emphasis ours] patients," with legitimate need illustrated through the example of a patient who was "60 years old, has chronic disabling osteoarthritis pain," and "whose history reveals no . . . personal or family history of drug abuse or addiction." Scientists then presented a counterexample of a younger patient who was "30 years old with . . . recent intravenous drug abuse," for whom opioid pain medication would not be appropriate.[88]

In another section of the statement by Drs. Chou et al. tailored specifically to the problem of "breakthrough pain" (a sudden magnification of pain among patients already treated for chronic pain), scientists emphasized that for this kind of pain there was no evidence of a connection between opioid pain relievers and addiction, before preemptively attributing any heightened risk to patients' preexisting vulnerability: "Although there is no evidence of the risk of aberrant drug-related behavior in relation to the availability of medication prescribed for breakthrough pain, it is reasonable to assume that access to a short-acting drug may increase the risk of such *behavior in those already engaging in them or at high risk to do so* [emphasis ours]."[89]

Much as opioid marketers had put forth the notion of a class of people with an in-built vulnerability to develop "addictive disease," these scientists assured that even though some drugs produced pleasurable reward, critical determinants of addiction rested also with the user. Addiction should not be considered as an effect of opioids. It was something that occurred "*in vulnerable individuals* [emphasis ours]when repeated rewarding drug use triggers a biologic change leading to a protracted drive to use the drug."[90]

By the early 2000s, scientists were devising instruments to assist prescribers in identifying appropriate opioid patients. Several of these were designed by scientists with known financial ties to industry.[91] They typically consisted of a short series of questions concerning patient history, with risk of addiction framed as an issue of patient characteristics, including criminality, prior illicit drug consumption, and history of mental illness.

One of the most widely promoted instruments was the Opioid Risk Tool,[92] developed in 2005 by Dr. Webster, a former president of the American Academy of Pain Medicine and also an author of numerous continuing medical education programs sponsored by Cephalon, Endo, and Purdue. The Opioid Risk Tool was published in *Pain Medicine*, the same journal that published various supplements funded by Endo, the company promoting Opana ER (an extended-release opioid similar to OxyContin). It was a five-question, one-minute self-reported patient questionnaire that purported to predict the risk of opioid dependence. To assess patients' "abuse liability" with opioids, the instrument questioned them about their prior drug use and criminality, with specific questions including (1) How often do you have mood swings? (2) How often do you smoke a cigarette within an hour after you wake up? (3) How often have you taken medication other than the way that it was prescribed? (4) How often have you used illegal drugs (for example, marijuana, cocaine, etc.) in the past five years? and (5) How often, in your lifetime, have you had legal problems or been arrested? Other academic researchers—several of them with known financial links to industry—devised similar screening tools, including the SOAPP, the revised SOAPP (SOAPP-R), and the Diagnosis, Intractability, Risk, Efficacy (DIRE) instrument.[93] Assessment tools like this were used to deflect concerns about the properties of the medication itself by implying that screens for prior drug use left those who screened negative safe from the addictive potential and overdose risk of opioids.

Finally, it is worth looking at how this splitting of opioid consumers into legitimate and illegitimate publics occurred at the level of clinical trials. Although opioid pain relievers had been promoted for patients with osteoarthritis since OxyContin came onto the market in 1996, it was actually not until 1999 that the first study of the effectiveness of controlled-release oxycodone for patients with osteoarthritis was published. The study, which was published in the *Journal of Rheumatology*, treated patients with four daily doses of opioid painkillers for one month and excluded patients with a history of drug addiction or alcoholism from participating. It noted that "controlled release oxycodone [OxyContin] was associated with a lower incidence of some side effects."[94] This trial was followed one year later with a second study by Roth and colleagues that assessed the efficacy of controlled-release oxycodone (the nonbranded name for OxyContin) among patients who were suffering from osteoarthritis.[95] Again, most of the patients included in the study were elderly, and patients with histories of criminality or drug addiction were excluded from participating. Although the race of study participants was not indicated, clinical trial participants in US-based studies at the time were disproportionately white, as was the image of the "universal" human that study participants represented (the proverbial 70 kg white male biomedical research subject).[96] The message was clear: OxyContin was safe, but the kinds of people who were deliberately excluded from its clinical trials were not: the young, those with a history of addiction or crime, and—by association, after a century of portrayals of "addicts" as racial others—those who were not white.

Splitting "True Addiction" from "Pseudoaddiction"

If the hard distinction between patients and abusers created the possibility for opioids to be considered as safe, at least for some people, there still remained a problem. How would clinicians react if their trustworthy (predominantly white) patients were to present at their clinics with obvious symptoms of drug addiction? Would clinicians still consider opioids to be safe? Would the newly approved opioids have transformed their trustworthy white, elderly, and veteran patients with no predisposition to addiction into "addicts"? The solution was a second order of category subdivision: splitting apart what *looked like* addiction into two categories, "true addiction" and "pseudoaddiction," could recast trustworthy patients showing signs of addiction, not as drug addicts, but as undertreated pain patients. Below, we outline the origin and germination of this idea across American medicine.

In 1989, David Weissman and David Haddox published an article that would become a critical instrument of opioid marketing, entitled "Opioid Pseudoaddiction: An Iatrogenic Syndrome." Haddox was a past president of the American Academy of Pain Medicine, an organization that received significant financial funding from Purdue. He later went on to become a senior medical director for Purdue. In the article, Weissman and Haddox introduced the term *pseudoaddiction* to describe an "iatrogenic syndrome of abnormal behavior" entailing behavioral symptoms that mimicked "true opioid psychologic dependence." They argued that behavioral symptoms such as "overwhelming and compulsive interest in the acquisition and use of opioid analgesics" were not symptoms of addiction because such symptoms were "caused by the undermedication of pain." In other words, patients who were presenting in clinics with behaviors typically associated with addiction were actually suffering from pseudoaddiction. According to Weissman and Haddox, the solution to this was to increase patients' dose of opioid pain medications on the basis of their self-reported level of pain.[97]

The paper, which was published in the prestigious journal *Pain*, presented the pharmaceutical industry with a fortuitous source of scientific legitimacy for its marketing campaign. Pharmaceutical manufacturers published thousands of copies of educational guides for clinical practitioners and designed dozens of continuing medical education programs teaching that pseudoaddiction was real.[98] For example, a Purdue pamphlet titled *Providing Relief, Preventing Abuse* urged doctors to look for pseudoaddiction, which it characterized as "the inaccurate interpretation of [drug-seeking] behaviors in patients who have pain that has not been effectively treated." Similarly, a clinical guide sponsored by opioid manufacturers Cephalon, Endo, and Purdue, titled *Responsible Opioid Prescribing*, taught that behaviors such as requesting drugs by name, demanding or manipulative behavior, hoarding, and seeing more than one doctor to obtain opioids were all signs of pseudoaddiction rather than true addiction.[99] These and various other guides produced by the pharmaceutical industry repeatedly cited the Weissman and Haddox paper.

Purdue also sponsored a continuing medical education program entitled "Path of the Patient: Managing Chronic Pain in Younger Adults at Risk for Abuse." In a specially devised role-play, a chronic pain patient tells his doctor that he is taking twice as many hydrocodone pills as directed. The narrator notes that because of pseudoaddiction, the doctor should not assume the patient is addicted even if he persistently asks for a specific drug, seems desperate, hoards medicine, or "overindulges in unapproved escalating doses." The role-play ends with the doctor treating the patient with a high-dose, long-acting opioid.

Endo Pharmaceuticals, manufacturer of Opana ER, took this idea a step further by sponsoring a National Initiative on Pain Control continuing medical education program in 2009 ("Chronic Opioid Therapy: Understanding Risk While Maximizing Analgesia"), designed specifically to teach clinicians about pseudoaddiction. To increase opioid prescriptions to patients who were showing signs of drug addiction, Endo even mandated that it would award grants to continuing medical education providers *only* if they taught clinicians to differentiate between addiction and pseudoaddiction.[100] Since Endo was a key funder of the National Initiative on Pain Control—responsible for developing, specifying, and reviewing content—this decision went on to have a profound effect on continuing medical education programs.

As clinicians made the rounds of industry-sponsored conferences and educational programs, and as the concept of pseudoaddiction populated pharmaceutical marketing materials, the addicted patient was severed from his or her addiction. Separation of true addiction from pseudoaddiction could remove the offending diagnosis (addiction) from the trustworthy patient, who could now be considered as an undertreated pain patient, rather than as a person addicted to opioids.

Although implicit, the racial logic of pseudoaddiction was clear: newly patented extended-release opioids such as OxyContin were marketed to white, "legitimate" pain patients for the white problem of treatable pain (since, as a group, physicians tended not to medicate Black or Latinx patients for the same diagnoses and pain symptoms). If a white, "legitimate" pain patient on extended-release opioids showed signs of opioid dependency, such as escalating one's requirements for opioids, showing an "overwhelming and compulsive interest in the acquisition and use of opioid analgesics," "requesting drugs by name," exhibiting "demanding or manipulative behavior," or seeing more than one doctor to obtain opioids, this was not addiction. It met the diagnostic criteria for a new, alternative condition, pseudoaddiction, that was reserved for the predominantly white patients who had access to primary care doctors, and whose doctors tended to recognized their suffering as legitimate. And the treatment for pseudoaddiction was neither rehabilitation nor incarceration, but treatment with increased doses of long-acting opioids. In essence, pseudoaddiction helped to preserve the Whiteness of patients who had long been protected from the public scrutiny and blame of an addicted identity in the bifurcated US system, where nonwhite drug use was criminalized and white prescription narcotics were deemed a medical necessity.

GHOSTLY WHITE

The rise of OxyContin can be fully understood only in relation to the racial unconscious of American white people and of the industries catering to them. Whiteness as unspoken, unacknowledged, and ultimately so buried that it becomes unconscious in everyday life is crucial to fostering racial capitalism. Racialized medical consumer markets, like racially motivated retraction of public benefits in favor of privatized health care, housing, education, and employment, can easily operate under cover of competition-based innovation, individual responsibility, and merit-based rewards if they hide their underlying ideology of Whiteness as a valuable and exclusive trait. Early twentieth-century race scholar W. E. B. Du Bois wrote about this as the veil that blinds white Americans to the humanity of Black people, and thus to the harms of the violent racial hierarchy.[101] Sociologist Pierre Bourdieu wrote about powerful social classes attributing their position in the hierarchy to their personal merit as *misrecognition*: they fail to see how educational and economic systems are actually structured to produce the hierarchy they inhabit because these systems seem natural: they are taken-for-granted elements of their worldview, like the water that surrounds a fish.[102] The case of OxyContin marketing illustrates how such misrecognition, as harnessed to produce profits for health industries, can harm those in high as well as low positions in social hierarchies.

Opioids also reveal the important role of class in racial capitalism. Working-class white people had early access to newly patented opioids, but they could not hold on to the same consumer protections and drug policy exceptions as middle-class and affluent white people, who were able to keep their private physician prescriptions despite reinvigorated narcotic regulation such as that of prescription drug monitoring programs. Middle-class and affluent white people later benefited from medicalization as the national response to opioid overdoses, but working-class white people could not afford the addiction medicine market (as detailed in chapter 6 on buprenorphine). Prescription opioid marketers quickly dropped white blue-collar workers with occupational injuries and military veterans when opioid regulations were reinvigorated, and these working-class opioid users were the first to turn to the illegal opioid market when they could not get prescriptions. This market lacked the protections of pharmaceutical-grade quality control, not to mention the legal protections of prescribed pharmaceuticals.

The OxyContin story also pulls back the curtain on our societal obsession with magic bullets. It shows how quasi-religious American beliefs in the power of new technologies to solve entrenched social problems such as addiction—beliefs that pharmaceutical manufacturers turned to their advantage in the form of professional and public trust of their claims about new products—come back to haunt us.

Of course, no amount of pharmaceutical splitting, or downsizing of government, or pharmaceutical deregulation, or universal neuroscience, or racial precision in medicine could hide the tsunami of overdose deaths that followed prescription opioid marketing, first among mostly middle-aged to older white people to whom the new opioids were marketed as aggressively as any pharmaceutical can be, and then among the young who got opioids through the growing street market of prescription opioids, and ultimately among still younger people who had come of age after the prescription opioid boom, during the twenty-first-century age of heroin infiltrating a small town, suburban, and rural America that was in prescription opioid withdrawal. As we shall see in the next chapter, creatively reimagined policy responses to this white opioid tsunami, as distinct from prior war on drugs policies, led to an even larger boost for the idea of racially precise pharmaceuticals.

CHAPTER 6

Buprenorphine's Silent White Revolution

"Charles deserves the credit for the heavy lifting."

Jerome Jaffe sat across from Helena Hansen in his Baltimore suite at a nonprofit addiction research institute, three blocks from the Johns Hopkins Medical Center. The year was 2011, and he was describing his collaboration in the late 1990s with Charles O'Keeffe, CEO of Reckitt Benckiser Pharmaceuticals, to pass the Drug Addiction Treatment Act of 2000 (DATA 2000), the federal legislation that quietly reversed eighty years of prohibition on private-office prescribing of opioid medications to treat opiate addiction. "[The manufacturers] were concerned that [buprenorphine] might become stigmatized the way methadone was if it were used for the treatment of addiction . . . that if it were limited to clinics the way that methadone was, that this would not be much of a breakthrough drug."

O'Keeffe had brought buprenorphine to Jaffe's attention as a potential alternative to methadone for treatment of opioid addiction. It was effective in preventing relapse, in the same way as methadone: it was an opioid, and because it bound to opiate receptors in the brain, patients did not crave other opioids. But the real innovation of buprenorphine lay in who could prescribe it. And that innovation came not from scientists but from a seasoned pharmaceutical executive: Charles O'Keeffe, who would become CEO of Reckitt-Benckiser Pharmaceuticals, manufacturer of buprenorphine. As Jaffe explained, in 1992, when he published the first clinical trial of buprenorphine, "It wasn't clear what would happen with buprenorphine . . . because the real issue was, could this be something that any doctor could prescribe, with some training, or would it be regulated in the same way [as methadone]. . . . [The credit] all goes to Charles O'Keeffe. He conceptualized it, and worked on it, what special magic he had."

Thirty years before, while serving as the first US drug czar (the director of the Office of National Drug Control Policy) under Richard Nixon in 1971, psychiatrist Jaffe had launched methadone as the primary weapon in Nixon's War on Drugs; he established the system of methadone clinics, regulated by the Drug Enforcement Administration (DEA), that we know today. But by the late 1990s, Jaffe reappeared in national drug policy to testify to Congress on the need for an alternative to methadone. In collaboration with O'Keeffe, he made the case for buprenorphine to be prescribed in the privacy of a doctor's office and taken at home, as a treatment that was free of the methadone's stigma, political baggage, and requirement for daily observed dosing.[1]

This was a silent revolution in US drug policy. Jaffe, O'Keeffe, and their supporters in Congress had done a remarkable thing by creating a legal portal for long-term, home-based opioid treatment of opiate addiction. The medication to be used was not even named in the new legislation—legislation that was barely reported in the media, that passed Congress without public comment or challenge by regulators, and that was slipped into a broad children's health bill in the final hour of congressional deliberation. In a US drug control system notorious for its hostility to and scrutiny of narcotics, Jaffe and O'Keeffe quietly paved the way for a new approach to addiction based on narcotic maintenance in private doctor's offices, an approach that US federal regulators had vigorously denounced for almost a century.

The new approach was made possible by a form of narcotic exceptionalism that would characterize the first two decades of the twenty-first century. Although not the intention of Jerome Jaffe, the exceptionalism required to legalize buprenorphine marshaled Whiteness based on the racial geography of pharmaceutical distribution. It created a distinct track of clinical intervention—instead of law enforcement—for "new," white opioid users. Only by uncovering the unspoken tools of Whiteness can we solve the puzzle of how one drug altered US drug policy without being named in law, becoming America's most federally promoted and most restricted prescription opioid at the same time.

We also can begin to answer the question, how did private practice treatment with buprenorphine—an opioid—become a primary policy response to the opioid crisis, even as the punitive War on Drugs was still in full force? The US incarceration rate peaked in 2008—representing a tenfold increase in number of incarcerated people since 1980, far surpassing that of every other country in the world, and driven significantly by drug law sentencing, with half of US federal prisoners carrying drug charges.[2] Thus incarceration rates were at an all-time high eight years *after* the Decade of the Brain, with its redefinition of addiction as a "chronic relapsing brain disease," and eight years *after* the legalization of office-based buprenorphine for opioid dependence. How did the federal government come to promote an opioid as the antidote to opioid addiction while simultaneously maximizing arrests in a war on drugs?

Sometime after interviewing Jerome Jaffe, Helena joined commuters on the Staten Island ferry in order to understand buprenorphine dissemination in communities. She passed Ellis Island and the Statue of Liberty as the ferry cruised from the crowded asphalt of Manhattan to Staten Island, New York City's whitest and most suburban borough, with its single-family homes, trimmed lawns, and tree-lined streets. Staten Islanders commuting home from Manhattan sipped coffee from the ferry café. On the walls were placards warning that "heroin addiction starts here" over a photo of an open bottle of prescription painkillers. Next to them, a website for New York's addiction treatment hotline, CombatHeroin.ny.gov, referred callers to buprenorphine prescribers.

By 2014 Staten Island had the highest ratio of buprenorphine-certified prescribers to residents in New York State.[3] A cadre of community generalist doctors took it upon themselves to get certified, doctors who had not before treated addiction. Helena's research team had observed public-sector doctors in other New York City boroughs routinely refer to poor, largely Black and Latinx addicted people as "med seeking" or looking for "a hot and a cot" (a meal and a bed) in the hospital. In contrast, Staten Island community doctors described their opioid-addicted patients as professionals, neighbors, and innocent youth—people with whom they identified, and for whom they were willing to undergo additional training. As one doctor told the team, "Most of the patients are difficult, but I [became certified] for them." Another connected race, youth, and blamelessness in a way that is now familiar: "These are smart, Irish American kids. They're smart and know right from wrong, and they didn't think they were doing anything wrong. The substance affects judgment, and suddenly they start lying, cheating, stealing, even within family, and without having had a criminal background."

In this chapter, we trace the emergence of buprenorphine as a white, middle-class treatment for opioid use disorder, as its advocates distinguished it from methadone and from punitive responses to opioid dependence. We then compare buprenorphine treatment among people with contrasting racial identities to examine buprenorphine as a technology of Whiteness: a vehicle by which Whiteness is defined and defended, and a medication that solidifies the white, middle-class social position of its users.

BUPRENORPHINE: THE SILENT REVOLUTION IN ADDICTION TREATMENT

Buprenorphine, sold commercially as Suboxone, was the only product owned by Reckitt Benckiser Pharmaceuticals, a subsidiary of Reckitt Benckiser Corporation, manufacturer of common household products including Lysol, Clearasil, and French's Mustard. At the time of our 2011 interview with Jerome Jaffe, Suboxone had become a blockbuster drug at well over a billion dollars in sales per year in the US alone. Addiction scientists writing for the *American Journal of Psychiatry* hailed buprenorphine as the primary breakthrough in addiction technology produced in the 1990s' "Decade of the Brain."[4] During the 1990s, the US Congress authorized an infusion of funds to the National Institute on Drug Abuse (NIDA) to identify the biomolecular causes of addiction and to develop pharmaceutical technologies to target those causes, largely through public-private partnerships. Reckitt Benckiser Pharmaceuticals received $23 million from NIDA to subsidize clinical trials of buprenorphine for opiate addiction.[5] Those studies were promising: they found lower rates of relapse to nonmedical opioid use with buprenorphine than without, and rates of relapse and treatment dropout similar to methadone's.[6]

Buprenorphine was a once-a-day tablet that could be prescribed by a general practitioner and taken at home, and it appeared to be safe for long-term use. NIDA billed buprenorphine as a targeted "smart" drug that directly stimulated opiate receptors on neurons to prevent drug cravings and relapse. Buprenorphine seemed to actually be a magic bullet, revealing addiction—formerly portrayed as a messy amalgam of moral failing and social conditions—to be a chronic disease that responded to pharmacotherapy. Addiction appeared to be much like asthma, diabetes, or hypertension, but located in the brain. The clinical trials of buprenorphine for opioid dependence were hailed by NIDA directors as providing further scientific evidence that addiction was a "chronic brain disease."[7]

But there was a hitch. Buprenorphine itself was an opioid. Originally developed in 1966 in the British laboratories of Reckitt Coleman Corporation (before that company merged with Benckiser Corporation), it was first touted in the 1970s as a "minimally addictive" opioid pain reliever, much as OxyContin would be two decades later.[8] Like OxyContin, buprenorphine was soon revealed to be addictive. Unlike OxyContin, buprenorphine is not as potent a pain reliever as morphine, so sales for pain relief were slow. It was not until the 1990s, when Congress was searching for a pharmaceutical solution to burgeoning white suburban and rural prescription opioid addiction, that buprenorphine found new life as a treatment for addiction.

In the 1960s, Dr. John Lewis's efforts in Reckitt Coleman's British laboratories to design a "nonaddictive" opioid pain reliever involved removing the group of atoms from opioid molecules that cause sensations of reward or pleasure, while preserving the group of atoms that bind to pain-relieving (Kappa) opioid receptors.[9] Such a smart drug would have been the holy grail of opioid manufacturers: a nonaddictive pain reliever with an opioid's unparalleled potency for pain, but not for pleasure. One of the fruits of Lewis's experiments was buprenorphine. Because it only partially activated opioid receptors in the brain, it was limited in its ability to cause pleasure, and it did not suppress breathing as much as other opioids so it had a lower risk of overdose, but it still relieved pain.

When Reckitt Coleman first marketed buprenorphine as an injectable for postsurgical pain in the 1970s, it came to the attention of Don Jasinski, then a young researcher at the US federal inpatient addiction treatment center nicknamed the "Narcotic Farm" in Lexington, Kentucky. As he told Helena in a 2011 interview, from the beginning he and his colleagues were excited about the potential of buprenorphine as an addiction treatment:

> I can tell you when I first heard about buprenorphine, it was in a disco in Mexico City. It was at a meeting of the Committee of Problems on Drug Dependence; we had been talking with John [Lewis], and the only place that stayed open late had been the disco, so we had this picture that he was drawing of chemical structures on my plane ticket in a disco in Mexico City at about 1 o'clock in the morning talking about buprenorphine and what had been the advantages of buprenorphine. . . . Part of this was a recognition that you could get a methadone-like drug but [it] would be better, safer. . . in the sense of less toxic, less physical dependence capacity, and perhaps more useful.

Shortly thereafter, in laboratories that had moved from Lexington to Maryland to become the campus of NIDA, Jasinski noted that heroin-dependent patients reported twenty-four-hour relief from withdrawal symptoms with buprenorphine. By the 1980s he began clinical trials of buprenorphine for opioid addiction, and he shared his preliminary findings with Reckitt executive Charles O'Keeffe. O'Keeffe had become known to NIDA researchers in the 1970s when he sold the US government urine toxicology kits to test returning Vietnam veterans for narcotics use. He later became a drug policy adviser to President Carter. O'Keeffe was interested in buprenorphine's potential as an addiction treatment, but he found other executives at Reckitt Coleman resistant to associating their pain reliever with a stigmatized heroin-using clientele. The received wisdom in the pharmaceutical industry at that time was that addiction was bad for business: historically no company had made notable returns on prescribed addiction treatments.

When he related his early work to bring addiction treatment to people who needed it, Helena noted O'Keeffe's eagerness to tell his story, the way he looked directly into her eyes and seemed to take pleasure in the interest she showed. He seemed sincere; he was proud of his accomplishment in directing national attention to a problem that had so long been criminalized and stigmatized. As O'Keeffe said,

> No pharmaceutical company has had any interest whatsoever in developing products for the treatment of opioid dependence. . . . From a pharmaceutical point of view, you have a patient population that is stigmatized, that has reached a point that they're not self-sufficient, they have no insurance, they can't pay for the drug, so you're dependent on government services to treat the patient. You have a patient population that is stigmatized, nobody wants to admit that they are a drug addict. You have a patient population that physicians don't want to treat, because many of them view this as bad acting, as criminal behavior rather than a disease, so why should anybody be interested in developing a drug for the treatment of this disease that nobody wants to treat? And nobody wants a treatment for? And if you do it, nobody's going to pay for it?

Events in global drug trade after the 1970s, however, created an unusual window for Reckitt Coleman to rescue their product, buprenorphine, from an untimely death as it was shown to be an addictive, low-potency painkiller. Following the 1970s rise in cocaine use by the white middle class, thriving Columbian cartels sought to expand to other products. Columbian cartels began planting heroin poppies in addition to coca bushes, with an eye to capturing the lucrative heroin market that, for centuries, had been dominated by Middle Eastern and East Asian growers.[10] Seeing potential heroin consumers in the middle class and affluent US populations that used powder cocaine, the cartels smuggled large shipments of high-purity heroin from Colombia to street distributors in New York and other major US cities, setting a low price that meant middle-class users could afford to snort instead of inject it. Snorting was a key distinction for middle-class users in those early years of the AIDS epidemic, when injection was associated with poverty and HIV risk.[11] Columbian cartels thereby facilitated the phenomenon of early 1990s "heroin chic" embodied and popularized by the fashion industry via the "junkie" appearance of supermodels such as Kate Moss.[12]

Marketing-fueled increases in prescription opioid use beginning in the 1990s provided another opportunity for a new drug to treat addiction. American media spotlighted prescription opioid addiction among middle-class and affluent white people such as Cindy McCain, wife of Senator John McCain, as well as astronomical increases in opioid prescribing overall.[13] By 1999, Congress was debating the best approach to a perceived national crisis of opioid use among "suburban youth."[14]

Long-acting, buprenorphine could suppress cravings for opiates and withdrawal symptoms for up to two days, making it useful for long-term treatment. And to boot, Reckitt Benckiser manufactured it together with naloxone, an opioid antidote that is absorbed into the bloodstream when injected but not when taken orally. The combination pill therefore caused opioid withdrawal symptoms if injected but not if taken orally as prescribed. Reckitt marketed this buprenorphine-naloxone combination under the name Suboxone as an opioid that technologically deterred abuse by punishing those who injected it, causing the painful cramps and diarrhea of withdrawal as the naloxone entered their bloodstream and reversed the action of the opioid buprenorphine. A doctor who was an early buprenorphine prescriber referenced philosopher Michel Foucault's account, in the book *Discipline and Punish,* of prison panopticons that submit inmates to constant surveillance when he told Helena: "Suboxone is a pharmacological panopticon."

Taking buprenorphine with benzodiazepines such as Valium or Ativan intensified its opioid high and at the same time raised the risk of overdose. This combination became common among injectors in France and Finland, where buprenorphine surpassed all other opioids as a recreational drug.[15] In addition, in Malaysia, where the combination pill Suboxone was widely distributed, people who inject drugs quickly learned to overlook the initial discomfort caused by the added naloxone and to inject

Suboxone nonmedically.[16] Curiously, US addiction specialists made no mention of the international cases that challenged Suboxone's image as an abuse-proof "smart drug" for addiction. We do not know whether this was due to US specialists' belief in the claims of Suboxone's manufacturer or to the political influence of the pharmaceutical industry in the US. To date, however, there is little evidence that buprenorphine has become a recreational drug in the US, where a variety of more potent opioids are readily available in the illegal market: studies of nonprescribed buprenorphine use in the US find that it is largely shared or sold among those who want to forestall withdrawal symptoms when they cannot procure their drug of choice, such as heroin or OxyContin.[17] In addition, as we detail in our concluding chapter, France demonstrated that the public health potential of buprenorphine is significant when it is widely available and combined with universal health insurance, social services, and harm reduction. Yet Reckitt-Benckiser overlooked the political differences between France and the US in order to tell a story about the molecular magic of buprenorphine that justified regulatory changes in the US to make the medication available through doctors' offices in the private market rather than as a part of a public health initiative.

By 2015, when opioid overdose made headlines as the leading cause of a historic decline in life expectancy among white Americans, federal agencies had already held up buprenorphine as a primary strategy for preventing opioid overdose deaths for over a decade.[18] Along with surveillance of doctors who prescribe opioid pain relievers, and distribution of naloxone overdose reversal kits to people at risk for overdose, the feds redoubled their efforts to certify physicians to use buprenorphine for addiction and to increase the number of buprenorphine patients that those doctors could treat.[19]

The story behind these developments illustrates yet more pathways by which opioids encode white race on their users, and by which white race re-encodes opioids as medication, rather than as addictive and punishable. Buprenorphine advocates ushered in a sea change in the US response to addiction. Prior to the 2000s, most addiction treatment programs other than methadone clinics were based on a drug-free mandate; they were designed to help people cope with life's stressors without substances. US drug policy up to 2002 had emphasized supply-side surveillance, interdiction, arrests, and punishment. After 2002, pharmaceutical maintenance became the gold standard of care, at least for those with access to buprenorphine-certified doctors. The magnitude of this medicalization of addiction initially was barely perceptible from the outside, but it soon came to shape the landscape of Whiteness in America, from the popular media's portrayal of white lifestyles to the intimacy of relations between family members and neighbors.

"WELCOME TO HEROIN ISLAND": STATEN ISLAND AS CASE STUDY IN WHITE OPIOIDS

A borough with twice the land mass and less than one-third the population of Manhattan, accessible only by ferry and bridge, Staten Island is distinguished from the rest of New York City by its suburban sprawl of drive-through malls interspersed with single-family homes, two-car garages, and tree-lined streets, rather than the high-rise buildings and subways of other boroughs. It is the enclave of successful Italian American and Irish American owners of small businesses, especially in construction, and of administrators of the New York Police Department and the New York Fire Department. City health officials told us that Staten Islanders have long had disproportionate access to opioid prescriptions because of a high rate of musculoskeletal injury in the fields of construction, law enforcement, and firefighting, combined with access to primary care physicians willing to prescribe opioids for injuries, and good prescription coverage from private health insurance plans. Ironically, the very agencies charged with enforcing drug laws and responding to drug overdoses had employees that were among the most exposed to opioid prescriptions. And as explained in chapter 1, although the small business owners and police and firefighter administrators that have homes in Staten Island may not have college or professional degrees, in terms of their stable incomes and their private insurance coverage, they make up an important part of the middle-class market that opioid manufacturers targeted in their direct-to-prescriber marketing campaigns, first with extended-release opioid pain relievers and later with buprenorphine.

Overall, Staten Island has been awash in opioids, with the highest opioid painkiller prescribing rate in New York City. As a result, by the 2010s, its overdose rate was three to four times that of any other borough, first by prescription opioids as the primary cause of overdose, then by heroin, and most recently by the ultrapotent synthetic opioid fentanyl.[20]

In order to make Staten Island a community case study of the middle-class, white neighborhoods that are the primary consumer market for buprenorphine, Helena's team of ethnographers, including the anthropology, public health, and social work students described in chapter 1, observed and conducted interviews in clinics, pharmacies, and harm reduction and community service organizations across Staten Island. They took field notes on the interactions of physicians, clinical staff, and pharmacists with patients in private community practices and local drugstores, and on meetings of community organizations that were attempting to address neighborhood opioid use and overdose. The team documented opioid-related messaging on the billboards, graffiti, and local media outlets in Staten Island neighborhoods. Team members also interviewed sixty-four Suboxone-prescribing physicians and seventy-seven Suboxone patients in public and private clinics across all boroughs of New York City, as well as forty-seven community pharmacists in Staten Island from 2014 to 2016. With these observations and interviews, Staten Island helped make legible the local symbolism and community responses surrounding opioids in suburban America.

Like the national media coverage of opioids, local media coverage on and about Staten Island played up the contrast between the island's suburban way of life and the inner-city grit of Black and Brown New York neighborhoods, such as the South Bronx, East Brooklyn, and Harlem, that have long been portrayed as overrun by drug trade. A Staten Island rap group called White Trash Clan (in reference to the Black 1990s gangster rap group Wu-Tang Clan) produced a music video called "My World Is Blue," in reference to the blue color of OxyContin tablets, that went viral on YouTube.[21] In a parody of Black hip-hop videos, the White Trash Clan, young white men dressed in polo shirts or collared shirts with blazers, ties, and baseball caps in the light blue shade of OxyContin tablets, playfully invert the markers of "white trash" which usually reference poor white people and images such as trailer parks or dilapidated shacks. They also invert the association of hip-hop music with Black housing project residents such as Wu-Tang Clan members. Instead of drug dealers driving down inner-city streets and toting guns, as one might see in Wu Tan Clan videos, White Trash Clan members dance their way down the aisles of a pharmacy, propellers rotating on their baseball caps, rapping, "I'm dope sick, but my doctor's the shit—180 pills a month and I got another script."

As they pop OxyContin tablets in their mouths, they tell viewers to "hide it from your parents" and say there is "only one chick in my life, her name is Roxy" (in reference to the prescription opioid Roxicodone). In the next frame, the "Blue Fairy" enters: a thin, white woman with a ponytail, wearing a light blue minidress and sequined wings, using her wand to sprinkle blue pixie dust over the group. Along with the male rappers, she presses a finger first to one nostril, and then the other, snorting the dust out of the air. The playful tone of the video highlights the joys of pharmaceutical-grade opioid use among young people who are above the law and have only to "hide it from [their] parents." It is a symbolic enactment of white middle-class privilege, with young men who snort dust in ties and polo shirts, upwardly mobile despite their opioid adventures, and young women who hold on to the innocence and charm of fairies while sharing in the opioid-induced fantasy world of young men.

Shortly after release of the video, in 2013, the woman playing the "Blue Fairy" was arrested for selling prescription opioids from an Edible Arrangements outlet in Staten Island, an outlet that professed to deliver fresh fruit bouquets, a common gift for middle-class people to send as a thank-you or to congratulate friends and colleagues on birthdays or promotions.[22] With her wings, spindly legs, and sequined shoes, she evoked not the gun-toting Black male dealer of classic rap videos, but Tinker Bell or Judy Garland in *The Wizard of Oz*. The judge sentenced her to mandatory drug rehabilitation.

In 2014, a local news channel revisited the White Trash Clan in a segment entitled "Welcome to Heroin Island" in reference to the wholesale transition that opioid users in Staten Island had made from prescription pills to heroin, as tamper-resistant prescription opioids replaced older formulations in the pharmacies and as state surveillance of prescribers shrank the clinical supply of opioid pain medications. Sifting through empty prescription bottles littering the ground in a city park, the lead rapper picks out a label: "Suboxone—it's for opiate withdrawals. . . . You literally can't walk anywhere in Staten Island without seeing some of these on the floor. . . . There's just so many kids on it, and then they get put on it long term."[23] Two years later, the news reported that the "Blue Fairy" had died of an overdose.[24]

According to the rapper, the island's population has gone through three cycles of opioids: from prescription painkillers, to heroin, and then to buprenorphine, commercially known as Suboxone, for treatment of opioid addiction. The last phase of buprenorphine prescriptions was facilitated by online marketing strategies by Reckitt-Benckiser Pharmaceuticals that target suburban, US white middle class markets like Staten Island. This marketing was enhanced by New York City Department of Health employees who made detailing visits to Staten Island community physicians to explain the advantages of offering buprenorphine treatment. As Department of Health workers told us, city officials had focused on Staten Island early in the opioid epidemic, in response to the disproportionate overdose death rate there, and in response to politically empowered community residents who demanded intervention. Some people would later ask, why was this attention to buprenorphine access not given in the majority-Black and -Latinx South Bronx, which reported the largest total number of heroin and opioid overdose deaths of any New York City borough in the same time period?

BUPRENORPHINE IN COMMUNITIES AND CLINICS

Our interviews with buprenorphine-prescribing Staten Island doctors revealed that they are agents in the social reproduction of the white middle class. Prescribers get adolescents back on track toward college and career, men back into management, and women back into motherhood. With buprenorphine, the treatment goal is the restoration of middle-class "normality" rather than a life in which jobs and housing are limited by a criminal record. In Staten Island doctors' offices, addicted patients are not punished or ignored by prescribers, as past cohorts of narcotics users have been; rather, in many cases, prescribers treat them as family.

Prescribers in the Family

Staten Island community physicians voluntarily undergo eight hours of certification training in order to prescribe buprenorphine, and they subject themselves to unannounced DEA inspections of records and to surveillance by the New York State Prescription Monitoring Program. Most Staten Island physicians that we interviewed had no prior experience treating addiction and had had to modify their practice for addicted patients. They saw themselves as rescuing a generation of people in their community who were not "drug seeking" or criminal but rather were unwitting victims of reckless prescribing of painkillers.

Staten Island doctors spoke of their opioid-using patients in ways that alternated between respectful and endearing, describing them as valued professionals needing support and as vulnerable, needing protection. Buprenorphine prescribers recognized that they were treating patients who sought privacy, and sought to preserve their social status, in ways that were incompatible with attending methadone clinics. As one physician told us: "People who come here are not criminals; they're teachers, nurses, policemen [laugh], CEOs." Then, echoing a discourse of blameless suburban youth that was prominent in popular media, he also referred to them as "kids" that had fallen victim to neurochemical control: "There was a huge overuse problem of narcotics [in Staten Island]. Once you are exposed, if your brain likes it, then you're on it. Most of the kids I see here are either injured or had an operation and they were started on something like Vicodin or Oxycodone 30. They go to dentists, or regular physicians without bad intentions."

Buprenorphine-prescribing physicians echoed the popular press in associating opioid dependence with forces outside the individual. They noted that opioid dependence had grown because of the opioid pain relievers that other doctors had made available. Some cited opioids' ubiquitous availability and their physiological effects. One provider theorized the possibility of preexisting "endorphin deficiency" that made patients susceptible to opioid dependence and, once they were dependent, made them need long-term buprenorphine treatment: "Let's say you have depression—that is because you may have a serotonin deficiency. Why can't it be that certain people have an endorphin deficiency? Some people are down to 2 mg [of buprenorphine] or less and they can't just come off of it."

Many physicians identified with their patients. In Staten Island, which they spoke of as a small, homogenous community in which patients were also neighbors, they felt they knew patients intimately. During one of our interviews, a buprenorphine prescriber described a young man who had relapsed and died of an overdose due to preexisting cardiovascular disease. She described how this patient had reminded her of her son and how his death had motivated her to continue treating opioid-dependent patients despite their relapses:

> We had a patient who never filled [her buprenorphine prescription], she had no motivation. Soon her sister got married, and I told her that if she wanted to follow her sister's footsteps and get married, she would have to be clean. Years later, she brought her husband and pictures of her family, she said she wants to get clean and have children now [crying]. We didn't really do anything for three days when we found out the other patient I told you about died. It was painful when he died. I have a thirty-seven-year-old [son]. It's a happy thing when you see someone move on.

This physician's tears and emotion, her familial narrative, with its focus on marriage, children, family photos, and other trappings of middle-class social reproduction as addiction treatment "success," demonstrate that her patients were not just patients. She spoke of them as though they were members of her own family, and her role as physician was maternal—to help guide them through developmental stages and ensure the future of the clan. The physician even tapped into a quotidian thread of female competition to motivate her patient, comparing her patient with her married sister to convince her to fill her buprenorphine prescriptions, prescriptions that ritually "cleaned" the patient and thereby prepared her for (respectable, middle-class) marriage.

This physician's stance toward her patients stood in sharp contrast to the "othering" that physicians often use to distance themselves from their addicted patients, avoiding interactions with addicted patients or discussing treatment decisions with them.[25] Such othering was missing among Staten Island physicians who felt addicted patients could have been their own children. Some physicians even blamed themselves for the widespread dependency on opioids. When asked if he had prior experience treating opiate addiction, one said, "Not in the sense of giving them treatment, only getting them addicted." Another said that by first prescribing OxyContin and then refusing to prescribe buprenorphine, his colleagues had "turned a pill problem into a heroin problem." He voiced a moral obligation to spend more time with opioid-dependent patients and to get addiction training: "Two of my patients were addicted to opioids and they wouldn't go to [a methadone] clinic for it. . . . They didn't want to be seen at the clinic with other drug addicts. I heard of Suboxone from one my colleagues; I read general Suboxone articles and went for training. I offered it to them and they agreed. Now, one is clean and the other is on 2 mg [of Suboxone]."

One general practitioner with no specific addiction medicine training stated: "I spend about thirty minutes per patient, but I think it's worthwhile especially if they're young. If I fix them at twenty-three, then they're good. If I don't spend the time with them and counsel them, if they don't get treatment, they all go to heroin eventually." Another generalist described a homegrown family therapy approach: "Anybody under the age of thirty, I try to get a responsible adult or parent as their monitor. If they get that, if they're helpful, then they might get with the program. If mother and father come in with them and talk to the patient all the time or if [the patient is] married and the spouse is clean, then they're more likely to be compliant."

Weekly urine toxicology exams, referrals to therapy groups, family involvement in treatment, and longer visits were some of the ways community physicians reinvented their practices in response to white opioids and demonstrated a kinship-based practice of care. They did not get insurance reimbursements for this extra time. Community doctors took it upon themselves to create an evolving office-based buprenorphine maintenance approach. Identifying with addicted patients, they included themselves in a form of pharmaceutically mediated family therapy.

The Slow Trickle-Down to Public Clinics

The course of buprenorphine dissemination to public clinics made visible two tracks of responses to opiate addiction in America; a white, middle-class track toward private office treatment and a Black and Latinx track toward public, punitive bureaucracies. By following Lucille, an African American army veteran living in the public housing projects on the Lower East Side of Manhattan, Helena and her ethnographic team saw how distinct the tracks can be.

Lucille first came to the emergency room of the largest public hospital in New York to find relief from a sensation of water and heaviness that she had felt in her left ear since turning fifty. The odd sensation slowed her down, which she felt she could not afford as the grandmother of a three-year-old boy whose father she had adopted two decades before, when his parents—her neighbors in her housing project— died of AIDS. As the clinic staff put Lucille through a neurological workup, they discovered that she had been using heroin regularly since she was in her midtwenties. She did not feel that heroin had interfered with her job in the army, nor with her life after the army. But she was tired of using heroin because she no longer enjoyed it; she simply used it in order to feel normal (to stave off withdrawal) and to keep up with her active grandson.

Lucille started attending group therapies at the hospital's outpatient addiction clinic daily. Her southern drawl and welcoming smile won her friends. She found herself drawn to the creative arts therapy groups, where her years working as a draftsman came through in her skill with art supplies. Lucille refused methadone maintenance. She had heard that methadone leached calcium from teeth and bones, and as she put it, "I already have a sweets problem, I don't need any more problems with my teeth." Also, she disliked the way that methadone clinics kept people hostage with daily clinic visits to get dosed, seemingly for life. As she said, "I seen people die on it."

To keep her withdrawal symptoms and cravings for heroin at bay, the clinic psychiatrist prescribed buprenorphine, which seemed to work well. Lucille showed up for groups each day and almost stopped thinking of heroin.

Then, one day, the clinic was no longer in her health insurance network. Her health insurance was a low-cost federal plan offered to families of veterans; she did not qualify for VA benefits because she had gone AWOL to attend to her husband when he was hospitalized. We tried to help find her a buprenorphine prescriber who would accept her insurance, but no buprenorphine-prescribing doctors participated in her insurance. After several calls to her insurance plan, a representative told us that if Lucille went to a twenty-eight-day inpatient rehabilitation facility to start buprenorphine, she could appeal for coverage of outpatient buprenorphine with an out-of-network physician. The only program we found that met these requirements was located thirty miles north of her home, in a wealthy suburb of New York City.

Lucille resisted the idea of entering a twenty-eight-day inpatient rehabilitation program because it would require her to find care for her grandson and to leave her disabled neighbors and her roommate, who depended on her daily visits. Ultimately, she made arrangements for them, reasoning that buprenorphine was worth the burdens of rehab admission.

On the way to the rehabilitation facility, Lucille related the many losses she had suffered, beginning with her mother, and then her brothers, one of whom had died of kidney disease and the other who had been brutally murdered by a jealous girlfriend. Her husband, whom she had married in Japan while both were serving in the army, had died of cancer while they were deployed. Tears welled up in her eyes when she said, "Because all my family died, I began to wonder, why am I still here, when they're not? . . . None of them did anything but go to church and live by what God wanted them to live by. Not the extracurricular stuff with substances and things that tear down your body. . . . Sometimes thinking about them gets overwhelming."

Her rehabilitation ended early when her landlord threatened eviction if she did not pay her rent in person. The rehab staff discharged her with a one-week supply of buprenorphine to hold her until she could see an outpatient prescriber. Finding again that no physicians that would accept her insurance, and not having completed rehabilitation in order to get out-of-network reimbursement, her buprenorphine ran out and she used heroin to stave off withdrawal.

After a few months of heroin, Lucille made calls to find other rehabilitation programs near the city that offered buprenorphine. She eventually found one in a predominantly white suburban Long Island town and arranged for admission. The program receptionist directed her to take a ninety-minute train ride from midtown Manhattan with a suitcase full of clothes for her stay. When she arrived at the program, the receptionist and intake staff looked at her and told her that they could not accept her because they did not have a doctor on call.

Although she did not explicitly name race or capitalism as factors, Lucille's attribution of the program's refusal of service to their marketing to an affluent white clientele that was consistent with racial capitalism. On the train returning home, Lucille related,

> If I wore my hair straightened, and had on a dress and heels and a nice mink coat, maybe I'd have been all right. But why would I need them then? This class [pointing in one direction] shouldn't mix with this class [pointing in the other direction]. And that's the nicest way I can put it. That's the only way I'm going to put it, because that's the way it is. . . . I'm tired. I would have been happier if it didn't turn out that way, I like happy endings (low sarcastic chuckle). I believe in fairy tales.

The landscape of buprenorphine treatment in New York City that Lucille encountered can be understood by examining the walls between biomedicine targeted to the private sector and biomedicine targeted to the public sector. Methadone maintenance was designed for Lucille's demographic: it was pioneered by 1960s researchers using poor Black subjects from Harlem, and by city officials who promoted it as a solution to white voters' fears of Black urban crime. As the first director of one of New York City's oldest and largest methadone clinics, Dr. Robert Newman, told us in an interview, methadone saw successive waves of rediscovery and support through the 1980s, when AIDS activists in New York City lobbied for methadone expansion as an injection-related HIV prevention measure, and in the 1990s, when conservative Republican mayor Rudolph Giuliani expanded methadone after pressure from wealthy campaign donors who had heroin-addicted children.[26]

By the time buprenorphine was approved for use in opioid addiction, New York City had substantial methadone services in public hospitals and a network of privately run Medicaid-accepting methadone clinics. Methadone clinic directors that we interviewed told us that many of their treatment slots went unfilled. When buprenorphine was first approved, methadone clinics saw themselves as in competition with it. Methadone clinics could not provide take-home prescriptions for buprenorphine; they were federally mandated to observe patients taking medications inside the clinic, including buprenorphine. By the second decade after buprenorphine's approval, methadone clinics were able to apply for state and federal waivers (X waivers) to provide take-home doses of buprenorphine.

But Medicaid and insurance companies had not worked out reimbursements for buprenorphine treatment. Whereas methadone treatment was reimbursed at a fixed weekly rate that lumped medication costs together with all ancillary services, including counseling, the costs of patented buprenorphine were not adequately covered in those rates. The cost of methadone averaged forty cents per dose, and buprenorphine averaged nine dollars per dose. Most methadone clinics were unable to reach agreements with insurers that would allow them to offer buprenorphine.[27]

Outside of methadone clinics, for decades the majority of addiction treatment programs in New York City had been "drug free" and had rejected the use of medication for addiction recovery. Their philosophy was that reliance on substances to cope with psychic or physical pain was the root of the problem and that addicted people needed to retrain themselves to cope using methods not based on substances. Many of these programs were therapeutic communities such as Phoenix House and Daytop Village that were based on the model of Synanon, a movement that began in the 1950s and defined addiction as a character flaw requiring adherence to community rules of conduct, enforced by prescribed punishments and group shaming, such as forcing relapsed members to stand in diapers at the center of a circle of peers, symbolizing that they had returned to the infancy of their recovery.[28]

Many of the drug counselors and therapists employed in public New York City clinics had been trained in the therapeutic community model, which rejected medication as a part of treatment. Buprenorphine put the staff of the few public clinics that offered it in an awkward position. Some public clinic counselors and therapists would contradict buprenorphine prescribers by advising patients that the goal was to gradually taper off buprenorphine and embrace a "drug-free" lifestyle, rather than stay on it long term. The contradiction between their character-based drug-free philosophies of treatment and that of buprenorphine maintenance was evident in their efforts to develop "treatment contracts" with patients that detailed the consequences of using other substances (such as cocaine) while taking buprenorphine, of sharing their buprenorphine with others, or of missing appointments, which could lead to reduction or discontinuation of buprenorphine. These measures had a punitive quality that was at odds with the concept of addiction as a chronic medical illness. As one public clinic physician critical of this practice asked, "Would you take insulin away from a diabetic who'd missed insulin doses?" Buprenorphine providers in private offices serving more affluent patients did not use such measures.

In addition, public clinic buprenorphine prescribers were often told that buprenorphine was better suited for "stable" and "reliable" patients: those with steady employment and the resources to adhere to treatment. These factors help to explain why, two decades after the legalization of office-based buprenorphine for opioid dependence, and fifteen years after New York City public hospital administrators promoted buprenorphine uptake by using buprenorphine prescriptions as a quality indicator for city hospitals, only one out of eleven public hospitals had a primary care buprenorphine service. National statistics show this pattern is widespread; US patients are over four times as likely to pay for buprenorphine out of pocket or with private insurance as they are to pay with Medicaid or Medicare.[29]

Prisons and jails are the institutions that house more people receiving mental health and addiction services than any other type of institution in the US.[30] A number of clinical trials of buprenorphine in prison and jail found their adherence after release to the community comparable to that of nonincarcerated populations and found the effectiveness of office-based buprenorphine comparable to that of methadone clinics.[31] Incarceration is itself a risk factor for overdose given that the risk of overdose among opioid-dependent people is elevated in the weeks after release, a period in which physiological tolerance for opioids is lowered by enforced abstinence during incarceration.[32] Release puts them at high risk for relapse, and likely to buy opioid mixtures that contain the ultrapotent synthetic opioid fentanyl. Despite these findings, however, advocates for jail and prison-based addiction treatment find corrections officials resistant to buprenorphine and methadone, which officials perceive as rewarding addicted criminals with pleasure.

Corrections officials have been faster to adopt long-acting injectable naltrexone, an opioid antagonist that blocks opioid receptors in the brains of addicted people, preventing them from feeling the effects of heroin or other opioids, while producing effects that are the opposite of opioids—they do not cause pleasure, they do not relieve pain, and under certain circumstances, they cause withdrawal symptoms. Naltrexone injections that can last from thirty to ninety days depending on the formulation are the medication most often used in jails and prisons.[33] While as of 2016, thirty states offered prerelease naltrexone in their correctional system, as of 2018 only three states reported that they offered prerelease buprenorphine.[34] Pharmaceutical executives and researchers involved in the development and marketing of injectable naltrexone told us that Vivitrol, the first injectable formulation of naltrexone to be approved for opioid dependence, had not initially sold well because private patients did not like its side effects and did not want to commit to a month of irreversible blockage of their ability to feel opioids. Neither had Vivitrol sold well among public insurance plans that did not want to take on its high up-front costs—up to $1,000 per monthly injection. But in the end, Vivitrol found a growing market in the correctional system, where its opioid-blocking properties were appealing to wardens and officials.

Alarming data suggest that long-acting naltrexone may put incarcerated people at higher risk for overdose after release, rather than lower risk,[35] given that naltrexone further lowers physiological tolerance to opioids, and given that inmates have limited access to health care, social services, and employment after release, posing barriers to maintaining naltrexone injections.

The take-home lesson is that private doctor–prescribed buprenorphine, part of what the *New York Times* described as a "kinder, gentler" response to opioid dependence than US war on drugs policies of the prior decades, fits poorly with the punitive logics of addiction intervention that continue to dominate in the sectors disproportionately encountered by low-income people of color: prisons, jails, and public clinics.[36]

THE PREQUEL: CORPORATE BRAIN SCIENCE BEFORE OXYCONTIN

Advocates for federal promotion of office-based buprenorphine maintenance portrayed it as a rational, modern, neuroscience-based approach to addiction—"medication-assisted treatment" or MAT—rather than as reversing a century of prohibition of private-office prescribing narcotics for addicted people. Cloaking this reversal in the neutral language of neuroscience, buprenorphine's advocates drew on a century-old system of narcotic segregation in the US, in which some drugs became illegal through association with nonwhite users, and other drugs were legal and deemed "medicines" reserved for white and middle-class consumers: in short, a system in which the Whiteness of certain drugs medicalized them.

From midcentury barbiturate tranquilizers and stimulant diet pills to 1960s Librium, Valium, and other sedative benzodiazepines sold as "mother's little helper," middle-class whites with private doctors had enjoyed a steady supply of prescribed psychoactive drugs that were both legal and dangerous, causing catastrophic overdose rates in their intended markets in the 1940s–60s.[37] The legal and prescribed status of these drugs sharply distinguished them from those in illicit drug markets created by early twentieth-century prohibition: markets that were located initially in poor southern and eastern European and Asian immigrant ghettoes of large early twentieth-century port cities including New York, San Francisco, and Chicago. By the late twentieth century, after the great northern migration of African American, Latin American, and Caribbean laborers from plantations to industrializing cities, illicit drug markets were located in burgeoning Black and Latinx neighborhoods of those same port cities.[38] There, organized crime found a ready supply of unemployed laborers and the cover of red-light districts, to which white consumers would commute in search of drugs, a history to which we return in the next chapter on heroin.

It also happened that in the 2000s, "medication-assisted treatment" for addiction provided by general physicians came of age during an era of high corporate returns on psychotropic drugs. The 1990s saw the fruits of the "Prozac revolution": the successful marketing of new antidepressants and antipsychotics billed as free of the side effects that would otherwise limit their use to specialists. Prozac, the first serotonin selective reuptake inhibitor (SSRI), was approved by the Food and Drug Administration (FDA) in 1987 as the first antidepressant safe for prescription by primary care doctors in ordinary practice. Previous classes of antidepressants, such as tricyclics and monoamine oxidase inhibitors, carried serious side effects ranging from seizure and coma to hypertensive emergency, and therefore required close monitoring by a psychiatrist. Prozac's approval and marketing for primary care prescribing was followed by large increases in the number of people diagnosed with and treated for depression. Prozac quickly became a blockbuster drug; by 1999 it represented 25 percent of the $10 billion revenue of Eli Lilly Company.[39]

Prozac served as a model for the development and marketing of new classes of psychotropic medications that had milder side effects than their predecessors and were suitable for primary care doctors to prescribe, from second-generation antidepressants to second-generation antipsychotics. Where Valium had long been marketed to women as "mother's little helper," Prozac was specifically marketed as a technological "fix" for the problems raised by white, middle-class feminists who had attacked medical sexism by pointing to the example of women who had become addicted to Valium after their physicians tried to sedate them into acceptance of housewifely drudgery. Prozac, its boosters pointed out, led to energy and assertiveness, not compliance, and it was not addictive.[40] Medications for mood disorders, anxiety, obsessive compulsive disorders, and eventually, addiction fell into the category of "lifestyle drugs" with expandable criteria for diagnosis, expandable indicated uses, and therefore an expandable number of patients that qualified for treatment.[41] From the 1980s on, the third, fourth and fifth editions of the American Psychiatric Association's *Diagnostic and Statistical Manual* (*DSM*) changed the official diagnostic system from one based on a patient's history and clinical appearance to one based on a checklist of symptoms—a change that greatly expanded the number of psychiatric diagnoses in the manual and made it easier to produce clinical trial evidence for the FDA and insurers that a pharmaceutical was effective in treating said diagnoses.[42] At the same time, "behavioral health care" increasingly fell under the purview of general doctors rather than psychiatric specialists; this was especially advantageous to pharmaceutical marketers, who understood that a much larger population of people visit primary care physicians than visit psychiatrists. By the 2000s, these shifts made psychotropic medications among the most lucrative drugs in the US.[43]

The interplay of race with these market forces was integral to the medicalization of addiction treatment heralded by DATA 2000, the federal law that legalized office-based buprenorphine. As described in the previous chapter on OxyContin, corporate strategists made use of the racial symbolism of drugs and the segregation of US health care to mainstream opioid pain relievers into primary care practice. Advocates of buprenorphine also saw the promise of primary care–based prescribing for expanding markets. As Donald Jasinski, a prominent addiction pharmacology researcher who had run the first clinical trials of buprenorphine for opiate dependence at NIDA in the 1970s, told us in a 2011 interview: "The treatment of addiction [with buprenorphine] and depression [with SSRIs] came about the same time. . . . If you're depressed now, you can go to the psychiatrist, but you can also go to your family practitioner . . . to bring it back into sort of the mainstream of medicine."

Yet the addiction specialists who advocated for buprenorphine's approval and dissemination did not always see the racial implications of office-based clinical care. Many of them explained in interviews that they were working against the stigma of addiction and resulting punitive drug policies; they assumed that expanding biomedical care for addiction would also lead to racial equality. For instance, when Helena mentioned national findings of racial inequalities in use of buprenorphine to former US drug czar Jerome Jaffe, he resisted the idea that race was a deciding factor in treatment and spoke optimistically about reducing the financial drivers of inequalities: "I think what you're seeing is that it's not necessarily an ethnic or racial, it is a socioeconomic issue. . . . The people who get on buprenorphine in most places are people who can afford to get on buprenorphine. . . . Here in Baltimore it has already changed, in that the city has provided public subsidy, and also the state has made it possible."

What Jaffe had not registered was that Baltimore was an exception to the national pattern of buprenorphine dissemination because Johns Hopkins University had hosted early clinical trials of buprenorphine and recruited study subjects from a large population of Black and Latinx heroin-dependent Baltimore residents for whom research participation was a route to free biomedical treatment. These trials created local physician familiarity with buprenorphine and facilitated buprenorphine's adoption in clinics across the city beginning in 2004, when the Baltimore city government declared buprenorphine access a priority, dedicating public and private foundation funding.[44] Baltimore illustrates that the drivers of buprenorphine's demographics are institutions, not individual prescribers.

The racial geography of buprenorphine across the US is the result of racial capital, operating in many sectors, from drug development and marketing to regulation and popular media coverage. Additionally, many buprenorphine researchers and advocates whom we interviewed echoed the view that office-based buprenorphine was a treatment modality that was most appropriate for "stable" patients who could reliably follow prescribed treatments on their own, outside of the daily observation requirements of methadone clinics. Addiction scientist Donald Jasinski told us in an interview, "The issue is that people who are on methadone may be people who need more services and help than those who are not. . . . [Those that] have a job, and are really adjusted and the major problem in their life if you solve their appetite for opiates [with buprenorphine] . . . they don't need the rest of the degree of psychosocial services." While Jasinski described his own addiction treatment unit at Johns Hopkins as treating a number of Medicaid-insured patients with buprenorphine, he acknowledged that nationally, buprenorphine had a niche among people who would look for a treatment and wouldn't want to go to methadone clinics because there was stigma associated with it. He noted a lot of buprenorphine patients who had jobs or positions that were in the public eye. While addiction research pioneers such as Jaffe and Jasinski doubtless strove for treatment equality, they echoed reports from other physicians that buprenorphine was designed for those who could afford it, who did not need the surveillance and control of a methadone program, and who could not professionally afford the stigma of methadone: implicitly, the white middle class.

Also, it is notable that Jerome Jaffe and Donald Jasinski were among the pioneering addiction researchers who entered the field with idealism about medical treatment for addiction as a way to overcome the stigma and marginalization of people who used drugs, including marginalization by race, ethnicity, and social class. They demonstrated the disconnect between, on one hand, scientists who approached their work with a "color-blind" ideology, an earnest belief in the universal nature of biology and the addicted brain and therefore of the causes of and interventions for addiction, and on the other hand pharmaceutical industry executives, who were acutely aware of the corporate imperative to cultivate market segments that could afford new products and whose political capital would reduce regulatory scrutiny. It is an illustration of the way that different aspects of Whiteness as an ideology—its invisibility in biomedical sciences as biological universals stand in for white subjects and its strategic deployment in racial capitalist industries— reinforce one another.

THE COLOR OF OPPORTUNITY

Up to the 1990s, the only pharmaceutical that had been shown effective for preventing relapse among people addicted to heroin and synthetic opioids was methadone. Since 1971, when Jerome Jaffe worked as Nixon's drug czar to promote methadone for heroin addiction, methadone had been associated in popular media and the American imagination with Black and Brown people in the inner cities, along with homeless Vietnam veterans. Methadone was President Nixon's first weapon in the war on drugs: a chemical means of control in unruly Black and Latinx city centers in the era of white flight to suburbs. The Rockefeller University researchers who developed methadone maintenance in the 1960s, Vincent Dole, Marie Nyswander, and Mary Jeanne Kreek, characterized heroin addiction as "chronic opioid receptor deficiency" in which the receptors on brain cells that bound to opioid molecules had become so depleted from chronic use of heroin or other opioids that they did not come back to normal levels, even long after the person stopped using opioids. As Dr. Kreek explained in an interview with Helena, beyond developing simple tolerance to opioids, Dole and his team thought that the brains of people with heroin addiction were permanently altered so that even if they abstained from opioids for months to years, they would not feel the effects of the physiological opioids, such as endorphins, that the body made to regulate its own pain. Dole's theory was that people with this opioid receptor deficiency needed long-term treatment with medical opioids, such as methadone, to control the craving and pain that they continuously felt without opioid supplementation. He saw this as analogous to insulin deficiency in diabetes, in which patients needed insulin supplementation to maintain their blood sugar balance.

Yet these researchers combined clinical metaphors with social indicators in their research reports: their landmark article reporting the success of methadone maintenance in a sample of African American heroin-addicted men in Harlem used outcomes that were unusual for the *Annals of Internal Medicine*: arrest and employment at six months.[45] This hybrid clinical-criminological frame for methadone, as a biotechnological solution to heroin use in the setting of racial segregation and urban divestment, persists today. In our team's visits to methadone clinics in many large cities, we have been disturbed by the dehumanizing omnipresence of security guards and the fastidiousness with which nurses inspect patients' mouths to make sure they have swallowed their medication and follow patients into bathrooms to observe them urinating into cups for drug testing.

Methadone has long been marked as a Black drug, which manifests in the criminalizing ethos created by DEA regulation of methadone clinics. Methadone maintenance treatment was developed in the 1960s in New York City, which at the time was estimated to be home to over 50 percent of illicit narcotics users in the US. As we detail in chapter 7, at the time media coverage fed white popular perceptions of heroin-related crime as the result of the immorality of urban Blacks and Latinxs, rather than as the result of racially concentrated unemployment and organized crime leaders who bribed police forces to turn a blind eye in those neighborhoods. Sensational reports of urban heroin as a result of Black and Latinx moral and family disintegration led to white political support for tough-on-crime policies. Political promotion and subsidy of methadone maintenance treatment emerged as a political compromise, first by conservative Democratic mayor Robert Wagner (1954–65), and then by liberal Republican mayor John Lindsay (1966–73), both of whom promoted methadone to satisfy, on one hand, drug law reformists calling for treatment over criminalization of addiction and, on the other hand, a conservative constituency calling for control of urban crime.[46] The racial associations of methadone maintenance treatment were thus central to debates about its role in drug policy and health care from its inception.

Socially progressive 1960s–70s commentators and activists in Black and Latinx communities decried promotion of methadone as a false "magic bullet" and a "cheap pharmaceutical" solution to lack of educational opportunities, employment, and racial discrimination. Civil rights and Black Power leaders suspected methadone to be a strategy to politically repress Black and Latinx constituents through sedation and control by white methadone doctors. White residents of New York City neighborhoods designated to house methadone clinics organized around "Not in My Backyard" sentiments and fears of an influx of Black and Latinx, addicted Medicaid patients, forcing the clinics to relocate to politically disempowered poor Black and Latinx neighborhoods.[47] As historian Mical Raz shows, 1970s methadone programs were largely inspired by politicians' desire to control crime, and from the beginning methadone "incorporated many aspects of surveillance and regulation, similar to those employed in the prison system, where the NTA [Narcotic Treatment Administration] was first developed. . . . [Methadone programs] helped lay the groundwork for the involvement of physicians in the creation of a punitive approach to drug policy."[48]

Thirty years later, these factors made methadone a hard sell to opioid-addicted white, middle-class people who could use their economic and race privilege to shelter themselves from this horrifying level of surveillance and institutionalized stigma. The racial associations of methadone treatment with urban, Black and Latinx heroin users had made possible its legalization as a crime-fighting measure but had also prevented its adoption into mainstream (i.e., white) medicine and had prevented regulators from approving methadone for use in less oppressive and less regulated settings, such as private doctors' offices. Methadone clinics remained in marginal neighborhoods geographically distant from general medical centers and were burdened by repressive federal regulation restricting methadone's use to licensed clinics that require daily observed dosing to prevent the drug's diversion. In the case of methadone, in other words, race undergirded its partial medicalization in specialized clinics separated from mainstream medicine and characterized by elements of law enforcement, including oversight by the DEA.

Vanguard addiction specialists who had run methadone programs in the 1970s and 1980s, including Robert Newman, who had been at Beth Israel Hospital in New York, and Herbert Kleber, who ran methadone research at a Yale-affiliated hospital during that period, told us in interviews that they had successfully lobbied for federal exemptions that allowed their clinics to run trials of office-dispensed methadone well into the 2000s. Through these trials, they provided a handful of patients with private office-based methadone dispensed on a monthly basis. But political support for wider deregulation of methadone was thin, in no small part because of methadone's racialized association with street drugs and crime.

Faced in the 1990s with what was described as rising opioid use among "suburban youth," members of Congress sought a medication that did not have the stigmatized associations of methadone.[49] This potential market for buprenorphine was not lost on Charles O'Keeffe, who reached out to his former Nixon administration contact Jerome Jaffe for help in crafting a strategy to expand the use of buprenorphine. As he and Jaffe saw it, federal law prohibiting generalist doctors from maintaining addicted patients on opioids was the major barrier. This prohibition of opioid maintenance dated to the 1920s. The period from the 1914 passage of the Harrison Act restricting doctors from prescribing narcotics to narcotics-dependent people through the 1920s was an era of widespread negative publicity surrounding so-called dope doctors whose practices consisted solely of morphine injections for opioid-addicted patients. Moral crusaders used racial imagery to build support for prohibitionist policies and to protect white privilege in an era of mass immigration and the racial segregation following the end of slavery. In the media and in Congress, they raised fears of unsuspecting white women being lured into sex slavery in so-called opium dens in Chinese immigrant neighborhoods, or being raped by "cocaine crazed" Negro men in the South.[50]

The Controlled Substances Act of 1970 continued the prohibition on private practice prescription of opioids for opioid addiction, which impeded the dissemination of buprenorphine. By the 1990s, however, the Decade of the Brain–era campaign to redefine addiction as a chronic brain disease was in full throttle. Jaffe and O'Keeffe partnered with key congressional representatives to position buprenorphine as an office-based addiction treatment by distinguishing it pharmacologically and symbolically from methadone. As O'Keeffe recounted to Helena in an interview:

> I looked at the Controlled Substances Act and said, you know, we could really fix this by one tiny little sentence, changing one sentence in the Controlled Substances Act. And not being a lawyer, I decided, well, it can't be

that simple, so I called [a lawyer], and he and I sat down in his office in Washington and did in fact write a piece of legislation that was simply a one-sentence change in the Controlled Substances Act and took it over to [Senator] Bliley, and said, this'll do it, if you can make it happen.

This one-sentence change in the law gave private doctors the right to prescribe Schedule III narcotics in their offices for treatment of addiction, where Schedule III was a class of narcotic thought to be at low risk for abuse. O'Keefe and Jaffe found insider support in Herbert Kleber, a psychiatrist who had been drug czar under President George H.W. Bush. Kleber started his research career conducting clinical trials of methadone-assisted heroin detoxification in the 1960s at the Lexington "Narcotic Farm" in Kentucky, and later led several studies of medication for addiction, including methadone, at Yale and Columbia Universities. Kleber worked with O'Keefe, Jaffe, and federal representatives to craft a key provision for buprenorphine into a congressional bill. Ultimately, that bill was DATA 2000, part of a children's mental health services bill that included a line on opioids for treatment of opioid addiction.

Methadone was Schedule II, according to the rating system introduced by the 1970 Controlled Substances Act. That meant it was considered to have high addictive potential and limited therapeutic use, as opposed to Schedule I drugs such as heroin, considered to have high addictive potential and no therapeutic use. Schedule III drugs were those with moderate addictive potential and high therapeutic use, such as the codeine used in cough syrup. As Herbert Kleber recounted to us in a 2012 interview, reflecting on the complexities of getting DATA 2000 passed during his tenure as deputy director of the Office of National Drug Control Policy: "The Drug Abuse Treatment Act doesn't mention buprenorphine by name, but what it says is that doctors can prescribe a maintenance drug if it is a Schedule III—methadone is a Schedule II—so it has to be Schedule III agents that are long acting and can be given in safety in doctors' offices. And in 2002 the FDA approved buprenorphine as [a Schedule III drug] having those characteristics." Without specifying buprenorphine as the designated medication, DATA 2000 reversed the precedent of the 1914 Harrison Act by permitting physicians to use Schedule III drugs for the office-based treatment of addiction.

David Pollack, a psychiatrist and health policy fellow charged with crafting health legislation for Democratic senator Ted Kennedy, was the Democratic lead in writing the bill that ultimately became DATA 2000. The bill was initially designed to reauthorize the Substance Abuse and

Mental Health Services Administration (SAMHSA) in order to boost support for community mental health and PTSD treatment in the wake of the Oklahoma City bombing of 1995 and the Columbine High School massacre of 1999. As Pollack told us in an interview, the unnamed buprenorphine provision (legalizing office-based Schedule III opioid maintenance) was not originally a part of the bill that he was designing. He first learned about buprenorphine at a lobbying lunch with Reckitt Benckiser Pharmaceutical CEO Charles O'Keeffe. There Pollack learned that a provision for buprenorphine had already been written into a bill on the House side, where it was sponsored by Republican representative Tom Bliley, chair of the House Finance Committee, who happened to be from Roanoke, Virginia, the headquarters of Reckitt Benckiser Pharmaceuticals. Pollack noted that the quiet "backdoor" addition of buprenorphine to the bill met with resistance from some senators, who threatened to block the bill because they had not been consulted. In the end, Republican Utah senator Orrin Hatch convinced Kennedy to include the buprenorphine provision in exchange for cosponsorship of a children's health insurance plan, which added billions of dollars to Medicaid funding.

In congressional hearings leading up to DATA 2000, National Institutes of Health and Department of Health and Human Services officials testified that office-based buprenorphine was the answer to the growing population of opioid-dependent "suburban youth," who were "not hardcore." As then-director of NIDA Alan Leshner explained, "Narcotic addiction is spreading from urban to suburban areas. The current [methadone] system, which tends to concentrate in urban areas, is a poor fit for the suburban spread of narcotic addiction."[51] Then-Department of Health and Human Services director Donna Shalala noted that buprenorphine, as an alternative to methadone, would serve a new kind of addict: "It would be available not just to heroin addicts but to anyone with an opiate problem, including citizens who would not normally be associated with the term addiction."[52] The racially coded language of the congressional debate pointed to the growing white clientele for opioid addiction treatment and to the need for an upper tier of addiction treatment for those with private doctors and with private insurance or the ability to pay doctors' fees out of pocket.

On October 8, 2002, the FDA approved buprenorphine for office-based prescription for opioid dependence. Out of fear of the widespread diversion and street sale of buprenorphine, the DEA and other federal regulators instituted special restrictions on buprenorphine's circulation in general medical practice. First, SAMHSA required physicians to complete an eight-hour course on buprenorphine patient management and an application to the DEA for an X waiver to prescribe buprenorphine in their office. Former Reckitt-Benckiser CEO Charles O'Keeffe described it this way in our interview:

> The concern of the DEA was that we had real problems back in the '70s with methadone, . . . some physicians who were basically methadone mills, who were simply selling prescriptions and selling methadone, making money and passing out methadone in the streets, we don't want to repeat that, so we sat and discussed how can we do it. So let's set a limit on the number of patients, and let's get it out to the mainstream practice of medicine where patients can be treated by physicians rather than going into the office, and more and more folks said, well, they need to be specialized, and American Society of Addiction Medicine came in, and the American Academy of Addiction Psychiatry came in and said what about training, maybe they should be trained physicians and how do you go about training. So we decided, yeah, ok, let's train the physicians if that'll make everybody happy, you gotta have eight hours of training and you gotta limit the number of patients.

This quote indicates that from Charles O'Keeffe's point of view, at the time he was forced to compromise by limiting access to buprenorphine to those who could go to specialized doctors who had undergone voluntary additional training in the use of buprenorphine in order to get certified. While O'Keeffe may not have started his campaign to legalize and market office-based buprenorphine treatment with the intent to limit its clientele by race and class, the political and economic imperatives of the pharmaceutical industry and its regulators forced those limits. This result illustrates the systemic forces of racial capitalism that funneled buprenorphine access to one market segment despite the apparently democratic intentions of the executive charged with crafting its marketing strategy.

In the buprenorphine training and certification system that was ultimately put into place, the DEA assigned certified prescribers an "X" number for pharmacies to validate and fill buprenorphine prescriptions. Holding an "X" number subjected prescribers to additional surveillance by the DEA, who conducted unannounced inspections of buprenorphine prescribers' offices and medical records. Prescribers holding an "X" number could elect to be listed in an internet-based buprenorphine physician locator service posted on SAMHSA's website and on a website sponsored by the manufacturer. This locator service allowed internet browsers looking for buprenorphine treatment to enter their zip code and produce a list of certified buprenorphine prescribers in their area.

Federal regulators capped the number of buprenorphine patients that a single physician could treat to thirty. Later, provisions were made that this cap could be raised if the prescriber had been prescribing for over a year and abided by regulations.

Buprenorphine was the first and only prescription medication to come with these special training and certification requirements, as well as limits on patient caseloads. Pharmaceutical executives and drug policy makers that we interviewed realized that the restrictions would limit access to buprenorphine and create inequalities in treatment, but stated that these restrictions were necessary to get office-based buprenorphine accepted by federal regulators. Many also acknowledged that white middle-class patients were the usual market segment for newly approved medications because they could afford the higher prices of newly patented medications and had access to prescribers. Implicit in their statements was that the Whiteness and middle-class status of the targeted market for buprenorphine were shored up by these restrictions, which helped to reassure federal regulators whose ideas about who was at risk for diversion, street sale, and nonmedical use of buprenorphine were influenced by stereotypes about the propensity of Black and Latinx people toward addiction and drug trafficking. Since US physicians more frequently prescribe opioid pain relievers to white patients and often believe that nonwhite patients are more likely to abuse opioids, racial stereotypes about addiction pervade clinical and regulatory practice.[53]

In our interviews with sixty-four buprenorphine prescribers across New York City, we were told that the certification requirements and the cap on the number of buprenorphine patients per prescriber were significant barriers to public clinic uptake of buprenorphine. Public-sector physicians and those working with low-income patients in Medicaid-accepting clinics tend to have large caseloads and thus no incentive to take on additional patients because they are not reimbursed accordingly. Moreover, they have little time to leave their practices for additional training. In our search of the SAMHSA-sponsored buprenorphine prescriber locator service, we found that as of 2015, fewer than 10 percent of those listed in New York City accepted Medicaid. In that year, only one of New York City's eleven public hospitals had a primary care–based buprenorphine clinic.[54]

The marketing strategy for buprenorphine used by its manufacturer, Reckitt-Benckiser, relied on the SAMHSA-sponsored online prescriber referral system and on public service announcements on websites sponsored by the manufacturer such as that of the National Alliance for

Advocates of Buprenorphine Treatment (naabt.org). The homepage of the website depicts a blond man in a business shirt in the lower left corner next to a tab labeled "Patients: Find a Buprenorphine Provider," which links to the SAMHSA physician locator service. On the same website, a blonde woman in a white blouse is pictured next to a tab labeled "Download and Print Info," with an Asian female doctor in a white lab coat in the lower right corner, next to a link labeled "Prescribers: Help Patients Now" (see figure 6, Introduction).

The same site features a link to the three-part webisode "Mike's Story," in which Mike, a middle-aged white diner owner in Ohio, is seated between two American flags, speaking of the ways buprenorphine rescued him from a prescription painkiller habit following his back injury at work and allowed him to return to coaching his son's baseball team and singing in his church choir. Mike stresses his "classic American upbringing" and the way that getting buprenorphine from a doctor, "like an ordinary patient," has "made all the difference in the world." In the plot of the ad, buprenorphine delivers Mike (back) into ordinary Whiteness: it normalizes both opioid addiction and treatment, associating them with everyday struggles in the heartland of (white middle-class) America.

This is a far cry from the violent and criminal Black and Latinx "dope fiends" depicted in the films and media coverage of the 1970s and from the "crackheads" of the 1980s–90s. The Whiteness of Mike's story and the other, almost exclusively white, images of buprenorphine patients on the naabt.org website retool the symbolic landscape of addiction, opening addiction medication markets that were previously too regulated and stigmatized for pharmaceutical companies to profit from.

As a number of the physicians that we interviewed pointed out, since primary care in the US is itself often limited to those who can pay and is segregated by race and class, a medication that requires regular primary care visits in itself inscribes the white race and middle class of the consumer. The efforts of the manufacturer of buprenorphine/Suboxone to associate its products with white middle-class consumers, and of regulators to restrict access to buprenorphine, were successful: in 2005, a nationally representative study showed that buprenorphine patients were 91 percent white and that over 50 percent had a college education, compared with methadone patients, who were 43 percent white and of whom 17 percent had a college education.[55] By 2015, among US patients diagnosed with opioid use disorder, whites were still three to four times as likely as Blacks to receive buprenorphine, and the vast majority paid for buprenorphine with cash or private insurance.[56]

WHITENESS IN A BOTTLE: PHARMACEUTICALLY RESTORING RACE AND CLASS

The cultural logic of the "chronic brain disease" model makes a diagnosis of opioid addiction safe for middle-class whites by asserting that addiction resides in a molecular imbalance of the brain, rather than in the personality or social environment of the person. It also asserts that molecular balance in the brain can be restored to a normal state, thereby restoring the addicted person to not only normal function but a normal status in society. The resulting mundane, blameless normality of both the addicted, imbalanced state and the pharmaceutically restored non-addicted self allows for broad public acknowledgment of white addiction. It does not threaten the dominant status of the racial group in question; rather, it bolsters the symbolic position of whites (and their diseases and personal struggles) as the American norm. The brain disease model of addiction, and the pharmaceutical solutions that it implicates, are interwoven with the cultural politics of white dominance and the imperatives of racial capitalism.

Not only does the brain disease model of addiction afford affected middle-class whites an escape valve from the racialized moral blame that has historically been attached to illegal narcotic use, but it also fits an economic logic of investment in pharmaceuticals as the primary response to problem drug use. A dominant discourse of buprenorphine advocates has involved the idea that if addiction is a brain disease, then the central factor in treatment success is pharmaceutical technology, rather than the psychosocial interventions that have historically been prescribed for addiction, such as psychotherapy and therapeutic communities. It does not lead to a focus on the social determinants of health, or to the social safety net provided in western Europe.

Addiction researchers, physicians, and policy makers advocating buprenorphine maintenance based on a brain disease model have taken an increasingly hard line that buprenorphine alone (without psychosocial intervention) is an effective treatment on its own and that regulators and health systems should not be burdened with requirements to provide psychosocial services in conjunction with it. In the early 2000s, just after buprenorphine was first approved for office-based use, addiction experts and legislators engaged in a delicate negotiation over the policies and

clinical language that would be used to designate buprenorphine maintenance. At addiction medicine and health policy meetings that we observed
in the early 2000s, brain disease advocates pushed for the medication to
be recognized as the primary therapeutic agent and lobbied against
requirements for psychotherapy that they saw as too cumbersome to
allow rapid dissemination of buprenorphine. An opposing group of
addiction specialists who saw addiction as inseparable from co-
occurring mood, anxiety, or psychotic disorders, as well as traumatic
experiences and social marginalization, insisted that buprenorphine regulation include provisions for psychosocial services. To placate both
sides of this divide, addiction specialists popularized the term *medication-assisted treatment* primarily to describe office-based buprenorphine,
although technically it could also refer to methadone maintenance. The
term *assisted* indicated that although medication was central, other elements of treatment, such as psychotherapy and counseling, would be
co-prescribed. The early 2004 guidance of SAMHSA directed buprenorphine prescribers to include mental health and social service referrals in
their treatment plans: "Candidates for buprenorphine treatment of opioid addiction should be assessed for a broad array of biopsychosocial
needs in addition to opioid use and addiction, and should be treated and/
or referred for help in meeting those needs. . . . An up-to-date listing of
community referral resources (e.g., therapy groups, support groups, residential therapeutic communities, sober-living options) should be given to
patients. . . . Referrals to social workers and case managers are often
beneficial in helping patients address legal, employment, and family
issues."[57]

In practice, however, government agencies and health insurance companies provided neither funding nor technical support to ensure that
such psychosocial assessments and referrals took place. National studies of buprenorphine prescribers found that 93 percent believed that
buprenorphine patients would benefit from formal counseling but that
only a minority stated that adequate counseling services were available
in their communities.[58] In the buprenorphine clinics that we observed
from 2009 to 2015 as part of our study of buprenorphine dissemination
in New York City, we found that many prescribers simply mentioned
twelve-step programs as a resource to buprenorphine patients. The
institutional barriers to integration of mental health and social services
with buprenorphine maintenance were enormous, even in public hospitals that had psychiatrists and social workers. Many public hospital
administrative meetings about buprenorphine were devoted to gaps in

communication, scheduling, and insurance reimbursements between primary care and psychiatry services. As the years passed, hospital administrators pronounced these gaps insurmountable and referrals were not tangibly improved. Primary care and psychiatric services had different intake and billing systems, patients who started buprenorphine in primary care had difficulty navigating the psychiatry intake requirements, and the hospital could not easily pay for psychiatric or psychological services to be rendered in the primary care clinic.

At the same time, buprenorphine advocates made increasingly bold claims that psychosocial services were not necessary. They cited a handful of negative clinical trials that combined buprenorphine with counseling and short-term cognitive behavioral therapy to argue that psychosocial services made no difference.[59] They did not question whether the structure of the trials (more communication with and logistical support for all study participants—including those in the control group—than in ordinary clinical practice), or the limited nature of the counseling (an additional fifteen-minute weekly session with a nurse employed by the research team) and therapy (twelve weeks of manual-guided cognitive behavioral therapy) might have influenced this finding. They did not cite the trials of buprenorphine that showed higher treatment adherence when combined with other psychotherapies,[60] nor did they wonder about approaches whose combination with buprenorphine had not been studied, ranging from treatment for co-occurring psychiatric disorders, to community-based and peer support, to social services such as housing, employment, or legal assistance. In our observation of addiction policy forums, we repeatedly heard buprenorphine advocates state that the research showed "medication alone is the treatment": that the medication corrects the biology of addictive behavior. Many of these advocates called for the term *medication-assisted treatment* to be replaced by the term *medication for addiction treatment*, or to replace the acronym *MAT* with *MOUD* (*medication for opioid use disorder*), indicating the stand-alone nature of buprenorphine's effectiveness. By the time that the American Society for Addiction Medicine issued its 2018 updated policy recommendations for buprenorphine regulation, its guidance on psychosocial aspects of care had been reduced to one sentence of advice, that prescribers "document provision of or referral for additional psychosocial treatment if indicated."[61]

The Whiteness of drug use is rarely as visible in drug policy as in the 2000s push to expand buprenorphine maintenance, but class was also a factor in the push. The intersection of white race with middle-class status drove the degree to which the pharmacological properties of a drug, as opposed to the social and moral condition of the user, were the dominant explanation for addiction. Two recent exceptions to the invisibility of white US drug use illustrate this intersection with social class. In the first, as described above in chapter 5, starting in the 1990s, the media portrayed methamphetamine addiction as a problem of poor white rural communities. Media images connecting rural methamphetamine use to crime, poverty, violence, and unchecked sexual activity actually told a story about the declining social and economic status of working-class white Americans.[62]

The second exception to the invisibility of US white drug use has been the nonmedical use of stimulants that are usually prescribed for attention deficit disorder (such as Ritalin and Adderall) but are often used off-label by middle-class and affluent whites for performance enhancement at school and work in the absence of ADHD symptoms. Affluent stimulant users are positively portrayed as hardworking leaders and entrepreneurs who use "neuroenhancers" rather than drugs of abuse.[63] Ironically, most of these stimulants contain methamphetamine analogues, so chemically they are in the same class of narcotics that were villainized and criminalized in media coverage of "crystal meth" addiction among rural whites.

The contrast of poor white methamphetamine "abuse" with affluent white stimulant "use" for performance enhancement highlights the intersection of class with race in the moral symbolism attached to drugs. The fact that methamphetamines were manufactured in home-based kitchen labs, while stimulants for performance enhancement were manufactured by pharmaceutical companies and prescribed by doctors, also illustrates that the distinction between licit and illicit narcotics that has created a medicalized, decriminalized space of white middle-class drug use is both a class- and race-based technique for maintaining two-tiered drug policies.

Along with class and race, gender plays a defining role in the degree to which drug users are seen as dangerous or vulnerable, culpable or deserving of care. On one hand, women who use narcotics are less likely to be portrayed in the media as violent or threatening. Middle-class white women have been disproportionately represented in popular media coverage of the "new face of opioid addiction," where their gender and class are deployed to create a sympathetic portrayal of white opioid-dependent people as blameless and deserving of care.[64] On the other hand, although women are less often incarcerated on drug charges, opioid use during pregnancy of both white and nonwhite women has been criminalized in response to reports of increasing rates of prenatal opioid exposures, and their parenting has become subject to intense surveillance by state agencies.[65] Women are also depicted as more easily addicted and harder to treat because of their biological vulnerabilities, which has led to gender-specific clinical responses, regardless of the lack of scientific consensus on the existence or nature of such biological differences.[66]

The symbolic intersections of race, class, and gender in the white opioid epidemic contrast with the heightened arrests and sentencing surrounding the crack cocaine epidemic of the 1980s–90s, a period in which popular media coverage depicted crack-using poor Black men as violent "superpredators" and poor Black women as "crack whores" who gave birth to babies with neurological damage.[67] Another contrasting example is that of marijuana laws in the late 1960s–1970s, which politicians relaxed in response to increases in marijuana use by middle-class, white college students, giving judges wide discretion that led to race and class inequalities in marijuana-related sentencing.[68] A key feature of the racial imagery implicating whites, however, is that it is often indirect or implicit, since as "the unmarked category against which difference is constructed, Whiteness never has to speak its name, never has to acknowledge its role as an organizing principle in social and cultural relations."[69] White race is usually not mentioned in media stories; instead, it operates through visual imagery, in coded terms such as *suburban*, or through references to white neighborhoods, thereby employing techniques of "color-blind" racism that buoy white privilege by not mentioning race.[70]

At the same time, pharmaceutical manufacturers see white, middle-class consumers as their highest-priority market. White, middle-class people are the primary target of a lucrative strategy of the past few decades to market and sell the idea of chronic disease and a form of prevention that requires lifelong maintenance on patented medication. Opioid maintenance regimens that are prescribed to prevent relapse are designed to keep addicted members of the white middle class in their positions as managers, mothers, and consumers in the service economy.

The fact that buprenorphine is less available to working-class whites, leaving them exposed to the structural and gendered violence of drug war–era institutions—drug courts, carceral systems, term-limited welfare, child protective services, foster care, and the daily surveillance of methadone clinics—further illustrates that narcotic laws reinforce intersecting power inequalities by race, class, and gender. Middle-class whites are protected by an exclusive clinical zone of narcotics use and treatment that provides them permissive law enforcement, medical care, and affordances of gender. This two-tiered structure of drug use has a history in the US that is over a century long. It has been based on distinctions between, on one hand, legal, prescribed drugs available to the white middle class—often to women who disproportionately saw doctors for chronic conditions such as pain, as well as for insomnia or anxiety to be managed by barbiturates, benzodiazepines, or other sedatives—and, on the other hand, illegal opiate trade that organized crime channeled to poor port city neighborhoods.[71]

PHARMACEUTICALS AS RACIAL PROSTHESIS

From the gender and family imagery of buprenorphine prescribers as first responders to opioid addiction in white suburban communities such as Staten Island, one might draw on sociologist Steve Garner's analysis of Whiteness as the basis for nation building in colonial states such as the US. In Garner's view, Whiteness is a situationally contingent quality used to sort those who belong inside the nation, with full citizenship, from those who belong outside the nation. In this frame, buprenorphine maintenance is a prosthetic device for the maintenance of the white nation.[72]

This function of buprenorphine became clear in our comparison of white, college-educated patients to Black and Latinx patients with less education in our interview sample of seventy-seven people who were being treated in the only two public buprenorphine clinics available in New York City between 2014 and 2017. The clinics hosted middle-class patients who had exhausted their savings and lost their jobs in the course of their opioid addiction, thus qualifying for Medicaid coverage, along with low-income patients who had rejected methadone treatment because of its requirement of daily observed dosing.

The impact of buprenorphine maintenance on their subjectivities and daily lives diverged depending on their race and class status. White, middle-class patients such as a filmmaker whom we will call Alexis spoke of the utility of buprenorphine for preserving her reputation and social capital in the competitive world of film: "I usually like to keep my addiction a very private thing. . . . Professionally speaking I have to be careful, you can lose grants, respect. . . . [With buprenorphine I have] normality—a sense that you can have a sense of goals and without having to depend on a group or a program, like the other options out there for us like [methadone maintenance and Narcotics Anonymous]. I'm able to travel and to have regular life."

Buprenorphine did allow employed people to keep their addiction "a very private thing" in many ways: at the time of our interview with her, buprenorphine was not a widely recognized drug name, and no employers tested for it on random urine screening of employees. While Alexis had found her way to the only public hospital in New York City to offer outpatient buprenorphine, private hospitals in the city ran cash-only buprenorphine clinics that did not even accept private health insurance, and private practice doctors charged fees of $1,000 and up for an initial half-hour buprenorphine induction visit.

Alexis was focused on the ways buprenorphine helped her maintain her productivity and her professional and personal social networks. She described her public image as "happy and productive" as a result. She saw her physician as an ally and advocate, someone from a similar background who could share her sense of accomplishment. Speaking of the doctor who wrote her first buprenorphine prescription, and whom she contacted years later to tell that she had stayed on buprenorphine treatment since leaving his practice, she said: "it was a very emotional and beautiful thing for him to see me healthy."

In contrast, low-income Black and Latinx patients in the same clinics were disproportionately referred by drug courts and lived in homeless shelters. Their experience of buprenorphine treatment was often alienating; it consisted of brief, monthly medical checks with a harried primary care doctor and little to no discussion of their social or psychological needs. One Puerto Rican man whom we will call Omar related that "they [first] gave me Suboxone inside of jail." After his release, he was compliant with his buprenorphine treatment on the threat of rearrest by his probation officer. He therefore experienced buprenorphine as an extension of police surveillance. When asked whom he turned to for support and help through his addiction treatment, he struggled to produce names, first considering his probation officer and his case manager at his homeless shelter but later dismissing both as untrustworthy. He ended by saying, "I have nobody. I feel lonely and alone."

In Omar's case, buprenorphine was less a tool for maintaining white, middle-class citizenship and more a technology of containment. Buprenorphine provided the chemical control of methadone but without the psychosocial services that methadone clinics are mandated to offer, such as therapy groups and social workers. Instead, for Omar, primary care–based buprenorphine represented stripped-down pharmaceutical "care," where the molecular safeguards of the "smart drug" buprenor-phine replaced the individual attention of a health care provider.

Other subtle negotiations over the symbolism and political status of buprenorphine took place in the clinic that provided both Alexis and Omar with their prescriptions. The prescribing doctors in the clinic, always wary of accusations that they were simply "replacing one addic-tive opioid with another," referred to buprenorphine treatment as "opi-oid maintenance therapy" rather than by older terms developed in ref-erence to methadone—"opiate replacement" or "opiate substitution" therapy. They kept detailed records in anticipation of unannounced inspections by the DEA officers charged with preventing buprenorphine "diversion"—that is, nonmedical uses and street sales of buprenorphine related to unscrupulous prescribing. These prescribers attempted to keep buprenorphine symbolically in the category of medication rather than potentially abusable opioid by telling patients to take buprenor-phine as prescribed "at the same time every day, with meals, like a vitamin," and never to crush tablets or snort them.

Office-based buprenorphine represents just one arm of an effort to create medicalized and therefore decriminalized channels for control of opioid use in white communities that would not be politically tenable targets for drug war law enforcement. Another arm of this effort has been the adoption of prescription drug monitoring programs, eventually enacted in all fifty states, that provide surveillance of prescribers and pharmacists, with sanctions against those who bypass mandated restric-tions on controlled substances. Here we see the workings of regulation, the third "technology of Whiteness" that was introduced in chapter 2.

Despite the regulatory breakthrough that office-based buprenorphine represented, in providing a less stigmatized and surveilled form of opi-oid maintenance treatment than methadone, its lower level of regula-tion can still pose a barrier to patients' access and reinforce the stigma of addiction treatment. Some doctors that we interviewed in Staten Island, faced with the legal liability of a New York State Prescription Drug Monitoring Program that mandates them to check a database for other controlled-substance prescriptions written for a patient before prescribing any narcotic, on threat of loss of their license and criminal charges, told us that they opted not to provide buprenorphine because they did not want to risk treating anyone with a history of problem use. Pharmacists told us that they decided not to stock buprenorphine in order to avoid the mandatory prescription data checks of, and stigma of, a substance-abusing clientele. Patients confirmed that pharmacies routinely refused to stock buprenorphine. Thus an unanticipated effect of prescription drug monitoring programs, which were designed to stem opioid overdose, is that they may paradoxically contribute to overdose risk, not only by redirecting opioid-dependent people to heroin, but also by reducing access to buprenorphine treatment in the very communities that they were intended to protect.[73]

The other side of this coin is that buprenorphine dissemination is beginning to reach public clinics such as Federally Qualified Health Centers, and even some jails and prisons—the product of advocacy by medical societies, patient advocacy groups, and pharmaceutical manufacturers seeking to expand their markets now that buprenorphine has gained acceptance as a safe (white) drug.[74]

Calls for equal access to buprenorphine as a health justice issue are gaining momentum. Their focus on medication is consistent with the American master narrative of progress through commercialized technologies. The danger is that mobilizing around access to medication would foreclose discussion of the fundamental policy and institutional drivers of racial and class inequalities in problem substance use. That is, singular attention to medication rather than social safety nets, economic revitalization, and restorative justice for communities that have been ravaged by targeted drug law enforcement threatens to leave unseen, intact, and even strengthened the very structures of inequality and exploitation that led to the opioid crisis in the first place.

RACIAL CAPITAL IN MEDICATION-ASSISTED TREATMENT

By 2012, ten years after its FDA approval, buprenorphine, in its commercial formulation Suboxone, was a blockbuster drug at $1.5 billion in US sales annually.[75] Generic Suboxone was not cleared for sale until 2019, even though Reckitt-Benckiser Pharmaceutical's patent had expired in 2009. Reckitt-Benckiser's legal team had blocked generic manufacturers from US markets for a decade, using myriad strategies such as declaring the original tablets to be at high risk for overdose by young children based on case reports.[76] A plethora of newly patented formulations of buprenorphine—extended-release injectables, implantables, and patches—entered the field. This explosion in capitalized medications for opioid use disorder coincided with the heightened economic insecurity of the white middle class in the wake of the 2008 economic crisis; a volatile service economy and the exportation of manufacturing

left few routes to success, with white men and women unable to reproduce the middle-class nuclear family structures of their parents, and
facing becoming the racial minority in the US by 2030. As Linda Alcoff
writes in *The Future of Whiteness,* white Americans are conscious of
their shrinking numerical dominance and feel called to defend their economic and political privilege in new ways.[77]

The white middle class faces the problem of reproducing itself in an
economy that no longer affords the insulation of white privilege as it did
in the postwar years of industrial growth. New York City, like much of
the US, has experienced cycles of expansion and contraction in the face
of illusory venture capital investments, globalized labor pools, and
mortgage bubbles that have displaced middle managers and small business owners along with the working class, creating subjectivities of personal insecurity and questioned self-worth.[78] Opioid manufacturers
such as Purdue Pharmaceuticals (of OxyContin) and Reckitt-Benckiser
(of Suboxone) could be seen as beneficiaries of disaster capitalism,[79] in
that opioids that are used nonmedically, and opioid maintenance treatment for opioid dependence, are commodities that help the white middle class to face the uncertainties of economic implosion and political
impotence.

Opioids have joined the panoply of drugs that are now being prescribed to reduce the risk of disease, rather than merely to treat diseased
states themselves. As Joe Dumit has noted, pharmaceutical manufacturers' current strategy for growing consumer markets is to change the
reference ranges for tests indicating normal, at-risk, and diseased states
and to get more and more people on chronic regimens—for conditions
such as heart disease, diabetes, and asthma—that are now prescribed
"for life."[80] In the case of white opioids, prior nonmedical opioid use is
now a lifetime risk factor for future opioid addiction: large numbers of
suburban whites meet criteria for buprenorphine maintenance treatment. Implicit in Dumit's argument is the idea that pharmaceutical companies are selling their maintenance regimes as ways of maximizing
health and the biological self to ward off risk and control an uncertain
future.[81] Buprenorphine works as a *pharmaceutical prosthesis* for privilege. It is prescribed to keep the white middle class in their privileged
position as managers and consumers in the service economy and to
ward off the vagaries of physical and existential pain as well as addiction. As prosthesis, however, this pharmaceutically bolstered social
position carries uncanny reminders of what is missing and stirs a "recognition that the world can be undone."[82] Like a phantom limb, the

former security of race and class dominance is not really there. And unlike the cholesterol, hypertension, and depression drugs of Dumit's marketers, white narcotics require ongoing distinction from regimes of Black and Brown narcotic control, a delicate balance with its costs. In the logic of the Greek *pharmakon,* opioids are both poison and cure in American racial politics: the symbolic and political apparatuses needed to sustain white narcotic privilege also create blind spots and prey on white vulnerabilities in the narrow therapeutic index of these psychoactive substances.

The centrality of Whiteness to the colonial foundations of US capitalism has long been documented by social analysts, including W.E.B. DuBois a century ago, in his seminal paper "The Souls of White Folk."[83] In the contemporary opioid epidemic, we might see medicalized opioids such as buprenorphine as a symbolic and political counterweight to the loss of white race and middle-class security, and therefore as a rallying point for the defense of white privilege. If white suburban youth can emerge from heroin addiction with their futures biomedically secured, their political dominance will be embodied in the consumer economy of twenty-first century biocapital.

There are drawbacks to this racial capitalist strategy, even for white people. Getting federal law reversed to legalize private office-based buprenorphine required mechanisms for limiting access to buprenorphine to the white middle class, a group that regulators saw as low risk for diverting buprenorphine to nonmedical uses and markets. Prescriber training and certification requirements, and targeted online marketing, have created a patchwork system in which many people do not have access to buprenorphine, or have discontinuous access due to scarce prescribers. They may encounter arduous prior authorization procedures as required by insurance companies, or pharmacists who refuse to stock buprenorphine because they don't want addicted clients. These elements undermine the principle of a maintenance medication, which requires consistent dosing to protect against relapse and its risks of overdose and infection. Thus structural racism is preventing effective public health intervention, including among white Americans.

Although the harms of the surreptitious pharmaceutical apartheid of buprenorphine maintenance appear to be about drugs, in fact they are just one instance of a broader effort to maintain the exclusive social space of Whiteness in American society. As David Roediger shows in *Working toward Whiteness,* his history of the integration of early twentieth-century white immigrants into the American middle class, in

America, *white* is a verb, not a noun.[84] Whiteness is the aspiration built into the American dream, Whiteness is the collective identity cementing the nation, and it provides some measure of safety for those who fall within it, but its ever-shifting bounds prompt continual efforts to protect Whiteness. Prescription opioids, and the maintenance opioids to treat dependence on them, show how lethal the promises of Whiteness can be.

CHAPTER 7

The Housewife's Return to Heroin (and Forays into Fentanyl)

In a close-up photo in the *New York Times,* a wiry young woman in a white buttoned shirt, her blond ponytail skirting the back of her collar, has her sleeves rolled up and her right arm flexed. Her pose would be that of a modern Rosie the Riveter, were it not for the tourniquet on her arm and the syringe that she holds between her teeth. The 2013 article below the photo describes epidemic heroin use in Maine following an explosion in prescription painkiller use.[1] While the article does not directly reference race or gender, the photo is clearly meant to challenge gendered and racialized stereotypes of heroin addiction. In fact, the image goes a step beyond, juxtaposing images of (white women's) liberation and of (narcotic) dependence.

In the years that followed, such images pervaded the national media, which featured stories such as that of a blonde school teacher from suburban Putnam County, New York, elegantly coiffed, with pearl earrings and a silk scarf: "'I'm a great mom,' Michelle told NBC News. 'I'm a teacher. I'm a daughter, a niece. I'm all of these great things and then I am a heroin addict showing up at a Fourth of July party with track marks." The article goes on to point out: "Addiction doesn't discriminate. And in recent years heroin has wound its way into American communities and touched people who wouldn't have considered using it just a decade ago."[2]

Deseret News of Salt Lake City put it this way: "This is the new face of heroin addiction in America: young, white and increasingly female."[3]

Bar graphs in the article were taken from a report in the *Journal of the American Medical Association* showing a sharp rise in the proportion of women using heroin, from the 1960s, when 17 percent of new users were women, to the 2010s, when 51 percent of new users were women.[4] The story was carried in newspapers throughout the country, from *The Oklahoman* to *Central Kentucky News*, next to the image of a fresh-faced young woman with long blonde hair cascading over her shoulders, Blake Landry, "once a promising high school soccer star . . . who started heroin when she was 20." She stands next to a stained-glass window in an Arizona chapel, where she is in recovery and counseling other young women. The article ends by quoting the director of the Drug Enforcement Agency in Landry's state: "Everything we do has to be about, 'Are we gonna be able to save these kids?'"[5]

The intersection of gender with race and class in news coverage of the "suburban opioid epidemic" reveals that white futures are thought to be at stake, both the futures of "kids" who use heroin and the futures of their children. In its imagery, white women convey blamelessness and vulnerability in a way that challenges the historically punitive, criminalizing, and racially othered ethos of US drug policy. It instead lends urgency to supportive community and policy responses to addiction by calling attention to the role of white addicted women in reproducing white society as mothers, daughters, and teachers. Media and clinical portrayals reflect a logic of a white racial rescue spawned by threatened futures in the era of substance-induced white downward mobility.

Young women may have been selectively featured in news coverage of white opioid addiction to evoke sympathy and protectiveness, yet the current heroin epidemic does have the distinction of being the first feminized wave of heroin use since the early twentieth century. One has to go all the way back to the late nineteenth century, when heroin was first introduced by Bayer Corporation, to find another time when the majority of those addicted to opiates were white middle-class women. Opiates were a common ingredient in over-the-counter patent medicines, and family doctors injected Victorian-era housewives with morphine for a range of complaints.[6] This opiate-consumer profile shifted thanks to medical reforms: by the time heroin was outlawed in 1924, it was confined to the male-dominated, immigrant circuits of street trade. There it remained for seventy years. Only in the 2000s did usage patterns change, thanks to a two-part development. First, loosened controls on pharmaceutical opioids helped encourage a rapid rise in addiction among white, middle-class women—as in the nineteenth century, the largest doctor-visiting demographic. Then, as an opioid addiction crisis grew, authorities tightened controls over pharmaceutical opioids, depriving addicted women of their medically sanctioned supply and pushing them to illicit heroin supplies.

The images of biologically based addiction among promising young white women, otherwise productive workers and nurturing mothers, that emerged in early 2000s media coverage of new heroin users stand in stark contrast to the criminalizing media images of the low-income urban African American and Latina crack cocaine–using women in the 1980s–1990s, which led to policy initiatives to mandate minimum drug sentencing and termination of parental and reproductive rights.[7]

In contrast, by the 2000s, heroin laws were humanized in some parts of the US. For example, local court systems developed diversion programs to channel those arrested on drug charges away from sentencing and toward treatment. Such initiatives were concentrated in empowered white affluent neighborhoods, while punitive, law enforcement responses to heroin remained intact in Black and Latinx neighborhoods as well as many poor white neighborhoods, including in Appalachia.[8] The fact that humanizing heroin initiatives were only partially available to working-class whites, leaving them exposed to the structural and gendered violence of drug war–era institutions—courts and carceral systems, term limited welfare, child protective services, foster care, and the surveillance of methadone clinics—further illustrates that narcotics interact with multiple axes of power, including class, gender, and race. White middle-class women are protected by differential law enforcement, clinical ideologies, and affordances of gender.

This two-tiered structure of drug use has a history in the US that is over a century long. It has been based on distinctions between, on one hand, legal, prescribed opioids (and other drugs) available to the white middle class—largely to women, who have disproportionately seen private doctors—and on the other hand illegal opioids that were geographically zoned to poor port city neighborhoods where drug trade has been permitted to flourish with a ready workforce among unemployed Black, Brown, and immigrant men.[9] The unique feature of the early twenty-first-century opioid "crisis" was the growing prominence of middle-class white people, including women, buying heroin in prohibition markets, something that challenges the historical system of distinguishing medical use of pharmacotherapies from illegalized substances of "abuse." The shifting associations of heroin made Whiteness in its co-constitution with class and gender more visible.

At the same time, the very language of a "new crisis" or "new epidemic" to describe the twenty-first-century increase in heroin use and overdose among whites denies the chronic losses sustained by Black and Latinx communities that experienced cyclical influxes of heroin in northern US cities in the 1950s, 1960s, and 1970s. The South Bronx, a low-income Black and Latinx section of New York City, reported the largest number of overdoses and the second-highest overdose death rate in New York City starting in 2017.[10]

Heroin use is epidemiologically complex. A growing number of drug researchers identify not just one heroin "epidemic" but multiple, interlocking, and simultaneous epidemics ranging from the affluent white suburbs to poor white rural areas and multiracial city centers.[11]

That very variability highlights a few ironies of heroin.

The popular narrative of heroin from its prohibition in 1924 to the end of the twentieth century has been remarkably consistent: that of a morally contaminating substance born of Black, Brown, and migrant underworlds—a substance that, left unchecked, tempts unsuspecting white youth and corrupts the moral fiber of suburban and rural America. Against this backdrop, the white middle-class image of new heroin users in the early 2000s may seem like an anomaly, or at least like the fulfillment of an apocalyptic prophecy of infection from inner cities. But the full history of heroin illustrates exactly the opposite. Time and time again, illegal substances that are portrayed as a new threat to (white) society—that are portrayed as deriving from the unrestrained excesses of Black, Brown, or immigrant "others"—actually began as medications for white middle-class patients, often women, that later spread out to Black, Brown, and migrant neighborhoods as white demand created local illegal economies of supply. That is: our most feared narcotics, including heroin, started with white middle-class consumers.

In the twenty-first century, heroin fits this pattern. The impetus for this symbolic inversion—from white initiation to Black and Brown initiation of new drug markets—lies in the racial capitalist imperative to create demand for new products in the largest and most affluent segment of American society (the white middle class) and then, as time passes and the disadvantages of that product become known, to offload distribution of, and blame for, the product onto racial/ethnic groups with less power to fend off its social costs.

Over the past century, then, heroin spread from white middle-class women to Black and Brown men and then back again to white women. That is because heroin began as white medicine, became illegal as it was associated with immigrant and racialized "others," and later resurged among whites when prescription opioids that were marketed to whites were legally restricted. Ironically, heroin panic has been used as a political driver of residential segregation (i.e., through white flight and policing of the boundaries between segregated neighborhoods as part of drug scares), at the same time that white heroin deaths were the result of medical segregation—of the targeted promotion of prescription opioids to white consumers that eventually created new markets for heroin in suburban, small town, and rural America. This is one way that white Americans ultimately suffered heavy casualties from racial narcocapitalism.

MODERN LYNCHINGS

In January of 2016, Maine's governor Paul LePage, when asked about the heroin problem in his predominantly white state, explained that Black drug dealers were coming into Maine and impregnating young, white girls: "These are guys with the name D-Money, Smoothie, Shifty—these types of guys—they come from Connecticut and New York, they come up here, they sell their heroin, they go back home. Incidentally, half the time they impregnate a young white girl before they leave, which is a real sad thing because then we have another issue we have to deal with down the road." Later, seeking to clarify his comments, he doubled down on the threat he believed men of color posed to Maine's white womanhood:

> You try to identify the enemy and the enemy right now, the overwhelming majority of people coming in, are people of color or people of Hispanic origin. . . . I made the comment that Black people are trafficking in our state, now ever since I said that comment I've been collecting every single drug dealer who has been arrested in our state. I don't ask them to come to Maine and sell their poison, but they come and I will tell you that 90-plus percent of those pictures in my book, and it's a three-ringed binder, are Black and Hispanic people from Waterbury, Conn., then Bronx and Brooklyn.[12]

In invoking both the supposed innocence of young white women and the threat of miscegenation, Governor LePage revealed in stark terms how racism and Whiteness are operating in the current heroin crisis. For LePage and many others, heroin's threat is explicitly racial: it is a Black drug that threatens white communities (as symbolized by the white women responsible for their social reproduction). The threat, in other words, emanates not just from heroin itself but from those historically associated with the drug, namely, Black and Brown men. White people are at risk not just of addiction but also of losing their Whiteness and white status as heroin facilitates a blurring of racial boundaries. To LePage and others like him, heroin use in white communities stands as both a symptom and a cause of a racial crisis, one that requires a political effort to rebuild the edifice of Whiteness by strengthening the policing of racial boundaries—including, implicitly, the wayward young white women who passively became impregnated by the D-Moneys, Smoothies, and Shiftys of the white racial imagination.

White authorities' use of drugs in maintaining racial boundaries and racist systems is not new. Fear of cocaine use as supposedly driving Black men to commit violence against their white employers and to rape white women played an important role in segregationist law enforcement a century ago, when Jim Crow was first built. America's severe and racially driven drug law enforcement serves a similar function to lynching—as a bulwark of segregation. Like sex, drugs tend to draw people across racial boundaries. In the case of drugs, this is because drug markets themselves are so spatially segregated, with white people commuting to informal markets physically located in immigrant and/or Black and Brown neighborhoods where segregationist policies and law enforcement allow the drug trade to take place. When people cross the lines of segregation in pursuit of drugs, white authorities use drug laws, like miscegenation laws, to reinforce those boundaries, often under the pretext of protecting white women as a symbol of the white nation. The targets of such campaigns—Black men—are prosecuted by the tens of thousands, in formal and popular venues, generating a stream of images of Black degradation, disgrace, arrest, and imprisonment that, together, demonize an entire "race" and reference the legacy of lynching. The same cultural productions implicitly convey a necessary corollary: that white people are inherently valuable and merit protection from the scourge of Black drug use. (The stories also bear a warning for white women, of course, reminding them of the consequences of trespassing racial boundaries.)

In this way, LePage's comments belong to a long segregationist tradition of American drug politics. And his racial logic was reflected in contemporaneous popular media coverage of what journalists dubbed the "heroin highway" to describe the traffic of heroin from inner cities and their implied Black and Latinx populations to white suburban and rural neighborhoods. The articles quote policy makers and law enforcement officials on drug trade routes running from Chicago to Kane County, Illinois; from Baltimore to suburban Maryland and rural

Virginia and West Virginia; from urban Paterson, New Jersey, to suburban Sussex County; from New York City to Long Island; from Cincinnati to Fort Thomas, Kentucky; from Atlanta to western North Carolina, and ultimately from Mexican cartels: "We want them to get out of our country, stop bringing that junk in."[13] These stories cemented the narrative of inner-city Black and Brown contagion spreading to white communities—an illicit and morally polluting chemical miscegenation.

While reflecting a racial order that continues to fuel mass incarceration of Black and Brown men, LePage's comments were construed by some as an outlier, cited "virally" across social media as retrograde and out of touch. This is because, in the early twenty-first century, historical developments have challenged the logic of heroin as a Black drug and a Black problem. Instead, white women themselves have become the face of the new heroin epidemic—not because they have been taken advantage of by predatory Black men, but because they have been taken advantage of by predatory Big Pharma.

Heroin's reconfiguration as white has not meant an end to the drug's value as a vehicle for reinforcing American racial hierarchies. Instead, it heralds new ways that white authorities use heroin to protect and preserve the sanctity of white women and their role in the social reproduction of the white people. These new technologies of Whiteness are not as explicitly racist as Governor LePage's remarks. Instead, in keeping with an era of "color-blind racism," they deploy seemingly race-neutral public health science, biomedical vocabularies of "chronic brain disease," and selectively medicalizing, decriminalizing policies to serve the needs of Whiteness. White supremacy is so deeply embedded in the US that Whiteness still finds ways to commandeer even laudatory goals to reproduce itself.

Yet every moment of change is also a moment of opportunity—a moment of flux when collective action can influence the arc of history. When Whiteness is deployed in new ways, its workings become—or can become—unusually visible, perhaps even jarringly so when compared to long-entrenched cultural practices. At these moments it is even more urgent to notice, to expose, and to analyze, to recognize and denaturalize the new racial stereotypes being built before our very eyes.

In this chapter, we work towards this goal in two ways. First, David traces the racial history of heroin, exploring how heroin became "Black" in the first place and how it became white again. This history is crucial context for understanding the present. On the one hand, it reveals how seemingly natural categories of race have, in fact, changed over time in response to purposeful human action. History frees us to imagine and pursue real justice. At the same time, however, deeper patterns of consistency reveal the operation of Whiteness as a system—malleable but always dedicated to the protection of race privileges. Present-day ironies and absurdities are not aberrations to be repaired in an otherwise rational drug policy but rather evidence of long-standing, structural injustices that require deep reimagining and reconstruction.

Second, Jules and Helena explore how responses to the twenty-first century's opioid crisis participate in the long history of malleable but consistent systems of Whiteness. Authorities used the crisis to reinforce the boundaries of Whiteness, marshaling sympathetic new stories about the wasted potential of addicted white Americans to push for new racially preferential policies to rebuild the promise of Whiteness during a time of economic challenges. This has led to obvious harms for the Black and Brown communities excluded from new, more humane approaches to addiction. But the white people who benefited from it also bore a cost, as their use of opioids, especially heroin, continued to rise and become even deadlier with the advent of fentanyl.

HEROIN'S HISTORIC JOURNEY FROM WHITE, TO BLACK, TO WHITE AGAIN

1. From White to Off-White

When Bayer Pharmaceuticals introduced Heroin in 1898, it was not a revolutionary medical advance. Rather, it was one more opium derivative entered into competition against existing medicines like morphine and codeine. It appeared to produce fewer gastrointestinal side effects, and, many observers hopefully noted, it did not seem to produce a "habit" in users.[14] This made it especially attractive as an alternative to morphine, which had developed an association with addiction after decades of unrestrained prescribing, often for middle-class white women suffering from "the pains of existence." But opioid prescribing for such purposes was already declining by the time Heroin was introduced, and the drug was most prominently advertised as a cough suppressant.

Nor did initial optimism about Heroin's addictiveness last. The realization in the early 1910s that the new wonder drug could produce a habit was disappointing but not in itself remarkable: this was a known quality of opiates that physicians had become accustomed to over the past half century. As one physician wrote: "Be not deceived . . . by its promoters. . . . [Heroin] is an opiate."[15]

The fact that it was addictive did not threaten Heroin's status as a medicine. In 1898 opiate addiction was still primarily produced in the course of medical care and was thus most common among white, respectable classes, especially women. Addiction was considered to be a horrifying tragedy when it occurred, but in this Heroin was not alone; all potent medicines inevitably carried the risk of horrifying tragedy. Authorities approached addicted people, like victims of other drug-related harms, with sympathy.[16]

Despite the disappointment, in other words, Heroin fit into the cultural slot of other opiates quite nicely, and medical literature about the drug had all the hallmarks of a "white" discourse. Physicians never mentioned the race of Heroin users or Heroin sellers and focused exclusively on the goal of helping the drug's potential consumers (i.e., "patients") with respiratory ailments and a variety of other disease states.

The absence of race in discussions of Heroin was possible, in part, because the racial status of Heroin's consumers had already been long established by 1898. Since the mid-nineteenth century, opioid sales in America had been informally divided between smoking opium and other opioids labeled as medicinal. White authorities associated smoking opium with Chinese or "Oriental" culture and portrayed addiction to it as a civilizational threat whose opening wedge was white women lured into "white slavery" by devious Chinese men. In this context, campaigns against smoking opium dovetailed with campaigns to restrict Chinese immigration and limit the rights of Chinese immigrants. By contrast, other opioids such as morphine, laudanum, and eventually Heroin were portrayed as medicines used primarily by white, native-born men and especially women. Cases of addiction in this context were used as evidence that pharmaceutical markets required stronger regulation by professional men in medicine and pharmacy. Smoking opium was a domain of criminals who required policing and punishment; medicinal opiates were a domain of commerce that required regulation and consumer protection.[17]

Heroin's status changed in the 1920s because of social and political factors. Most important were the consequences of reformers' turn-of-the-century push to restrict sales of opiates to formal medical channels and to limit sales even within those channels. The goal, in part, was to criminalize smoking opium. One element of this push was to define nonmedical opiate use as one of the threatening "vices" attributed to the urban "dangerous classes" in America's fast-growing and largely immigrant cities. Importantly, these were concentrated in what reformers called "vice districts," where municipal authorities had quarantined informal market infrastructure. Not coincidentally, these neighborhoods also happened to be where authorities segregated racialized communities: Chinese immigrants, southern and eastern European immigrants, and (eventually) African Americans. To combat vice and impose their moral order on vice districts, reformers successfully built new policing and punitive powers for local, state, and national governments. Activities such as the sex trade, gambling, drinking, and drug taking that had been disreputable (and subject to a range of repressions) now became criminal and subject to even more intense repression.[18]

The immediate practical result for informal market consumers was an even greater need to hide those activities from view. For nonmedical opiate users, this meant abandoning their traditional smoking opium—bulky and smelly, thus ill-suited for illicit traffic—in favor of the more compact and scent-free Heroin. Here timing mattered a great deal: in the 1900s, when reformers began their campaigns, Heroin, unlike morphine, was not yet widely recognized as addictive and was thus easier to purchase. By the time authorities moved to restrict sales of Heroin, it dominated America's most important nonmedical drug markets (especially New York City).[19]

Heroin, which had been relatively unremarkable as a medicine, began to take on a distinctive identity once it was adopted by informal urban markets. This even happened literally, as "Heroin" became "heroin," losing its brand-name association with the Bayer pharmaceutical company.

Heroin's distinctiveness was shaped, and strengthened, by the new invisibility of opiate addiction in other sectors of American society. Outside of New York and other major cities, for example, morphine supplied through medical channels remained a major drug of addiction for native-born, white, respectable people with privileged access to medical care. But this medical supply was officially discouraged and technically even illegal and was thus relatively clandestine. By the 1920s heroin and its urban consumers may have wished to be clandestine, but antivice policing made it increasingly difficult for them to maintain their habits without becoming visible to authorities. Soon these drug consumers, increasingly referred to with the derogatory term *junkies*, had come to stand alone as the face of addiction in America. Heroin's status as a drug of abuse became so entrenched, in fact, that in 1924 it ceased to be considered a "medicine" at all: Congress passed a special law just to prohibit the importation of opium to make heroin. It became, in effect, a fully criminalized substance.[20]

Unlike the trade in pharmaceuticals, the nonmedical heroin trade was not evenly spread throughout the US. Pharmaceutical medicines enjoyed a distribution system involving literally hundreds of thousands of physicians and pharmacists dispersed throughout the nation, but heroin's markets continued to be much more geographically and spatially concentrated. Opium poppies were not grown within the US, and heroin was illegal, so all heroin had to be smuggled in. As Eric Schneider has shown, this immediately favored port cities, and especially New York City, which had both the nation's largest port and the largest illicit infrastructure for unloading and distributing smuggled goods. Once heroin was in the US, preparation and retail sales required a second, substantial illicit infrastructure. This was no small matter; it took time to develop a significant and experienced managerial and sales force and to establish locales shielded from police. Even in port cities like New York, only some neighborhoods had this infrastructure: the "urban vice districts" marked by sex work, disreputable entertainment, and, in general, a thriving informal economy existing with the implicit (or sometimes explicit) protection of police happy to have such activities quarantined away from "respectable" neighborhoods.[21]

In major cities like New York at this time, these neighborhoods tended to be populated by so-called new immigrants, their children, and the poorer, disreputable native-born whites who ended up living among them. Hailing from eastern and southern Europe (e.g., Italy, Russia, Poland), these immigrants would today be understood as white, but at the time they belonged to a racial category that has since ceased to exist: off-white, you might say—not exactly white, but definitely not Black either. Native-born whites recognized them as having distinctive, and inferior, racial characteristics.[22] Cleaning up urban "vice" and cleaning up these racially stigmatized populations were, in many senses, one and the same thing.

This type of supposedly inferior white person posed new problems for America's racial order, in part because of their potential assimilability. Naturalized European immigrants automatically enjoyed the right to vote, for example, and, of course, sexual boundaries were more difficult to police in the absence of clearly visible differences such as skin color. This helps explain the popularity in America of racial sciences that measured skull shapes or assessed "Intelligence Quotient" (IQ), and the ruthless regime of residential segregation that separated immigrant families from native-born whites, as well as from the (relatively small) African

American communities in cities outside the South. It also helps explain the draconian restriction of immigration from eastern and southern Europe implemented in 1924—the same year as laws restricting the "immigration" of heroin.[23]

One of the most influential expressions of the supposed immigrant threat was the campaign for what was called eugenics: "breeding up the American stock" by persuading superior (or "eugenic") people to have more children and forcing inferior (or "dysgenic") people to have fewer. Eugenics was first embraced by elite scientists but soon became a widely popular social phenomenon, with "better baby contests" for the eugenic and often-involuntary sterilization for the dysgenic.[24] The eugenics campaign focused not only on immigrants themselves but also on whites ignorant or immoral enough to consider having sex with them— dysgenic or "feeble-minded" young women, for the most part.[25]

Heroin fit perfectly with this version of racial threat, just as smoking opium before it had helped sensationalize the threat of "Oriental" men. Native-born white moral crusaders immediately (and, ironically, correctly) saw heroin sales and use as belonging to, while also helping to further, the whole panoply of dysgenic behaviors that they saw unfolding in "urban vice districts." Under the influence of heroin—or in the desperate need to get more heroin—young women could be trapped in "white slavery" (i.e., sex work) that not only was immoral but also threatened the future of the race.

In the 1930s, after a decade of limited immigration, the "new" immigrants began to make their way into full membership in Whiteness, most prominently by joining the New Deal political coalition.[26] Interestingly, this same political moment saw the creation of a federal narcotics institute in Lexington, Kentucky, colloquially known as the "Narcotic Farm," which combined a prison, a research center, and a working farm for patient/inmates: "a 'New Deal for Addicts,'" as it was called. The "Narcotic Farm" was a prison where people with addiction could be quarantined so as to protect "normal" criminals, but it was also a treatment center where experts hoped they could be redeemed—a process consonant with the wider cultural attempt to redeem immigrant "stock" and dysgenic whites as respectable members of white society.[27]

2. From Off-White to Black

Heroin traffic also plummeted during Great Depression and World War II, which was not surprising given the overall decline in global trade during those years. When trade resumed after World War II, the landscape had shifted. The "Great Migration" had slowly introduced African Americans into the urban vice districts formerly occupied by immigrants and "dysgenic" whites, who were now completing their path to respectable Whiteness through federal programs such as the GI Bill and the Federal Housing Authority that encouraged them to climb into the middle class through a variety of subsidies to help them move into the suburbs, receive a college education, or start a small business.[28] As they left, these newly minted American whites did not take cities' illicit market infrastructure with them; that remained in the neighborhoods they abandoned. But those neighborhoods were now populated by a different and even more deeply racialized community: African Americans, who, thanks to a dense network of interrelated banking, real estate, and housing practices, were forcibly segregated there.

As historian Eric Schneider has shown, the consequences of this spatial "zoning" of the informal economy and of recently arrived families into the same neighborhoods was both predictable and brutal: a young generation of African Americans was exposed to the heroin trade and heroin use at a much greater rate than the children of families who had been subsidized to move out of those neighborhoods. An explosion of heroin addiction soon took root in the 1940s. It began in jazz clubs, where nonconformist, marijuana-smoking musicians and their clientele had already created countercultural communities resistant to reformers' antivice moral campaigns. It spread through personal and commercial networks whose densest hubs were physical locations in urban neighborhoods—jazz clubs, cafeterias, and so on.[29]

The generation of heroin users who emerged within these places was predominantly African American. Police quarantined heroin trafficking to the urban neighborhoods where African American families lived, meaning that African American children—especially the teenagers and young adults most at risk for addiction—lived amid easy heroin availability as well as the local knowledge required to purchase and use it. "Heroin had just about taken over Harlem," Claude Brown remembered in his memoir *Manchild in the Promised Land*: "It seemed to be a kind of plague. Every time I went uptown, somebody else was hooked, somebody else was strung out. People talked about them as if they were dead. You'd ask about an old friend, and they'd say 'Oh, well, he's strung out.' It wasn't just a comment or an answer to a question. It was a eulogy for someone. He was just dead, through."[30]

The policing quarantine was explicitly designed to keep drug activity out of "white" neighborhoods. This, in turn, meant that selling heroin to white consumers produced considerably more police scrutiny and potential legal consequences. Heroin sellers were thus very reluctant to sell to whites; white teenagers eager to try the drug were usually rebuffed unless they had a personal connection to someone who could vouch for them.[31] These protections were in addition to the semi-intentional market structuring of segregation, which meant that only families of color were forced to raise children amid easy, unregulated heroin availability.

Despite this, mass-media portrayals of heroin during the 1950s remained whiter than ever. This was because authorities' interest in heroin remained almost exclusively focused on supposed threats to white Americans—even as communities of color experienced most of the actual harms of unregulated prohibition markets for heroin. Thus, in popular culture, heroin shifted from being the province of immigrants and dysgenic whites to being a terrifying threat lurking in middle-class "teen space," in the suburbs, among bobby-soxers. Popular accounts like the comic books *Trapped!* and *Holiday of Horrors* portrayed good white neighborhoods invaded by sinister "pushers" who lured young people into a life of deviance and despair.[32] Everyone was white, but the ever-Blackening city loomed large at the margins of the story, and the overall narrative arc was not lost on a population immersed in the racial fantasies of "white flight," which sanctified the suburbs in part by contrasting them to dangerous, wild, Black cities always threatening to invade.[33]

Thus, even though heroin remained associated in popular culture with white users, its racial status had changed significantly. Socially speaking, the neighborhoods where heroin markets were located were now Black and Brown. Culturally speaking, heroin was now being portrayed as an insidious invader threatening white suburban youth, with the invader at least implicitly being understood as the (racially) dark cities lying just outside the suburbs.

Framed in this way, race became an important tool for understanding—or, more accurately, for purposefully misunderstanding—illicit heroin markets. Even though heroin sellers actively resisted selling to whites, especially to white youths, reformers focused much of their anger on an invented figure of the heroin "pusher" who sought to infiltrate white, suburban America to "hook" kids. This enabled very harsh new policing laws such as those passed federally in 1951 and 1956, which, among other things, pioneered the tactic of mandatory-minimum jail sentences for drug "pushers."

The focus on "pushers" left open a space for a relatively sympathetic response to the still putatively white victims of the heroin menace. Even though the 1950s were the height of America's punitive campaign against narcotics, they also saw the first stirrings of a carefully crafted resistance coming from reformers in law, medicine, and the academy. No one questioned the demonization of drug "pushers," but a few experts began to raise doubts about the automatic criminality of people addicted to heroin—and a smaller few even raised the possibility that maintenance, rather than punishment, might be the best response.[34] These reformers spoke in the universalist language of Whiteness: the race of their sympathetic addicts was never mentioned.

These racial dynamics are captured fairly well in the only Hollywood film from this era about addiction, *The Man with the Golden Arm* (1955). The movie tracked the career of Frankie Machine, an addicted jazz drummer and poker dealer, played sympathetically by Frank Sinatra. Frankie gets a chance at a "straight" life after a stint at the federal Narcotic Farm in Lexington, Kentucky. For Americans accustomed to interpreting whitened mass culture—African American music played by white bands, et cetera—this film conveyed both that (Italian-heritage) whites like Frankie's character could be redeemed, while also indicting the whitened but clearly African American urban jazz scene as the source of temptation and vice.[35]

The relatively small burst of heroin use after World War II, Eric Schneider recounts, was just a rehearsal for a larger, and ultimately more consequential, epidemic of heroin addiction that struck American cities in the 1960s. All of the same factors were involved, only more intensely. New transportation technologies increased the volume of heroin being smuggled—and increased the value of port cities able to handle the traffic. Racial segregation meant that the crucial neighborhoods gained ever more African American and Latinx people as the Great Migration reached its high point. The cost of rent rose even as economic opportunities, which had been "fleeing" along with whites since the end of the war, all but disappeared. Unemployment among people of color, especially youth, reached crisis proportions. Meanwhile, heightened antidrug policing led to a proliferation of jobs in the informal drug economy: sellers now needed lookouts, steerers (to vet customers), runners (to restock supplies so sellers were never in possession of large quantities), and so on. Heightened policing also favored hiring youths, who would face lesser criminal penalties if they were caught. The police focus on breaking up urban gangs ironically decimated one of the few social structures that welcomed youths of color and effectively discouraged drug taking (leaders felt it made gang members unreliable). Aside from being (often) the only game in town, poorly paid and dangerous jobs in the drug economy also benefited from some social cachet thanks to the first generation of African Americans to successfully break into the profitable higher echelons of the business—romantic self-styled outlaws like "Bumpy" Johnson.[36]

Most important of all, however, was racial segregation that quarantined young people of color and the heroin trade in the same neighborhoods. Police were central to this too, and with a final brutal irony: widespread corruption meant that police were often actively involved in drug trafficking, meaning that all the collateral damage their activities produced was often designed to take control of, rather than to stop, the heroin trade, and to keep it "out of sight" in segregated neighborhoods.[37]

The result was predictable: a new and destructive wave of heroin use that emerged with almost scalpel-like precision in America's poorest urban neighborhoods. African American and Latinx people were more likely to be heroin consumers, and the structural crises battering their neighborhoods meant that their using was more likely to lead to addiction and its many attendant problems. Popular culture portrayals of heroin use and addiction continued to focus on the fate of young white "hippies" whose rebellious forays into Black urban neighborhoods gave them access to informal heroin markets, but people of color became increasingly visible as heroin sellers and consumers.

The mid-1960s urban heroin epidemic came at a pivotal moment in America's racial history. After attaining historic success in the battle against Jim Crow–style segregation in the South, civil rights activists increasingly focused their attention on cities across the US, where a system of inequality hinging on residential segregation was often obscured as "informal" or de facto. The new campaigns, often grouped together as "Black Power," confronted a surging backlash from northern white Americans who suddenly faced demands for change, not in the faraway South, but in their own neighborhoods. Conservative politicians, who had been on the defensive in the face of civil rights activists' clear moral vision, began to stitch together a new coalition that repackaged white racial interests to avoid the moral taint of overt racism. Thus, for example, they announced their belief in racial equality and opposed what they described as racial preferences like affirmative action and school busing. "Color-blind conservatism," as one historian later called it, styled itself as following the model of civil rights heroes even as it rejected any solution to racial inequality that acknowledged the existence of race.[38]

But conservatives' most important, and most successful, move was to focus on crime. After all, by the 1970s no one could deny that American cities—home to the majority of people of color outside the South—were experiencing terrifying waves of crime. Indeed, African American communities themselves were demanding that authorities do something about crime in their neighborhoods.[39] But if African Americans hoped for better policing and more economic opportunity, conservative politicians saw different possibilities in the urban crime wave. Sensationalizing urban crime could be used as proof that liberal policies had failed and used to craft a new narrative of individual moral culpability that would crowd out stories of structural inequality. At the same time, crime rates could be used to heighten whites' fears of the city and to intensify their commitment to protecting their suburbs from any "invasion" by African American or Latinx people. Meanwhile, this strategy maneuvered liberals into the unenviable position of appearing to defend violent criminals by casting them, too, as victims.[40]

In this political context, the racially disparate heroin epidemic was especially useful as a symbol. And as a result, addiction among urban racial minorities became spectacularly visible, a quick go-to metaphor that conjured white people's political interests without explicitly articulating a white racial politics—or, at least, while creating a plausible deniability. As a symbol of urban racial decline and danger, heroin had finally completed its long journey from white medicine to Black drug.

3. A "Black" Drug in the Civil Rights Era

Just because heroin was sold preferentially in communities of color did not mean that African Americans and Latinx people were the only ones using heroin. Far from it. In fact, the late 1960s saw white "countercultural" youth pushing against the spatial boundaries of race in many cities, most famously the Haight-Ashbury neighborhood in San Francisco and Greenwich Village and East Village in New York City. Already skeptical of their parents' warnings about drugs because of their own experience with marijuana, these young urban explorers were unafraid of new drug experiences, including heroin. It did not take long before the relatively small, exclusive ranks of white heroin users had expanded dramatically. Meanwhile, Black and white soldiers serving in the Vietnam War also gained access to heroin markets, since the war unfolded in the so-called Golden Triangle where the vast majority of the world's opium was grown and processed.[41]

The mere existence of white heroin users did not necessarily disrupt the drug's new racial status. Instead it gave the drug even more political utility, since it provided lurid evidence that racialized cities posed a real and urgent threat to "mainstream"—that is, white—Americans. But at the same time, the presence of white victims required that drug policy maintain the kind of complexity embodied in the 1950s-era distinctions between "pushers" and "addicts." Dire punishments could be aimed at the former, but some form of rehabilitation needed to be preserved for the latter. This complexity, in fact, characterized the approach of President Richard Nixon when he oversaw a thorough transformation of the nation's federal drug policies and structures in 1970. On the one hand, punitive policing (for "pushers") was enhanced by the introduction of "no-knock" police raids and the transfer of policing from the old Federal Bureau of Narcotics, in the Treasury Department, to a new Drug Enforcement Administration in the Justice Department. On the other hand, opportunities for rehabilitation (for "addicts") were significantly expanded through funding for drug treatment, including, importantly, methadone maintenance as well as "therapeutic communities" and other programs based loosely on the model of Alcoholics Anonymous.[42]

The "medicalization" of heroin addiction was ambiguous and short-lived—at least in comparison to the more durable punitive policies that characterized what Nixon himself called a "war on drugs." The first politician to fully grasp the value of heroin as a political symbol was New York governor Nelson Rockefeller, who in the early 1970s was worried about his moderate reputation in an increasingly conservative Republican Party. New York City had been one of the centers of the 1950s pushback against punitive drug policies and had been home to a number of nominally progressive efforts to treat addiction as a sickness rather than a crime. Pointing to the city's spiraling crime rate, and claiming to have support from African American community leaders as well as suburban whites, Rockefeller announced in 1973 that these efforts had failed and that the time had come to stop being "soft" on drugs. Instead, he pushed for the draconian, punitive policies known as the "Rockefeller Drug Laws," whose central feature was long, mandatory prison sentences for even relatively minor crimes such as drug possession.[43]

Rockefeller's laws represented a rebalancing rather than a total transformation of American drug policy. It threatened the racialized pusher/user divide but did not entirely eliminate it. The laws did impose steep penalties for possession as well as selling, but it was drug "pushers" who came in for the harshest condemnation—though now described, in "color-blind" terms, as harming Black communities as well as white ones. Meanwhile, white suburbs received implicit and explicit assurances that their drug-using children were not the ones the governor had in his crosshairs—they were the victims, not the criminals. This was illustrated by marijuana possession charges, over which judges exercised significant discretion, deeming white youth victimized users and Black arrestees pushers.[44] Even so, the supposedly "medicalized" responses to white users' addiction were themselves shaped by a political impetus to demonstrate "tough love" to wayward youths. Therapeutic communities, for example, emphasized total abstinence and often complete psychic and moral reconstruction—a process that could be as harsh and moralistic as prison. Patients receiving methadone maintenance, meanwhile, were subjected to minute surveillance and punishment for any transgressions. Both forms of "treatment" were advertised as tools to reduce crime, and their effectiveness was measured almost exclusively by their impact on crime rates. Both were thus seamlessly integrated into the growing carceral response to drug use despite their optimistic rhetoric.

Although Rockefeller's approach was disastrous when judged as a response to a public health crisis, it was immediately successful as a political move. Conservative and liberal politicians alike competed to impose harsh punishments on drug "pushers" and "junkies" and to blame them for the nation's urban crisis.[45] By the end of the 1970s, heroin had become synonymous with the decline of America's nonwhite cities and with the threat those cities posed. It was a hardy political template, rejuvenated in the 1980s when the same structural factors that had given rise to heroin use in central cities produced a different drug crisis surrounding "crack," a cheap, smokable version of cocaine.

4. The Return of White Heroin Use

Something peculiar happened to heroin in the half century after Rockefeller clinched its transformation into a Black drug: it became white again, featuring centrally in newly refashioned cultural dramas of supposedly cataclysmic white decline, whose purpose, as always, was to muster the deployment of resources to shore up the privileges of White-ness. In the 1990s, the media began reporting on "new" heroin users—white middle-class youth and young adults. Indeed, middle-class, white heroin use was growing. This change in the demographics of heroin consumption was due in part to an influx of heroin from newly planted poppy fields in Colombia, whose cartels were competing with estab-lished Middle Eastern and Asian heroin distributors by dramatically lowering the price and increasing the purity of the heroin they sold in the United States cities. This development attracted middle-class users, who found they could snort instead of injecting the purer heroin.[46] "In what came to be known as "heroin chic," the upsurge in white heroin use coincided with the portrayal of heroin use in popular culture, including fashion photography. Based in the desire to create images of gritty realism, heroin chic created "a trope of the junkie as the ultimate, authentic critic who withdraws from society."[47]

These images typically portrayed emaciated models in urban, poor settings. Rizzo notes that heroin chic was predicated on references (albeit silent ones) to Blackness. She notes:

> Placing Black models in lower-class settings that evoke heroin use would be to create a situation that seemed too "real." It would conform to racist social expectations, and would reduce the possibility of identification between the ad's target audience—the angst-ridden white, middle-class hipster—and the product. Yet, the sense of style in the photos, the use of haute couture dress, and the attitude of the models all come together to suggest "coolness," and particularly the coolness of the heroin-using rebel. These models are "safe" because of their Whiteness, but exude a form of "coolness" potentially coded as "Black" which makes them desirable.[48]

Then-president Clinton pointed out the jarring juxtaposition of her-oin (widely perceived as Black) with the presumed innocence of whites. In May 1997, following the death from an overdose of the fashion pho-tographer Davide Sorrenti, Clinton came out strongly against "heroin chic" imagery. He noted that, when he was growing up, heroin was deeply feared as the worst possible drug. He said: "There were these horrible images associated with it—strung-out junkies lying on street corners in decidedly unglamorous ways." In contrast, he noted, "In the press in recent days, we've seen reports that many of our fashion leaders are now admitting—and I honor them for doing this—they're admitting flat-out that images projected in fashion photos in the last few years have made heroin addiction seem glamorous and sexy and cool."[49]

Heroin chic "whitened" heroin but did not disrupt the drug's traditional racial politics in America. Informal heroin markets continued to be physically located in urban spaces where racialized and marginalized populations had been segregated. Thus its sudden emergence among white youths could still be portrayed as an alien invasion, where it did not belong, and against which authorities must act decisively. The decisive action involved punitive action against so-called pushers (the 1990s was the decade when mass incarceration really began to heat up, thanks in part to drug arrests) combined with protections and treatment for innocent white youth ensnared by heroin.

5. Returning Full Circle: Heroin Becomes White Again

At the same time that heroin chic was emerging and being criticized, prescription opioids began to hit the market, creating a new generation of largely white heroin users. Nearly 90 percent of the people who tried heroin in the first decade of the new millennium were white.[50] Many of these new heroin users got their start with prescription opioids and turned to heroin, in part as a result of policy responses that cracked down on the prescription opioid supply.

The National Institute on Drug Abuse estimated that in 2012, 2.1 million people in the United States suffered from substance use disorders related to prescription opioid pain relievers. Ironically, it is also racism that likely kept the numbers of Black and Latinx people addicted to prescription opioids relatively low. Prescription opioids are more readily available in white communities than in communities of color. Numerous studies have shown that African Americans, in particular, are denied access to pain medication even when it is compellingly warranted. For example, Blacks are 34 percent less likely than whites to be prescribed opioids for back pain, abdominal pain, and migraines, and 14 percent less likely to be prescribed such medications for pain from traumatic injuries or surgery. Pharmacies in poor white neighborhoods are fifty-four times as likely as pharmacies in poor neighborhoods of color to have "adequate supplies" of opioids.[51] Not surprisingly, then, rates of overdose death from prescription opioids are higher among whites than Blacks: whites have had the "privilege" of almost unfettered access to prescription opioids, facilitated by higher rates of insurance and access to physicians.

Addiction to prescription opioids is at least in part a driver of the current wave of heroin use. In a study that pooled data from 2002 to

2012, the incidence of heroin initiation was nineteen times higher among those who reported prior nonmedical pain reliever use than among those who did not (0.39 vs. 0.02 percent).[52] Still, while non-medical prescription opioid use is a growing risk factor for starting heroin use, only a small fraction of people who use pain relievers switch to heroin use. Many who use opioids nonmedically are not actually those for whom the medication is prescribed; according to the National Survey on Drug Use and Health, 75 percent of all nonmedical opioid use starts with people using medication obtained from a friend, family member, or dealer. And, according to general population data from the National Survey on Drug Use and Health, fewer than 4 percent of people who had used prescription opioids nonmedically started using heroin within five years.[53] Maia Szalavitz notes: "A Cochrane review of opioid prescribing for chronic pain found that less than one percent of those who were well-screened for drug problems developed new addictions during pain care; a less rigorous, but more recent review put the rate of addiction among people taking opioids for chronic pain at 8–12 percent."[54] The boom in pharmaceutical opioid sales, in other words, finally landed white families in the same pickle that racialized families had been grappling with for nearly a century: raising children amid easily accessible, poorly regulated opioid markets.

While new addictions to heroin are relatively rare among those prescribed prescription pills, it is clear that our policy responses to the prescription pill crisis have contributed to an increase in heroin use. According to the National Institute on Drug Abuse: "Growing evidence suggests that abusers of prescription opioids are shifting to heroin as prescription drugs become less available or harder to abuse. For example, a recent increase in heroin use accompanied a downward trend in OxyContin abuse following the introduction of an abuse-deterrent formulation of that medication."[55]

Prescription opioids and heroin have similar chemical properties and effects, especially when administered by the same method, making heroin appealing to those addicted to prescription opioids who cannot access pills easily. The initial policy response to prescription opioids was to crack down on their supply without offering any meaningful alternative or route out of addiction. In addition to abuse-deterrent formulations, which make prescription opioids difficult to crush and inject, there have been a number of efforts to discourage the prescribing of pain medications and an increase policing of physicians' prescribing practices.[56] For example, prescription drug monitoring programs, which require physicians to check a database before prescribing pain medications to patients, have been associated with a decrease in prescribing and an increase in heroin use.[57] Unless accompanied by new addiction treatment programs, these supply-side tactics leave those addicted with few alternatives but to turn to heroin.

Those transitioning from pills to heroin note that heroin is cheaper, is more available, and provides a better high. And the price of heroin has decreased in recent years.[58] In one study of people in treatment for opioid addiction, 94 percent said they chose to use heroin because prescription opioids were "far more expensive and harder to obtain."[59]

The number of past-year heroin users in the United States nearly doubled between 2005 and 2012, from 380,000 to 670,000. The Centers for Disease Control and Prevention (CDC) counted 10,574 heroin overdose deaths in 2014, which represents more than a fivefold increase of the heroin death rate from 2002 to 2014.[60] In 2017, the CDC reported that for the first time ever, more than 50,000 people had died from drug overdoses in the US, outnumbering deaths from automobile accidents. Rates of drug overdose are increasing among all racial groups, but for the first decade and a half of this century the greatest increases were among whites. Between 1999 and 2015, rates for non-Hispanic Blacks increased 63 percent, and for Hispanic people 43 percent. Among whites during the same period, the increase was 240 percent. Increasingly heroin rather than prescription drugs is driving these deaths; in 2015, the percentage of drug overdose deaths involving heroin (25 percent) was triple the percentage in 1999 (8 percent). By 2020, overdose death rates had accelerated at unprecedented rates for all ethnic-racial groups in the midst of the COVID pandemic; however, for the first time since 1999, the overdose death rate among Black Americans exceeded that of white Americans, with the highest overdose death rate among Native Americans.[61]

THE ENDANGERED WHITE AMERICAN

The outpouring of sentiment in media coverage surrounding the heroin overdose death of actor Philip Seymour Hoffman in 2014 crystallized a decade of media fascination with the white prescription opioid–cum-heroin user. Through the 2000s, news headlines had sounded the call of the most recent American moral panic surrounding drugs—this time among white, suburban youth and the middle-aged white housewife next door: on Fox News "The New Face of Drug Addiction," on NBC News "Painkiller Use Breeds New Face of Heroin Addiction," on Today

"Hooked: A Teacher's Addiction," and on ABC News "Heroin in Suburbia: The New Face of Addiction" and "The New Face of Heroin Addiction."[62] Although the race and ethnicity of the protagonists in these stories were rarely explicitly mentioned, it was clear from the photos, the surnames, and the locales (Vermont; Maine; Newton, Massachusetts, West Los Angeles) that the novelty was their Whiteness and the shock that (presumed white and middle-class) readers would experience from realizing that "they are just like us!"

The assumption in the media accounts is that white communities have heretofore been free from drugs; these neighborhoods are not the expected place to find drug use. As one news reporter puts it: "This isn't about inner cities and successive generations of unemployed addicts. This about suburbia, and rural America—Amish country, for heaven's sake—and middle-class high school students who have seen their lives unexpectedly derailed."[63] Underlying this surprise is the assumption that drug use is to be expected and generational in poor, ethnic minority urban communities, but not in suburban and rural white America. White drug use is always defined in relation to stereotypes and assumptions about drug use in communities of color.

These white heroin users are not only "new" but largely blameless. Media accounts of how white people become addicted to heroin typically follow one of three tropes: (1) a young person started using the prescription medications of their parents or grandparents; (2) the person "fell in with a bad crowd"; or (3) the person was prescribed painkillers for an illness or injury and then became addicted to them. This story from suburban Minneapolis is typical: "Ashton, 20, grew up in North Branch in a loving, supportive family. He was a stellar student and athlete until he found a new crowd in middle school. They smoked weed and drank on the weekends. Seeking acceptance, he became a user, then a dealer, which gave him ready access to cocaine, meth and ecstasy. After his father had back surgery, Ashton and his friends scavenged his supply of pain medication."[64]

Ashton moved on to heroin despite his loving, supportive family and his stellar performance in school and in sports—neither he nor his family was to blame. He simply fell in with a new crowd, and he had ready access through his dealing connections and through the prescriptions from his father's back surgery. Given our deeply rooted fears about and stigma surrounding drug use and drug users, these explanations about why and how Ashton began using drugs help construct him as someone who, despite his drug use and his drug dealing, is sympathetic and relatable.

Similarly, iatrogenic medicine (people getting hooked as the result of a doctor's prescription and care) is a common explanation for how people eventually became addicted to heroin in white communities—one that helps lay the blame somewhere beyond the individual user, casting him or her as an "innocent victim." The *Tampa Tribune* explains how one woman fell victim: "In fall 2010, Julie Schenecker 'fell into a severe depression,' the documents state. 'During this time she began to pull away from friends and family and began to undergo a series of surgeries that resulted in her addiction to pain killers, in particular Oxycontin.'"[65]

In contrast, in stories about Black and Latinx people who use drugs, the criminality of their actions is the story. Steiner and Argothy argue in their analysis of the courts that "the contemporary drug war promulgates a profoundly racist illusion that represents white illicit drug abuse as a private health problem and Black illicit drug abuse as a public 'criminal' activity."[66] The causal backstories about addiction afforded to white people are important, not just for explaining the supposedly new white opioid epidemic, but also for keeping them blameless and offering a rationale for keeping white users out of the drug war.

This racial logic has enabled a broader political project to be built out of the opioid crisis. This project was most potently exemplified in 2015 in a story widely reported in the mainstream media. Anne Case and Angus Deaton had reported in the *Proceedings of the National Academy of Sciences* their finding of a significant decline in life expectancy for middle-aged whites, reversing a decades-long trend of increasing longevity. They noted that drug overdose, suicide, and alcohol-related liver disease were driving the premature deaths of poorly educated, middle-aged whites to such an extent as to affect the life expectancy of the entire cohort of middle-aged white Americans. Meanwhile, the life expectancy for middle-aged Black and Latinx people continued to increase during the same period, although middle-aged Blacks still had a significantly higher mortality rate than whites. Case and Deaton noted that deaths among middle-aged whites were also associated with increased reports of pain and mental distress and could be linked to economic insecurity.[67] These so-called deaths of despair, along with the rapid approach of the loss of whites' majority (it is estimated that by 2043, people of color will outnumber whites in the US), led to increased racial anxiety. The thousands of drug overdose deaths among people of color barely got mentioned, while the news of increasing white deaths created a tsunami of alarm, an outpouring of media coverage, and new approaches to drug policy.

Demographer Shannon Monnat conducted analyses showing that in geographic regions hard hit by these deaths, Trump did amazingly well, as much as 10 to 16 percent better than Romney in 2008. Class and economic despair seemed to be driving much of this. According to Monnat: "In the kinds of places that I'm talking about, jobs have been declining for at least three decades, and the dignity of work has been replaced by suffering and the feeling that the people in power don't care about them. . . . All of these things are working together to drive Trump's over-performance. And they're really reflecting larger systemic social and economic problems that go beyond drugs, alcohol and suicide mortality."[68] An in-depth analysis of "the addiction crisis" in the *Washington Post* in 2016 similarly observed: "The most compelling predictor of any U.S. county's partisan shift between 2012 and 2016 was not race, income or education levels but health. The most dramatic changes in voting patterns happened in counties with low life expectancy and high rates of diabetes, obesity and heavy drinking."[69]

Trump rarely spoke directly about drugs during his campaign, but when he did, he played to the racial anxieties of many white working-class voters. He promised to use the Wall (along the US-Mexico border) to keep out heroin, while deporting "gang members [and] drug dealers." Addressing the rise in overdose deaths at a campaign rally in Ohio, he said: "We need the wall. We need to stop illegal immigration. We will stop it. We're not going to have drugs pouring into our country and destroying our youth." As in the reefer madness scare of the 1930's, Trump's rhetoric fomented fear of Mexican drugs and Mexican immigrants poisoning the presumed white and innocent American countryside. He called for the literal building of walls to protect whites from people of color and the drugs associated with them. The day after his inauguration, Trump posted a statement about his approach to law enforcement, which read in part: "Our job is not to make life more comfortable for the rioter, the looter, or the violent disrupter. Our job is to make life more comfortable for parents who want their kids to be able to walk the streets safely. . . . President Trump is committed to building a border wall to stop illegal immigration, to stop the gangs and the violence, and to stop the drugs from pouring into our communities. . . . It is the first duty of government to keep the innocent safe."[70]

Drugs, and particularly heroin, in this view, are part of what is threatening the sanctity of white life—the threat against which we need to be protected. White heroin use is rooted, not in any structural causes or problems inherent in white poor communities, but in external threats from Mexicans abroad. To protect innocent and valued white life, we need to build literal walls to keep out Mexicans and to increase "law and order" to control Black Americans, referred to here as rioters, looters, and violent disrupters.

This kind of racist rhetoric has proven successful in mobilizing many white people and expresses both an identification with white supremacy and deep-rooted fears about its precarity. As noted above, there is a strong association between declining white life expectancy and "deaths of despair," including opioid overdoses and pain, economic insecurity, and mental distress. This raises the question of what is causing whites, especially poor, middle-aged whites, so much pain and distress. As Samuel Preston, a professor of sociology at the University of Pennsylvania, said in response to the Case and Deaton article: "This [declining life expectancy] is a vivid indication that something is awry in these American households."[71] Scholars of Whiteness, like Linda Alcoff, have posited that the impeding loss of majority status along with the moral emptiness of the Whiteness at the core of the mythical American dream causes anxiety that can be easily mobilized by racist rhetoric and actions (not to mention that white elites have long offered illusory race privilege to win white working-class loyalty).[72]

Others, including most famously W. E. B Du Bois and James Baldwin, have posited that there is a cost for whites in maintaining their Whiteness. Perhaps this cost is now finally coming due for white Americans in the form of declining life expectancy. As more and more attention is brought to bear on the socially constructed nature of Whiteness, its threatened status, the extraordinary damage it creates, and the violence and inhumanity inherent in maintaining Whiteness are being exposed perhaps in new ways. The Movement for Black Lives is just one example of efforts to reveal and repudiate the brutality of white supremacy. With these kinds of exposures, whites are confronted with both the emptiness of Whiteness and the moral erosion of their own values and humanity. As Baldwin puts it:

> This moral erosion has made it quite impossible for those who think of themselves as white in this country to have any moral authority at all—privately, or publicly. The multitudinous bulk of them sit, stunned, before their TV sets, swallowing garbage that they know to be garbage, and—in a profound and unconscious effort to justify this torpor that disguises a profound and bitter panic—pay a vast amount of attention to athletics. . . . But this cowardice, this necessity of justifying a totally false identity and of justifying what must be called a genocidal history, has placed everyone now living into the hands of the most ignorant and powerful people the world has ever seen: And how did they get that way? By deciding that they were white. By opting

for safety instead of life. By persuading themselves that a Black child's life meant nothing compared with a white child's life. By abandoning their children to the things white men could buy. By informing their children that Black women, Black men and Black children had no human integrity that those who call themselves white were bound to respect. And in this debasement and definition of Black people, they debased and defamed themselves.[73]

Although Baldwin wrote forty years ago, TV remains a favorite source of torpor for white Americans (many of whom did in 2016 elect a reality TV star as president), but so too do opioids and heroin. What we are suggesting is that part of why many white Americans are using heroin and prescription pills—some of the reason they are dying "deaths of despair"—is rooted in the toxic nature of Whiteness itself. Drugs are a way to medicate, to forget, to deny the reality that Whiteness is hollow.

WASTED WHITENESS: WHITE DRUG USE AS TRAGEDY

White people who use heroin are not only sympathetic in popular media because of how and why they started using drugs. Their stories are depicted as particularly tragic because they are seen to have wasted their tremendous potential—more was hoped of them and for them. The idea that whites who use drugs are squandering their privilege and putting their status at risk has been noted in analyses of both stoner films and the reality TV show *Intervention*. Sears and Johnson claim that stoner films are on one level about "the specter of seeing white domination go 'up in smoke'—via wasting, as opposed to hoarding, white privilege."[74] In her analysis of *Intervention*, Daniels notes that "virtually every episode of *Intervention* follows this form of wasted Whiteness and squandered white privilege."[75] According to Daniels, producers of this show intentionally construct the stories in each episode around white subjects as a way to challenge the stereotype of addiction. Within these media narratives, portrayals of white drug simultaneously challenge stereotypes of addiction afflicting primarily Black and Brown people and reinforce the expectations that white people should fulfill their privileged potential to be "productive" neoliberal citizens.

In our systematic content analysis of one hundred randomly selected national news articles on heroin and opioids published in 2001 and 2011, we found that media accounts of white drug use go out of their way to humanize the person using drugs, to explain how he or she defies the stereotype of a drug user, and then to describe the potential that the individual tragically lost. These are accounts of personal, individualized tragedy—not the impersonal arrest reports that characterize media accounts of drug use in Black and Latinx communities.[76]

These stories, which are often about the tragic death of a young person due to opioid overdose, create an identification between the imagined white reader and the victim. The underlying assumption is that the reader is white, and the victim is often contrasted to a "real addict"—an unnamed other freighted with stigma. As a story from the *Roanoke Times*, "It Happened to a Bright Kid Like Ian," puts it: "I'm not talking about homeless, bum-looking street people—I'm talking about relatively affluent, well-dressed, high-achieving Volvo-driving kids, kids who belong to the honor societies, who play soccer and lacrosse, kids headed to the good schools."[77]

The stories about white drug use also go out of their way to reassure us that these individuals, even though they use drugs, are familiar folks. The media accounts are replete with references to how the people in these stories "could be you." As one woman noted: "It's the person in line beside you at Publix, the woman next to you in the pew at church."[78]

Once the identification between the reader and the victim has been made, the stories generally recount the tremendous potential that was lost to drugs or to overdose death. This account below is typical of many of these stories, which describe a relatively young person who got addicted to drugs and lost everything, including his life: "John Garrighan was a smart, precocious musician who at 14 formed a pop-punk band that, by the time he was 22, had toured nationally and sold thousands of albums. After eight years of shooting up, dozens of stints at rehabilitation clinics and then relapses, he overdosed in the restroom of a Squirrel Hill coffee shop on Jan. 29 and died the next day."[79]

The story goes on to talk about how his brother, parents, and friends are mourning, not just his death, but his lost potential. Often these stories are told by bereft parents or friends either as opinion pieces or as extensive quotes by the reporters. In this story from Batesville, Indiana, a father is quoted at length talking about the death of his daughter to a high school auditorium filled with students: "Manda was the best thing that ever happened in my life, and even though Manda had two parents who loved her unconditionally, had good friends, went to good schools and had good teachers . . . she let the beast of drug addiction take over her."[80]

Significantly, drug addiction is an external threat, a "beast," not an inherent flaw in Manda's good character; that character was tragically overcome by the "beast." Generally accompanied by a picture of the lost loved one, these accounts often go into great depth about the person's life: what they did in school, who their friends were, what they hoped to do in the future, what hobbies they enjoyed. We found no stories of overdose deaths in Black and Latinx communities, although we know overdose happens in those communities as well. Rather, as noted above, we found arrest stories. The only details of the individuals involved included name, age, and criminal charge. The individuals in those stories were not afforded particulars about their lives, their families, their hopes and aspirations.

The stories of the deaths of white people are considered tragic in part because of the underlying assumption of promise and privilege lost. Because of drugs, people normally expected to be "productive" cannot fulfill the obligations and expectations that (a neoliberal) society has for them. As Lane DeGregory of the *Tampa Bay Times* notes, with the increasing opioid crisis in white communities, "Hard workers can no longer hold jobs. Smart students drop out. Good moms neglect their kids, drain their bank accounts, steal from family members."[81] Part of the implied tragedy is that of squandered Whiteness and a system of advantages to which Black and Latinx people have limited access. The ways that this systemic advantage is built on racial inequality go unflagged. Nor do these accounts of white opioid use mention the criminal justice system that disproportionately disciplines Black and Latinx people.

HEROIN DEPENDENCE AS DISABILITY

One way that wasted Whiteness can be partially reclaimed is by considering addiction as a disability. Although a discourse of addiction as a disabling "chronic brain disease" has permeated the institutions that interface with people who use drugs across races, for Black and Latinx urban heroin users, fears of their violence and welfare dependency have led to pharmaceutical containment—to co-occurring psychiatric diagnoses and to sedating medications that qualify them for Social Security benefits while reducing their risk of committing crime. For white heroin users, federal and state legislatures, pharmaceutical manufacturers, and community physicians have conjointly developed a new apparatus of private office opioid maintenance designed to rescue white youth—to endow them with "pharmaceutical citizenship," that is, through psychotropics that "bring the patient back into (middle-class consumer) society."[82] These contrasts make visible the convergence of biological and political vulnerabilities in the efforts of middle-class whites to reproduce their privilege: that is, to stay in mid- to upper-level service industry jobs and stave off the need for public benefits. US middle-class whites face a crisis of social reproduction in the face of a volatile, globalized service economy that is exporting jobs, as well as growing individual debt and credit financing with increasing rates of foreclosure and bankruptcy. In this setting, exclusive, patented pharmaceuticals serve as a commoditized racial rescue agent in the epoch of disaster capitalism.

Below we trace the impact of disabilities-framing responses to patients being treated for heroin addiction whom we followed over four years in New York City: Ruben, a Puerto Rican whose Social Security benefits require him to take multiple psychotropic medications, and Jonathan, a white college student whose opioid maintenance medication allows him to complete his degree and plan a career.

Ironically, during the very period of the ascendance of methadone maintenance for Black and Latinx heroin addiction—from 1972 to 1996—federal law made disability from drug and alcohol addiction eligible for Social Security benefits. The 1970s had seen liberalization of public attitudes toward public entitlement programs, which led Congress to allow Social Security payments for applicants with alcoholism or drug addiction as a primary disabling diagnosis.[83] By 1996, the Ronald Reagan and post-Reagan discourse of "personal accountability" led to a reversal of this law. In 1994, in the midst of mounting media coverage of welfare abuses and pressure on Congress to cut entitlement programs, *Dateline* and *60 Minutes* aired exposes of overdose deaths from drugs purchased with Social Security checks. Reporters claimed that "the Social Security Department is the largest supplier of drug and alcohol to addicts in America" and that the Social Security Administration's Drug Addiction and Alcoholism program was "a misguided enabler of addiction."[84]

The year 1996 was a watershed: the federal government abruptly discontinued Social Security beneficiaries who had qualified with an alcoholism or drug dependence diagnosis, and the new Personal Responsibility and Work Opportunity Reconciliation Act imposed five-year lifetime limits on welfare eligibility across the board. This meant a sea change for low-income Americans whose families and neighborhoods had subsisted on SSI and welfare payments. Caseloads shifted as alcohol- and drug-dependent Social Security beneficiaries either got recertified under another psychiatric diagnosis or lost disability benefits, and as masses of people formerly on welfare applied for Social Security under a psychiatric diagnosis. As a result, Social Security rolls increased fourfold between 1996 and 1998, with young adults representing the fastest-growing group,[85] and the largest single area of growth in mental and psychiatric disorders.[86]

This growth created a virtual industry of Social Security qualification, replete with a new class of "neurocrats" who evaluate the veracity of psychiatric claims,[87] including state-funded case managers trained to coach clients off state welfare rolls and onto the federally funded SSI program to save the state funds, and private lawyers who demand as much as 25 percent of awarded monthly Social Security checks.[88] Qualifying and recertifying for Social Security payments on the basis of psychiatric disability requires clinical assessments and medical records that demonstrate functional impairment from mental illness. Social Security applicants are advised to stay on high-dose antipsychotics and mood stabilizers as evidence of severe, disabling symptoms, despite their side effects, in order to strengthen their case for disability benefits.

As a result, maintenance medications, such as antipsychotics and mood stabilizers combined with methadone, and Social Security payments based on co-occurring psychiatric disorders enable low-income, opioid-addicted people to survive but also marginalize them socially and economically. The multiple, sedating psychotropic regimens of SSI beneficiaries contrast with those of middle-class opioid-dependent people, whose doctors limit medications with side effects that interfere with function at school and work.

Ruben's story makes the landscape of Social Security disability payments and medical maintenance visible. Ruben is New York Puerto Rican, born in the Lower East Side projects of Manhattan and the oldest of twelve children. He is the son of a Korean War veteran who returned home with one arm, and with a morphine-cum-heroin habit that Ruben discovered in high school when he accidentally walked in on his father's war buddy injecting his father's remaining arm.

Ruben's father died of AIDS and his mother of alcohol-related organ failure a few years later. Ruben moved out, determined to become a taxpaying, substance-free citizen. Eventually, however, while he was driving Access-a-Ride vans for seniors and disabled children, his boss introduced him to heroin. He later discovered that his boss was making a sizable side income providing free heroin samples to his employees and later, as they needed larger quantities over time, charging them for heroin by docking their pay.

Ruben violently confronted his boss about this narcotic entrapment, left his job, became homeless, and ended up at Bellevue's methadone clinic. There his psychiatrist helped him qualify for Supplemental Security Income (SSI) based on his unpredictable angry explosions, for which he got a bipolar disorder diagnosis. SSI checks allowed him to pay his rent in unlicensed supportive housing; he signed over $500 per month from his Social Security check for a closet-sized room and a shared bathroom with eighteen other men in a rundown walkup on a notoriously dangerous strip in Brownsville, Brooklyn. Social Security also made him eligible for Medicaid coverage, which paid for his methadone and psychiatric treatment.

Ruben's clinic introduced him to art therapy. Over the subsequent three years he spent hours every day in the clinic's studio. He eventually joined an "outsider art" movement in the city and began identifying himself an artist. Emboldened by the fact that his art was being displayed and sold in galleries, he called his estranged brother and sister and arranged to meet them at his sister's house. On his arrival, his sister, who over the years had referred to Ruben as "crazy" and "the addict" (despite her own history of crack cocaine use), waved away Ruben's printed invitation to a gallery show of his work, saying, "You still on heroin?" Ruben left her house vowing never to return, and thankful that he had not told her about his bipolar diagnosis.

In Ruben's mind, working for pay and living independently would make him an adult, a citizen, someone who could answer to his sister. Ironically, it was Ruben's effort to enter the licit service economy, as an Access-a-Ride driver, that led him to heroin. With a psychiatric disability, he became eligible for housing and art therapy. Without it, Ruben most likely would have ended up on the default route of addicted working-class Puerto Ricans: prison.

Ironically, 1996, the year that the federal government excluded addiction as the basis for SSI eligibility, and the year that welfare reform instituted time limits on benefits, was the same year that Purdue Pharmaceuticals marketed OxyContin as a "minimally addictive pain reliever" in suburban and rural America, sowing the seeds for a separate heroin epidemic started by privatized, industry-led initiatives.

As suburban and rural white prescription opioid users transitioned to heroin once tamper-resistant opioid formulations and new prescription monitoring laws made prescription opioids hard to get and to use, heroin poisoning deaths in New York City increased, accelerating in 2014 after a long negative trend, with the largest increase in largely white and suburban Staten Island.[89] Of heroin users surveyed, 80 percent had used prescription opioids first, compared to 1 percent who had used heroin before prescription opioids.[90] Media coverage of whites as the "new face of heroin" was followed by calls for a "gentler war on drugs."[91] Media and community movements mobilized in support of white narcotic exceptionalism to shelter suburban and rural users from drug war reasoning. A geographically distinct network of community physicians provided buprenorphine maintenance, designed to maintain addicts' function and membership in the broader community by mainstreaming their treatment in primary care clinics.

This biomedicalizing movement is rooted in a concept of addiction as a chronic brain disease requiring pharmaceutical treatment, as illustrated by the biography of Jonathan, a white man in his twenties living with his parents in suburban Queens. Jonathan's father himself was unable to work because of a severely debilitating chronic condition for which he was prescribed opioids, opioids that Jonathan stole from his father and took with friends, and that eventually led them to heroin as their tolerance and need for supplies went up. Jonathan's heroin use led his parents to bring him to the same public addiction clinic that Ruben attended, where Jonathan also participated in art therapy groups. Unlike Ruben, who accepted that he would probably be on Social Security Disability payments for the rest of his life, Jonathan, and his psychiatrist, who prescribed him buprenorphine and antidepressants, were preoccupied with his taking a developmental step from his youthful heroin use and mood swings into adult responsibilities and financial independence. Group therapy, especially art therapy, was a way to wrest Jonathan away from his high school friends, who got high in their parents' basements. In art therapy, Jonathan discovered his love for the video camera, and on his therapist's advice he enrolled in City College to study film production. His doctor never suggested that he apply for Social Security: rather, he framed Jonathan's "chronic relapsing brain disease" as one to be medically managed, to allow him to finish college and find competitive work.

On good days, Jonathan attended college classes and worked part time in a department store, imagining that a future film production internship would one day land him artistically satisfying jobs. On bad days, Jonathan's depression and nihilistic thoughts about never earning enough to move out of his parents' apartment led him to relapse. His vulnerability was brought home by the overdose death of a long-term friend who had been progressing in job training but had decided to become "drug free" and wean himself off opioid maintenance treatment before he died. Tears welled in Jonathan's eyes when he learned of his friend's death: "He hadn't called me for a long time. I guess he didn't want me to know he wasn't doing well. When I did see him he looked skinny, he was probably already back to using."

Jonathan was younger and more middle class than most of the other patients in the public hospital addiction clinic in which his parents had enrolled him. His counselors and psychiatrist at the clinic discussed his case in different terms than those of most other patients; they spoke of his developmental stage and his need to accept a new identity as someone who was disabled but who could grow into a bright future with appropriate medical and psychological support. In contrast to Ruben's counselors, who saw their job as keeping Ruben out of jail, the problem that Jonathan's counselors implicitly identified his problem as whether he could reproduce the middle-class life he grew up with in an economy that might no longer afford him the insulation of white privilege that it had in the postwar years of industrial growth.

THE BOUNDARIES OF WHITENESS

Making heroin white did not eliminate the problems of heroin use among Black and Brown people. While attention has gone to heroin use among whites over the past two decades, communities of color not only have historically borne the brunt of heroin but continue to suffer today. While until 2017 the rate of increase for heroin deaths was highest among whites, it then rose in communities of color: from 2013 on, overdose rates increased the fastest among Black Americans.[92]

Even as calls for treatment and harm reduction grow in white communities, the war on drugs rages on in communities of color. Racist policing, disparate sentencing, and gross racial disparities in incarceration persist, reaffirming the link between Black and Latinx drug use and criminality in the public imagination and subjecting people of color to the criminal justice system and its devastating collateral consequences as reflected by disparities in overall drug arrests.[93] Though white people make up nearly two-thirds of the overall US population, they constitute only 28.4 percent of all drug arrests, while African Americans make up 45.0 percent and Latinx 24.0 percent of drug arrests.[94]

While people of color bear the brunt of the costs of racializing drug policy, it is important to recognize another unpleasant fact made invisible by white heroin: the cost borne by white communities. However much they may target communities of color, punitive drug laws are blunt instruments that also harm many white drug consumers, especially low-income white people. Recent analyses of incarceration data, for example, have shown that the number of new Black prison inmates fell by about 25 percent and the number of Hispanic inmates fell by about 30 percent from 2006 to 2013. In contrast, the number of new white inmates fell by only about 8 percent. However, a deeper dive into the data reveals that the real uptick in white prisoners stems from small, rural counties (described as "mostly white and politically conservative counties"), where people are about 50 percent more likely to go to prison than people in populous counties.[95] It appears, in another of US history's ironies, that poor whites have fewer protections when they live in rural, predominantly white places without the legacy of civil rights activism and resulting institutions that provide alternatives to incarceration such as public addiction services and harm reduction.

Race, which has always played a pivotal role in our portrayals of drug use and addiction, is intertwined with class. For example, according to the CDC, while heroin use has risen among all income levels, heroin addiction rates among people who make less than $20,000 a year are 3.4 times higher than in people who make over $50,000.[96] And while much of the media coverage has focused on young, suburban heroin users, poor white rural areas are among the hardest hit. Policies in response to white drug use, which have trended toward the more compassionate and therapeutic, are not evenly distributed across class and geography.

In the case of methamphetamine, another drug largely coded as white, we saw punitive responses directed at a highly stigmatized group of white poor rural users. Methamphetamine has been constructed as a white drug used in poor rural communities, one that denotes declining white status and cultural anxieties about white social position.[97] Meth users have been "constructed as the bottom of the white racial-economic spectrum: 'white trash.'"[98] Interestingly, meth users, though disparaged, are less linked to violence and are portrayed in a more contextualized and sympathetic way than crack users.[99] Similarly, Tunnell argues that when OxyContin first emerged in rural, poor Appalachia, it was socially constructed as "hillbilly heroin," a white drug.[100] This intersection of Whiteness and class is also apparent in sympathetic media coverage of nonmedical use of stimulants (such as Ritalin, Adderall) by middle-class and affluent white entrepreneurs and hard workers facing escalating academic and job pressures.[101] When an epidemic—like the current heroin problem—is coded as a middle-class white, largely suburban problem, different representational strategies and interventions are invoked. Individual white drug users are portrayed as largely blameless victims of their own biology, and deserving of help, such as treatment and prevention of complications like overdose and infection.[102] In contrast, the (re)criminalization of heroin in poor, white, politically conservative areas may demonstrate that there, poor rural whites serve as quasi-racialized "others"; they are incarcerated and their children placed in foster care at rates that approach those of Blacks in racially segregated US cities.[103]

A DEADLY FENTANYL FOOTNOTE TO WHITE DISASTER CAPITALISM

At a 2017 drug policy conference, a physician working in the Rhode Island prison system held up his pen to demonstrate how fentanyl, the synthetic opioid that was rapidly infiltrating the street opioid supply, differed from heroin: "Just to give you perspective, this pen is about the size of a day's worth of heroin." He then took the cap off of the pen.

> And now, for fentanyl, we're not even talking about this cap. We're talking about the tip of this pen as the amount of fentanyl that could kill someone who is tolerant to a pen's worth of heroin. I've seen it many, many times. People drop dead from a pen tip's worth of fentanyl, and many of them don't even know there's fentanyl in what they are taking. You bet that it is easier for smugglers to get fentanyl wherever they're going; think about how much money you can make from a supply the size of this pen!

As he explained, not only is fentanyl forty times more potent than heroin and far less costly to produce, but it lingers in the bloodstream thirty to forty times longer than heroin. He cited a study of an outbreak of emergency room admissions for fentanyl overdose in a one-week period: seventeen out of eighteen patients with confirmed fentanyl overdose required additional doses of the opioid reversal agent naloxone after eight hours, and four required continuous infusions of naloxone. This fit with the belief among physicians that more naloxone was required to reverse fentanyl than to reverse heroin, and the knowledge that fentanyl's effects outlast those of naloxone.[104]

Fentanyl, first synthesized in Belgium by Paul Janssen of Janssen Pharmaceuticals in 1959, first appeared in street markets in 1979 in California under the name "China White." For a decade it was used mostly in suburban West Coast neighborhoods.[105]

It is well documented that by the 2000s, after the successful marketing of prescription opioids paved the way for heroin trade to move from large port cities into small town and rural America, and as prescription drug monitoring and tamper-resistant opioid formulations left prescription opioid–dependent people stranded and desperate, heroin became a cheaper and more available opiate of last resort.[106] A first wave of prescription opioid overdose deaths starting in 2000 was thus followed by a second wave of heroin overdose deaths between 2007 and 2015. Fentanyl and related ultrapotent synthetic opioids led to a third wave of opioid trade, starting in 2013. Mostly produced in China but entering the US through Canada and Mexico, fentanyl is more efficiently smuggled and is now widely mixed into heroin and other illegally sold drug supplies, often without the knowledge of consumers. State narcotics bureaus reported an increase of fentanyl in street supplies of 1400 percent from 2015 to 2017, and overdose deaths from synthetic opioids—primarily fentanyl—rose 174 percent in the top eight most burdened states from 2013 to 2014.[107]

Unlike heroin, which is consciously sought out by most users, when fentanyl first reached street markets, not all people who purchased it, knowingly or unknowingly, found its effects pleasant. Some reported that it put them to sleep and others that it made them lash out uncontrollably.[108] Further, many feared the ease with which those injecting fentanyl overdosed. Most of them knew well the danger of overdose from fentanyl, having seen firsthand many people die from fentanyl-laced supplies. Those interviewed about their use of fentanyl-laced heroin supplies described elaborate ways that they attempted to judge the presence or absence of fentanyl in street supplies, sought out trusted dealers who would be honest about the contents of their supplies, and used fentanyl testing strips—which are now available from harm reduction centers and even pharmacies in some regions—to assess the contents of their purchases.[109] The shifting terrain of unknown "heroin" contents appears to be widening power differentials based on the ability of consumers to protect themselves. In a series of studies, women were twice as likely as men to report unintentional exposure to fentanyl.[110] Black people who die of overdose are more likely than white people to have been exposed to fentanyl,[111] and rates of death involving fentanyl exposure are rising faster for Black and Latinx Americans than for white Americans.[112] Importantly, fentanyl-related overdose is also rising among recently incarcerated people,[113] and it is a key factor in the disproportionate rise of overdose deaths among Black people.[114]

Fentanyl exposure, then, is the latest iteration of a century-long cycle of racialized harms from drugs that were initiated by white middle-class consumption but later spread to, and concentrated among, people of color (as well as those marginalized by gender and class). White middle-class consumers, predictably, have used their resources to shield themselves from the least desirable effects of those drugs. They are more likely to be able to test their supplies and to pay more for supplies with known contents from known sellers; they also appear to be distancing themselves socially and politically from those who are now left holding the bag of fentanyl in the latest chapter of our epic American opioid crisis.

CHAPTER 8

From Racial Capitalism to Biosocial Justice

Our breath unfurled in the November chill of Downtown East Side, Vancouver's major docking and shipping port. For over a century, Downtown East Side had been home to single-room occupancy hotels, bars, and brothels serving longshoremen and seasonal dock workers. Over the decades, as machines replaced human workers on the docks, the demand for formal port labor dried up, making room for heroin trade in the 1960s–70s, for crack in the 1980s–90s, and then, by the 2000s, back to what was sold as heroin but was often actually an ultra-potent synthetic opioid like fentanyl. More recently, affluent people were moving to Vancouver, drawn by its breathtaking views of the harbor and surrounding mountains, as well as thriving technology and media industries. They pushed housing prices up and, with that, homelessness among low-income East Side residents. This morning, those who had spent the night on the steps of its office buildings circled an unmarked door, waiting for it to open. It was the entrance to INSITE, the harm reduction center and safe injection facility that, for decades, had distinguished Vancouver as a world center for overdose prevention. A young woman with a nose ring ushered us through a side door to give us a tour before opening for business. Leading us through brightly lit rooms, she explained that the injection booths had been adapted from hair salon booths, which was why they featured three-way mirrors framed by rows of lightbulbs. The bulbs and mirrors helped clients see their arms clearly and thus avoid the skin abscesses that were a compli-

cation of missed veins. Abscesses could progress to life-threatening sep-
tic shock by the time they were seen by a doctor. Clients avoided hospitals; in their experience, hospital staff were likely to humiliate or ignore
them because of their drug use. That was why INSITE employed medical staff. Showing us the exam room where she treated infections and
wounds and, at times, gathered evidence of sexual assault, our guide
told us that she had become a registered nurse just so she could work at
INSITE.

Mulling over the statistic that not a single lethal overdose had
occurred at INSITE despite thousands of onsite injections over three
decades, we walked three blocks further to a women's safe injection site
called Sister Space. Overstuffed couches surrounded a long kitchen table
where women ate meals together. As a client watered the green vines
framing the windows, the director explained that women needed a safe
space because so many of them had been assaulted on the streets. These
are poor women, she reminded us. To survive, many stay with abusive
men or do sex work under violent conditions. Their children are often
taken by child protective services, on the basis of urine tests for drug use
alone and many times without indication of danger to their children.
She pointed out that wealthy and middle-class women in Canada also
use drugs but are protected by their financial and social resources from
child removal. Atira, the organization sponsoring Sister Space, founded
on principles of gender, race, and socioeconomic justice, recognized
child removal as a central issue facing women who use drugs. Child
removal fostered intergenerational transmission of trauma, as many of
the women at risk for overdose and child removal had themselves been
removed from their parents. Their own children faced elevated risk of
drug use, child removal, and overdose when placed in foster care. To
break this cycle, Atira had done the seemingly impossible: convinced
the Vancouver child protective services to allow poor women to keep
custody of their children even if still using drugs. Atira ran a housing
facility for women and their children that provided twenty-four-hour
child care, early childhood education, and academic support for school-
aged children. This had been especially important for their First Nations
clients, whose own foster care placement had been triggered by parental
drug and alcohol use, while their traumatic separation from their own
children by foster care in turn intensified their drug and alcohol use and
later put their children at risk of having their grandchildren taken into
state custody. Atira described foster care as a form of cultural genocide
of Indigenous people.

Our Canadian colleagues showed us that overdose prevention is an opportunity to rethink public policy in relation to race, drugs, and the greater societal good. The United States has, unfortunately, pursued very different policies that do not merely ignore but actually worsen structural injustices and the social determinants of (ill) health. Psychoactive substances and drug policies in the United States are racially segregated into legal medications in clinical spaces and drugs of abuse in the criminal justice system. Health care and social services are relegated to an unequal and insufficient private market. The results are clear: rising death rates and foster care placements for US Black, Latinx, Indigenous, and white people alike.

THE INVISIBLE (WHITE) HAND OF THE MARKET

In a 2017 special report to the *New England Journal of Medicine* entitled "The Role of Science in Addressing the Opioid Crisis," Nora Volkow, director of the US National Institute on Drug Abuse (NIDA), and Francis Collins, director of the National Institutes of Health (NIH, of which NIDA is one part), begin and end a report to clinicians on NIH opioid research programs by referencing the central importance of "public-private partnerships." Their vision is for NIH to aggressively fund pharmaceutical and biotechnology companies for opioid-related basic science, drug development, and market testing. They also cite their success in lobbying the US Food and Drug Administration (FDA) for streamlined regulatory review and accelerated approvals of newly patented, abuse-deterrent pain medications and addiction treatments, stating, "Our goal is to cut in half the time typically required to develop new safe and effective therapeutics."[1] They end the essay with statements that solidify the conflation of science with industry that infuses the entire report: "Recent NIH–industry partnerships, such as the Accelerating Medicines Partnership, demonstrate the power of public–private collaboration in speeding the development of new medications. Ending the opioid crisis will require this kind of collaboration. . . . As we have seen repeatedly in the history of medicine, science is one of the strongest allies in resolving public health crises. . . . With our [corporate] partners, the NIH will take an 'all hands on deck' approach to developing and delivering the scientific tools that will help end this crisis and prevent it from reemerging in the future."[2]

This conflation of scientific with corporate enterprise—note the slippage from "industry partnerships" to "science is one of the strongest allies in resolving public health crises"—implies that large companies with profit-driven investors are the only viable engine of scientific progress. Ironically, what public-private partnerships do in practice is to channel large amounts of public, taxpayer dollars to private companies, while further weakening regulatory oversight of their products. This channels public funds away from public infrastructure development that might disseminate existing technologies to those whose health is most at risk. The products of public-private partnerships—newly patented pharmaceuticals and biotechnologies—have not historically driven public health improvements; rather, social interventions and service system infrastructures have. In fact, in light of the revelations from corporate files made public in class action lawsuits against opioid manufacturers, for-profit pharmaceutical and biotechnology developments, along with relaxed regulation and accelerated FDA approvals, have been, not agents of public health promotion, but rather "one of the strongest drivers" of the opioid crisis.

Yet US federal opioid policies of the second decade into the opioid crisis have followed an ingrained pattern: investment of public dollars into privatized "solutions" with a focus on pharmaceuticals as "treatment." Under former president Obama, the 2016 Comprehensive Addiction and Recovery Act (CARA) and the 21st Century Cures Act of 2018 authorized over $1 billion for distribution by the US Health and Human Services Administration. In 2017, President Trump declared the opioid crisis a public health emergency, and his Presidential Opioid Commission recommended an additional $27 billion for opioid initiatives; the commission, along with the 21st Century CURES Act and the NIH HEAL initiative, focused on access to medications to treat opioid use disorder, on development of new pharmaceuticals for opiate use disorder, and on new, lower-risk medications for pain.[3]

The federal government's medication-oriented response to illicit opioid use is a remarkable departure from the punitive policies of the US "war on drugs." But at the same time, that response has not evenly replaced punishment across white, Black, and Latinx communities. This is consistent with a century-long, racially segregating pattern of support for legal narcotics for the white middle class. It is also consistent with a racially capitalized system of private-sector drug development and dissemination for white consumers.

First, while buprenorphine and methadone as medications for opioid use disorder are clinically effective in reducing nonprescribed substance use and overdose deaths,[4] these medications alone, without accompanying systemic interventions, cannot reverse the overdose epidemic. Opioid-related mortality continues to rise, and it increased significantly after the emergence of COVID,[5] across the US where access to medications is limited and racially disparate. The federal opioid agenda has allocated few resources for public health systems development, harm reduction, social needs, poverty, and structural racism as barriers to care and recovery, criminal justice reform, and reaching marginalized and stigmatized populations.[6] Yet investment in public health and social service infrastructures is key to stemming deaths among groups marginalized from health care by ethnicity, race, gender, and poverty.

Given the political strength of the pharmaceutical industry in the US to set drug prices and its influence on drug regulation, including FDA approvals for opioids, as well as the industry's ties to leading opioid researchers, the prominence of drug development and public-private research partnerships in the NIH HEAL Initiative is not surprising.[7] Current US opioid research policy provides significant public funding for patentable new technologies for pain relief and for treatment of opioid use disorder. Because the prices set for newly patented technologies are high, such technologies are likely to benefit only those individuals with the resources to pay for them. Effective medication for opioid use disorder has been available for over fifty years, yet because of systemic barriers it is not reaching people who need it. Rather than continuing to focus on new technologies, US policy that effectively reduced opioid deaths would shift the research agenda toward social determinants of health and would fund health and social service infrastructures to promote overall survival.[8]

OF HOME AND HARM

Descending the subway platform, we noticed a buildup of empty plastic bags and wrappers on the sidewalks of the abandoned warehouses and treeless streets of the South Bronx neighborhood that was home to a leading harm reduction center. A few people walked briskly ahead of us, holding their collars up against the November chill. We opened a metal door to a multistory gray cinder block building with a small BOOM!Health logo on the window. Warm air poured over us, and a spry Latinx woman looking to be in her sixties, with a denim jacket that showed the edge of a tattoo, greeted us from her seat. After calling the program director down to meet us, she told us how much she loved her job. "These people, they are family, they are like gold. I'm a former user myself. I've been here twenty years, first as a client. I'm here to save our community." She called out to people who entered by name, laughing with them as they shook off the chill from outside.

The program director offered us a guided tour of the building. The first floor was for distribution of safe injection equipment and naloxone overdose reversal kits, as well as premade lunch bags for people who were hungry but on the go. Many clients are living in the parks and have nowhere else to go, he explained. He brought us upstairs to show us the cafeteria, the lounge chairs where people rest while being monitored for signs of overdose, shower stalls, clothes-washing machines, and meeting rooms for therapy groups. Shown the weekly calendar of therapy groups, we saw titles that referenced trauma, a women-only group, LGBTQ issues, and navigating sex work. The next floor featured a pharmacy and a clinic run by a local teaching hospital. As the director explained, "This is a one-stop shop! And also a place where people can feel at home. It is hard out there. We hire peers—people who have used themselves—so the people who work here understand where the clients are coming from."

We thought of Vancouver-based addiction doctor Gabor Maté's observation that the opposite of addiction is not abstinence but rather connection.[9] Some of our colleagues took exception to his statement, pointing out that using drugs is all about connections. But the spirit of Maté's words seemed apt. His book highlights the extensive trauma histories that his addicted patients from Downtown Eastside of Vancouver reported: many had experienced severe childhood abuse and deprivation, foster care, and repeated abuse as adults from sexual partners, family members, and clients in sex and drug industries. What Maté alludes to, but does not name explicitly, is the structural violence of extremes of power and wealth that created the conditions for such widespread trauma. His patients sit at the lower extreme, and Canadian elites at the other, including those currently buying and developing land in Downtown Eastside, thereby displacing long-term residents along with their jobs and small businesses. If we follow the logical thread of Maté's quote, the synonym for addiction is disconnection—not disconnection from drug trade networks, of course, but disconnection from the fabric of supportive families and neighbors that leaves children and adults bare to the world of encroaching disaster capitalism industries, including informal narcotics trade and even prescription drugs.

When journalist Naomi Klein coined the term *disaster capitalism* to describe the government or corporate practice of taking advantage of major disasters to adopt liberal economic policies that the population would be less likely to accept under normal circumstances, she was thinking of more acute disasters—hurricanes, war, terrorist attack, stock market crashes.[10] But what did Downtown Eastside residents share with unemployed white Americans in the deindustrializing Rust Belt of former mining and manufacturing towns? What did they share with the South Bronx, which burned down in the 1960s–80s because of "benign neglect" and "planned shrinkage" by New York City government officials, who closed firehouses in an attempt to clear the land of Black and Latinx workers stranded by the early waves of manufacturing's departure for Asia and disinvestment from city centers? What Downtown Eastside Vancouver, the Middle American Rust Belt, and the South Bronx all share is the decades-long state- and industry-sponsored disintegration of neighborhoods and the social ties that sustain them, a disintegration whose race- and class-patterned mental health and physical health consequences psychiatrist and urbanist Mindy Fullilove tracks in her multi-city study *Root Shock*.[11] And which entities have profited from such devastation? Among others, elaborate infrastructures of both prescribed and street-traded narcotics.

As drug historian Nancy Campbell has noted, harm reduction is an international movement based on care for, and creativity of, the very people that New York City planners, US manufacturing and mining industries, Vancouver developers, and multinational opioid manufacturers see as disposable.[12] The lives saved are not only physical, they are also social and productive. BOOM!Health, Sister Space, and INSITE are places where the lived histories and nimble survival strategies of participants are recognized and where people solve collective problems and at times organize politically to push back against police repression and gentrification. In fact, drug users' unions have emerged in many places across North America, including North Carolina, San Francisco, New York, Vancouver, and more. Not only have they organized around access to syringes and overdose prevention as well as less repressive policing, they have also lobbied for policies that provide for affordable housing and other structural reforms to address the economic and social inequalities driving harms from drugs. When COVID-19 first emerged in US cities, public health officials predicted large-scale relapse and overdose among people with opioid use disorder who would be left without clinical services or recovery support groups. While many of their predictions came to fruition, harm reduction organizations formed the front line of creative COVID responses despite insecure funding and despite the fact that many of their services remain illegal in the majority of US states.[13] Anthropologist and harm reduction activist Jennifer Carroll noted that harm reduction organizations like the Urban Survivors' Union quickly pioneered virtual safe injection sites where people monitored each other for signs of overdose using their cell phones, provided home delivery of buprenorphine and other medications, and wrote online guides to navigating the increasingly volatile and therefore lethal street drug supply during COVID containment.

Harm reduction sites are not places where drugged people totter on the edge of physical and social death, like zombies; rather, they are sites of vitality and community in the face of unspeakable loss: loss of lives, of relationships, and also of ways of life. They are also, in a practical sense, sites of valuable innovation, pushing the envelope of our understanding of drug use, drug addiction, and drug policy—the generative source of the most important ideas transforming our thinking and practices around these issues.

TED'S STORY

There are yet other places that foster community and vitality in the face of intergenerational trauma, loss, and despair. Ted met Helena when he found safe harbor in a dilapidated corner of New York City's oldest public hospital. A New York–born Puerto Rican, he had grown up in the South Bronx in a turbulent time. Born in the early 1970s, he and his family lived through waves of displacement as city officials first practiced "benign neglect"—disinvestment from Black and Latinx city center neighborhoods as white residents fled for gated communities in the suburbs, as real estate developers sought to clear the land for more profitable uses, and as officials practiced "planned shrinkage," the deliberate closing of fire stations and other essential services in city centers in order to empty properties by accidental fires and arson. Fully 40 percent of the housing stock in the South Bronx burned to the ground during Ted's childhood. This led to massive displacement of residents from social networks made up of local grocers, church leaders, and neighbors who were "aunties" and "uncles." For decades such networks had sustained poor neighborhoods like his, providing regularity and safety for children whose parents often struggled to manage odd jobs and/or substance use.

Ed's methadone clinic counselors referred him to creative art therapy on the second floor of the hospital's old wing. Because he rarely spoke, his counselors thought he would respond to visual art as a nonverbal therapeutic medium. For months, he sat quietly in the corner of the art room, working methodically on elaborate sketches based on photographs he took at local parks. Over time, he joined the filmmaking group, a therapeutic group co-founded by an art therapist and by a patient who was a professional filmmaker. Group members took turns storyboarding and scripting film projects, making sets, arranging lighting and costumes, operating microphones and cameras, then editing the resulting footage into short films that were shown throughout the hospital. The video camera captivated Ted: he spent hours testing its settings and finding perfect angles for shots. His footage was the most often picked for final edits because he established intimacy with his subjects. But despite that intimacy, Ted's own life and thoughts remained a mystery to us.

In those years—2008–9, just before New York State privatized its Medicaid programs—public health insurance still paid for extended treatment for substance use disorder, including psychotherapy and creative arts therapy groups. Two years into his work behind the camera, we were able to coax Ted to appear in front of the camera. Using pictures of his family members to prompt his personal story, we first got him to speak of his parents. He had idolized his father: "He was the one that got me interested in astronomy. He always took time off to speak with me about the wonders of the stars, the different shapes and sizes. . . . I remember seeing *Star Wars* with [him]. . . . We was close, we was very close."

Ted had lost his father as a young boy, to mysterious circumstances. "I never knew the cause of death of my father. Maybe it was a heart attack or something." And years later, after his own son and daughter were born, he lost his mother to alcoholic cirrhosis of the liver: "One day we was arguing . . . she went for a beer. She was not supposed to take one more ounce of alcohol, because the doctor told her you can't take one more ounce. And she started throwing up blood. . . . The whole bathroom was full of blood, and my kids went to the next-door neighbor—they were panicking—they called the ambulance, 'Grandma is bleeding!' She made it to the hospital, but she died in the hospital."

Ted moved his traumatized wife and two children to Puerto Rico. For a time, he worked in a factory and supported his family as his third child—his youngest daughter—was born. But the thriving heroin market in Puerto Rico lured the grieving Ted. Full of shame and secrecy, he suddenly left his family for New York, where he lived on the streets.

Five years passed without communication with his family in Puerto Rico.

Ted eventually found himself in a family shelter with his brother. Beds in men's shelters in New York were hard to come by and were dangerous; violence and even murder by intoxicated residents were common. But by requesting housing together, Ted and his brother qualified for a safer family shelter that offered physical and mental health screens. Upon learning of his heroin use, shelter staff recommended methadone.

Along with daily supervised methadone doses, Ted enrolled in an intensive outpatient clinic that had been started thirty years prior by a psychiatrist who was also a visual artist. The clinic was built around a kitchen in which patients cooked and ate meals together. Two hallways led to group meeting rooms that hosted visual art, music therapy, film-making, community performances, and workshops on managing anger, coming to terms with trauma, and spirituality. The clinic founder and a group of patients took a plot of land wedged between the hospital and a major highway that had been deemed unsuitable for parking, shipped in donated soil, trees, seeds, and irrigation supplies, and created a lush oasis called the Sobriety Garden. From March to November, they gathered in the garden for self-fashioned horticultural therapy. Side by side they worked the soil and coaxed seed into flowers and vegetables, symbolically enacting recovery with their spades and wheelbarrows, turning compost to revive the soil and create symbiotic microecologies.

Ted spent his afternoons in the garden with the clinic's camera, getting close-ups of Monarch butterflies on milkweed and raspberries on the vine. While discussing his photos with the photo group, he finally spoke of his children back in Puerto Rico. His oldest daughter would turn seventeen that year, and his youngest daughter six. His son, Ted Jr., would be in high school. Members of the filmmaking group encouraged Ted to call his children.

Ed decided to use the clinic's office phone to call his father-in-law in Puerto Rico, with whom his children and wife had been living when he left the island five years before. Members of the filmmaking group stood by in the room next door.

After ten minutes of suspense, Ted entered the group meeting room with a smile on his face. His wife had sobbed with relief. She and his children had thought he was dead. Over the months that followed, the filmmaking group took up a collection to send Ted to Puerto Rico to see his children. Ted boarded a plane with two weeks of methadone doses in his backpack; he had successfully lobbied the methadone program to dispense an unusual number of take-home doses. Miraculously, he got his fourteen bottles of methadone through airport security without questions.

Upon Ted's arrival to Puerto Rico, his daughters and son expressed joy that he was alive. None asked him why he had left. Ted did not explain the past five years, nor did he mention his methadone treatment or therapy groups at the hospital. Two weeks later he returned to New York alone but was determined to wean himself off of methadone and to give his children a "normal" life:

> When I was on heroin, it was a horrible lifestyle. When I got on methadone, okay, I became normal, so to speak . . . with the exception that you depend on your medication to function. . . . That's the one thing, that if you don't have it, then you go through hell. That's what I would start from, to become a normal person, I have to get off that medication, not depend on no medication to function, and from there, to live independent like anyone else: to be self-sufficient. My daily dose is 13 milligrams. Come Friday, really, Friday, I'm going to be on 10. Three milligrams [less] every two weeks . . . I'm on the brink of being on single digits, you know, from 10 I go down to 7, then 4, wow. That makes me very excited, because, to think that soon I'll be all the way down to 3 and then maybe zero—if I can just get off it pain free, aww, that would be great, great, great. There's not a soul on this planet that's gonna be more at peace than me.

When asked if he had fears about going off of methadone, he replied, "Absolutely, I have fears, I don't know how I'm going to react when I go all the way down to zero. When the moment comes when they dispense the medication right there, the liquid goes right there, that last drop 'zzzt' . . . [but] I wanna have my kids in my life. . . . Then everything would be complete."

Ted was singular in his focus on becoming "drug free," a ubiquitous sentiment among methadone patients across the country. Methadone patients are not immune to the influence of the cultural premium that Americans put on "independence," the opposite of the dependence that methadone symbolizes.

Ted did wean himself off methadone. Once he did so, however, his insurance no longer covered his therapy groups. The filmmaking group threw him a "graduation" party with cake and balloons, amid promises to stay in touch.

Three months later, Ted's brother contacted the filmmaking group. He was going to the city morgue to identify Ted's body. Ted had been found dead in his shelter bed. The coroner had found fentanyl in his blood.

Numb, we held a memorial for Ted at the hospital chapel, showing his best photos and footage from our interviews of him. We all thought of his children back in Puerto Rico, reeling from having lost their father—twice. What none of us knew for sure was, how much was his relapse was due to weaning himself off methadone? Certainly, many studies had shown a high likelihood of relapse after discontinuing methadone.[14] And Ted's body had no tolerance to the ultrapotent fentanyl that now permeated the New York "heroin" market. The biomedical establishment identified methadone as the crucial element of "treatment," and his health insurance made his coverage contingent on methadone. But then again, what might have been possible if he'd continued his art therapy and filmmaking groups, with all of the daily care and attention that fellow group members gave him through the ups and downs of recovery? It was striking how much Ted had gained a sense of meaning, purpose, and connection in therapy groups—groups that had structured his days and anchored him in the midst of rotating shelter rooms, his efforts to reconnect with his children, and the physiological roller coaster of a methadone taper.

Could it be that Ted's story—on the surface of it, a validation of the idea that medication must be maintained to prevent relapse—is actually a story of the importance of the psychosocial support system that was tied to Ted's daily methadone doses? It is worth noting how rare that constellation of psychosocial supports—the arts, community gardening, and group therapy—is among addiction treatment programs. An accident of the clinic director's creative vision, this constellation was not found in any other addiction program in New York and would be difficult to find anywhere in the US, especially in a public hospital serving low-income people of all races. Could Ted's story also be a fable of what might have been in an alternate realm of health justice through cutting-edge social technologies for treating addiction?

THE FRENCH CONNECTION (OR THE MYTH OF MAGIC BULLETS)

As the failed promises of OxyContin's sustained-release capsule and the inability of buprenorphine marketing to stem overdoses have shown, biotechnology cannot stop the harms of narcotics without systemic and social intervention. To underscore this point, we turn to an international comparison often made by American advocates of buprenorphine expansion. In France, where buprenorphine was adopted for general physician treatment of opiate dependence in 1995, buprenorphine was billed, not as a stigma-reducing agent for a white middle-class market, but as a public health intervention to stem overdose and HIV among low-income, largely immigrant and nonwhite heroin injectors. Buprenorphine was widely adopted among primary care doctors in poor communities, in a country with universal health care. The opioid overdose rate in France dropped 80 percent in the first five years after buprenorphine's approval.[15] Contrast this with the US, where by 2020 opioid overdoses were five times as high as they had been when buprenorphine was approved in 2002.[16]

From our interviews with white and nonwhite people trying to access buprenorphine and stay on buprenorphine, we suggest that the public health potential of buprenorphine is limited by the race- and class-segregated, market-driven US health care system, in which patients have patchy insurance coverage and tenuous access to prescribers. France has universal health care and a robust social safety net; these are critical elements to their success with buprenorphine. Buprenorphine and methadone are now largely provided through a network of community-based centers located in areas of high drug traffic. Centers provide free, integrated addiction medication and general health care, harm reduction services including clean syringes and safe injection rooms with medical supervision to prevent overdose, and comprehensive social services including housing and income support.

However, our comparison of US opioid policy with that of France, in collaboration with sociologist Marie Jauffret-Roustide of INSERM, Paris, the French equivalent of NIH, alerted us that there is even more to the story of buprenorphine in France.

First, why does the most widely cited time sequence graph of overdose deaths and people on buprenorphine treatment prepared by French researchers Marc Auriacombe and colleagues stop at 1999, five years after the introduction of buprenorphine in France (figure 16)? That is because, after 1999, the overdose rate in France increased again, and by 2010 it had almost returned to its highest recorded level, even though by 2010 buprenorphine use had dramatically expanded in France. This suggests that other factors, in addition to buprenorphine, played a role in reducing the overdose rate by 1999. A late 1990s influx of crack cocaine into previously heroin-dominated French markets may be one of them. And it turns out Auriacombe's work was not widely cited in

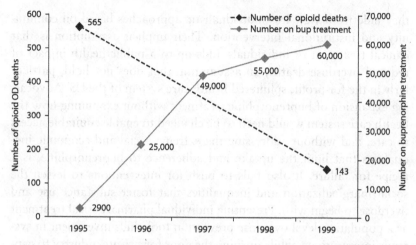

FIGURE 16. Opioid overdose deaths by number of buprenorphine patients in France, 1995–99. Source: Marc Auriacombe et al., "Buprenorphine Treatment and Opioid Overdose in France," *American Journal on Addictions* 13, Suppl. 1 (2004): S17-S28.

France because his research was supported by Schering Plough, which held the license to buprenorphine in France, so he was considered to have conflicts of interest.

The other point is, looking at the French overdose peak in 1995, the largest number of annual ODs was 565. Not 565,000, as it might be in the US, but just 565 in a country of 60 million people. France has never had an overdose crisis of the proportion we've seen in the US. Why not? In the 1990s, direct-to-consumer and direct-to-prescriber marketing was illegal in France, and France had a national drug-purchasing body that independently assessed pharmaceutical company claims about the clinical advantage and safety of new drugs. OxyContin was never marketed in France.

This should make us skeptical about the power of the private market to protect the public and rectify inequalities in health. In our for-profit health care system, buprenorphine maintenance has followed the pattern predicted by the theorists of fundamental causes of disease, sociologists Bruce Link and Jo Phelan: that new biotechnologies will widen, rather than narrow, health inequalities if social drivers of health are not addressed.[17]

Advocates of the brain disease model of addiction present their model as the antidote to moralistic responses. By framing individual clinical treatment as *the* health-promoting alternative to incarceration, they hide from view less individualistic approaches based on community and institutional intervention. Their implicit assumption is that clinical treatment of individuals adds up to a public health impact of reduced overdose deaths, an assumption that does not hold, particularly in the for-profit, splintered health care system of the US. Advocating expansion of buprenorphine treatment without examining how the health care system would need to be changed to enable equitable access to care, and without addressing the extreme social and economic inequalities that limit the uptake and adherence to buprenorphine, is a recipe for failure. It also fails to push for interventions to lessen the social marginalization and inequalities that foster substance use and overdose to begin with. Presenting individual pharmaceutical treatment as a population-level overdose prevention tool chills investment in systemic interventions, while opening the door for private industry to capitalize on our societal hope for magic technological bullets.

ADDICTION IS BIOSOCIAL

Let's reconsider what it could mean to define addiction as a chronic brain disease. Neuroscientists are increasingly seeing the brain as a plastic, socially responsive organ that has evolved to adapt to complex social systems.[18] Emerging life science models of neuroplasticity, epigenetics (the way that gene expression is influenced by social exposures, sometimes in ways that are heritable), and the microbiome (the ways microorganisms in the human gut are influenced by social exposure and in turn affect physiology) have underscored that human biology is not fixed or genetically predetermined but rather dynamically shaped in interaction with environment. These more sophisticated biological models call on us to invest in research on the biological impact of social systems, and of interventions that create healthy social contexts, including a well-regulated pharmaceutical industry, biomedical research that is driven by public interest and not by profit, racially equitable economic development, a robust social safety net, and recovery support networks that give dignity, meaning, and structure to people's lives.

If we were to take seriously the widespread comparison of substance use disorder with diabetes, asthma, and hypertension, we'd recognize that each of these conditions has strong social determinants and that success in their prevention and treatment requires social connection, stable housing, access to fresh foods, and safe, unpolluted, walkable neighborhoods. These preventive measures have strong race and class gradients that geographically concentrate in affluent, empowered neighborhoods.[19] As we've argued in this book, their race and class gradients are actively produced by public policies, scientific discourse, and corporate marketing strategies that capitalize on assumptions of white middle-class morality and deservedness versus other less valued constituencies. In order to change these gradients of health and disease, life and death, those assumptions, including those about the white middle class, must be made conscious and visible. When racial assumptions are visible, health advocates can promote new social technologies of policies, scientific discourse, and corporate behavior that draw on different goals: the goals of racial and economic justice.

REINTERPRETING "DEATHS OF DESPAIR" AS CALLS FOR RACIAL AND ECONOMIC JUSTICE

Anne Case and Angus Deaton's report on the decline in US white life expectancy was unusual in that its authors were not epidemiologists but economists.[20] Their analysis of root causes of overdose, as well as suicides and cirrhosis, lay not in neuroreceptors or genetics but in the deindustrialization of American Rust Belt towns where the departure of manufacturing and mining industries left behind high unemployment and social disintegration. A sociological study following their report showed overdose rates were linked to thin social networks,[21] and ethnographies of deindustrializing, working-class white areas with high overdose rates found that their shrinking economic opportunities were accompanied by the weakening or disappearance of community institutions such as neighborhood clubs and public school sports teams, leaving youth and older generations without a sense of belonging or optimism for the future.[22] Accordingly, Case and Deaton have popularized the idea that overdoses are "deaths of despair."

Their argument is persuasive. Its logic prescribes social and economic revitalization through policies that promote social integration as well as stable employment with livable wages and benefits, not just the expansion of access to medications and public-private partnerships to develop, quickly approve, and disseminate new medications for addiction, as currently prioritized in the NIH HEAL Initiative and the CURES Act. But Case and Deaton's focus on whites makes the analysis incomplete and makes Black and Latinx overdose deaths invisible. Case and Deaton do not explain why Black and Latinx life expectancy did not decline in the time period of their study; but as this book details, white people were the target for the long-acting opioids that were patented in the 1990s, with relaxed federal regulation and aggressive ethnic marketing in white communities through the 2000s, followed by transition to heroin as access to prescriptions was restricted. In addition, Black and Latinx people had already seen their own overdose crisis thirty to forty years prior, with the ethnic marketing of heroin to inner-city neighborhoods from the 1960s through the 1980s. Those heroin deaths were followed by crack cocaine–related deaths and incarceration in the 1980s–90s. It is worth noting that blue-collar workers in Black and Latinx neighborhoods were often barred from unions, were last hired, first fired, and saw massive unemployment much earlier than white workers, who were initially protected by industrial discrimination. These earlier Black and Latinx opioid and crack crises were not seen as health crises; rather, they were reported in popular press as epidemics of crime, leading to white flight from cities and further disinvestment in Black and Latinx city neighborhoods.[23] Those neighborhoods were left with the survivors of earlier drug crises. Survivors of large-scale drug-related deaths in urban, low-income Black and Latinx neighborhoods were not the focus of marketing for the newly patented long-acting opioids of loosely regulated pharmaceutical companies of the 1990s–2000s, nor were they initially the target of the expanding Latin American heroin trade that took advantage of the new opioid markets in suburban, small town, and urban white America that prescription opioid manufacturers had opened.

Though opioid manufacturers, and the suburban and small-town heroin cartels that followed them, initially bypassed Black and Latinx neighborhoods for white markets, by 2017 the US Centers for Disease Control reported that Black middle-aged men were the group with the fastest-rising overdose rate.[24] They are disproportionately incarcerated on drug charges, have low physiological tolerance to opioids upon release from jail and prison, have a high risk of relapse, and live in settings where few social or medical services are available and where the ultrapotent fentanyl is predominant in street opioid markets. In the case of Black and Latinx people, ongoing criminalization of (as opposed to clinical care for) opioid use disorder has had serious biological consequences. And it is worth noting, on the heels of widespread protests against racially targeted police killings in the US as orchestrated by the Movement for Black Lives and others, that one of the key differences between Black and white communities in the US is their level of policing based on drug law enforcement. Deaths of despair now abound in white, Black, and Brown communities across the US. Addressing them effectively requires us to acknowledge racial capitalism as the common root of despair and to prioritize racial justice to the benefit of all.

HOPE FOR ALL?

In Staten Island, New York, the district attorney collaborated with community groups lobbying on behalf of members with opioid use disorder to create a novel approach called Project HOPE. As of 2017, those people arrested in Staten Island on low-level drug charges, such as possession of small amounts of illegal drugs, have been given the option of bypassing a sentencing hearing and instead getting referred to addiction treatment and being matched with someone who is in recovery from addiction as a peer support person and health care system navigator. The program has been hailed as a success, reporting that by 2019, 81 percent of those eligible for the program were being diverted from sentencing and directed to treatment.[25]

In the same time period, of all boroughs of New York City the largest total number of overdoses were in the Bronx,[26] which had no Project HOPE. In contrast to Staten Island, the South Bronx has the neighborhoods with the highest poverty rate in New York City and the poorest congressional district in the US, with a predominantly Latinx and Black population.[27] The South Bronx has the highest incarceration rate in the city,[28] with a reputation for police brutality and stop-and-frisk policy enforcement.[29] While in white suburban Staten Island the district attorney swiftly reoriented toward treatment referral as a part of Project HOPE, in the Bronx courts continue to churn arrestees through drug-related sentencing, putting those incarcerated at even greater risk of overdose after their release. The downstream effects of incarceration and other forms of residential displacement in the Bronx have been well documented by community health researchers, who point out that incarceration harms the health of residents in the neighborhoods that send the most people to prison: even neighborhood rates of premature birth and neonatal mortality are strongly related to the percentage of neighborhood residents serving time in jail or prison.[30] Ultimately, the criminalization of drug use and the breakup of neighborhood support networks in disinvested city centers kill people, just as the racially selective marketing of narcotics for pain in white suburban and rural communities kills people.

Yet programs like Project HOPE will not solve these structural inequalities. Problem drug use cannot be addressed through reforms in the criminal legal system or changes in policing alone. Courts should not be primary entry points to care for substance use disorder, and police should not be primary first responders to overdose. That is, people with problem substance use should not go through law enforcement to get services. Many community activists in disinvested, heavily policed neighborhoods are now lobbying for systems of community-based mutual aid instead of 911 and other police-driven crisis responses.[31] And of course, we cannot limit ourselves to crisis response or individual-level solutions to structural problems. Funding more treatment, as is emphasized in the current US federal opioid response, does not change the root causes of the escalating overdose calamity in the US.

We might use the case of white opioids to update Cedric Robinson's insights about the role of race in capitalism.[32] Health care and biotechnology make up one of the largest economic sectors worldwide. Ours is a biomedical economy that depends not only on cheap labor but also on consumption of high-cost pharmaceuticals driven by accumulating diagnoses. Opioids, which create physiological dependence calling for escalating doses to ward off withdrawal, and thus create a population of people diagnosed with opioid use disorder, who are then prescribed opioids for that dependence, drive a closed circle. Add this to a neuroscientific cultural logic that (1) propagates the image of the universal brain with a hidden, implicit white racial identity; (2) thereby erases social environment as a factor in drug use; (3) and leads to further translation of neuroscience into racialized biotechnologies, while (4) using neuroscientific claims—that addiction is located in neuroreceptors in the brain and thus amenable to wholly technological solutions (for those who can pay for them)—to bolster racialized marketing of these new biotechnologies.

While Robinson's analysis of racial capital focused on the ways nonwhites provided expendable labor for global, colonial capital, opioids today show that Whiteness is key to understanding the cycle of biotechnology consumption. As our pharmaceutical executive informants explained to us, white middle-class markets drive demand for patented drugs in pursuit of magic bullets, as such patients use their privilege and private income to pay for "cutting-edge technology." Then, closer to the end of a drug's patent life, when the shortcomings of the drug have become apparent, pharmaceutical companies look to patent new formulations of the drug in order to keep their legal monopoly on their rights to sell the drug, while marketing the original formulation to nonwhite, publicly insured patients that extend sales of the drug just before patent expiration. For example, opioid use is now rising among Black and Latinx people, and simultaneously, twenty years after the FDA approval of buprenorphine for opioid use disorder, buprenorphine is finally gaining market share in public clinics and is beginning to penetrate jail and prison systems. At the same time, federal funds are subsidizing newly patented formulations of opioids, both for pain and for addiction treatment.

Where does this leave us? First, addressing the root causes of epidemic drug deaths among whites and nonwhites alike requires pushing back against the racial capitalism of pharmaceutical and biotech industries while promoting race and class justice in economic and health policy. As the current opioid crisis has taught us, the racial calculus underlying drug development and regulation, pharmaceutical marketing, and drug law enforcement is ultimately harmful to all racial constituencies. It hinges on a racial capitalism that first privileges the white markets that are consumers of new biotechnologies, and to which marketers have the least restricted access, through private doctors and flexible payment schemes. It also privileges the sales potential of biomedical technologies over population health promotion.

At the end of this chapter, we provide specific and personal examples of how we should use concern about the current opioid crisis to move beyond the racial capitalism driving new drug development and to invest in the following:

1. Universal health care with the components necessary to address social determinants of health and psychosocial needs through integrated harm reduction services, trauma-informed psychotherapy, treatment for psychiatric comorbidities such as mood and anxiety disorders, peer navigation and community health workers, recovery networks of support, and assistance with housing, employment, income, education, and basic needs. Ted's story, above, illustrates the good that can come of more comprehensive health care, which in his case, at its best, involved not only medications but also housing, social services, psychotherapy, including art therapy, and a supportive network of peers.

2. Ending criminalization and promoting harm reduction as a national response to overdose, instead of relying on local initiatives. Focusing on locally initiated arrest diversion initiatives such as Staten Island's Project HOPE, rather than repealing federal and state-level drug laws that privilege empowered communities, virtually ensures that court-sanctioned decriminalization and treatment will focus on the white middle class. It deepens inequalities by race, class, and neighborhood, and it also leaves

even the most privileged people vulnerable to the vagaries of the geographic space in which they happen to encounter law enforcement or overdose. We should make community-based mutual aid organizations, such as harm reduction and peer-led groups, rather than criminal legal systems, the first line of overdose prevention and support services for problem drug use.

3. Development of, and research on, the social structures and biosocial processes that mitigate addiction and overdose, including social innovations such as peer-based recovery networks, the use of the arts, urban gardening, and community-based organizations including spiritual or religious organizations. Such social technologies currently receive almost no public research and addiction response funding; these are left to private foundations and donors as isolated demonstration projects, limiting their reach, while public investment would establish such interventions as "evidence based" among health and human services administrators.

4. Strengthening regulation of pharmaceutical manufacturers and disentangling regulatory body officials from industry interests, not only during safety reviews but throughout the federal research and purchasing systems. This includes the bodies that set NIH research priorities and that review Veterans Affairs, Medicare, and Medicaid pharmaceutical benefits.

5. Racial justice initiatives. These include racial impact assessments of new drug policies, such as those that the Black and Hispanic Caucuses of the New York State Legislature have proposed, modeled on the environmental impact assessments of the federal Environmental Protection Agency. They also include explicit redress of the harms to Black, Latinx, and Indigenous communities that have been targeted for decades by the war on drugs through heightened policing and incarceration. Such redress would operate through investment in economic development and public services in neighborhoods that have long been disinvested by city officials. The New York and California marijuana legalization laws are examples of such an approach. These laws allow those with low-level marijuana convictions to have their records expunged, requalifying them for a host of housing, education, and small business loan programs for which a criminal record made them ineligible. In addition, through cannabis social equity programs, low-income people who live in neighborhoods disproportionately affected by drug law enforcement and those who have been convicted of marijuana-related crimes are given preference in newly legalized marijuana-related business ventures, as business owners, employees, or tenants of such

businesses. Such social equity programs are also being initiated in other states that have legalized medical marijuana, including Florida, Maryland, Ohio, and Pennsylvania.[33]

These proactive measures will move us beyond incarceration and commercial biomedicine as responses to drugs, toward a public health and racial justice approach that reduces the harm to both whites and nonwhites of our racialized drug industries. Rather than promoting individualized, commercialized solutions to our overdose crisis, we need to see overdose as rooted in long-standing inequalities that require community organizing and a social movement for policies that push back against the vagaries of unrestricted racial capitalism, through policy change and community revitalization. We must build on the political legacy and innovations of harm reduction movements without limiting ourselves to preventing overdose or infection: we must shift our institutions away from the violent racial order that has caught so many Americans in its crosshairs.

Racially segregated drug policies and lucrative yet lethal prescription narcotic marketing can be sustained only if there is a separate route to categorize and discipline drug use among whites, and that route must appear, at least on its face, to be race neutral. It has costs that are borne by white people who pay inflated prices, and sometimes pay with their lives. The ambiguity of the Greek word *pharmakon*—its dual meaning of "medicine" and "poison"—is exploited in America's white "war on drugs that wasn't," in which unprecedented profits are made in the liminal space between licit and illicit pharmaceutical sales, a space that is protected by its symbolic Whiteness.

CODA—HOW INDIVIDUALS CAN WORK TOWARD SYSTEMIC CHANGE

As this book argues, the racial identities and the lethality of opioids are overdetermined by multiple, overlapping systems that shape popular culture, medical-scientific authority, corporate financial incentives, and political power. The toxic racialization of drugs is multifaceted and systemic, so simply raising the awareness of individuals will not change it. Yet the actions of individuals are important. As the anthropologist Margaret Mead famously said, "Never doubt that a small group of thoughtful, committed citizens can change the world; indeed, it's the only thing that ever has." The key word in this quote is *group*: that is, change requires collective action.

In this last section, we as authors describe our attempts at collective action. We offer them with humility, recognizing that problems of race and drugs are deeply rooted in many sectors of our society and that they have no single solution. We reiterate that magic bullets are a myth, whether those magic bullets are newly patented pharmaceuticals or a shift in policy, in media coverage, or in medical practice. Change will require actions in all of those areas, and more.

Critical, Structural Clinical Practice (as told by Helena Hansen)

Without knowing it, I pursued joint training in medicine and social science—cultural anthropology—in order to help change the culture of medicine. I came of age during the height of AIDS activism and took a job in the New Jersey branch of the National AIDS Fund my first year after college. My desire to change the culture of medicine had a lot to do with the way people who used drugs were treated by doctors, nurses, and other medical professionals in the midst of the AIDS pandemic.

New Jersey was the epicenter of AIDS among women and children in the US. AIDS was concentrated among poor, Black, and Latinx women in New Jersey's cities, including Newark, Elizabeth, Trenton, and Camden. By the 1980s, these cities were in the throes of profound disinvestment of public funding and infrastructure. They had been abandoned by white flight during the civil rights era and race riots of the 1960s to '70s, when residents of the white neighborhoods moved to suburban areas, taking their tax base with them. The cities were further impoverished by the 1980s closure of manufacturing plants as industries pursued ever cheaper labor pools overseas, as well as by the weakening of labor unions and further reductions of state and federal payments for city infrastructure. In that period, the pharmaceutical and insurance industries that had headquarters in New Jersey thrived on state and federal subsidies and tax breaks for corporations, paid for by reductions in government funds for public services and benefits. New Jersey had the country's richest suburbs and poorest cities; the residents of poor city neighborhoods saw shrinking employment and state assistance. To survive, many turned to the informal drug economy. This created a perfect storm of crack cocaine, heroin, and sex trades in those neighborhoods, and, with time, HIV.

The underfunded hospitals and clinics of these New Jersey cities drowned in the onslaught of drug trade–related violence and disease. Clinicians often responded by refusing to treat people with HIV, claiming the right to protect themselves from exposure, or by discharging desperate patients to the streets when staffing and supplies were short, while blaming patients for their "choices." Women were shamed for their drug use by judges and social workers, who placed their children in foster care while giving the mothers advice to complete drug treatment and parenting classes when treatment, and assistance with basic survival needs including housing and food, were nowhere to be found. A generation of children lost their parents and lost connections to their neighborhoods of origin, while being told that they were damaged by their parents' drug use, and while navigating stigma and exclusion in schools that had no funding for mental health or social support. Meanwhile, their mothers often died on the streets without medical attention. For many years, the very definition of AIDS that qualified patients for the few existing treatments and public benefits left out the signs of AIDS that were most common in women, such as cervical cancer, because early AIDS policies were geared toward men who had sex with men.

A few brave doctors, nurses, and therapists joined forces with AIDS activist organizations to change that. They testified to Congress to get the official definition of AIDS to include diseases that were common to women with AIDS and their children; they held "die-ins" on the steps of Newark's city hall and the New Jersey statehouse to get funding for housing and income assistance for families that were decimated by AIDS; they founded dedicated clinics and residential facilities for women and families with AIDS. They also ran needle and syringe exchange programs to stem HIV transmission, illegally and with donated funds, at a time when the federal government ignored the evidence that they saved lives in order to please voters who saw AIDS as punishment from God for people who had made immoral "choices." Together, these brave clinicians and the grassroots activists with whom they partnered, many of whom were HIV positive themselves, actually changed federal laws.

With time, these activists brought about remarkable changes. The NIH began mandating that committees and commissions charged with setting HIV/AIDS research funding priorities include members who were themselves HIV positive. The Ryan White CARE Act passed in Congress, infusing states with federal funding for HIV and AIDS services. The community councils that oversaw distribution of those funds were mandated to include HIV-positive members and representatives from the neighborhoods most affected by HIV. The problems of racial capitalism's disinvestment from US cities were not solved, but the political participation of marginalized people in health policy and health systems was significantly enhanced by AIDS activism.

Inspired by these breakthroughs, I devoted myself to bringing into academic medicine research on how communities, institutions, and policies influence health. I also sought out ways to practice medicine differently, to practice in a way that supported health and recovery through collective support by fostering a sense of belonging, positive identity, and creativity. Fortunately, as a psychiatry intern I found my way to the public addiction clinic that I have described in this book, led by an addiction psychiatrist who is also an accomplished visual artist, Dr. Annatina Miescher. It was Dr. Miescher's vision, and the vision of the talented art therapists and addiction counselors that she gathered, most of whom had lived experience of addiction, that led to the rich tapestry of art therapy, filmmaking, music therapy, and community gardening as part of addiction treatment that we describe in chapters 1, 6, and 7.

Yet turning insights from the practice of collective recovery, as well as observations about the ways biomedicine can reinforce race and class hierarchies, into formal knowledge that can inform policy and medical practice required me to master research methods and ways of thinking about the body and about health care that are foreign to medical research—and that challenge fundamental assumptions of medicine. For instance, in biomedicine, the simplest explanation for population differences is assumed to be the most likely to be true. This is a version of Occam's Razor, a European philosophical principle of knowledge that dates back at least seven centuries and that guides biomedical researchers to simplify variables and the causal relationships between them. This book has provided examples of how Occam's Razor works in opioid research: biomedical researchers reduce race to quasi-biological categories and reduce the cause of addiction to the bonding of molecules to brain cells. To tell the story of opioids and race that we have presented here, I had to seek out complexity: to analyze the narratives of pharmaceutical ads and executives, regulatory agencies, neuroscientists, prescribers, and patients in relation to the histories and political economic systems of the places in which they work and live. And I had to read against the grain: to question whether biomedical scientists and practitioners are doing what they claim, and often believe, that they are doing. This is the type of critical self-reflection that I hope to help foster among my colleagues in medicine.

But how to use critical self-reflection to practice medicine differently? Twenty years after I began medical school and graduate school in social science, I found myself lecturing medical school students, residents, and faculty about the insights I had gained from AIDS activism—insights about the power of clinician collaboration with socially and economically marginalized people. With psychiatrist-historian Jonathan Metzl, I formed a movement with likeminded colleagues in medical schools across the US that we call "structural competency."[34] We sought out and publicized examples of clinical practitioners who had addressed health inequalities by collaborating with community-based organizations, with nonhealth service sectors such as housing agencies, law enforcement, schools, and city planners, and with policy makers to change the structures—the community resources, service institutions, and policies—that explain health outcomes better than patients' personal choices or genes. Reorienting clinicians to this way of intervening also requires a shift from *social determinants of health*, a term borrowed from public health that clinicians use to describe patients' risk factors for disease, such as unstable housing or criminal-legal system involvement, toward *structural drivers of health*, which refers to institutional or policy-level causes of these risk factors, such as urban planning that razes low-income housing to enable developers to build luxury real estate, or drug law enforcement and sentencing that target poor Black and Brown neighborhoods.

Introducing clinicians to structural explanations for health inequalities, and encouraging clinical practitioners to intervene on community, institutional, and policy levels, is an uphill battle. Medical practice, and reimbursements for medical services, focus on the bodies and behaviors of individual patients. Most practitioners graduate from clinical training without any teaching on the ways that neighborhood conditions, public policies, and the inner workings of local institutions, including clinics and hospitals themselves, shape their patients' health. Clinical professors often fail to explain racial inequalities in myriad health problems, from drug-related issues to hypertension or diabetes, or they reference yet-to-be-identified genetic differences, or they attribute inequalities to "cultural differences" that imply that certain groups have pathological beliefs and behaviors, part of the culture-of-poverty theory that for decades justified US policies of control and blame of the urban poor.

Clinicians are fundamentally practitioners. They don't learn from abstract theory, they learn techniques by "seeing one, doing one, teaching one." Training clinicians to intervene on structural drivers of health inequalities often requires creating new clinics and collaborations so that they can put structural interventions into practice. These interventions can work on many levels. The first level of intervention is the low-hanging fruit of what can be done inside clinics in the course of everyday clinical care. The examples I give my clinical colleagues include social prescribing, which means partnering with social service organizations or community health workers who can take a "prescription" that a clinician writes a patient for a social need, such as help applying for Social Security Disability benefits, and can make it happen—for example, guide the patient through the process of applying. Another example is to form medical-legal partnerships with law students or pro bono lawyers so that patient problems that lend themselves to legal advocacy can be addressed. For instance, among low-income people many health problems can be traced to negligent landlords who may fail to test for and clean up lead paint in older buildings, leading to lead poisoning among children. Also, landlords may try to evict tenants who show signs of serious psychiatric problems, in violation of the Americans with Disabilities Act. Legal action is often expedient in these cases, and when larger population-level patterns are found, lawyers and clinicians together can pursue changes to local, state, or federal laws to protect patients' health. Yet another example is that clinics are beginning to train and hire community health workers, and, in particular, people with lived experience of problems with substance use or serious mental health problems who have found ways to cope with them, otherwise known as "peer navigators," to work as a part of clinical teams. Community health workers and peer navigators are insiders to the groups they serve and have the benefit of personal knowledge and experience managing the health problems, as well as the systemic barriers, faced by patients.

A second level of intervention that I advocate for clinicians is to partner with community organizations to do on-site health interventions. When it comes to addressing racial inequalities in substance-related harms, strong examples include clinical practitioners who are working with grassroots harm reduction organizations, such as BOOM!Health, described above, and other trusted, culturally resonant community organizations to provide harm reduction and treatment for substance-related problems on-site with the support of peers and trained community members. For example, psychiatrist Ayana Jordan and psychologist/community organizer Chyrell Bellamy partnered with Black and Latinx churches in New Haven, Connecticut, to create Imani Breakthrough, a comprehensive harm reduction, addiction treatment, and peer-based recovery support program located in churches.[35] As Ayana and Bellamy explain, low-income Black and Latinx people who use substances often experience demeaning and even violent treatment in mainstream biomedical clinics. They may have seen clinicians about their substance use only in the setting of jails, prisons, or understaffed emergency rooms and may associate professional help with these punitive settings. Relocating services in trusted churches and staffing them with community members changes the dynamic of care. Other examples abound of creative partnerships between clinicians and community gardens, art centers, and environmental justice organizations to address health problems.

A third level of intervention involves clinicians partnering with non-health sectors such as housing agencies, legal aid organizations, parks and recreation, or schools in order to address medical needs together with social needs in community sites, and also to redesign public services so that they promote health. One physician who has taken this approach to its logical end is psychiatrist Mindy Fullilove. She undertook decades of research documenting the ways that intentional race and class segregation of US city neighborhoods, combined with the displacement of low-income people from their housing by policies such as urban renewal, has fueled health problems ranging from HIV and harmful substance use to psychiatric illness, diabetes, and hypertension.[36] Dr. Fullilove then collaborated with urban planners and architects to redesign cities, taking down barriers that segregated neighborhoods, such as highway overpasses, and replacing them with parks and common spaces that featured murals honoring city history and the works of local artists.[37] As she explains, she no longer treats individual patients. Instead, she treats the pathologies of cities.

And then there is the fourth level of intervention, which is for clinicians to advocate for health-promoting public policies. Since clinical training does not usually teach health professionals how to influence policy, this requires special preparation. For instance, in New York City, a group of health practitioners, formerly incarcerated people, and disenchanted criminal legal system officials formed an organization called From Punishment to Public Health, whose goal is to divert people with mental health and substance use problems away from jails and prisons and toward health care. Reforming punitive drug laws is one of their priorities, and to accomplish this, together with the Drug Policy Alliance, they train clinical practitioners to give testimony to policy makers about the ways drug laws endanger those who are sentenced—

disproportionately low-income people of color with preexisting psychiatric conditions. They also enlist political organizers who train clinicians to write op-eds and engage popular media for policy change.

While these approaches initially strike many clinical practitioners as "too political" and as going beyond their realm of expertise, growing numbers of practitioners, especially those still in training, recognize the limits of their current tools. Doctors and nurses were reporting high rates of professional burnout and related turnover at record numbers even before COVID-19;[38] they described frustration with institutional and social barriers to their patients' improvement. When surveyed, US physicians rate social needs as among the largest barriers to their patients' improvement but say that they do not know how to address them.[39] Structural intervention enables clinicians to uphold their oath to help the sick. It is the key to self-preservation not only for patients but also for clinicians themselves.

Public-Facing Scholarship (as told by David Herzberg)

The stories we tell about drugs matter. They shape how we understand and respond to drugs at every level from our personal feelings to our policies and practices. Too often, the stories we tell are ones we inherited, unreflectively, from the past: they are old stories, originally written long ago, by people whose intentions and values we do not share. They are the stories of Whiteness, serving that system's purposes while making things worse for the actual people and communities we care about.

History, like other humanities disciplines, can be a powerful tool for challenging those inherited stories and offering truer accounts. These accounts are truer not just because they fit the evidence rather serving a political agenda. They are also truer because they reckon directly with political agendas—with how the workings of power have shaped not only events but also stories about events. They can free us to be more deliberate in our decisions and, when needed, to head in new directions more consonant with our values.

For these reasons I try to make my work as a historian as available as possible to the public. In part this means researching subjects that are directly relevant to present-day issues and openly acknowledging the present-day implications of what I find. It means writing as simply and directly as possible so that the ideas can be more easily understood by anyone interested in them. It also means taking opportunities to tell stories about drugs beyond the important but also restricted networks of scholarly books and journals. I teach hundreds of college students, graduate students, and medical students every year. I give public presentations or do workshops with anyone interested: health care workers, community and advocacy groups, medical societies, retirement homes—whoever. I talk to media. I testify in court. And often I talk to people who, for whatever reason, don't have a better place to turn for personal advice.

I do all this as part of my job as a professor and historian. But the unique power of stories is that we all tell them. True, some people have louder bullhorns and their words reverberate more broadly. Politicians, medical leaders, journalists, and other authorities have a lot of power to shape "the narrative." But the stories they tell don't work simply because we hear them. Rather, they rely on us to *tell* them: to make use of them to understand our lives and events around us, to communicate with friends, and to decide how to act. We are all storytellers, and we all shape the story.

Unfortunately, most of the stories about drugs we have available to us—the ones handed down to us from the past—are designed to weaponize our real and legitimate fears, to distort and magnify them to serve the demands of Whiteness and its assorted political needs. Rejecting that terror and approaching addiction with empathy and common sense is, in its own way, a radical act. As this book has shown, important elements of racial capitalism depend on us thinking irrationally and fearfully about addiction. Most of us do not feel very powerful in the face of such systems. One thing we can do is try not to allow our personal struggles to contribute to them and, in doing so, to push back against them.

I hope that history can help people in this effort. The past is a laboratory of human endeavor. It is the closest thing we have to a series of social experiments that reveal the results of particular strategies, concepts, policies, and approaches to drugs and addiction. If we can see this past through the "whiteout" of received stories, we can use those results to help us make good choices today. I'll conclude now by summarizing some of the most useful conclusions that I have drawn from this historical laboratory.

- Desegregate drugs. Our current drug policy architecture was built over one hundred years ago by white elites using concepts and policies common at the time that we now recognize and reject as "segregation." We don't have to accept this architecture if we no longer want to achieve those goals. Dividing drug sellers and drug users into arbitrary categories based at least partly on race has not been an effective way to protect the public from drug risks (or to make drug benefits available to the public). Corporate profit seeking has catapulted white markets into nearly continual crisis, while prohibition markets and punitive policing have wreaked even worse havoc on racialized communities. The most effective drug policies have emphasized two things: robust regulation (rather than prohibition) to subordinate profit to consumer well-being, and care (rather than punishment) for consumers harmed despite the protections. In the US, the closest approximation of such policies was in "white markets" during periods of reformist creativity: white markets for opioids after the nineteenth-century crisis but before the first drug war hardened in the 1920s, and white markets for sedatives and stimulants in the early 1970s before the second drug war hardened later that decade. Before Rockefeller and Nixon pushed the US back to punitive prohibition as the 1970s wore on, consumer protections even expanded for the first time beyond white markets with methadone maintenance—stigmatized and punitively policed, but still an extension of quality-controlled pharmaceuticals to poorer, racialized consumers long defined as fundamentally "nonmedical."

· Destigmatize drugs. Drug use is not abnormal or a cause for shame. I try to talk simply, equivalently, and in a matter-of-fact way about all forms of drug use—medical or nonmedical, legal or illegal, to ease suffering or to pursue pleasure, or just out of curiosity. I try to make clear the distinction between drug use (a common human behavior) and drug harms (often the result of social injustice). One way I have found that seems effective sometimes is to adopt familiar terms like *consumer* to describe people who use drugs, which shifts the context through which to understand their behavior by highlighting similarities with other common consumer activities (such as driving cars, using space heaters, skiing, cooking with a gas grill, or lifting weights, all of which also carry risks that must be carefully managed).

· Destigmatize addiction. The use of racial stigma to associate drug effects such as tolerance, dependence, and desire with social categories such as shame, criminality, and downward social mobility was built by particular people at particular times in the past, to accomplish particular goals. Specifically, it was built by the same "reformers" who developed the many hierarchical policies that, together, we now refer to as "segregation." Policies have reinforced this coupling over the past century, but we do not have to continue doing so. If we push back against the inherited racism embedded in our concepts and practices, we can approach "addiction" frankly, pragmatically, and with empathy as a potential drug side effect, like other drug side effects, that some consumers will experience. Antiracist thinking can give us the freedom to reduce consumers' risk of experiencing addiction and, just as importantly, to reduce the harms of addiction itself by decoupling it from shame, criminality, and downward social mobility. Among its many other harms, racist thinking prevents us from taking commonsense, pragmatic, and effective steps to maximize the benefits and minimize the risks of drugs.

· Don't fall for "addiction porn." The pharmaceutical industry has been responsible for many false and harmful stories about drugs and addiction. Individual drug risks become public health crises not because drugs or the people who use them are bad but because corporate profit seeking has prevented us from properly gauging and managing their real risks. Historically, reformers have used "addiction porn"—prurient, often racialized, stories of addiction—to whip up (white) political support to reform Pharma. But doing so distracts from what most needs reforming, namely, corporate behavior, and, at best, can lead only to a pyrrhic victory: new regulations that make white markets safer at the cost of increasing stigma and reinforcing drug war thinking for everyone else.

· Don't fall for prohibition. Prohibition is not a solution to bad behavior in the pharmaceutical industry, any more than it is a solution to "street" drug use. History has few reliable laws, but evidence has shown repeatedly that prohibition does not eliminate drug markets. Rather, it has been a destructive way to regulate those markets. I use the term prohibition markets to emphasize the way that prohibition has its own predictable incentives that do not eliminate but rather shape how markets function. Those incentives are perverse and harmful. They select for the easiest-to-smuggle products, which are often the most potent and thus carry the highest risks for consumers (think here of the shift from smoking opium to injection heroin after the 1909 prohibition of smoking opium, or of the shift from heroin to fentanyl in the early twenty-first century). They encourage or even require sellers to focus on evading authorities rather than providing reliable, high-quality products and truthful information for consumers. And so forth. All markets are regulated. The question is, by whom and for what purposes. Prohibition markets do not serve the interests or safety of consumers—the people drug policy is supposedly designed to protect.

- Don't fall for free markets. It is tempting to push back against drug war prohibitions by calling for complete consumer freedom. But free markets are not the goal. Like prohibition markets, free market incentives privilege sellers' goals over consumer well-being. In no other commercial context do we take businesses' or corporations' good behavior on faith; we know they must be regulated to ensure that they don't place profits above the public good. Drugs are not a magical exception to this rule. Business regulations inevitably restrict consumer freedoms: we cannot buy cars without safety features and pollution controls, or houses that do not meet code. For especially desirable and especially dangerous products like drugs, we do not accept "Let the buyer beware" as the rule of the market. Instead, we arrive at a "least worst" solution that balances profits, freedoms, and the public good. Complete consumer freedom is a libertarian fantasy. Markets will never provide universal safe access to basic needs. That requires politics: deliberate, collective action.

Drug Policy Reform (as told by Jules Netherland)

In this final section, as we look at solutions, I will focus on what I've learned as a drug policy reformer with the hopes that it is instructive for others. I do so with humility and the belief that there are no right or wrong answers, just efforts to make meaningful change and learn from past mistakes. We have tried to make the case that racial capitalism relies on a system of Whiteness and that white privilege and Black disadvantage are embedded in our social, political, and economic structures. This kind of analysis is critically important to help guide solutions, particularly revealing the limitations of race-neutral policies. For example, in places where marijuana has been legalized or decriminalized, the total number of arrests declines dramatically. This is good news; fewer people overall are going to jail and prison. But even when those numbers steeply decline, the racial disparities persist. That is, even when a small number of people are being arrested for drug use, people of color remain far more likely than white people to be arrested because changing the law did nothing to address racial disparities per se. Communities of color remain overpoliced, and the racial bias of law enforcement persists. When we talked to people who use drugs in Oregon about the passage of the law there to decriminalize personal possession of all drugs, they told us that they feared "net widening." They believed that police would find other reasons to arrest people of color if they could no longer arrest them for drug possession. Indeed, many drug policy reformers believe that, even if we succeed in dismantling our most punitive drug policies, the criminal legal system will find other ways to criminalize people of color, such as through "crimes of poverty," like loitering and failure to pay fees.

Similarly, early efforts to legalize marijuana markets were "race neutral" and did little to benefit communities of color and redress the harms of marijuana prohibition in those communities. In fact, the emerging legal marijuana market is predominantly white, and some markets disadvantage people of color by excluding those with a drug conviction from participating in the industry. Given the gross racial disparity in drug arrests, such policies effectively keep more people of color out of the industry, even though those very same groups bore the brutal brunt of prohibition in the first place. Because white privilege and anti-Black racism operate systemically, even well-meaning policy change, like marijuana legalization, can replicate them.

What, then, are we to do? Clearly white supremacy and racial capitalism harm individuals, and we will always need services and supports to help mitigate those harms. But until we look upstream and address the root causes of these harms, we will fail to make meaningful change. For white people, a first necessary though insufficient step is to understand how systems of racial capitalism and white privilege work. As James Baldwin puts it: "Not everything that is faced can be changed, but nothing can be changed until it is faced."[40] White people must start by facing systems of white privilege. We hope that this book has helped reveal how Whiteness is working within the current opioid crisis. However, because Whiteness is a system of unearned advantage that operates at every level, individual awareness will never be enough to dismantle it. Rather, solutions require systemic interventions.

The war on drugs is a tool of Whiteness and racial capitalism that has infiltrated multiple sectors, including our housing, immigration, employment, education, and public welfare systems, in ways that cannot be disentangled from racism in the US.[41] The belief that some people who use drugs (people of color and poor people) are deeply flawed and morally corrupt has justified policies that prevent people with drug arrests or convictions from accessing public housing, professional licenses, jobs, and financial aid for college. Drug testing is used to keep people who use drugs from working or retaining custody of their children—absent any evidence of their unfitness as employees or parents. Drug arrests are routinely used to deport immigrants. Some drug use—mostly that by poor people of color—props up a vast array of policies and practices that are directly tied to the ability of individuals and communities to survive and thrive. Those who have more contact with the systems of the state—public housing, public education, public welfare, child protective services, probation, or parole—are more likely to face surveillance, policing, and drug testing that impedes their ability to benefit from the very systems that purport to help them.

As a longtime activist and drug policy reformer—and as a white person—I face a number of dilemmas and questions every day when I think about what to do in the face of these deeply entrenched and complex systems of Whiteness and racial capitalism. Given how intricately racism is woven into the fabric of our laws, policies, and practices, is reform even possible? Can the systems of the state—law enforcement, capitalism, health care, social services—be changed in ways that do not perpetuate racism, or do they need to be abolished entirely? Should we be working for community-based systems of mutual aid rather than working to prop up an inherently racist and failed state? Given how distant radical reform seems, should we be spending our time and energy on incremental reforms that can at least relieve the suffering of some now? And whose decisions are these? I don't have the answers, but I'd like to share a few things I've learned.

First, we must reject race-neutral policies and give very careful consideration to how our policies can explicitly redress the harms of racism. For example, as we described above, the law to legalize marijuana in New York took specific steps to expunge the records of those arrested under prohibition (predominantly young Black and Latinx men), ensure that people of color would benefit from the newly formed industry, and redirect revenues from the sales of marijuana into those communities most harmed by prohibition. As drug policy reformers look to legal markets for currently illicit drugs, they must also confront the danger inherent in racial capitalism and commercialization—forces that, unchecked, could increase, rather than decrease, drug harms, particularly for people of color. A safe, legal supply of a drug is far preferable to an illicit one that carries, not only the risk of an unknown, potentially contaminated product, but also the risk of criminalization and all of its collateral consequences. But we know racial capitalism is seldom good for communities of color, so as we explore newly regulated drug markets, we must think creatively about new kinds of markets, such as cooperatives and compassion clubs, where interests are driven by those who can most benefit from a legally regulated supply rather than large commercial interests. Similarly, when we work on criminal justice reforms, such as drug decriminalization, we need an analysis that explicitly addresses concerns about net widening and ensures that we are not merely shifting racial disparities into another sector of the criminal legal system. The Movement for Black Lives understands the importance of honoring Black life in a culture that does everything to denigrate it. It is this kind of centering of Black life and interests that must replace race-neutral policy making and inform our drug policy.

Second, drug policy reformers must engage with other reform movements. As we noted, drug policy affects housing, employment, immigration, child welfare, health care, education, and public welfare. Therefore, housing policy is drug policy. Immigration policy is drug policy. Welfare reform is drug policy. If we care about drug policy, we also have to care about fights for basic income, affordable education, and universal health care. Reforming drug policy means engaging with all of these systems, exposing drug war logic wherever it occurs, and understanding that these are intersectional issues that require broad coalitions working together for change.

Third, we need visionary change. I long for a world without police, without a prison industrial complex, without a system of racial capitalism that strips people of their humanity while filling the coffers of a greedy few. I am an abolitionist who believes that many (maybe most) of the systems of the state are so inherently racist and corrupt that they cannot be saved. I embrace movements for mutual aid, and I understand why communities are developing systems for mutual support and accountability that circumnavigate 911 and the involvement of the criminal legal system. I have seen how the very organizations and agencies intended to help people, particularly people who use drugs, penalize and entangle them more deeply in a system that dehumanizes them.

Yet I have also seen how incremental reforms, like drug decriminalization, can help hundreds of thousands of individuals avoid the collateral consequences of a drug arrest or conviction. I have seen how even an inequitable and deeply flawed medical marijuana program can help alleviate pain and suffering. Incremental change can have value, but we must continually interrogate any incremental reforms to make sure that they are not undermining that larger vision of a racially just and humane future.

Fourth, people of color and those directly affected by the war on drugs should lead movements for reform. Even those of us who are well-intentioned whites cannot know and cannot see all the ways in which Whiteness is operating. I try to step back and listen to leaders of color and those directly affected by the war on drugs about what they want and need, the ways they see Whiteness operating in a given situation, and the trade-offs they feel are worth making or not. Those are not my decisions to make. It is time for us who are white to learn from leaders of color how we can be most helpful rather than assuming we have the answers. This likely means abdicating positions of leadership and power so that new leaders can step up.

Fifth, we should not rely on the trope of white innocence to leverage policy change. I understand the temptation and the impetus for using Whiteness to move policy forward. When white people came into focus as the "victims" of the opioid crisis, policy advocates, like me, suddenly had new openings and opportunities to try and move white legislators toward important reforms. Unfortunately, as we have seen, too often the innocent, white drug user is constructed in relation to an imagined guilty, morally bankrupt, user of color or a drug seller who is also presumed to be Black or Latinx. And when we rely on the opening of drug use as a "white problem," we end up with solutions, like buprenorphine, that primarily benefit white individuals and communities, while communities of color are left with punitive criminal legal responses and their legacies of harm. Moreover, we at best ignore and at worst perpetuate the racist history of the war on drugs against people of color when we focus on drug problems as white.

Finally, and here I can speak only for myself, I have come to believe that there are no right answers or easy solutions. There is only working in community with others, continuing to deepen my analysis, learning from and holding myself accountable for my mistakes, and recognizing my own limitations. The terrible costs of Whiteness have been and will always be borne mostly by people of color, and yet Whiteness costs white people too. We have described the ways in which Whiteness and racial capitalism have hurt poor whites and led to disinvestment in important infrastructure and services that could benefit all of us, but I believe there are more personal costs to Whiteness as well for white people. A system of Whiteness can only be maintained by—on some level—participating in the delusion that people of color are less human than white people. How else could white people condone or even tolerate structures and practices that criminalize, denigrate, and literally kill people of color? Drugs have been used as a proxy for race, entangling Blackness, criminality, and drug use. We have allowed ourselves to be taught and to believe that people who use drugs (some of them anyway) are less than human, and the minute we do that, I believe that we ourselves become less human. At the risk of being deemed overly sentimental and trite, I keep returning to a truth I've always known but perhaps in moments allowed myself to forget, that radical transformation, of even the most entrenched systems of oppression, is grounded in radical love, the kind of love that abhors othering and cannot withstand the kinds of divisions, deceptions, and denigration propped up by the lies of Whiteness and racial capitalism. The call to better, more intentional policy reform, the call to transform structures, the call to repair harms of the drug war, is for me also a call to transform hearts. So one place to start transforming our drug policies is to unconditionally love people who use drugs and to recognize their full dignity and humanity even as we commit ourselves more fully to dismantling the systems of Whiteness and racial capitalism that dehumanize them in the first place.

Glossary

ADDERALL Amphetamine prescribed for ADHD (attention deficit hyperactivity disorder).

AMPHETAMINE Psychostimulant drug with both licit and illicit formulations in the US; illicit form commonly referred to as "meth" or "crystal meth."

BENZODIAZEPINE Class of drugs with depressant effects, meaning that they slow down central nervous system activity. Taken with opioids, they can intensify an opioid high while increasing risk of overdose.

BUPRENORPHINE Synthetic opioid developed in 1966 as a pain reliever, approved by the FDA in 2002 for treatment of addiction. A "partial agonist," it only partially activates brain opioid receptors. Touted for its "ceiling effect," such that, once a certain moderate dose is reached, increasing the dose will not increase the drug's effect, including its effect on breathing; consequently at higher doses the risk of death by overdose is lower than with full agonist opioids.

CDC Centers for Disease Control and Prevention.

CODEINE Opioid prescribed to treat mild to moderate pain; also in "cough syrup."

CPDD College on Problems of Drug Dependence.

CRACK COCAINE Solid form of cocaine derived from more expensive powder cocaine; became racially coded as Black in the 1980s and subjected to harsh minimum sentencing laws (*See* Powder cocaine).

CRT Critical Race Theory

DATA 2000 Drug Addiction Treatment Act, passed in 2000, enabling certified physicians to prescribed buprenorphine for opioid use disorder in outpatient clinics.

DEA Drug Enforcement Administration, federal law enforcement agency under the US Department of Justice.

DECRIMINALIZATION Lessening or termination of criminal penalties related to an act, article, or behavior, sometimes retroactively. Regulated permits or fines might still apply. For example, after marijuana possession was first decriminalized in New York City, it was still illegal to burn it or have it in public view, allowing for low-level marijuana charges to persist. *See* Legalization.

DPA Drug Policy Alliance.

DRUG CZAR Term for person who directs US drug policies, appointed by president.

DRUG-INDUCED HOMICIDE LAWS Statutes authorizing prosecution of drug-related deaths; these laws establish criminal liability for individuals who provide controlled substances to another person who dies as a result.

FDA Food and Drug Administration, federal agency of the Department of Health and Human Services.

FENTANYL Synthetic opioid, first synthesized in Belgium by Janssen Pharmaceuticals in 1959. Arrived in street markets in 1979 in California under the name "China White." Since 2013, illicitly manufactured fentanyl overdoses have increased rapidly in many US states.

GOOD SAMARITAN LAW Law protecting any volunteer giving aid to an injured person in an emergency.

GOOD SAMARITAN 911 LAW Provides limited protection from arrest, charge, or prosecution for people seeking emergency medical assistance at the scene of a suspected drug overdose. Passed in New York in 2011 and later was copied across many states.

HARRISON ACT Passed in 1914, federal law that formalized the distinction between medical and nonmedical substances and prohibited office-based maintenance of opioid-addicted patients using opioids.

HEROIN Natural opioid derived from poppy plant, illicit in the US.

HIV Human immunodeficiency virus.

HYDROCODONE Opioid prescribed to treat severe pain. Pain-relieving effects similar to morphine's.

IATROGENIC Refers to harm, disease, or other ill effect caused by medical activity, including diagnosis, intervention, error, or negligence.

JIM CROW State and local statutes enacted after the US Civil War that legally enforced racial segregation and racial discrimination.

LEGALIZATION Removing a prohibition against something currently not legal. Creates a legally regulated market for production and sales. *See* Decriminalization.

LIBRIUM Trade name for Chlordiazepoxide, a benzodiazepine with tranquilizing effects.

LONG-ACTING OPIOIDS Also referred to as extended-release opioids, designed to slowly release opioid contents into the body for a longer temporal effect and less frequent dosing.

MAT Medication for addiction treatment (a term that emphasizes the medication's stand-alone effectiveness), formerly called medication-assisted treatment (a term for treatment that, though making medication central, involves and recognizes the importance of co-prescribing other elements, such as psychotherapy and counseling).

METHADONE Opioid medication used for pain relief and for opioid addiction. For opioid addiction, patients are required to attend methadone-specific clinics for observed daily dosing and regular urine testing.

MORPHINE Opioid prescribed to treat severe pain.

MOUD Medication for opioid use disorder; refers to methadone, buprenorphine, and naltrexone.

NALOXONE Opioid antidote absorbed into the bloodstream when injected, but not active when taken orally. Used to reverse overdose (brand name Narcan).

NALTREXONE Opioid antagonist; blocks opioid receptors in the brains of addicted people, preventing them from feeling effects of opioids. *See* Vivitrol (brand name).

NARCOTIC Originally referred to any substance that dulled the senses and relieved pain. Term lacks clarity as some use it to refer to any illicit substance, while official institutions define it as opioids alone.

NARCOTIC FARM US federal in-patient addiction treatment center in Lexington, Kentucky.

NIDA National Institute on Drug Abuse

NIH National Institutes of Health.

OPANA Prescription opioid pain reliever with active ingredient oxymorphone, prescribed for moderate to severe pain, sometimes used to help anesthesia work during surgery.

OPIATE Natural opioids such as heroin, morphine, and codeine.

OPIOID Natural, synthetic, or semisynthetic chemical that interacts with opioid receptors in the body.

OPIOID ANTIDOTE Agent such as naloxone that acts as an antagonist to opioids, competitively binding to *mu* opioid receptors in the body to reverse the signs and effects of opioid intoxication.

OXYCONTIN Opioid pill manufactured by Purdue Pharma and approved by the FDA in 1996, marketed as a "minimally addictive pain reliever" on the basis of its patented sustained-release capsule technology, which in theory could lower the reward for users by preventing an initial rush of pleasure. *See* Sustained-release capsule technology

OXYCODONE Semisynthetic opioid, active ingredient of OxyContin. Considered slightly more potent than morphine in analgesic effects with a shorter half-life and more predictable metabolism.

POWDER COCAINE Stimulant drug extracted from coca plant; rose in popularity in the 1970s among white middle class and affluent in the US. More expensive than crack cocaine, which was racially coded as Black and subjected to harsh minimum sentencing. *See* Crack cocaine

PRESCRIPTION DRUG MONITORING PROGRAM Electronic database that tracks controlled substances.

PROBUPHINE Implantable form of buprenorphine that lasts six months; designed to provide a constant, low-level dose of buprenorphine to patients.

PROZAC The first serotonin selective reuptake inhibitor (SSRI), FDA approved in 1987 as the first antidepressant safe for prescription by primary care doctors. Previous classes required close monitoring by a psychiatrist.

PSEUDOADDICTION Term used to describe patients with pain who exhibited behaviors like those seen in other patients who were labeled as "addicts," such as dependence, withdrawal, isolation, risk taking, obsession, and financial and relationship difficulties. The term was promoted by pharmaceutical companies to argue that patients with pseudoaddiction should be treated with increased opioid dosages rather than less.

PURDUE PHARMA Pharmaceutical company principally owned by the Sackler family. Markets and sells opioids including OxyContin, among other products.

ROCKEFELLER DRUG LAWS Passed in 1977 in New York, these laws implemented harsh minimum sentencing for minor offenses including drug possession, driving mass incarceration in the following years; these laws were later copied in many US states.

ROXICODONE Brand-name opioid pain reliever like OxyContin; oxycodone is active opioid ingredient.

SAMHSA Substance Abuse and Mental Health Services Administration.

SCHEDULE I DRUG Considered to have high addictive potential and no therapeutic use; includes heroin.

SCHEDULE II DRUG Considered to have high addiction potential and limited therapeutic use; includes methadone.

SCHEDULE III DRUG Considered to have moderate addictive potential and high therapeutic use; includes codeine and buprenorphine.

SCS Supervised consumption site, also known as overdose prevention center, a place where people who use drugs can legally inject or consume drugs under supervision.

SSRI Serotonin selective reuptake inhibitor.

SUBOXONE The brand-name combination buprenorphine/naloxone, designed so that buprenorphine is the only active ingredient when the medication is taken orally as prescribed but so that, if injected, naloxone is activated and triggers opioid withdrawal.

SUSTAINED-RELEASE CAPSULE TECHNOLOGY Designed to release drug at a predetermined rate to maintain a constant drug concentration in the body for a specific period of time while reducing side effects.

TAMPER-RESISTANT FORMULATION OF OXYCONTIN Designed to make it harder to crush, snort, or inject by forming a viscous substance difficult to consume by those means. Also known as "abuse deterrent."

VALIUM Benzodiazepine with tranquilizing effects commonly prescribed to treat seizure and anxiety disorders. Also referred to as "mother's little helper."

VIAGRA Medication used to treat male erectile dysfunction, made by Pfizer.

VIVITROL First injectable formulation of naltrexone approved for opioid dependence. Injections last from thirty to ninety days and block the effects of opioids, including pleasure and pain relief. Most common medication offered in correctional facilities for opioid addiction. See Naltrexone.

WITHDRAWAL Period of feeling acute symptoms following termination of opioid use, common signs of which can include anxiety, "goose bumps," diarrhea, vomiting, fever, yawning, insomnia, restlessness, body aches, sweating, rapid heart rate, rapid breathing, high blood pressure, hallucinations, and seizures.

X WAIVER Requirement of prescribers of buprenorphine since its approval for use in the treatment of addiction. Prescribers undergo training, then apply for the waiver through the DEA. Restricts the number of patients who can receive buprenorphine from that prescriber; subjects prescribers to additional oversight.

Notes

CHAPTER I. PHARMAKON OF RACIAL POISONS AND CURES

1. Everette May and Arthur Jacobson, "Committee on Problems of Drug Dependence: A Legacy of the National Academy of Sciences. A Historical Account," *Drug and Alcohol Dependence* 23, no. 3 (1989): 183–218.

2. David Herzberg, *White Market Drugs: Big Pharma and the Hidden History of Addiction in America* (Chicago: University of Chicago Press, 2020).

3. On marketing that targeted white neighborhoods and on drug representatives' language about "trustworthy" and "legitimate" patients, see Commonwealth of Massachusetts v. Purdue Pharma L.P. et al., Superior Court C.A. No. 1884-cv-01808 (BLS2), January 31, 2019. On physicians' attribution of lower addiction risk to white patients, see Leslie R. M. Hausmann et al., "Racial Disparities in the Monitoring of Patients on Chronic Opioid Therapy," *Pain* 154, no. 1 (2013): 46–52, and Vickie L. Shavers, Alexis Bakos, and Vanessa B. Sheppard, "Race, Ethnicity, and Pain among the US Adult Population," *Journal of Health Care for the Poor and Underserved* 21, no. 1 (2010): 177–220. On physicians' attribution of higher pain tolerance to Black patients, see Keith Wailoo, *Pain: A Political History* (Baltimore: Johns Hopkins University Press, 2014).

4. Karin A. Mack, Christopher M. Jones, and Leonard J. Paulozzi, "Vital Signs: Overdoses of Prescription Opioid Pain Relievers and Other Drugs among Women—United States, 1999–2010," *Morbidity and Mortality Weekly Report* 62, no. 26 (2013): 537–42.

5. Michael Agar and Heather Schacht Reisinger, "Using Trend Theory to Explain Heroin Use Trends," *Journal of Psychoactive Drugs* 33, no. 3 (2001): 203–11; Ansley Hamid et al., "The Heroin Epidemic in New York City: Current Status and Prognoses," *Journal of Psychoactive Drugs* 29, no. 4 (1997): 375–91.

6. Michelle Alexander, *The New Jim Crow* (New York: New Press, 2010).

7. ScienceDaily, "Opioids Now Most Prescribed Drug Class in America," April 6, 2011, www.sciencedaily.com/releases/2011/04/110405161906.htm.

8. National Institute on Drug Abuse, *Prescription Drug Abuse*, Research Report Series, October 2011, www.drugabuse.gov/sites/default/files /rxreportfinalprint.pdf.

9. Sentencing Project, "Criminal Justice Facts," accessed 2019, www .sentencingproject.org/criminal-justice-facts/.

10. A. Stanton et al., "Expanding Treatment of Opioid Dependence: Initial Physician and Patient Experiences with the Adoption of Buprenorphine," May 5, 2006.

11. Pooja A. Lagisetty et al., "Buprenorphine Treatment Divide by Race/ Ethnicity and Payment," *Journal of the American Medical Association— Psychiatry*, prepublished May 8, 2019, https://jamanetwork.com/journals /jamapsychiatry/article-abstract/2732871.

12. Reynolds Farley, "Trends in Racial Inequalities: Have the Gains of the 1960s Disappeared in the 1970s?," *American Sociological Review* 42, no. 2 (1977): 189–208.

13. Agar and Reisinger, "Using Trend Theory."

14. Vincent P. Dole and Marie E. Nyswander, "A Medical Treatment for Diacetylmorphine (Heroin) Addiction," *Journal of the American Medical Association* 193, no. 8 (1965): 646–50; Vincent P. Dole, Marie E. Nyswander, and Mary Jeanne Kreek, "Narcotic Blockade," *Archives of Internal Medicine* 118, no. 4 (1966): 304–9.

15. Eric Schneider, *Smack: Heroin and the American City* (Philadelphia: University of Pennsylvania Press, 2011); Mical Raz, "Treating Addiction or Reducing Crime? Methadone Maintenance and Drug Policy under the Nixon Administration," *Journal of Policy History* 29, no. 1 (2017): 58–86.

16. Helena Hansen and Samuel K. Roberts, "Two Tiers of Biomedicalization: Methadone, Buprenorphine, and the Racial Politics of Addiction Treatment," in *Critical Perspectives on Addiction,* Advances in Medical Sociology 14, ed. Jules Netherland (Bingley, UK: Emerald Group, 2012), 79–102.

17. Anne Case and Angus Deaton, "Rising Morbidity and Mortality in Midlife among White Non-Hispanic Americans in the 21st Century," *Proceedings of the National Academy of Sciences* 112, no. 49 (2015): 15078–83.

18. Michael J. Zoorob and Jason L. Salemi, "Bowling Alone, Dying Together: The Role of Social Capital in Mitigating the Drug Overdose Epidemic in the United States," *Drug and Alcohol Dependence* 173 (2017): 1–9.

19. Dorothy E. Roberts, "Punishing Drug Addicts Who Have Babies: Women of Color, Equality, and the Right of Privacy," *Harvard Law Review* 104, no. 7 (1990): 1419–82; Marc Mauer, "Race, Class, and the Development of Criminal Justice Policy 1," *Review of Policy Research* 21, no. 1 (2004): 79–92.

20. US Office of National Drug Control Policy, "Office of National Drug Control Policy: President's Commission on Opioids," 2017, https://trumpwhite house.archives.gov/ondcp/the-administrations-approach/presidents-commission-opioids/.

21. Francis Collins, Walter Koroshetz, and Nora Volkow, "Helping to End Addiction over the Long-Term: The Research Plan for the NIH HEAL

Initiative," *Journal of the American Medical Association* 320, no. 2 (2018): 129–30.

22. Steven Epstein, *Inclusion: The Politics of Difference in Medical Research* (Chicago: University of Chicago Press, 2008), 234.

CHAPTER 2. HOW TO SEE WHITENESS

1. PolicyAdvice, "The State of the Healthcare Industry: Statistics for 2021," accessed August 6, 2021; IBIS World, "Biotechnology in the US—Market Size, 2005–2027," accessed July 31, 2021, www.ibisworld.com/industry-statistics /market-size/biotechnology-united-states/.

2. Nikolas Rose, *The Politics of Life Itself: Biomedicine, Power, and Subjectivity in the Twenty-First Century* (Princeton, NJ: Princeton University Press, 2006).

3. Stefan Helmrich, "Species of Biocapital," *Science as Culture* 17, no. 4 (2008): 463–78; K.S. Rajan, *Biocapital* (Durham, NC: Duke University Press, 2006); K. Birch and D. Tyfield, "Theorizing the Bioeconomy: Biovalue, Biocapital, Bioeconomics or . . . What?," *Science, Technology, and Human Values* 38, no. 3 (2013): 299–327; E. Kowal, "Orphan DNA: Indigenous Samples, Ethical Biovalue and Postcolonial Science," *Social Studies of Science* 43, no. 4 (2013): 577–97; C. Novas, "The Political Economy of Hope: Patients' Organizations, Science and Biovalue," *BioSocieties* 1, no. 3 (2006): 289–305; Michel Foucault, *The History of Sexuality: An Introduction* (New York: Vintage, 1990); G. Burchell, A. Davidson, and M. Foucault, *The Birth of Biopolitics: Lectures at the Collège de France, 1978–1979* (New York: Springer, 2008); C. Hayden, "From Market to Market: Bioprospecting's Idioms of Inclusion," *American Ethnologist* 30, no. 3 (2003): 359–71; Harriet A. Washington, *Deadly Monopolies: The Shocking Corporate Takeover of Life Itself—and the Consequences for Your Health and Our Medical Future* (New York: Anchor Books, 2012); S. Greene, "Indigenous People Incorporated? Culture as Politics, Culture as Property in Pharmaceutical Bioprospecting," *Current Anthropology* 45, no. 2 (2004): 211–37; Janis H. Jenkins, *Pharmaceutical Self: The Global Shaping of Experience in an Age of Psychopharmacology* (Santa Fe, NM: School for Advanced Research Press, 2010); Emily Martin, "The Pharmaceutical Person," *BioSocieties* 1, no. 3 (2006): 273–87; Paul Rabinow, "Artificiality and Enlightenment: From Sociobiology to Biosociality," *Politix* no. 2 (2010): 21–46; S. Gibbon and C. Novas, eds., *Biosocialities, Genetics, and the Social Sciences* (New York: Routledge, 2008); Adriana Petryna, *Life Exposed: Biological Citizens after Chernobyl* (Princeton, NJ: Princeton University Press, 2013); D. Heath, R. Rapp, and K.S. Taussig, "Genetic Citizenship," in *A Companion to the Anthropology of Politics,* ed. David Nugent and Joan Vincent (Blackwell, 2007), 152–67.

4. Birch and Tyfield, "Theorizing the Bioeconomy," 300.

5. Harriet A. Washington, *Medical Apartheid: The Dark History of Medical Experimentation on Black Americans from Colonial Times to the Present* (New York: Doubleday, 2006); Dorothy E. Roberts, *Fatal Invention: How Science, Politics, and Big Business Re-create Race in the Twenty-First Century* (New York: New Press, 2011); Alondra Nelson, *The Social Life of DNA: Race, Reparations,*

and Reconciliation after the Genome (New York: Beacon Press, 2016); Michael Montoya, *Making the Mexican Diabetic: Race, Science, and the Genetics of Inequality* (Berkeley: University of California Press, 2011); Duana Fullwiley, *The Enculturated Gene: Sickle Cell Health Politics and Biological Difference in West Africa* (Princeton, NJ: Princeton University Press, 2011); Troy Duster, *Backdoor to Eugenics* (New York: Routledge, 2003); Keith Wailoo, A. Nelson, and C. Lee, eds., *Genetics and the Unsettled Past: The Collision of DNA, Race, and History* (New Brunswick, NJ: Rutgers University Press, 2012); J. Marks et al., eds., *Revisiting Race in a Genomic Age* (New Brunswick, NJ: Rutgers University Press, 2008); Catherine Bliss, *Race Decoded: The Genomic Fight for Social Justice* (Redwood City, CA: Stanford University Press, 2020); Ruha Benjamin, *People's Science: Bodies and Rights on the Stem Cell Frontier* (Redwood City, CA: Stanford University Press, 2013); Ann Morning, *The Nature of Race: How Scientists Think and Teach about Human Difference* (Berkeley: University of California Press, 2011); T. Keel, *Divine Variations: How Christian Thought Became Racial Science* (Redwood City, CA: Stanford University Press, 2018); Samuel Roberts, *Infectious Fear: Politics, Disease, and the Health Effects of Segregation* (Chapel Hill: University of North Carolina Press, 2009); Lundy Braun, *Breathing Race into the Machine: The Surprising Career of the Spirometer from Plantation to Genetics* (Minneapolis: University of Minnesota Press, 2014); Jonathan Kahn, *Race in a Bottle: The Story of BiDil and Racialized Medicine in a Post-genomic Age* (New York: Columbia University Press, 2012).

6. Randall Hansen and Desmond King, *Sterilized by the State: Eugenics, Race, and the Population Scare in Twentieth-Century North America* (Cambridge: Cambridge University Press, 2013); Edwin Black, *War against the Weak: Eugenics and America's Campaign to Create a Master Race* (Washington, DC: Dialog Press, 2012); Stefan Kuhl, *The Nazi Connection: Eugenics, American Racism, and German National Socialism* (New York: Oxford University Press, 2002).

7. Arlene Dávila, *Latinos, Inc.: The Marketing and Making of a People* (Berkeley: University of California Press, 2012).

8. Nancy Scheper-Hughes, "Parts Unknown: Undercover Ethnography of the Organs-Trafficking Underworld," *Ethnography* 5, no. 1 (2004): 29–73; Petryna, *Life Exposed*; Rebecca Skloot, *The Immortal Life of Henrietta Lacks* (New York: Broadway Paperbacks, 2017).

9. Steven H. Woolf and Laudan Aron, eds., *US Health in International Perspective: Shorter Lives, Poorer Health* (Washington, DC: National Academies Press, 2013).

10. L. Anderson, "Private Interests in a Public Profession: Teacher Education and Racial Capitalism," *Teachers College Record* 121, no. 6 (2019): 1–38.

11. Kimberle Crenshaw et al., eds., *Critical Race Theory: The Key Writings That Formed the Movement* (New York: New Press, 1996).

12. Richard Delgado and Jean Stefancic, *Critical Race Theory: An Introduction*, 3rd ed. (New York: NYU Press, 2017).

13. M. E. Fine et al., *Off White: Readings on Race, Power, and Society* (New York: Taylor and Frances/Routledge, 1997); Ruth Frankenberg, *White Women, Race Matters: The Social Construction of Whiteness* (New York: Routledge,

1993); M.W. Hughey, "The (Dis) Similarities of White Racial Identities: The Conceptual Framework of 'Hegemonic Whiteness,'" *Ethnic and Racial Studies* 33, no. 8 (2010): 1289–1309; F.W. Twine and C. Gallagher, "The Future of Whiteness: A Map of the 'Third Wave,'" *Ethnic and Racial Studies* 31, no. 1 (2008): 4–24.

14. R.L. Allen, "Whiteness and Critical Pedagogy," *Educational Philosophy and Theory* 36, no. 2 (2004): 121–36; Jessie Daniels, *White Lies: Race, Class, Gender and Sexuality in White Supremacist Discourse* (New York: Routledge, 1997); Matt Wray, *Not Quite White: White Trash and the Boundaries of Whiteness* (Durham, NC: Duke University Press, 2006).

15. David Roediger, *Working towards Whiteness: How America's Immigrants Became White* (New York: Basic Books, 2006).

16. W.E.B. Du Bois, *The Souls of Black Folk* (Chicago: A.C. McClurg, 1903); Roediger, *Working towards Whiteness*.

17. Cheryl Harris, "Whiteness as Property," *Harvard Law Review* 106, no. 8 (1993): 1707–91.

18. Pierre Bourdieu, "The Forms of Capital," in *Handbook of Theory and Research for the Sociology of Education*, ed. J.G. Richardson (New York: Greenwood Press, 1986).

19. P. Frymer, "Acting When Elected Officials Won't: Federal Courts and Civil Rights Enforcement in US Labor Unions, 1935–85," *American Political Science Review* 97, no. 3 (2003): 483–99.

20. M. Fletcher, "White High School Dropouts Are Wealthier Than Black and Hispanic College Graduates: Can a New Policy Tool Fix That?," *Washington Post*, March 10, 2015, www.washingtonpost.com/news/wonk/wp/2015/03/10/white-high-school-dropouts-are-wealthier-than-black-and-hispanic-college-graduates-can-a-new-policy-tool-fix-that/.

21. B.P. Bowser, *The Black Middle Class: Social Mobility—and Vulnerability* (Boulder, CO: Lynne Rienner, 2007).

22. Richard Dyer, *White* (London: Routledge, 1997).

23. J.R. Feagin, *The White Racial Frame: Centuries of Racial Framing and Counter-framing* (New York: Routledge, 2020).

24. Charles W. Mills, *The Racial Contract* (Ithaca, NY: Cornell University Press, 2014), 18.

25. J.C. Mueller, "Producing Colorblindness: Everyday Mechanisms of White Ignorance," *Social Problems* 64, no. 2 (2017): 219–38.

26. On how Whiteness shapes housing, see S. Low, "Maintaining Whiteness: The Fear of Others and Niceness," *Transforming Anthropology* 17, no. 2 (2009): 79–92. On how it shapes education, see Zeus Leonardo, *Race, Whiteness, and Education* (New York: Routledge, 2009). On how it shapes politics, see J.R. Feagin, *White Party, White Government: Race, Class, and US Politics* (New York: Routledge, 2012). On how it shapes law, see Ian H. Lopez, *White by Law: The Legal Construction of Race*, Critical America 21 (New York: NYU Press, 1997). On how it shapes social science research methods, see Eduardo Bonilla-Silva and T. Zuberi, *White Logic, White Methods: Racism and Methodology* (Lanham, MD: Rowman and Littlefield, 2008). On how it shapes our understandings of society, see Feagin, *White Racial Frame*; George Lipsitz, *The Posses-*

sive Investment in Whiteness: How White People Profit from Identity Politics (Philadelphia: Temple University Press, 2006); and Mills, Racial Contract.

27. Allen, "Whiteness and Critical Pedagogy"; Karen Brodkin, How Jews Became White Folks and What That Says about Race in America (New Brunswick, NJ: Rutgers University Press, 1998); D. Hartmann, J. Gerteis, and P.R. Croll, "An Empirical Assessment of Whiteness Theory: Hidden from How Many?," Social Problems 56, no. 3 (2009): 403–24; Hughey, "(Dis) Similarities"; M. McDermott and F.L. Samson, "White Racial and Ethnic Identity in the United States," Annual Review of Sociology 31 (2005): 245–61.

28. Jessie Daniels and Amy J. Schulz, "Constructing Whiteness in Health Disparities Research," in Gender, Race, Class, and Health: Intersectional Approaches, ed. A.J. Schulz and L. Mullings (San Francisco: Jossey-Bass, 2006), 89–127; Jessie Daniels, "Intervention: Reality TV, Whiteness, and Narratives of Addiction," in Netherland, Critical Perspectives on Addiction, 103–28; B.K. Rothman, The Book of Life: A Personal and Ethical Guide to Race, Normality, and the Implications of the Human Genome Project (New York: Beacon Press, 2001); J. Malat, S. Mayorga-Gallo, and D.R. Williams, "The Effects of Whiteness on the Health of Whites in the USA," Social Science and Medicine 199 (2018): 148–56; Jonathan M. Metzl, The Protest Psychosis: How Schizophrenia Became a Black Disease (Boston: Beacon Press, 2010); Jonathan M. Metzl, Dying of Whiteness: How the Politics of Racial Resentment Is Killing America's Heartland (New York: Basic Books, 2019).

29. Ashley W. Doane and Eduardo Bonilla-Silva, "Rethinking Whiteness Studies," in White Out: The Continuing Significance of Racism, ed. Ashley W. Doane and Eduardo Bonilla-Silva (New York: Routledge, 2013), 11–26.

30. C. Amutah et al., "Misrepresenting Race: The Role of Medical Schools in Propagating Physician Bias," New England Journal of Medicine 384, no. 9 (2021): 872–78; L.N. Borrell et al., "Race and Genetic Ancestry in Medicine: A Time for Reckoning with Racism," New England Journal of Medicine 384, no. 5 (2021): 474–80.

31. C.C. Gravlee, "How Race Becomes Biology: Embodiment of Social Inequality," American Journal of Physical Anthropology 139, no. 1 (2009): 47–57; M. Montoya, Making the Mexican Diabetic.

32. Eduardo Bonilla-Silva, Racism without Racists: Color Blind Racism and Persistence of Racial Inequality in the U.S. (Lanham, MD: Rowman and Littlefield, 2003).

33. Julie Netherland and Helena B. Hansen, "The War on Drugs That Wasn't: Wasted Whiteness, 'Dirty Doctors,' and Race in Media Coverage of Prescription Opioid Misuse," Culture, Medicine, and Psychiatry 40, no. 4 (2016): 664–86.

34. David Herzberg, Happy Pills in America: From Miltown to Prozac (Baltimore: Johns Hopkins University Press, 2009).

35. James Baldwin, "On Being White—and Other Lies," in The Cross of Redemption: Uncollected Writings, ed. Randall Kenan (New York: Vintage, 2011), 168–69, originally published in Essence, April 1984.

36. Michel Foucault, Security, Territory, Population: Lectures at the Collège de France, 1977–1978 (London: Springer Press, 2007).

37. Marcel Mauss, "Les techniques du corps," *Journal de Psychologie* 32, no. 3–4 (1934).

38. Friedrich Nietzsche, *On the Genealogy of Morals,* trans. Reginald John Hollingdale (New York: Vintage Books, 1989).

39. J. Melamed, "Racial Capitalism," *Critical Ethnic Studies* 1, no. 1 (2015): 76–85; P. Halewood, "Citizenship as Accumulated Racial Capital," *Columbia Journal of Race and Law* 1 (2011): 313–25; J. R. Feagin and S. Elias, "Rethinking Racial Formation Theory: A Systemic Racism Critique." *Ethnic and Racial Studies* 36, no. 6 (2013): 931–60; N. Molina, "The Long Arc of Dispossession: Racial Capitalism and Contested Notions of Citizenship in the US-Mexico Borderlands in the Early Twentieth Century." *Western Historical Quarterly* 45, no. 4 (2014): 431–47.

40. Alan Leshner, "Addiction Is a Brain Disease, and It Matters," *Science* 278, no. 5335 (1997): 46.

41. Thomas McLellan et al., "Drug Dependence, a Chronic Medical Illness: Implications for Treatment, Insurance, and Outcomes Evaluation," *Journal of the American Medical Association* 284, no. 13 (2000): 1689–95.

42. George H. W. Bush, Presidential Proclamation 6158, July 17, 1990, Library of Congress, Project on the Decade of the Brain, www.loc.gov/loc/brain/proclaim.html.

43. On the whitening of heart disease, see Anne Pollock, *Medicating Race: Heart Disease and Durable Preoccupations with Difference* (Durham, NC: Duke University Press, 2012). On the whitening of lung disease, see Braun, *Breathing Race.* On the 70 kg white male research subject, see Epstein, *Inclusion.*

44. David W. Baker, "History of the Joint Commission's Pain Standards: Lessons for Today's Prescription Opioid Epidemic," *Journal of the American Medical Association* 317, no. 11 (2017): 1117–18.

45. On drug reps' counseling prescribers to direct OxyContin to "trustworthy" patients, see Commonwealth of Massachusetts v. Purdue Pharma L.P. et al., Superior Court C.A. No. 1884-cv-01808 (BLS2), January 31, 2019. On physicians' greater tendency to prescribe pain relievers to white patients, see Ian Chen et al., "Racial Differences in Opioid Use for Chronic Nonmalignant Pain," *Journal of General Internal Medicine* 20, no. 7 (2005): 593–98; Mark J. Pletcher et al., "Trends in Opioid Prescribing by Race/Ethnicity for Patients Seeking Care in US Emergency Departments," *Journal of the American Medical Association* 299, no. 1 (2018): 70–78; and Michael Joynt et al., "The Impact of Neighborhood Socioeconomic Status and Race on the Prescribing of Opioids in Emergency Departments throughout the United States," *Journal of General Internal Medicine* 28, no. 12 (2013): 1604–10. On physicians' greater tendency to suspect nonwhite patients of drug abuse, see Hausmann et al., "Racial Disparities"; Shavers, Bakos, and Sheppard, "Race, Ethnicity, and Pain."

46. T. Cicero and H. Surratt, "Effect of Abuse-Deterrent Formulation of OxyContin," *New England Journal of Medicine* 367, no. 2 (2012): 187–89.

47. Jerome H. Jaffe and Charles O'Keeffe, "From Morphine Clinics to Buprenorphine: Regulating Opioid Agonist Treatment of Addiction in the United States," *Drug and Alcohol Dependence* 70, no. 2 (2003): S3–S11.

48. Jaffe and O'Keeffe, "From Morphine Clinics."

49. US Census Bureau, "Law Enforcement, Courts, and Prisons: Arrests, 2009," Section 5 of the Statistical Abstract of the United States: 2012, www .census.gov/compendia/statab/cats/law_enforcement_courts_prisons/arrests.html.

50. Substance Abuse and Mental Health Services Administration, *Results from the 2009 National Survey on Drug Use and Health*, vol. 1, *Summary of National Findings* (Rockville, MD: Office of Applied Studies, 2010.

51. Christopher M. Jones et al., "Vital Signs: Demographic and Substance Use Trends among Heroin Users—United States, 2002–2013," *Morbidity and Mortality Weekly Report* 64, no. 26 (2015): 719–25.

52. Rebecca Haffajee, Anupam B. Jena, and Scott G. Weiner, "Mandatory Use of Prescription Drug Monitoring Programs," *Journal of the American Medical Association* 313, no. 9 (2015): 891–92.

53. Drug Addiction Treatment Act of 1999, S9111, Cong. Rec.—Senate (106th Cong.), 1999, S1092.

54. Drug Addiction Treatment Act of 2000, S9113, Cong. Rec.—Senate (106th Cong.), 2000.

55. Helena Hansen et al., "Buprenorphine and Methadone Treatment for Opioid Dependence by Income, Ethnicity and Race of Neighborhoods in New York City," *Drug and Alcohol Dependence* 164 (2016): 14–21.

56. Food and Drug Administration, "Timeline of Selected FDA Activities and Significant Events Addressing Opioid Misuse and Abuse," accessed 2018, www.fda.gov/drugs/information-drug-class/timeline-selected-fda-activities-and-significant-events-addressing-opioid-misuse-and-abuse.

57. Art Van Zee, "The Promotion and Marketing of Oxycontin: Commercial Triumph, Public Health Tragedy," *American Journal of Public Health* 99, no. 2 (2009): 221–27.

58. Van Zee, "Promotion and Marketing."

59. Gery P. Guy Jr. et al., "Vital Signs: Changes in Opioid Prescribing in the United States, 2006–2015," *Morbidity and Mortality Weekly Report* 66, no. 26 (2017): 697–704.

60. Netherland and Hansen, "War on Drugs That Wasn't."

61. K.D. Bertakis et al., "Gender Differences in the Utilization of Health Care Services," *Journal of Family Practice* 49, no. 2 (2000): 147–52.

62. Center for Substance Abuse Research, University of Maryland, College Park, "Suboxone® Sales Estimated to Reach $1.4 Billion in 2012—More than Viagra® or Adderall®," *CESAR FAX* 21, no. 49 (December 10, 2012), http:// db.cesar.umd.edu/cesar/cesarfax/vol21/21-49.pdf.

63. K. Eban, "OxyContin: Purdue Pharma's Painful Medicine," *CNN Money* (blog), November 9, 2011, http://features.blogs.fortune.cnn.com/2011/11/09 /OxyContin-purdue-pharma/.

64. BusinessWire, "The $11.9 Trillion Global Healthcare Market: Key Opportunities and Strategies (2014–2022)—ReearchAndMarkets.com," June 25, 2019, www.businesswire.com/news/home/20190625005862/en/11.9-Trillion-Global-Healthcare-Market-Key-Opportunities.

65. Lawrence Scholl et al., "Drug and Opioid-Involved Overdose Deaths—United States, 2013–2017," *Morbidity and Mortality Weekly Report* 67, no. 5152 (2019): 1419–27.

CHAPTER 3. GOOD SAMARITANS IN THE WAR ON DRUGS
THAT WASN'T

1. C. T. Baca and K. J. Grant, "What Heroin Users Tell Us about Overdose," *Journal of Addictive Diseases* 26, no. 4 (2007): 63–68.

2. Dean G. Skelos, "Senate Gives Final Legislative Approval to 'Good Samaritan' Law," New York State Senate, press release, June 20, 2011, www .nysenate.gov/newsroom/press-releases/dean-g-skelos/senate-gives-final-legislative-approval-%E2%80%9Cgood-samaritan%E2%80%9D-law.

3. Mariame Kaba, *We Do This 'Til We Free Us: Abolitionist Organizing and Transforming Justice* (Boston: Haymarket Books, 2021), 4.

4. C. C. Poindexter, "Passage of the Ryan White Comprehensive AIDS Resources Emergency Act as a Case Study for Legislative Action," *Health and Social Work* 24, no. 1 (1999): 35–41.

5. Nixon Foundation, "Public Enemy Number One: A Pragmatic Approach to America's Drug Problem," June 29, 2016, www.nixonfoundation.org/2016 /06/26404/.

6. Dan Baum, "Legalize It All: How to Win the War on Drugs," *Harper's Magazine,* April 2016, https://harpers.org/archive/2016/04/legalize-it-all/.

7. Tom Precious, "Lessons from 1977 Resonate in 2019 Marijuana Debate in Albany," *Buffalo News,* August 3, 2019, https://buffalonews.com/news/local /govt-and-politics/lessons-from-1977-resonate-in-2019-marijuana-debate-in-albany/article_59484c56-4d50-5e55-a057-e36e79116ac6.html.

8. Drug Policy Alliance, "A Brief History of the War on Drugs," accessed June 12, 2022, https://drugpolicy.org/issues/brief-history-drug-war.

9. Craig Reinarman and Harry G. Levine, "Crack in the Rearview Mirror: Deconstructing Drug War Mythology," *Social Justice* 31, nos. 1/2 (2004): 182–99.

10. Richard Dvorak, "Cracking the Code: De-coding Colorblind Slurs during the Congressional Crack Cocaine Debates," *Michigan Journal of Race and Law* 5 (1999): 611–63; K. M. Kilty and A. Joseph, "Institutional Racism and Sentencing Disparities for Cocaine Possession," *Journal of Poverty* 3, no. 4 (1999): 1–17.

11. Drug Policy Alliance, "Brief History."

12. Drug Policy Alliance, "Brief History"; Julilly Kohler-Hausmann, *Getting Tough: Welfare and Imprisonment in 1970s America* (Princeton, NJ: Princeton University Press, 2019).

13. Michelle Alexander, *New Jim Crow,* 9.

14. Josiah D. Rich, Sarah E. Wakeman, and Samuel L. Dickman, "Medicine and the Epidemic of Incarceration in the United States," *New England Journal of Medicine* 364, no. 22 (2011): 2081–83, https://dx.doi.org/10.1056%2FNEJMp1102385.

15. Matthew Bigg, "Report Says U.S. Jails More Blacks Than Whites for Drugs," Reuters, December 4, 2007, www.reuters.com/article/us-usa-drugs-race/report-says-u-s-jails-more-blacks-than-whites-for-drugs-id-USN0453686820071205; Erica A. Goode, "Incarceration Rates for Blacks Dropped, Report Shows," *New York Times,* February 27, 2013, www.nytimes .com/2013/02/28/us/incarceration-rates-for-blacks-dropped-report-shows.html; Michelle Alexander, *New Jim Crow.*

16. Loïc Wacquant, *Punishing the Poor: The Neoliberal Government of Social Insecurity* (Durham, NC: Duke University Press, 2009); Carl Hart, *High Price: A Neuroscientist's Journey of Self-Discovery That Challenges Everything You Know about Drugs and Society* (New York: Harper Collins, 2013).

17. Marijuana Arrest Research Project, "Reports, Publications, Testimony." Spring 2020, http://marijuana-arrests.com/reports-publications-testimony.html.

18. American Civil Liberties Union, *A Tale of Two Countries: Racially Targeted Arrests in the Era of Marijuana Reform* (New York: American Civil Liberties Union, 2020), www.aclu.org/report/tale-two-countries-racially-targeted-arrests-era-marijuana-reform.

19. Benjamin Mueller, Robert Gebeloff, and Sahil Chinoy, "Surest Way to Face Marijuana Charges in New York: Be Black or Hispanic," *New York Times,* May 13, 2018, www.nytimes.com/2018/05/13/nyregion/marijuana-arrests-nyc-race.html.

20. Zinzi D. Bailey, Justin M. Feldman, and Mary T. Bassett, "How Structural Racism Works: Racist Policies as a Root Cause of U.S. Racial Health Inequities," *New England Journal of Medicine* 384 (2021): 770.

21. Kaba, *We Do This*, 32.

22. Katherine Seelye, "In Heroin Crisis, White Families Seek Gentler War on Drugs," *New York Times,* October 30, 2015, www.nytimes.com/2015/10/31/us/heroin-war-on-drugs-parents.html.

23. M. D. Lassiter, "Impossible Criminals: The Suburban Imperatives of America's War on Drugs," *Journal of American History* 102 (2015): 126–40.

24. Herzberg, *White Market Drugs*.

25. Nancy D. Campbell, *OD: Naloxone and the Politics of Overdose* (Cambridge, MA: MIT Press, 2020).

26. National Harm Reduction Coalition, "Harm Reduction Resource Center," accessed 2020, https://harmreduction.org/resource-center/.

27. Prescription Drug Abuse Policy System, "Naloxone Overdose Prevention Laws," 2017, http://pdaps.org/datasets/laws-regulating-administration-of-naloxone-1501695139.

28. Mark Faul et al., "Disparity in Naloxone Administration by Emergency Medical Service Providers and the Burden of Drug Overdose in U.S. Rural Communities," *American Journal of Public Health* 105, no. S3 (2015): e26-e32.

29. North Carolina Harm Reduction Coalition, "US Law Enforcement Who Carry Naloxone," accessed 2020, www.nchrc.org/law-enforcement/us-law-enforcement-who-carry-naloxone/.

30. J. Murphy and B. Russell, "Police Officers' Views of Naloxone and Drug Treatment: Does Greater Overdose Response Lead to More Negativity?," *Journal of Drug Issues* 50, no. 4 (2020): 455–71.

31. Federal Bureau of Investigation, "2018 Crime in the U.S," Unform Crime Reporting, 2018, https://ucr.fbi.gov/crime-in-the-u.s/2018/crime-in-the-u.s.-2018.

32. Megan Twohey, "Mike Pence's Response to HIV Outbreak: Prayer, Then a Change of Heart," *New York Times,* August 7, 2016, www.nytimes.com/2016/08/08/us/politics/mike-pence-needle-exchanges-indiana.html.

33. Grant Smith, Drug Policy Alliance, personal communication, 2021.

34. H. Hansen and Roberts, "Two Tiers of Biomedicalization"; H. Hansen et al., "Buprenorphine and Methadone Treatment."

35. "War on Drugs Requires New Tactics: Our View," *USA Today,* May 16, 2016, www.usatoday.com/story/opinion/2016/05/16/heroin-safe-injections-vancouver-opioids-overdose-editorials-debates/84421772/.

36. Drug Enforcement Agency, "National Take Back Initiative," accessed February 18, 2013, www.deadiversion.usdoj.gov/drug_disposal/takeback/.

37. Secure and Responsible Drug Disposal Act (2010), S.3397, 11th Cong., www.congress.gov/bill/111th-congress/senate-bill/3397.

38. Jane Carlisle Maxwell, "The Pain Reliever and Heroin Epidemic in the United States: Shifting Winds in the Perfect Storm," *Journal of Addictive Diseases* 34, nos. 2–3 (2015): 127–40.

39. Tami L. Mark and Rita Vandivort-Warren, "Spending Trends on Substance Abuse Treatment under Private Employer-Sponsored Insurance, 2001–2009," *Drug and Alcohol Dependence* 125, no. 3 (2012): 203–7.

40. Janet R. Cummings et al., "Race/Ethnicity and Geographic Access to Medicaid Substance Use Disorder Treatment Facilities in the United States," *JAMA Psychiatry* 71, no. 2 (2014): 190–96.

41. Drug Policy Alliance, *An Overdose Death Is Not a Murder: Why Drug-Induced Homicide Laws Are Counterproductive and Inhumane,* report (New York: Drug Policy Alliance, 2019), https://drugpolicy.org/sites/default/files/dpa_drug_induced_homicide_report_0.pdf.

42. Valena Elizabeth Beety et al., "Drug-Induced Homicide Defense Toolkit," Ohio State Public Law Working Paper No. 467, October 4, 2019, http://dx.doi.org/10.2139/ssrn.3265510.

43. Christopher Ingraham, "White People Are More Likely to Deal Drugs, but Black People Are More Likely to Get Arrested for It," *Washington Post,* September 30, 2014, www.washingtonpost.com/news/wonk/wp/2014/09/30/white-people-are-more-likely-to-deal-drugs-but-black-people-are-more-likely-to-get-arrested-for-it/.

44. A. Brown and S. Atske, "Black Americans Have Made Gains in U.S. Political Leadership, but Gaps Remain," Pew Research Center, Fact Tank, January 22, 2021, www.pewresearch.org/fact-tank/2021/01/22/black-americans-have-made-gains-in-u-s-political-leadership-but-gaps-remain/.

45. Reflective Democracy Campaign, "Reflective Democracy Research Findings Summary Report," October 2017, https://wholeads.us/wp-content/uploads/2019/04/2017-report-corrected-4.2019.pdf.

46. K. Evers-Hillstrom, "Majority of Lawmakers in 116th Congress Are Millionaires," OpenSecrets, April 23, 2020, www.opensecrets.org/news/2020/04/majority-of-lawmakers-millionaires/; B. Birken and J. Schmidt, "The Average Net Worth of Americas—by Age, Education and Ethnicity," *Forbes*, April 23, 2021, www.forbes.com/advisor/investing/average-net-worth/.

47. James Foreman, *Locking Up Our Own: Crime and Punishment in Black America* (New York: Farrar, Straus and Giroux, 2017).

48. Diane Richardson, "More Funds Needed for Opioid Abuse," New York Assembly video clip, uploaded June 17, 2016, https://nyassembly.gov/mem/Diana-C-Richardson/video/7898/.

CHAPTER 4. "MOTHER'S LITTLE HELPERS"

1. Food and Drug Administration, "Tranquilizers: Use, Abuse, and Dependency," *FDA Consumer*, October 1978, 21.

2. Richard Hughes and Robert Brewin, *The Tranquilizing of America: Pill Popping and the American Way of Life* (New York: Warner Books, 1979), 3.

3. Scott Michels, "Heroin in Suburbia: New Face of Addiction," ABC News, September 29, 2008, https://abcnews.go.com/TheLaw/story?id=5494972&page=1.

4. Cara Buckley, "Young and Suburban, and Falling for Heroin," *New York Times*, September 25, 2009, www.nytimes.com/2009/09/27/nyregion/27heroin.html.

5. Myron Brenton, "Women, Drugs, and Alcohol," *Redbook*, May 1979, 27, 190.

6. Eric Eyre, "Drug Firms Poured 780M Painkillers into WV amid Rise of Overdoses," *Charleston Gazette-Mail*, December 17, 2016, www.wvgazettemail.com/news-health/20161217/drug-firms-poured-780m-painkillers-into-wv-amid-rise-of-overdoses#sthash.fIRPMoj8.dpuf.

7. Roland Berg, "Drugs: The Mounting Menace of Abuse," *Look*, August 8, 1967, 11–28.

8. Richard Nixon, address to the American Medical Association, June 22, 1971, Atlantic City, NJ, in *Advertising of Proprietary Medicines: Hearings before the Subcommittee on Monopoly of the Select Committee on Small Business, US Senate, 92nd Congress, First Session* (Washington, DC: Government Printing Office, 1971), 926–27.

9. Michels, "Heroin in Suburbia."

10. Dylan Lovan, "Appalachia's Approach to Drugs at Odds with AG's Policy," ABC News, May 15, 2017, www.wtvq.com/2017/05/15/appalachias-approach-drugs-odds-ag-policy/.

11. *Cincinnati Commercial*, "Opium Eating," *Daily Union and American*, March 4, 1866, 4.

12. "The Opium Habit's Power," *New York Times*, January 6, 1878, 5.

13. Edward Huntington Williams, "Negro Cocaine 'Fiends' Are a New Southern Menace," *New York Times*, February 8, 1914, SM12.

14. David Courtwright, *Dark Paradise: A History of Opiate Addiction in America* (Cambridge, MA: Harvard University Press, 1982); Joseph Gabriel, "Restricting the Sale of Deadly Poisons: Pharmacists, Drug Regulation, and Narratives of Suffering in the Gilded Age," *Journal of the Gilded Age and the Progressive Era*, July 2010, 313–36.

15. Courtwright, *Dark Paradise*.

16. Carl Trocki, *Opium, Empire and the Global Political Economy: A Study of the Asian Opium Trade 1750–1950* (London: Routledge, 1999); but see also Frank Dikotter, Lares Laamann, and Zhou Xun, *Narcotic Culture: A History of Drugs in China* (Chicago: University of Chicago Press, 2004).

17. Diana L. Ahmad, *The Opium Debate and Chinese Exclusion Laws in the Nineteenth-Century American West* (Reno: University of Nevada Press, 2014); Doris Provine, *Unequal under Law: Race in the War on Drugs* (Chicago: University of Chicago Press, 2007); Nayan Shah, *Contagious Divides: Epidemics and Race in San Francisco's Chinatown* (Berkeley: University of California Press, 2001).

18. "Chinese in New York," *New York Times,* December 26, 1873, 3.

19. *Journal of the American Medical Association* Editorial Board, "The United States Opium Commission," *Journal of the American Medical Association* 51, no. 8 (1908): 678–79.

20. Harry Hubbel Kane, *Drugs That Enslave: The Opium, Morphine, Chloral, and Hashisch Habits* (Philadelphia: Presley Blakiston, 1881), 17.

21. "The Opium Habit's Power," *New York Times,* December 30, 1877, 8.

22. "The Opium Habit," *Catholic World,* September 1881, 827.

23. Supplemental Treaty between the United States and China, Concerning Intercourse and Judicial Procedure, October 5, 1881, 22 Stat. (1864–83): 828.

24. An Act to Prohibit the Importation and Use of Opium for Other Than Medicinal Purposes, Pub. L. No. 221, ch. 100, 35 Stat. 614 (1909).

25. Courtwright, *Dark Paradise.*

26. Herzberg, *White Market Drugs.*

27. Caroline Jean Acker, *Creating the American Junkie: Addiction Research in the Classic Era of Narcotic Control* (Baltimore: Johns Hopkins University Press, 2002).

28. Philip Bump, "Rep. Steve King Warns That 'Our Civilization' Can't Be Restored with 'Somebody Else's Babies,'" *Washington Post,* March 12, 2017, www.washingtonpost.com/news/politics/wp/2017/03/12/rep-steve-king-warns-that-our-civilization-cant-be-restored-with-somebody-elses-babies/.

29. Williams, "Negro Cocaine 'Fiends.'"

30. Courtwright, *Dark Paradise.*

31. Herzberg, *White Market Drugs.*

32. Herzberg, *White Market Drugs.*

33. Lawrence Kolb, "Drug Addiction: A Study of Some Medical Cases," *Archives of Neurology and Psychiatry* 20, no. 1 (1928): 182.

34. David Musto, *The American Disease: Origins of Narcotic Control* (New York: Oxford University Press, 1999).

35. Acker, *Creating the American Junkie.*

36. Acker, *Creating the American Junkie.*

37. Schneider, *Smack.*

38. Samuel Hopkins Adams, "Control for the Devil's Capsules," *American Weekly,* July 20, 1947.

39. Bill Davidson, "The Thrill-Pill Menace," *Saturday Evening Post,* December 4, 1965.

40. Centers for Disease Control and Prevention, "Leading Causes of Death, 1900–1998," accessed June 19, 2022, www.cdc.gov/nchs/data/dvs/lead1900_98.pdf.

41. Herzberg, *White Market Drugs*; Nicolas Rasmussen, *On Speed: The Many Lives of Amphetamine* (New York: New York University Press, 2008).

42. Rollo May, *The Meaning of Anxiety* (Eastford, CT: Martino Fine Books, 1950), 344–45, cited in Herzberg, *Happy Pills in America.*

43. "Tension and the Nerves of the Nation . . . Psychiatry Eyes the Breaking Point," *Newsweek,* March 5, 1956, 54–58.

44. Herzberg, *White Market Drugs.* For regulations enabling rather than quashing drug markets, see Gabriel, "Restricting the Sale of Deadly Poisons."

45. Nicolas Rasmussen, "Goofball Panic: Barbiturates, 'Dangerous' and Addictive Drugs, and the Regulation of Medicine in Postwar America," in *Prescribed: Writing, Filling, Using, and Abusing the Prescription in Modern America*, ed. Jeremy A. Greene and Elizabeth Siegel Watkins (Baltimore: Johns Hopkins University Press, 2012); Kathleen Frydl, *The Drug Wars in America, 1940–1973* (New York: Cambridge University Press, 2013); Herzberg, *White Market Drugs*.

46. Vera Connolly, "Lethal Lullaby," *Collier's*, October 19, 1946, 95–97.

47. Juvenile Delinquency (National, Federal and Youth-Serving Agencies), Part 1: Hearings before the United States Senate Committee on the Judiciary, Subcommittee to Investigate Juvenile Delinquency in the U.S., 83rd Cong., 1st sess., November 19, 20, 23, 24, 1953, 290–96, https://searchworks.stanford.edu/view/11021292.

48. Frydl, *The Drug Wars in America;* Herzberg, *White Market Drugs*.

49. Schneider, *Smack*.

50. Herzberg, *White Market Drugs*.

51. Raz, "Treating Addiction or Reducing Crime?"; Claire D. Clark, *The Recovery Revolution: The Battle over Addiction Treatment in the United States* (New York: Columbia University Press, 2017).

52. Lizabeth Cohen, *A Consumers' Republic: The Politics of Mass Consumption in Postwar America* (New York: Alfred A. Knopf, 2003); Lawrence B. Glickman, *Buying Power: A History of Consumer Activism in America* (Chicago: University of Chicago Press, 2009).

53. Controlled Substances Act, Pub. L. No. 91–513, 84 Stat. 1236 (October 27, 1970).

54. Herzberg, *White Market Drugs;* David T. Courtwright, "The Controlled Substances Act: How a 'Big Tent' Reform Became a Punitive Drug Law," *Drug and Alcohol Dependence* 76, no. 1 (2004): 9–15, http://dx.doi.org/10.1016/j.drugalcdep.2004.04.012; Joseph F. Spillane, "Debating the Controlled Substances Act," *Drug and Alcohol Dependence* 76, no. 1 (2004): 17–29, https://doi.org/10.1016/j.drugalcdep.2004.04.011.

55. Herzberg, *White Market Drugs;* Rasmussen, *On Speed*.

56. Craig Reinarman and Harry Levine, *Crack in America: Demon Drugs and Social Justice* (Berkeley: University of California Press, 1997); Kohler-Hausmann, *Getting Tough*.

57. Herzberg, *White Market Drugs*.

CHAPTER 5. OXYCONTIN'S RACIAL PRECISION

1. Commonwealth of Massachusetts v. Purdue Pharma L.P. et al., Superior Court C.A. No. 1884-cv-01808 (BLS2), January 31, 2019.

2. John Seewer and Geoff Mulvihill, "Deal with OxyContin Maker Leaves Families Angry, Conflicted," Associated Press, September 2, 2021, https://apnews.com/article/business-health-6c2ad3d4164f3711eb5c2d443d23a75e.

3. US Council of Economic Advisors, "The Full Cost of the Opioid Crisis: $2.5 Trillion over Four Years," October 28, 2019, https://trumpwhitehouse.archives.gov/articles/full-cost-opioid-crisis-2-5-trillion-four-years/.

4. Seewer and Mulvihill, "Deal with OxyContin Maker."

5. Brian Mann, "The Sacklers, Who Made Billions from OxyContin, Win Immunity from Opioid Lawsuits," NPR, September 1, 2021, www.npr.org /2021/09/01/1031053251/sackler-family-immunity-purdue-pharma-oxcyontin-opioid-epidemic.

6. Pletcher et al., "Trends in Opioid Prescribing"; Chen et al., "Racial Differences."

7. Canadian Agency for Drugs and Technologies in Health, "Opioid Formulations with Tamper-Resistant or Abuse-Deterrent Features: Products and Policies," Environmental Scan, March 2017, www.cadth.ca/sites/default/files/pdf /ES0298-EH0034_Abuse_Deterrent_Opioid_Formulations.pdf.

8. Katie Warren and Taylor Nicole Rogers, "The Family behind Purdue Pharma: Meet the Sacklers, Who Built Their $13 Billion Fortune Off the Controversial Opioid," *Business Insider,* March 23, 2020, www.businessinsider .com/who-are-the-sacklers-wealth-philanthropy-oxycontin-photos-2019-1.

9. Young Hee Nam et al., "State Prescription Drug Monitoring Programs and Fatal Drug Overdoses," *American Journal of Managed Care* 23, no. 5 (2017): 297–303.

10. Daniel Ciccarone, Jeff Ondocsin, and Sarah G. Mars, "Heroin Uncertainties: Exploring Users' Perceptions of Fentanyl-Adulterated-and-Substituted 'Heroin,'" *International Journal of Drug Policy* 46 (2017): 146–55; Sam Quinones, *Dreamland: The True Tale of America's Opiate Epidemic* (New York: Bloomsbury, 2015).

11. Martin, "Pharmaceutical Person."

12. Anita Hardon, *Chemical Youth: Navigating Uncertainty in Search of the Good Life* (London: Palgrave Macmillan, 2020).

13. Herzberg, *Happy Pills in America.*

14. Patrick Radden Keefe, "The Family That Built an Empire of Pain: The Sackler Dynasty's Ruthless Marketing of Painkillers Has Generated Billions of Dollars—and Millions of Addicts," *New Yorker,* October 23, 2017, www .newyorker.com/magazine/2017/10/30/the-family-that-built-an-empire-of-pain; Patrick Radden Keefe, *Empire of Pain: The Secret History of the Sackler Dynasty* (New York: Doubleday, 2021).

15. Herzberg, *White Market Drugs,* 241–81.

16. Wailoo, *Pain.*

17. Lucille Joel, "The Fifth Vital Sign: Pain," *American Journal of Nursing* 99, no. 2 (1999): 9.

18. Brooke A. Chidgey, Katharine L. McGinigle, and Peggy P. McNaull, "When a Vital Sign Leads a Country Astray: The Opioid Epidemic," *Journal of the American Medical Association—Surgery* 154, no. 11 (2019): 987–88; D. A. Tompkins, J. G. Hobelmann, and P. Compton, "Providing Chronic Pain Management in the 'Fifth Vital Sign' Era: Historical and Treatment Perspectives on a Modern-Day Medical Dilemma," *Drug and Alcohol Dependence* 173 (2017): S11-S21.

19. Kelly M. Hoffman et al., "Racial Bias in Pain Assessment and Treatment Recommendations, and False Beliefs about Biological Differences between Blacks and Whites," *Proceedings of the National Academy of Sciences* 113, no. 16 (2016): 4296–4301.

20. Wailoo, *Pain*.

21. Helena Hansen, Philippe Bourgois, and Ernest Drucker, "Pathologizing Poverty: New Forms of Diagnosis, Disability, and Structural Stigma under Welfare Reform," *Social Science and Medicine* 103 (2014): 76–83.

22. Herzberg, *White Market Drugs*.

23. Wailoo, *Pain*.

24. Wailoo, *Pain;* Joanna Bourke, *The Story of Pain: From Prayer to Painkillers* (New York: Oxford University Press, 2014); Hoffman et al., "Racial Bias."

25. Marcia Meldrum, "A Brief History of the Multidisciplinary Management of Chronic Pain," in *Chronic Pain Management: Guidelines for Multidisciplinary Program Development*, ed. Michael Schatman and Alexandra Campbell (Boca Raton, FL: CRC Press, Taylor and Francis, 2007); Bourke, *Story of Pain*.

26. Jane Porter and Hershel Jick, "Addiction Rare in Patients Treated with Narcotics," letter to editor, *New England Journal of Medicine* 302, no. 2 (1980): 123.

27. Kathleen Foley, "Current Issues in the Management of Cancer Pain: Memorial Sloan-Kettering Cancer Center," in *New Approaches to Treatment of Chronic Pain: A Review of Multidisciplinary Pain Clinics and Pain Centers*, ed. Lorenz K. Y. Ng, NIDA Research Monograph 36 (Washington, DC: Government Printing Office, 1981), 169–81.

28. US Senate Finance Committee, *Findings from the Investigation of Opioid Manufacturers' Financial Relationships with Patient Advocacy Groups and Other Tax-Exempt Entities*, report, December 16, 2020, www.finance.senate.gov/imo/media/doc/2020-12-16%20Finance%20Committee%20Bipartisan%20Opioids%20Report.pdf.

29. Herzberg, *White Market Drugs*.

30. Wailoo, *Pain*.

31. "Worker's Comp System Hit by Opioid Crisis," News Service of Florida, April 25, 2018, https://wusfnews.wusf.usf.edu/2018-04-25/workers-comp-system-hit-by-opioid-crisis.

32. Chris Laws, *Narcotics in Workers Compensation*, National Council on Compensation Insurance, NCCI Research Brief, May 2012, www.gwca.info/articles/II_narcotics-wc.pdf.

33. Kenneth D. Tunnell, "Cultural Constructions of the Hillbilly Heroin and Crime Problem," in *Cultural Criminology Unleashed*, ed. J. Ferrell et al. (London: Routledge, 2016), 136.

34. Tunnell, "Cultural Constructions."

35. Shannon M. Monnat, "Opioid Crisis in the Rural US," in *Rural Families and Communities in the United States*, ed. Jennifer E. Glick, Susan M. McHale, and Valarie King (Cham: Springer, 2020), 117–43; Laura Radel et al., *Substance Use, the Opioid Epidemic, and the Child Welfare System: Key Findings from a Mixed Methods Study*, Office of the Assistant Secretary for Planning and Evaluation, ASPE Research Brief, March 7, 2018, https://aspe.hhs.gov/sites/default/files/private/pdf/258836/SubstanceUseChildWelfareOverview.pdf.

36. Daniel Ciccarone, "The Triple Wave Epidemic: Supply and Demand Drivers of the US Opioid Overdose Crisis," *International Journal on Drug Policy* 71 (2019): 183.

37. Case and Deaton, "Rising Morbidity and Mortality."

38. On race in the architecture of scientific technologies, see Braun, *Breathing Race*. On race in drug development strategies, see Sandra Soo-Jin Lee, "Racializing Drug Design: Implications of Pharmacogenomics for Health Disparities," *American Journal of Public Health* 95, no. 12 (2005): 2133–38; Jonathan Kahn, "Exploiting Race in Drug Development: BiDil's Interim Model of Pharmacogenomics," *Social Studies of Science* 38, no. 5 (2008): 737–58; Kahn, *Race in a Bottle*. On race in the attribution of racial differences in obesity, heart disease, and diabetes to biological-genetic heredity, see Anthony Ryan Hatch, *Blood Sugar: Racial Pharmacology and Food Justice in Black America* (Minneapolis: University of Minnesota Press, 2016), and M. Montoya, *Making the Mexican Diabetic*. For studies on the reproduction of white privilege in the medical sciences, see Michael Rodríguez-Muñiz, "Bridgework: STS, Sociology, and the 'Dark Matters' of Race," *Engaging Science, Technology, and Society* 2 (2016): 214–26.

39. On infrastructures of racialization in the pharmaceutical industry, see S. Lee, "Racializing Drug Design."

40. Daniels and Schulz, "Constructing Whiteness," 94.

41. Craig Reinarman, "Addiction as Accomplishment: The Discursive Construction of Disease," *Addiction Research and Theory* 13, no. 4 (2005): 307–20; Suzanne Fraser, David Moore, and Helen Keane, *Habits: Remaking Addiction* (London: Springer, 2014).

42. Epstein, *Inclusion*.

43. Nora Volkow, "Addiction Is a Disease of Free Will," National Institute on Drug Abuse, June 12, 2015, www.drugabuse.gov/about-nida/noras-blog/2015/06/addiction-disease-free-will.

44. Courtwright, *Dark Paradise*.

45. Herzberg, *Happy Pills in America*.

46. Nora Volkow and Ting-Kai Li, "The Neuroscience of Addiction," *Nature Neuroscience* 8, no. 11 (2005): 1436.

47. Volkow and Li, "Neuroscience of Addiction."

48. Caroline Jean Acker, "How Crack Found a Niche in the American Ghetto: The Historical Epidemiology of Drug-Related Harm," *BioSocieties* 5, no. 1 (2010): 70–88, https://doi.org/10.1057/biosoc.2009.1; Nancy D. Campbell, "Toward a Critical Neuroscience of 'Addiction,'" *BioSocieties* 5, no. 1 (2010): 89–104, https://doi.org/10.1057/biosoc.2009.2.

49. Suparna Choudhury and Jan Slaby, eds., *Critical Neuroscience: A Handbook of the Social and Cultural Contexts of Neuroscience* (New York: John Wiley and Sons, 2016).

50. On biological determinism and depression, see Andrew Lakoff, *Pharmaceutical Reason: Knowledge and Value in Global Psychiatry* (Cambridge: Cambridge University Press, 2006); Andrew Lakoff, "The Right Patients for the Drug: Managing the Placebo Effect in Antidepressant Trials," *BioSocieties* 2, no. 1 (2007): 57–71, https://doi.org/10.1017/S1745855207005054; Joao Biehl, "Life of the Mind: The Interface of Psychopharmaceuticals, Domestic Economies, and Social Abandonment," *American Ethnologist* (2004): 475–96.

51. Campbell, "Toward a Critical Neuroscience," 101.

52. Helena Hansen and Mary E. Skinner, "From White Bullets to Black Markets and Greened Medicine: The Neuroeconomics and Neuroracial Politics of Opioid Pharmaceuticals," *Annals of Anthropological Practice* 36, no. 1 (2012): 167–82, https://doi.org/10.1111/j.2153-9588.2012.01098.x.

53. For the 2001 total marketing figure, see Van Zee, "Promotion and Marketing"; for the 1996–2002 medical journal advertising figure, see Fred Schulte, "How America Got Hooked on a Deadly Drug," *Kaiser Health News*, June 13, 2018, https://khn.org/news/how-america-got-hooked-on-a-deadly-drug/.

54. US Senate Homeland Security and Governmental Affairs Committee, *Fueling an Epidemic: Exposing the Financial Ties between Opioid Manufacturers and Third Party Advocacy Groups*, HSGAC Minority Staff Report, 2018, www .hsgac.senate.gov/imo/media/doc/REPORT-Fueling%20an%20Epidemic-Exposing%20the%20Financial%20Ties%20Between%20Opioid%20Manufacturers%20and%20Third%20Party%20Advocacy%20Groups.pdf.

55. Commonwealth of Massachusetts v. Purdue Pharma L.P. et al., Superior Court C.A. No. 1884-cv-01808 (BLS2), January 31, 2019; Commonwealth of Virginia, ex rel. Mark R. Herring, Attorney General, v. Purdue Pharma L.P., Purdue Pharma Inc., and The Purdue Frederick Company, 2018, www.oag.state.va.us /consumer-protection/files/Lawsuits/Purdue-Complaint-Unredacted-2018-08-13. pdf, 29; State of Tennessee, ex rel. Herbert H. Slatery III, Attorney General and Reporter, v. Purdue Pharma L.P., 2018, www.tn.gov/content/dam/tn/attorneygeneral /documents/foi/purdue/purduecomplaint-5-15-2018.pdf, 17.

56. Douglas C. McDonald, Kenneth Carlson, and David Izrael, "Geographic Variation in Opioid Prescribing in the US," *Journal of Pain* 13, no. 10 (2012): 988–96.

57. J. A. Inciardi and T. J. Cicero, "Black Beauties, Gorilla Pills, Footballs, and Hillbilly Heroin: Some Reflections on Prescription Drug Abuse and Diversion Research over the Past 40 Years," *Journal of Drug Issues* 39, no. 1 (2009): 101–14; Tunnell, "Cultural Constructions."

58. Scott E. Hadland et al., "Association of Pharmaceutical Industry Marketing of Opioid Products with Mortality from Opioid-Related Overdoses," *Journal of the American Medical Association Network Open* 2, no. 1 (2019): e186007–e186007.

59. Susan Reynolds Whyte, Sjaak Van der Geest, and Anita Hardon, *Social Lives of Medicines* (New York: Cambridge University Press, 2002).

60. Parker and Hansen, "How Opioids Became 'Safe.'"

61. Rose, *Politics of Life Itself*; Martin, "Pharmaceutical Person"; Jenkins, *Pharmaceutical Self*.

62. On the personality of Valium, see Herzberg, *Happy Pills in America*. On that of Viagra, see Emily Wentzell, "Marketing Silence, Public Health Stigma and the Discourse of Risky Gay Viagra Use in the US," *Body and Society* 17, no. 4 (2011): 105–25, https://doi-org.manchester.idm.oclc.org/10.1177% 2F1357034X11410449. On that of Haldol, see Metzl, *Protest Psychosis*.

63. Wentzell, "Marketing Silence."

64. Nathan Greenslit, "Depression and Consumption: Psychopharmaceuticals, Branding, and New Identity Practices," *Culture, Medicine and Psychiatry* 29, no. 4 (2005): 477–502.

65. Parker and Hansen, "How Opioids Became 'Safe.'"

66. Van Zee, "Promotion and Marketing."

67. Andrew Ohio, "New Details Revealed about Purdue's Marketing of OxyContin," *STAT*, January 15, 2019, 15–16, www.statnews.com/2019/01/15 /massachusetts-purdue-lawsuit-new-details/.

68. Van Zee, "Promotion and Marketing"; John Temple, *American Pain: How a Young Felon and His Ring of Doctors Unleashed America's Deadliest Drug Epidemic* (Guilford, CT: Rowman and Littlefield, 2015); Melina Sherman, "Opiates for the Masses: Constructing a Market for Prescription (Pain) Killers," *Journal of Cultural Economy* 10, no. 6 (2017): 485–97.

69. Anna Lembke, *Drug Dealer, MD: How Doctors Were Duped, Patients Got Hooked, and Why It's So Hard to Stop* (Baltimore: Johns Hopkins University Press, 2016); Barry Meier, *Pain Killer: A "Wonder" Drug's Trail of Addiction and Death* (Emmaus, PA: Rodale, 2003).

70. Lembke, *Drug Dealer, MD.*

71. US Senate Homeland Security and Governmental Affairs Committee, *Fueling an Epidemic.*

72. David Healy and Dinah Cattell, "Interface between Authorship, Industry and Science in the Domain of Therapeutics," *British Journal of Psychiatry* 183, no. 1 (2003): 22–27.

73. Sergio Sismondo, "Ghost Management: How Much of the Medical Literature Is Shaped behind the Scenes by the Pharmaceutical Industry?," *PLOS Medicine* 4, no. 9 (2007): e286, https://doi.org/10.1371/journal.pmed.0040286.

74. Phillip Wininger, "Pharmaceutical Overpromotion Liability: The Legal Battle over Rural Prescription Drug Abuse," *Kentucky Law Journal* 93, no. 1 (2004): 269–94.

75. Van Zee, "Promotion and Marketing."

76. Massachusetts Attorney General's Office, Commonwealth of Massachusetts vs. Purdue Pharma LP, 2019.

77. Ohio, "New Details Revealed."

78. Ohio Attorney General's Office, State of Ohio ex rel. Mike DeWine, Ohio Attorney General, Plaintiff v. Purdue Pharma L.P., N.E. 1. Common Pleas Court of Ross County, Ohio, 2017.

79. The ad, under the title "JAMA Ad 2002" (bdr:927749), can be found in the Brown Digital Repository, https://repository.library.brown.edu/studio/item /bdr:927749/.

80. State of Ohio ex rel. Mike DeWine, Ohio Attorney General, Plaintiff v. Purdue Pharma L.P.; Commonwealth of Massachusetts v. Purdue Pharma LP; Florida Attorney General's Office, State of Florida, Office of the Attorney General, Department of Legal Affairs v. Purdue Pharma L.P., et al., 2018, http:// faca.fl-counties.com/sites/default/files/2018–05/State%20of%20Florida%20 Complaint.pdf.

81. US Senate Homeland Security and Governmental Affairs Committee, *Fueling an Epidemic.*

82. Derek McGinnis, *Exit Wounds: A Survival Guide to Pain Management for Returning Veterans and Their Families* (Washington, DC: Waterford Life Science, 2009), 106–10.

83. Massachusetts Attorney General's Office, Commonwealth of Massachusetts v. Purdue Pharma L.P., 2019.

84. American Pain Foundation, testimony, in *Senate Health, Education, Labor and Pensions Committee Hearing to Examine the Effects of the Painkiller OxyContin, Focusing on Risks and Benefits*, 107th Cong., 2nd sess., February 12, 2002, www.govinfo.gov/content/pkg/CHRG-107shrg77770/pdf/CHRG-107shrg77770.pdf, summarized in MSI Corporation v. Purdue Pharma L.P. et al., September 10, 2018, p. 20, http://healthdocbox.com/Substance_Abuse /120373315-Case-2-18-cv-cb-document-1-filed-08-21-18-page-1-of-92-in-the-united-states-district-court-for-the-western-district-of-pennsylvania.html.

85. Office of Attorney General, State of Kansas, State of Kansas v. Purdue Pharma, Case number 2019-CV-000369, 2019.

86. T. Altilio et al., *Treatment Options: A Guide for People Living with Pain* (Baltimore: American Pain Foundation, 2007), 15.

87. Seddon R. Savage et al., "Definitions Related to the Medical Use of Opioids: Evolution towards Universal Agreement," *Journal of Pain and Symptom Management* 26, no. 1 (2003): 655–67, https://doi.org/10.1016/S0885-3924(03)00219-7; David Haddox et al., "The Use of Opioids for the Treatment of Chronic Pain: A Consensus Statement from the American Academy of Pain Medicine and the American Pain Society," *Clinical Journal of Pain* 13, no. 1 (1997): 6–8, www.jpain.org/article/S1526-5900(08)00831-6/fulltext; Roger Chou et al., "Clinical Guidelines for the Use of Chronic Opioid Therapy in Chronic Noncancer Pain," *Journal of Pain: Official Journal of the American Pain Society* 10, no. 2 (2009): 113–30, https://doi.org/10.1016/j.jpain.2008.10.008; Martin E. Hale et al., "Efficacy and Safety of Controlled-Release versus Immediate-Release Oxycodone: Randomized, Double-Blind Evaluation in Patients with Chronic Back Pain," *Clinical Journal of Pain* 15, no. 3 (1999): 179–83.

88. R. Chou et al., "Clinical Guidelines," 114.

89. R. Chou et al., "Clinical Guidelines," 123.

90. Savage et al., "Definitions," 657.

91. Lembke, *Drug Dealer, MD*.

92. Lynn R. Webster and Rebecca M. Webster, "Predicting Aberrant Behaviors in Opioid-Treated Patients: Preliminary Validation of the Opioid Risk Tool," *Pain Medicine* 6, no. 6 (2005): 432–42.

93. Inflexxion Inc., "Screener and Opioid Assessment for Patients with Pain (SOAPP)® Version 1.0-SF," 2008, www.mcstap.com/docs/SOAPP-5.pdf; Stephen F. Butler et al., "Validation of the Revised Screener and Opioid Assessment for Patients with Pain (SOAPP-R)," *Journal of Pain* 9, no. 4 (2008): 360–72; Miles J. Belgrade, Cassandra D. Schamber, and Bruce R. Lindgren, "The DIRE Score: Predicting Outcomes of Opioid Prescribing for Chronic Pain," *Journal of Pain* 7, no. 9 (2006): 671–81.

94. Jacques R. Caldwell et al., "Treatment of Osteoarthritis Pain with Controlled Release Oxycodone or Fixed Combination Oxycodone Plus Acetaminophen Added to Nonsteroidal Antiinflammatory Drugs: A Double Blind, Randomized, Multicenter, Placebo Controlled Trial," *Journal of Rheumatology* 26, no. 4 (1999): 862.

95. S.H. Roth et al., "Around-the-Clock, Controlled-Release Oxycodone Therapy for Osteoarthritis-Related Pain: Placebo-Controlled Trial and Long-Term Evaluation," *Archives of Internal Medicine* 160, no. 6 (2000): 853–60.

96. Epstein, *Inclusion*.

97. David E. Weissman and J. David Haddox, "Opioid Pseudoaddiction: An Iatrogenic Syndrome," *Pain* 36, no. 3 (1989): 363–66.

98. New York Attorney General's Office, People of the State of New York v. Purdue Pharma L.P. et al., 2018, https://ag.ny.gov/sites/default/files/400016_2018_the_people_of_the_stat_v_the_people_of_the_stat_summons_complaint_2.pdf; Ohio Attorney General's Office, State of Ohio ex rel. v. Purdue Pharma L.P., 2017; Florida Attorney General's Office, State Of Florida v. Purdue Pharma L.P., 2018; Virginia Attorney General's Office, "Herring Sues Sackler Family for Role in Opioid Crisis, Trying to Illegally Enrich Themselves and Shield Company Money," press release, September 11, 2019, https://www.oag.state.va.us/consumer-protection/index.php/news/359-september-11-2019-herring-sues-sackler-family-for-role-in-opioid-crisis-trying-to-illegally-enrich-themselves-and-shield-company-money.

99. Purdue Pharmaceuticals, *Providing Relief, Preventing Abuse: A Reference Guide to Controlled Substance Prescribing Practices*, brochure, 2007; Scott Fishman, *Responsible Opioid Prescribing: A Physician's Guide* (Washington, DC: Waterford Life Sciences, 2007).

100. Ohio Attorney General's Office, State of Ohio ex rel. Mike DeWine, Ohio Attorney General, Plaintiff, v. Purdue Pharma L.P., 2017.

101. Du Bois, *Souls of Black Folk*.

102. Bourdieu, "Forms of Capital."

CHAPTER 6. BUPRENORPHINE'S SILENT WHITE REVOLUTION

1. Jaffe and O'Keeffe, "From Morphine Clinics."

2. Sentencing Project, "Criminal Justice Facts"; Federal Bureau of Prisons, "Inmate Statistics: Offenses," accessed 2019, www.bop.gov/about/statistics/statistics_inmate_offenses.jsp.

3. US Census Bureau, "Quick Facts: New York County, New York (Manhattan Borough)," accessed 2014, www.census.gov/quickfacts/table/HSD410214/36061; US Census Bureau, "Quick Facts, Richmond County (Staten Island Borough)," accessed 2014, www.census.gov/quickfacts/table/PST045215/36085; New York City Department of Health and Mental Hygiene, "Opioid Misuse in New York City," paper presented at the New York City Department of Health and Mental Hygiene, May 5, 2014.

4. Frank Vocci, Jane Acri, and Ahmed Elkashef, "Medication Development for Addictive Disorders: The State of the Science," *American Journal of Psychiatry* 162, no. 8 (2005): 1432–40.

5. Jaffe and O'Keeffe, "From Morphine Clinics."

6. Richard P. Mattick et al., "Buprenorphine Maintenance versus Placebo or Methadone Maintenance for Opioid Dependence (Cochrane Methodology Review)," *Cochrane Library*, no. 4 (2003), www.dronet.org/lineeguida/ligu_pdf/Oppiacei.pdf; Richard P. Mattick et al., "Buprenorphine Maintenance

versus Placebo or Methadone Maintenance for Opioid Dependence," *Cochrane Database of Systematic Reviews*, no. 2 (2004), www.cochranelibrary.com/cdsr /doi/10.1002/14651858.CD002207.pub4/abstract.

7. Ruben D. Baler and Nora D. Volkow, "Drug Addiction: The Neurobiology of Disrupted Self-Control," *Trends in Molecular Medicine* 12, no. 2 (2006): 559–66.

8. Nancy D. Campbell and Anne M. Lovell, "The History of the Development of Buprenorphine as an Addiction Therapeutic," *Annals of the New York Academy of Sciences* 1248, no. 1 (2012): 124–39.

9. Alan Cowan and John Lewis, *Buprenorphine: Combatting Drug Abuse with a Unique Opioid* (New York: Wiley Liss, 1995).

10. Merrill Singer, *Drugging the Poor: Legal and Illegal Drugs and Social Inequality* (Long Grove, IL: Waveland Press, 2007).

11. Hamid et al., "Heroin Epidemic"; Agar and Reisinger, "Using Trend Theory."

12. Amy Spindler, "The 90's Version of the Decadent Look," *New York Times*, May 7, 1996, www.nytimes.com/1996/05/07/style/the-90-s-version-of-the-decadent-look.html.

13. Amy Silverman and Jeremy Voas, "Opiate for the Mrs.," *Phoenix New Times*, September 8, 1994, www.phoenixnewtimes.com/news/opiate-for-the-mrs-6432986; Jim Edwards, "One Nation, on Vicodin: Narcotic Painkillers Are Most-Used U.S. Drugs," CBS News, April 20, 2011, www.cbsnews.com/news /one-nation-on-vicodin-narcotic-painkillers-are-most-used-us-drugs/.

14. Julie Netherland, "Becoming Normal: The Social Construction of Buprenorphine and New Attempts to Medicalize Addiction" (PhD diss., City University of New York, 2011).

15. Hannu Alho et al., "Abuse Liability of Buprenorphine–Naloxone Tablets in Untreated IV Drug Users," *Drug and Alcohol Dependence* 88, no. 1 (2007): 75–78; V. Pauly et al., "Estimated Magnitude of Diversion and Abuse of Opioids Relative to Benzodiazepines in France," *Drug and Alcohol Dependence* 126, nos. 1–2 (2012): 13–20.

16. R. Bruce et al., "Lack of Reduction in Buprenorphine Injection after Introduction of Co-formulated Buprenorphine/Naloxone to the Malaysian Market," *American Journal of Drug and Alcohol Abuse* 35, no. 2 (2009): 68–72; B. Vicknasingam et al., "Injection of Buprenorphine and Buprenorphine/Naloxone Tablets in Malaysia," *Drug and Alcohol Dependence* 111, nos. 1–2 (2010): 44–49.

17. Alexander Bazazi et al., "Illicit Use of Buprenorphine/Naloxone among Injecting and Noninjecting Opioid Users," *Journal of Addiction Medicine* 5, no. 3 (2011): 175–80; Chris-Ellyn Johanson et al., "Diversion and Abuse of Buprenorphine: Findings from National Surveys of Treatment Patients and Physicians," *Drug and Alcohol Dependence* 120, nos. 1–3 (2012): 190–95.

18. Case and Deaton, "Rising Morbidity and Mortality"; Substance Abuse and Mental Health Services Administration, Center for Substance Abuse Treatment, *Clinical Guidelines for the Use of Buprenorphine in the Treatment of Opioid Addiction*, Treatment Improvement Protocol (TIP) Series, No. 40 (Rockville, MD: Substance Abuse and Mental Health Services Administration, 2004), www.ncbi.nlm.nih.gov/books/NBK64234/.

19. Substance Abuse and Mental Health Services Administration, *Expanding the Use of Medications to Treat Individuals with Substance Use Disorders in Safety Net Settings*, September 2014, www.thenationalcouncil.org/wp-content /uploads/2020/01/Expanding_the_Use_of_Medications_to_Treat_Individuals_ with_SU_Disorders_in_Safety_Net_Settings.pdf.

20. New York City Department of Health and Mental Hygiene, "Opioid Misuse."

21. White Trash Clan, "My World Is Blue," music video, July 16, 2012, www.youtube.com/watch?v=1kOoyWVDNZc.

22. Aaron Katersky, "'Blue Fairy' Arrested in New York Drug Bust," ABC News, February 15, 2013, https://abcnews.go.com/Blotter/blue-fairy-arrested-york-drug-bust/story?id=18511865.

23. Mike Spies, Dave Gutt, and James Peterson, "Welcome to Heroin Island," *Vocativ*, August 21, 2014, www.vocativ.com/underworld/drugs/heroin-staten-island/index.html.

24. Andy Mai and John Annese, "S.I. Woman Who Played Blue Fairy in Drug Video Found Dead," *New York Daily News*, March 2, 2016, www.nydailynews .com/new-york/s-woman-played-blue-fairy-drug-video-found-dead-article -1.2549764.

25. Joseph O. Merrill et al., "Mutual Mistrust in the Medical Care of Drug Users," *Journal of General Internal Medicine* 17, no. 5 (2002): 327–33.

26. Stopthedrugwar.com, "New York Mayor Giuliani Reverses Himself on Methadone," *Drug War Chronicle*, January 22, 1999, http://stopthedrugwar .org/chronicle-old/075/giuliani.shtml.

27. Soteri Polydorou et al., "Integrating Buprenorphine into an Opioid Treatment Program: Tailoring Care for Patients with Opioid Use Disorders," *Psychiatric Services* 68, no. 3 (2017): 295–98.

28. Frederick B. Glaser, "The Origins of the Drug-Free Therapeutic Community," *British Journal of Addiction* 76, no. 1 (1981): 13–25; Clark, *Recovery Revolution*.

29. Lagisetty et al., "Buprenorphine Treatment Divide."

30. Council of State Governments, "Jails Have Become the Largest Provider of Mental Health Treatment in Our Nation," CSG Justice Center media clip, June 2, 2017, https://csgjusticecenter.org/mental-health/media-clips/jails-have-become-the-largest-provider-of-mental-health-treatment-in-our-nation/.

31. Stephen Magura et al., "Buprenorphine and Methadone Maintenance in Jail and Post-release: A Randomized Clinical Trial," *Drug and Alcohol Dependence* 99, nos. 1–3 (2009): 222–30; Joshua D. Lee et al., "Buprenorphine-Naloxone Maintenance Following Release from Jail," *Substance Abuse* 33, no. 1 (2012): 40–47.

32. Ingrid A. Binswanger et al., "Release from Prison—A High Risk of Death for Former Inmates," *New England Journal of Medicine* 356, no. 2 (2007): 157–65.

33. German Lopez, "How America's Prisons Are Fueling the Opioid Epidemic," *Vox*, March 26, 2018, www.vox.com/policy-and-politics/2018/3/13 /17020002/prison-opioid-epidemic-medications-addiction.

34. On states offering prerelease naltrexone, see Victoria Kim, "Naltrexone Is Now Being Offered to Inmates in 30 States," *The Fix,* July 14, 2016, www.thefix.com/naltrexone-now-being-offered-inmates-30-states. On states offering prerelease buprenorphine, see G. Lopez, "How America's Prisons Are Fueling the Opioid Epidemic."

35. R. Saucier, D. Wolfe, and N. Dasgupta, "Correction to: Review of Case Narratives from Fatal Overdoses Associated with Injectable Naltrexone for Opioid Dependence," *Drug Safety* 41, no. 10 (2018): 989.

36. Seelye, "In Heroin Crisis."

37. Herzberg, *White Market Drugs;* Rasmussen, *On Speed;* Frydl, *The Drug Wars in America.*

38. Schneider, *Smack;* Musto, *American Disease;* Courtwright, *Dark Paradise.*

39. Herzberg, *Happy Pills in America;* Anna Moore, "Eternal Sunshine," *The Guardian,* May 13, 2007, www.theguardian.com/society/2007/may/13/socialcare.medicineandhealth.

40. Herzberg, *Happy Pills in America;* Jonathan M. Metzl, *Prozac on the Couch* (Durham, NC: Duke University Press, 2003).

41. David Healy, "Shaping the Intimate: Influences on the Experience of Everyday Nerves," *Social Studies of Science* 34, no. 2 (2004): 219–45.

42. Allan V. Horwitz, *Creating Mental Illness* (Chicago: University of Chicago Press, 2002).

43. Haiden A. Huskamp, "Prices, Profits, and Innovation: Examining Criticisms of New Psychotropic Drugs' Value," *Health Affairs* 25, no. 3 (2006): 635–46, https://doi.org/10.1377/hlthaff.25.3.635.

44. Open Society Institute–Baltimore, *Using Buprenorphine to Treat Opioid Addiction,* OSI-Baltimore Brief, May 24, 2016, www.osibaltimore.org/wp-content/uploads/Buprenorphine-Brief.pdf.

45. Dole, Nyswander, and Kreek, "Narcotic Blockade."

46. Samuel Roberts, "'Rehabilitation' as Boundary Object: Medicalization, Local Activism, and Narcotics Addiction Policy in New York City, 1951–62," *Social History of Alcohol and Drugs* 26, no. 2 (2012): 147–69.

47. H. Hansen and Roberts, "Two Tiers."

48. Raz, "Treating Addiction," 60.

49. Netherland, "Becoming Normal."

50. Musto, *American Disease.*

51. Drug Addiction Treatment Act of 1999, Cong. Rec.—Senate (106th Congress), S1092.

52. Drug Addiction Treatment Act of 2000, Cong. Rec.—Senate (106th Congress), S9113.

53. On physicians more frequently prescribing opioid pain relievers to whites, see I. Chen et al., "Racial Differences," Pletcher et al., "Trends in Opioid Prescribing," and Joynt et al., "Impact of Neighborhood Socioeconomic Status." On physicians' belief that nonwhite patients are more likely to abuse opioids, see Hausmann et al., "Racial Disparities," and Shavers, Bakos, and Sheppard, "Race, Ethnicity, and Pain."

54. H. Hansen et al., "Buprenorphine and Methadone Treatment."

55. A. Stanton et al., "Expanding Treatment."

56. Lagisetty et al., "Buprenorphine Treatment Divide."

57. Substance Abuse and Mental Health Services Administration, Center for Substance Abuse Treatment, *Clinical Guidelines*.

58. L. A. Lin et al., "Perceived Need and Availability of Psychosocial Interventions across Buprenorphine Prescriber Specialties," *Addictive Behaviors* 93 (2019): 72–77.

59. D. A. Fiellin et al., "Counseling Plus Buprenorphine-Naloxone Maintenance Therapy for Opioid Dependence," *New England Journal of Medicine* 355, no. 4 (2006): 365–74; D. A. Fiellin et al., "A Randomized Trial of Cognitive Behavioral Therapy in Primary Care-Based Buprenorphine," *American Journal of Medicine* 126, no. 1 (2013): 74.e11.

60. Marek C. Chawarski, Mahmud Mazlan, and Richard S. Schottenfeld, "Behavioral Drug and HIV Risk Reduction Counseling (BDRC) with Abstinence-Contingent Take-Home Buprenorphine: A Pilot Randomized Clinical Trial," *Drug and Alcohol Dependence* 94, nos. 1–3 (2008): 281–84; Iván D. Montoya et al., "Influence of Psychotherapy Attendance on Buprenorphine Treatment Outcome," *Journal of Substance Abuse Treatment* 28, no. 3 (2005): 247–54.

61. American Society for Addiction Medicine, "Regulation of Office-Based Opioid Treatment," public policy statement, January 17, 2018, www.asam.org /advocacy/public-policy-statements/details/public-policy-statements/2021 /08/09/regulation-of-office-based-opioid-treatment.

62. William Garriott, *Policing Methamphetamine: Narcopolitics in Rural America* (New York: New York University Press, 2011); T. Linnemann and D. Kurtz, "Beyond the Ghetto: Police Power, Methamphetamine and the Rural War on Drugs," *Critical Criminology* 22 (2014): 339–55; N. Murakawa, "Toothless," *Du Bois Review: Social Science Research on Race* 8 (2011): 219–28.

63. A. Arria and R. DuPont, "Nonmedical Prescription Stimulant Use among College Students: Why We Need to Do Something and What We Need to Do," *Journal of Addictive Diseases* 29 (2010): 417–26; M. Talbot, "Brain Gain: The Underground World of 'Neuroenhancing' Drugs," *New Yorker*, April 27, 2009, www.newyorker.com/magazine/2009/04/27/brain-gain.

64. Helena Hansen, "Assisted Technologies of Social Reproduction: Pharmaceutical Prosthesis for Gender, Race, and Class in the White Opioid 'Crisis,'" *Contemporary Drug Problems* 44, no. 4 (2017): 321–38.

65. Stephen W. Patrick and Davida M. Schiff, "A Public Health Response to Opioid Use in Pregnancy," *Pediatrics* 139, no. 3 (2017): e20164070.

66. Nancy D. Campbell, *Using Women: Gender, Drug Policy, and Social Justice* (New York: Routledge, 2000).

67. D. Roberts, "Punishing Drug Addicts"; Nancy D. Campbell, "'Regulating Maternal Instinct': Governing Mentalities of Late Twentieth-Century US Illicit Drug Policy," *Signs: Journal of Women in Culture and Society* 24, no. 4 (1999): 895–923.

68. Lassiter, "Impossible Criminals."

69. George Lipsitz, "The Possessive Investment in Whiteness," in *White Privilege: Essential Readings on the Other Side of Racism,* 2nd ed., ed. Paula S. Rothenberg (New York: Worth, 2004), 67.

70. Bonilla-Silva, *Racism without Racists.*

71. Herzberg, *Happy Pills in America*; Schneider, *Smack.*

72. Steve Garner, *Whiteness: An Introduction* (New York: Routledge, 2007).

73. On how prescription drug monitoring programs redirect opioid-dependent people to heroin, see David S. Fink et al., "Association between Prescription Drug Monitoring Programs and Nonfatal and Fatal Drug Overdoses: A Systematic Review," *Annals of Internal Medicine* 168, no. 11 (2018): 783–90.

74. On buprenorphine use in Federally Qualified Health Centers, see L. Caton et al., "Expanding Access to Medications for Opioid Use Disorder in Primary Care: An Examination of Common Implementation Strategies," *Journal of Addiction Research and Therapy* 11, no. 407 (2020): 2, https://doi.org/10.4172/2155-6105.1000407. On buprenorphine use in jails and prisons, see Noa Krawczyk et al., "Expanding Low-Threshold Buprenorphine to Justice-Involved Individuals through Mobile Treatment: Addressing a Critical Care Gap," *Journal of Substance Abuse Treatment* 103 (2019): 1–8, and Kelly E. Moore et al., "Effectiveness of Medication Assisted Treatment for Opioid Use in Prison and Jail Settings: A Meta-analysis and Systematic Review," *Journal of Substance Abuse Treatment* 99 (2019): 32–43. On medical societies' advocacy of wider buprenorphine dissemination, see American Society for Addiction Medicine, "ASAM's Commitment to Addressing Racial Injustice and Health Disparities," letter to members, June 12, 2020, www.asam.org/docs/default-source/membership/asam-letter-on-racial-injustice-and-health-disparities-final.pdf.

75. Drugs.com, "Suboxone Sales Data," last updated February 2014, www.drugs.com/stats/suboxone.

76. Greg Stohr and Susan Decker, "Supreme Court Justice Refuses to Block Generic Suboxone Film," Bloomberg, February 19, 2019, www.bloomberg.com/news/articles/2019-02-19/supreme-court-justice-refuses-to-block-generic-suboxone-film.

77. Linda Alcoff, *The Future of Whiteness* (New York: John Wiley and Sons, 2015).

78. Katherine S. Newman, *Falling from Grace: The Experience of Downward Mobility in the American Middle Class* (Berkeley: University of California Press, 1999).

79. Naomi Klein, *The Shock Doctrine: The Rise of Disaster Capitalism* (New York: Macmillan, 2007).

80. Joe Dumit, *Drugs for Life: How Pharmaceutical Companies Define Our Health* (Raleigh, NC: Duke University Press, 2012); Paul Rabinow and Nikolas Rose, "Biopower Today," *BioSocieties* 1 (2006): 195–217.

81. Rabinow and Rose, "Biopower Today"; Rose, *Politics of Life Itself.*

82. Emily Cohen, "From Phantoms to Prostheses," *Disability Studies Quarterly* 32, no. 3 (2012): 18, https://doi.org/10.18061/dsq.v32i3.3269.

83. W. E. B. Du Bois, "The Souls of White Folk," in *Darkwater: Voices from within the Veil* (New York: Harcourt, Brace and Howe, 1920), chap. 2.

84. Roediger, *Working towards Whiteness.*

CHAPTER 7. THE HOUSEWIFE'S RETURN TO HEROIN

1. Katherine Seelye, "Heroin in New England, More Abundant and More Deadly," *New York Times,* July 19, 2013, A11.

2. Linda Carroll, "Hooked: A Teacher's Addiction and the New Face of Heroin," *Today,* April 8, 2014, www.today.com/health/hooked-teachers-addiction -new-face-heroin-2D79496263.

3. Kelsey Dallas and Sandy Balazic, "The New Face of Heroin Addiction," *Deseret News,* February 19, 2015, www.deseret.com/2015/2/19/20558592/the-new-face-of-heroin-addiction.

4. T. J. Cicero et al., "The Changing Face of Heroin Use in the United States: A Retrospective Analysis of the Past 50 Years," *Journal of the American Medical Association Psychiatry* 71 (2014): 821–26.

5. Dallas and Balazic, "New Face."

6. Courtwright, *Dark Paradise.*

7. D. Roberts, "Punishing Drug Addicts"; Campbell, "'Regulating Maternal Instinct'"; Reinarman and Levine, *Crack in America.*

8. Travis Linnemann, *Meth Wars: Police, Media, Power* (New York: New York University Press, 2016).

9. Herzberg, *Happy Pills in America*; Herzberg, *White Market Drugs.*

10. Denise Paone et al., *Unintentional Drug Poisoning (Overdose) Deaths in New York City, 2000–2016,* New York City Department of Health and Mental Hygiene, Epi Data Brief No. 89, June 2017, www1.nyc.gov/assets/doh/downloads /pdf/epi/databrief89.pdf.

11. Ciccarone, Ondocsin, and Mars, "Heroin Uncertainties."

12. Scott Thistle, "LePage: Over 90 Percent of Drug Dealers Busted in Maine Are Black or Hispanic," *Press Herald,* August 24, 2016, www.pressherald .com/2016/08/24/gov-lepage-says-most-drug-traffickers-arrested-in-maine-are-Black-or-hispanic/.

13. Karen Zatkulak, "News 13 Investigates: Heroin Highway," ABC 13 News, November 20, 2017, https://wlos.com/news/news-13-investigates/news-13-investigates-heroin-highway. See also Gloria Casas, "'Heroin Highway' between Kane and Chicago Thriving, Officials Say," *Chicago Tribune,* March 30, 2017, www.chicagotribune.com/suburbs/aurora-beacon-news/ct-abn-aurora-heroin-st-0330-20170329-story.html; Jennifer Donelan, "7 On Your Side Presents 'Heroin Highway,'" ABC/WJLA, February 14, 2016, https://wjla.com /features/hooked-on-heroin/7-on-your-side-presents-heroin-highway; Svetlana Shkolnikova, "On Route 23, or 'Heroin Highway,' A Growing Suburban Demand for Drugs Meets Urban Supply," northjersey.com, March 11, 2019, www.northjersey.com/story/news/crime/2019/03/11/nj-route-23-heroin-high-way-demand-drugs-meets-urban-supply/2955089002/; "Brown: Drug Operation Turned Long Island Expressway into 'Heroin Highway,'" CBS, January 13, 2012, https://newyork.cbslocal.com/2012/01/13/brown-drug-ring-turned-long-island-expressway-into-heroin-highway/; "Fort Thomas Police Launch Heroin Highway Interdiction; Arrests Made," WKRC Local 12 News, February 19, 2016, https://local12.com/news/local/fort-thomas-police-launch-heroin-high-way-interdiction-arrest-made.

14. David Herzberg, *White Market Drugs,* chap. 3.

15. George E. Pettey, "The Heroin Habit: Another Curse," *Alabama Medical Journal* 15 (1902–3): 180. See also John Phillips, "Prevalence of the Heroin Habit: Especially the Use of the Drug by 'Snuffing,'" *Journal of the American Medical Association* 59, no. 24 (1912): 2146–47.

16. Courtwright, *Dark Paradise.*

17. Herzberg, *White Market Drugs;* Shah, *Contagious Divides;* Ahmad, *Opium Debate.*

18. Acker, *Creating the American Junkie.*

19. Courtwright, *Dark Paradise.*

20. Herzberg, *White Market Drugs.*

21. Schneider, *Smack.*

22. Roediger, *Working toward Whiteness;* Matthew Frye Jacobson, *Whiteness of a Different Color* (Cambridge, MA: Harvard University Press, 1999).

23. Mae M. Ngai, *Impossible Subjects: Illegal Aliens and the Making of Modern America* (Princeton, NJ: Princeton University Press, 2004).

24. Wendy Kline, *Building a Better Race: Gender, Sexuality, and Eugenics from the Turn of the Century to the Baby Boom* (Berkeley: University of California Press, 2001); Alexandra Minna Stern, *Eugenic Nation: Faults and Frontiers of Better Breeding in Modern America,* 2nd ed. (Berkeley: University of California Press, 2015).

25. Michael Rembis, *Defining Deviance: Sex, Science, and Delinquent Girls, 1890–1960* (Urbana: University of Illinois Press, 2013).

26. Roediger, *Working towards Whiteness;* Lisa McGirr, *The War on Alcohol: Prohibition and the Rise of the American State* (New York: Norton, 2016).

27. On hopes for redeeming people with addiction at the Narcotic Farm, see Nancy D. Campbell, *Discovering Addiction: The Science and Politics of Substance Abuse Research* (Ann Arbor: University of Michigan Press, 2007). On attempts to redeem immigrant whites, see Lisa McGirr, *The War on Alcohol: Prohibition and the Rise of the American State* (New York: Norton, 2016), 28.

28. Thomas Sugrue, *The Origins of the Urban Crisis: Race and Inequality in Postwar Detroit* (Princeton, NJ: Princeton University Press, 2005); Eric Avila, *Popular Culture in the Age of White Flight* (Berkeley: University of California Press, 2006); Lizabeth Cohen, *A Consumers' Republic: The Politics of Mass Consumption in Post-War America* (New York: Alfred A. Knopf, 2003).

29. Schneider, *Smack.*

30. Claude Brown, *Manchild in the Promised Land* (New York: Simon and Schuster, 2011), 169.

31. Schneider, *Smack.*

32. Schneider, *Smack.*

33. Avila, *Popular Culture.*

34. Kathleen Frydl, *The Drug Wars in America, 1940–1973* (New York: Cambridge University Press, 2013); Campbell, *Discovering Addiction.*

35. Otto Preminger, *The Man with the Golden Arm,* screenplay by Walter Newman and Lewis Meltzer (United Artists, 1955).

36. Schneider, *Smack.*

37. Schneider, *Smack.*

38. Matthew Lassiter, *The Silent Majority: Suburban Politics in the Sunbelt South* (Princeton, NJ: Princeton University Press, 2006).

39. Michael Fortner, *Black Silent Majority: The Rockefeller Drug Laws and the Politics of Punishment* (Cambridge, MA: Harvard University Press, 2016).

40. Schneider, *Smack*.

41. Jeremy Kuzmarov, *The Myth of the Addicted Army: Vietnam and the Modern War on Drugs* (Boston: University of Massachusetts Press, 2009); Alfred McCoy, *The Politics of Heroin: CIA Complicity in the Global Drug Trade* (Chicago: Lawrence Hill Books, 2003).

42. Claire D. Clark, "'Chemistry Is the New Hope': Therapeutic Communities and Methadone Maintenance," *Social History of Alcohol and Drugs* 26, no. 2 (2012): 192–216; Clark, *Recovery Revolution*; Spillane, "Debating the Controlled Substances Act"; Courtwright, "Controlled Substances Act."

43. Kohler-Hausmann, *Getting Tough*; S. Roberts, "'Rehabilitation' as Boundary Object."

44. Lassiter, "Impossible Criminals."

45. Kohler-Hausmann, *Getting Tough*.

46. Hamid et al., "Heroin Epidemic."

47. Mary Rizzo, "Embodying Withdrawal: Abjection and the Popularity of Heroin Chic," *Michigan Feminist Studies* 15 (2001), http://hdl.handle.net/2027/spo.ark5583.0015.004.

48. Rizzo, "Embodying Withdrawal."

49. William Clinton, *Public Papers of the Presidents of the United States: William Clinton, 1997* (Scottsdale, AZ: Best Books, 1998).

50. Cicero et al., "Changing Face of Heroin Use."

51. Chris Hayhurst, "Moving Away from Opioid Reliance," *APTA Magazine*, October 1, 2018, www.apta.org/apta-magazine/2018/10/01/moving-away-from-opioid-reliance.

52. P. K. Muhuri, J. C. Gfroerer, and C. Davies, "Associations of Nonmedical Pain Reliever Use and Initiation of Heroin Use in the United States," *CBHSQ Data Review* (Substance Abuse and Mental Health Services Administration), August 2013, www.samhsa.gov/data/sites/default/files/DR006/DR006/nonmedical-pain-reliever-use-2013.

53. Muhuri, Gfroerer, and Davies, "Associations."

54. Maia Szalavitz, "Opioid Addiction Is a Huge Problem, but Pain Prescriptions Are Not the Cause," *Scientific American, MIND* guest blog, May 10, 2016, https://blogs.scientificamerican.com/mind-guest-blog/opioid-addiction-is-a-huge-problem-but-pain-prescriptions-are-not-the-cause/.

55. Nora Volkow, "America's Addiction to Opioids: Heroin and Prescription Drug Abuse," National Institute on Drug Abuse Archives, May 14, 2014, https://archives.drugabuse.gov/testimonies/2014/americas-addiction-to-opioids-heroin-prescription-drug-abuse.

56. On abuse-deterrent formulations, see Cicero, "Changing Face of Heroin Use."

57. Silva S. Martins et al., "Prescription Drug Monitoring Programs Operational Characteristics and Fatal Heroin Poisoning," *International Journal of Drug Policy* 74 (2019): 174–80.

58. Goege Unick et al., "The Relationship between US Heroin Market Dynamics and Heroin-Related Overdose, 1992–2008," *Addiction* 109, no. 11 (2008): 1889–98.

59. Cicero, "Changing Face of Heroin Use."

60. Centers for Disease Control and Prevention, "Today's Heroin Infographics," July 7, 2015, www.cdc.gov/vitalsigns/heroin/infographic.html.

61. Holly Hedegaard, Margaret Warner, and Arialdi M. Miniño, "Drug Overdose Deaths in the United States, 1999–2015," Centers for Disease Control and Prevention, NCHS Data Brief No. 273, February 2017, https://stacks.cdc.gov /view/cdc/44356?utm_source=miragenews&utm_medium=miragenews&utm_ campaign=news. Joseph Friedman and Helena Hansen, "Evaluation of Increases in Drug Overdose Mortality Rates in the US by Race and Ethnicity before and during the COVID-19 Pandemic," *JAMA Psychiatry* 79, no. 4 (2022): 379–81, doi:10.1001/jamapsychiatry.2022.0004.

62. Jonathan Lee, "The New Face of Drug Addiction," Fox News, July 19, 2013, http://fox40.com/2013/07/19/new-face-of-drug-addiction/; Yardena Schwartz, "Painkiller Use Breeds New Face of Heroin Addiction," NBC News, June 19, 2012, http://dailynightly.nbcnews.com/_news/2012/06/19/12303942-painkiller-use-breeds- new-face-of-heroin-addiction?lite; Carroll, "Hooked"; Michels, "Heroin in Suburbia"; "The New Face of Heroin Addiction," ABC News, October 30, 2010, http://abcnews.go.com/2020/video/face-heroin-addiction-12009941.

63. Joanne Ostrow, "Heroin's Harsh Reality," *Denver Post*, January 2, 2001, http://extras.denverpost.com/scene/ost102.htm.

64. Caryn Sullivan, "Prescription Drugs: Lock Your Cabinets, and Know the Risks," *St. Paul Pioneer Press,* May 27, 2011, www.carynsullivanscribe.com /prescription-drugs-lock-your-cabinets-and-know-the-risks/.

65. Josh Poltilove, "Julie Schenecker's Attorney: Dad Should Never Have Left Kids with Her," *Tampa Tribune,* December 5, 2011.

66. Benjamin D. Steiner and Victor Argothy, "White Addiction: Racial Inequality, Racial Ideology, and the War on Drugs," *Temple Political and Civil Rights Law Review* 10 (2001): 444.

67. Case and Deaton, "Rising Morbidity and Mortality."

68. Quote from Zoe Carpenter, "Did the Opioid Epidemic Help Trump Win?" *The Nation,* December 7, 2016, www.thenation.com/article/archive/did-the-opioid-epidemic-help-donald-trump-win/. See Kathleen Frydl, "The Oxy Electorate: A Scourge of Addiction and Death Siloed in Fly-Over Country," *Medium.com,* November 16, 2016, https://medium.com/@kfrydl/the-oxy-electorate-3fa62765f837.

69. Joel Achenbach, "I Spent a Year Studying America's Addiction Crisis—and Found No Easy Answers," *Washington Post,* December 30, 2016, https:// medium.com/thewashingtonpost/i-spent-a-year-studying-americas-addiction-crisis-and-found-no-easy-answers-85efe4dc65a4; Frydl, "The Oxy Electorate."

70. Q. Jurecic, "Trump Administration Releases 'Briefing Issues' on Foreign Policy and Security," *Lawfare* (blog), January 20, 2017, www.lawfareblog .com/trump-administration-releases-briefing-issues-foreign-policy-and-security.

71. Gina Kolata, "Death Rates Rising for White Middle-Aged Americans, Study Says," *New York Times*, November 5, 2015, www.nytimes.com/2015 /11/03/health/death-rates-rising-for-middle-aged-white-americans-study-finds .html.

72. Alcoff, *Future of Whiteness*.

73. Baldwin, "On Being White," 168.

74. Cornelia Sears and Jessica Johnson, "Waste," *Media/Culture Journal* 13, no. 4 (2010), https://doi.org/10.5204/mcj.286.

75. Daniels, "*Intervention*," 117.

76. Netherland and Hansen, "War on Drugs That Wasn't."

77. Bernie Day, "It Happened to a Bright Kid Like Ian," *Roanoke Times*, October 29, 2011, www.roanoke.com/webmin/opinion/it-happened-to-a- bright-kid-like-ian/article_dbdb0437-c827-525f-9221-8d8f2731d5e3.html.

78. Lane DeGregory, "A Young Woman Struggles with Oxy Addiction and Recovery," *Tampa Bay Times*, December 17, 2011, republished December 28, 2011, at *Psychology of Pain* (blog), http://psychologyofpain.blogspot.com/2011/.

79. "Addiction's Toll: The Scourge of Heroin Strikes Too Close to Home," *Pittsburg Post-Gazette*, July 31, 2011, www.post-gazette.com/opinion/editorials /2011/07/31/Addiction-s-toll-The-scourge-of-heroin-strikes-too-close-to-home /stories/201107310204.

80. Diane Raver, "Heroin Death: 'She Thought It Would Be Fun,'" *Batesville Herald-Tribune*, March 25, 2011. .

81. DeGregory, "Young Woman Struggles."

82. Stefan Ecks, "Pharmaceutical Citizenship: Antidepressant Marketing and the Promise of Demarginalization in India," *Anthropology and Medicine* 12, no. 3 (2005): 239–54.

83. Sharon Hunt and Jim Baumohl, "Drink, Drugs and Disability: An Intro- duction to the Controversy," *Contemporary Drug Problems* 30 (2003): 9–76; Kohler-Hausmann, *Getting Tough*.

84. Hunt and Baumohl, "Drink, Drugs and Disability," 39.

85. L. Jans, S. Stoddard, and L. Kraus, *Chartbook on Mental Health and Disability in the United States*, InfoUse Report (Washington, DC: US Depart- ment of Education, National Institute on Disability and Rehabilitation Research, 2004); M. Wiseman and S. Wamhoff, "The TANF/SSI Connection," *Social Security Bulletin* 66, no. 4 (2005–6): 21–23; D. Lakdawalla, J. Bhattacharya, and D. Goldman, "Are the Young Becoming More Disabled?," *Health Affairs* 23, no. 1 (2004): 168–76.

86. R. E. Drake et al., "Reducing Disability," *Health Affairs* 28, no. 3 (2009): 761–70.

87. Kelly Ray Knight, *Addicted, Pregnant, Poor* (Durham, NC: Duke Uni- versity Press, 2015).

88. H. Hansen, Bourgois, and Drucker, "Pathologizing Poverty."

89. Substance Abuse and Mental Health Services Administration, "National Survey Shows Continued Reduced Levels of Prescription Drug Use among Young Adults," news release, September 2013, www.samhsa.gov/newsroom /advisories/1309033910.aspx.

90. New York City Department of Health and Mental Hygiene, "Opioid Misuse in New York City."

91. Seelye, "In Heroin Crisis."

92. D. Furr-Holden et al., "African Americans Now Outpace Whites in Opioid-Involved Overdose Deaths: A Comparison of Temporal Trends from 1999–2018," *Addiction*, August 27, 2020, https://doi.org/10.1111/add.15233.

93. Federal Bureau of Investigation, "Arrests by Race, 2014," in *Crime in the United States, 2014*, https://ucr.fbi.gov/crime-in-the-u.s/2014/crime-in-the-u.s.-2014/tables/table-43.

94. Mark Motivans, "Federal Justice Statistics, 2011–2012," *Bureau of Justice Statistics Bulletin*, January 2015, www.bjs.gov/content/pub/pdf/fjs1112.pdf.

95. Ty Wright, "A Small Indiana County Sends More People to Prison Than San Francisco and Durham, NC, Combined. Why?," *New York Times*, September 2, 2016, www.nytimes.com/2016/09/02/upshot/new-geography-of-prisons.html.

96. Centers for Disease Control and Prevention, "Today's Heroin Infographics," July 7, 2015, www.cdc.gov/vitalsigns/heroin/infographic.html.

97. Murakawa, "Toothless"; Garriott, *Policing Methamphetamine*; Eugene Raikhel and William Garriott, *Addiction Trajectories* (Durham, NC: Duke University Press, 2013); Linnemann and Kurtz, "Beyond the Ghetto."

98. Murakawa, "Toothless," 223.

99. Murakawa, "Toothless."

100. Tunnell, "Cultural Constructions."

101. Talbot, "Brain Gain"; Arria and DuPont, "Nonmedical Prescription Stimulant Use."

102. Netherland and Hansen, "War on Drugs That Wasn't."

103. Linnemann, *Meth Wars*.

104. M. E. Sutter et al., "Fatal Fentanyl: One Pill Can Kill," *Academic Emergency Medicine* 24, no. 1 (2017): 106–13.

105. Gary L. Henderson, "Designer Drugs: Past History and Future Prospects," *Journal of Forensic Science* 33, no. 2 (1988): 569–75.

106. Quinones, *Dreamland*; Sarah G. Mars et al., "'Every "Never" I Ever Said Came True': Transitions from Opioid Pills to Heroin Injecting," *International Journal of Drug Policy* 25, no. 2 (2014): 257–66.

107. Daniel Ciccarone, Jeff Ondocsin, and Sarah G. Mars, "Heroin Uncertainties: Exploring Users' Perceptions of Fentanyl-Adulterated-and-Substituted 'Heroin,'" *International Journal of Drug Policy* 46 (2017): 146–55.

108. Ciccarone, Ondocsin, and Mars, "Heroin Uncertainties."

109. N. P. Weicker et al., "Agency in the Fentanyl Era: Exploring the Utility of Fentanyl Test Strips in an Opaque Drug Market," *International Journal of Drug Policy* 1, no. 84 (2020): 102900.

110. Sanjana Mitra et al., "Elevated Prevalence of Self-Reported Unintentional Exposure to Fentanyl among Women Who Use Drugs in a Canadian Setting: A Cross-sectional Analysis," *International Journal of Drug Policy* 83 (2020): 102864, https://doi.org/10.1016/j.drugpo.2020.102864.

111. Peter Phalen et al., "Fentanyl Related Overdose in Indianapolis: Estimating Trends Using Multilevel Bayesian Models," *Addictive Behaviors* 86 (2018): 4–10.

112. Merianne Spencer et al., *Drug Overdose Deaths Involving Fentanyl, 2011–2016*, Centers for Disease Control, National Vital Statistics Reports, March 21, 2019, https://stacks.cdc.gov/view/cdc/77832.

113. Lauren Brinkley-Rubinstein et al., "Risk of Fentanyl-Involved Overdose among Those with Past Year Incarceration: Findings from a Recent Outbreak in 2014 and 2015," *Drug and Alcohol Dependence* 185 (2018): 189–91.

114. Furr-Holden et al., "African Americans."

CHAPTER 8. FROM RACIAL CAPITALISM TO BIOSOCIAL JUSTICE

1. Nora D. Volkow and Francis S. Collins, "The Role of Science in Addressing the Opioid Crisis," *New England Journal of Medicine* 377, no. 4 (2017): 394, https://doi.org/10.1056/nejmsr1706626.

2. Volkow and Collins, "Role of Science," 394.

3. Bipartisan Policy Center, "Tracking Federal Funding to Combat the Opioid Crisis," March 2019, https://bipartisanpolicy.org/wp-content/uploads/2019/03/Tracking-Federal-Funding-to-Combat-the-Opioid-Crisis.pdf.

4. Marc R. Larochelle et al., "Medication for Opioid Use Disorder after Nonfatal Opioid Overdose and Association with Mortality: A Cohort Study," *Annals of Internal Medicine* 169, no. 4 (2018): 137–45, https://doi.org/10.7326/m17-3107.

5. Joseph N. Friedman et al., "Racial/Ethnic, Social, and Geographic Trends in Overdose-Associated Cardiac Arrests Observed by US Emergency Medical Services during the COVID-19 Pandemic," *JAMA Psychiatry* 78, no. 8 (2021): 886–95, https://doi.org/10.1001/jamapsychiatry.2021.0967.

6. Brendan Saloner et al., "The Affordable Care Act in the Heart of the Opioid Crisis: Evidence from West Virginia," *Health Affairs* 38, no. 4 (2019): 633–42, https://doi.org/10.1377/hlthaff.2018.05049; Nabarun Dasgupta, Leo Beletsky, and Daniel Ciccarone, "Opioid Crisis: No Easy Fix to Its Social and Economic Determinants," *American Journal of Public Health* 108, no. 2 (2018): 182–86, https://doi.org/10.2105/ajph.2017.304187.

7. On the pharmaceutical industry's power to set drug prices, see Aaron S. Kesselheim, Jerry Avorn, and Ameet Sarpatwari, "The High Cost of Prescription Drugs in the United States: Origins and Prospects for Reform," *Journal of the American Medical Association* 316, no. 8 (2016): 858–71. On the pharmaceutical industry's influence on drug regulation, see John Abraham, "The Pharmaceutical Industry as a Political Player," *The Lancet* 360, no. 9344 (2002): 1498–1502. On the pharmaceutical industry's influence on FDA approvals for opioids, see Richard D. DeShazo et al., "Backstories on the US Opioid Epidemic. Good Intentions Gone Bad, an Industry Gone Rogue, and Watch Dogs Gone to Sleep," *American Journal of Medicine* 131, no. 6 (2018): 595–601, https://doi.org/10.1016/j.amjmed.2017.12.045. On the pharmaceutical industry's ties to leading opioid researchers, see Tim Schwab, "US Opioid Prescribing: The Federal Government Advisers with Recent Ties to Big Pharma," *BMJ* 366 (2019): l5167, https://doi.org/10.1136/bmj.l5167. On the prominence of drug development in the HEAL initiative, see Collins, Koroshetz, and Volkow, "Helping to End Addiction."

8. Elizabeth A. Bowen and Andrew Irish, "A Policy Mapping Analysis of Goals, Target Populations, and Punitive Notions in the U.S. Congressional Response to the Opioid Epidemic," *International Journal of Drug Policy* 74 (December 2019): 90–97, https://doi.org/10.1016/j.drugpo.2019.09.014.

9. Gabor Maté, *In the Realm of Hungry Ghosts: Close Encounters with Addiction* (Mississauga, ON: Knopf Canada, 2008).

10. Klein, *Shock Doctrine*.

11. Mindy Thompson Fullilove, *Root Shock: How Tearing Up City Neighborhoods Hurts America, and What We Can Do about It* (New York: New Village Press, 2004).

12. Campbell, *OD*.

13. E. Nadelmann and L. LaSalle, "Two Steps Forward, One Step Back: Current Harm Reduction Policy and Politics in the United States," *Harm Reduction Journal* 14, no. 1 (2017): 1–7.

14. Gráinne Cousins et al., "Risk of Mortality on and off Methadone Substitution Treatment in Primary Care: A National Cohort Study," *Addiction* 111, no. 1 (2016): 73–82.

15. Marc Auriacombe et al., "French Field Experience with Buprenorphine," *American Journal on Addictions* 13, Suppl. 1 (2004): S17-S28.

16. Centers for Disease Control and Prevention, "Drug Overdose Deaths," accessed 2018, www.cdc.gov/drugoverdose/data/statedeaths.html.

17. Bruce G. Link and Jo Phelan, "Social Condition as Fundamental Causes of Disease," *Journal of Health and Social Behavior* 36, extra issue (1995): 80–94.

18. Robin I.M. Dunbar, "The Social Brain: Mind, Language, and Society in Evolutionary Perspective," *Annual Review of Anthropology* 32, no. 1 (2003): 163–81; Richard J. Davidson and Bruce S. McEwen, "Social Influences on Neuroplasticity: Stress and Interventions to Promote Well-Being," *Nature Neuroscience* 15, no. 5 (2012): 689–95.

19. William C. Cockerham, Bryant W. Hamby, and Gabriela R. Oates, "The Social Determinants of Chronic Disease," *American Journal of Preventive Medicine* 52, no. 1-S1 (2017): S5-S12.

20. Case and Deaton, "Rising Morbidity and Mortality."

21. Zoorob and Salemi, "Bowling Alone, Dying Together."

22. Susan Starr Sered, "The Opioid Crisis and the Infrastructure of Social Capital," *International Journal of Drug Policy* 71 (2019): 47–55.

23. Schneider, *Smack*.

24. Furr-Holden et al., "African Americans."

25. New York State Criminal Justice Knowledge Bank, "Heroin Overdose Prevention and Eduction (HOPE) Program," October 2018, https://knowledgebank.criminaljustice.ny.gov/heroin-overdose-prevention-and-education-hope-program.

26. Amy Yensi, "Bronx Continues to See Highest Number of Opioid Overdose Deaths," *NY1 News*, November 23, 2019, www.ny1.com/nyc/all-boroughs/news/2019/11/23/the-bronx-continues-to-see-highest-number-of-opioid-overdose-deaths.

27. Phys.org, "New York's Poorest Area has 44% Living in Poverty," November 20, 2015, https://phys.org/news/2015-11-york-poorest-area-poverty.html.

28. Chris Sommerfeldt and Reuven Blau, "New Website Shows Crotona Park East and Morrisania in the Bronx Have City's Highest Rate of Jailed Residents," *New York Daily News*, January 19, 2016, www.nydailynews.com/new-york/people-city-jails-bronx-neighborhoods-article-1.2501101.

29. Marina Carver, "NYPD Officers Say They Had Stop and Frisk Quota," CNN, March 26, 2013, www.cnn.com/2013/03/22/justice/new-york-stop-and-frisk-trial/index.html.

30. Ernest Drucker, *A Plague of Prisons: The Epidemiology of Mass Incarceration in America* (New York: New Press, 2013); Rodrick Wallace, "Urban Desertification, Public Health and Public Order: 'Planned Shrinkage,' Violent Death, Substance Abuse and AIDS in the Bronx," *Social Science and Medicine* 31, no. 7 (1990): 801–13; Fullilove, *Root Shock*.

31. Dean Spade, *Mutual Aid: Building Solidarity during This Crisis (and the Next)* (London: Verso Books, 2020).

32. Cedric Robinson, *Black Marxism: The Making of the Black Radical Tradition* (London: Zed Books, 1983).

33. Brentin Mock, "California's Race to the Top on Cannabis," Bloomberg, February 5, 2018, www.bloomberg.com/news/articles/2018-02-05/trading-cannabis-for-racial-equity-in-california.

34. Helena Hansen and Jonathan M. Metzl, eds., *Structural Competency in Mental Health and Medicine: A Case-Based Approach to Treating the Social Determinants of Health* (New York: Springer, 2019); Jonathan M. Metzl and Helena Hansen, "Structural Competency: Theorizing a New Medical Engagement with Stigma and Inequality," *Social Science and Medicine* 103 (February 2014): 126–33, https://doi.org/10.1016/j.socscimed.2013.06.032.

35. C.D. Bellamy et al., "A Collaborative Culturally-Centered and Community-Driven Faith-Based Opioid Recovery Initiative: The Imani Breakthrough Project," *Social Work in Mental Health* 19, no. 6 (2021): 1–10.

36. Fullilove, *Root Shock*.

37. Mindy Thompson Fullilove, *Urban Alchemy: Restoring Joy in America's Sorted-Out Cities* (New York: NYU Press, 2013).

38. T.D. Shanafelt et al., "Burnout and Satisfaction with Work-Life Balance among US Physicians Relative to the General US Population," *Archives of Internal Medicine* 172, no. 2018 (2012): 1377–85; Rachel Willard-Grace et al., "Burnout and Health Care Workforce Turnover," *Annals of Family Medicine* 17, no. 1 (2019): 36–41.

39. Robert Wood Johnson Foundation, "Health Care's Blind Side," December 1, 2011, www.rwjf.org/en/library/research/2011/12/health-care-s-blind-side.html.

40. James Baldwin, "As Much Truth As One Can Bear: To Speak Out about the World as It Is," *New York Times Book Review*, January 14, 1962, BR38.

41. Drug Policy Alliance, *Uprooting the Drug War*, report (New York: Drug Policy Alliance, 2021), https://drugpolicy.org/resource/uprooting-drug-war.

Bibliography

ABC News. "The New Face of Heroin Addiction." October 30, 2010. http://abcnews.go.com/2020/video/face-heroin-addiction-12009941.

Abraham, John. "The Pharmaceutical Industry as a Political Player." *The Lancet* 360, no. 9344 (2002): 1498–1502.

Achenbach, Joel. "I Spent a Year Studying America's Addiction Crisis—and Found No Easy Answers." *Washington Post*, December 30, 2016. https://medium.com/thewashingtonpost/i-spent-a-year-studying-americas-addiction-crisis-and-found-no-easy-answers-85efe4dc65a4.

Acker, Caroline Jean. *Creating the American Junkie: Addiction Research in the Classic Era of Narcotic Control.* Baltimore: Johns Hopkins University Press, 2002.

———. "How Crack Found a Niche in the American Ghetto: The Historical Epidemiology of Drug-Related Harm." *BioSocieties* 5, no. 1 (2010): 70–88. https://doi.org/ 10.1057/biosoc.2009.1.

Adams, Samuel Hopkins. "Control for the Devil's Capsules." *American Weekly*, July 20, 1947.

Agar, Michael, and Heather Schacht Reisinger. "Using Trend Theory to Explain Heroin Use Trends." *Journal of Psychoactive Drugs* 33, no. 3 (2001): 203–11.

Ahmad, Diana L. *The Opium Debate and Chinese Exclusion Laws in the Nineteenth-Century American West.* Reno: University of Nevada Press, 2011.

Alcoff, Linda. *The Future of Whiteness.* New York: John Wiley and Sons, 2015.

Alexander, Michelle. *The New Jim Crow.* New York: New Press, 2010.

Alexander, Monica J., Mathew V. Kiang, and Magali Barbieri. "Trends in Black and White Opioid Mortality in the United States, 1979–2015." *Epidemiology* 29, no. 5 (2018): 707–15.

Alho, Hannu, David Sinclair, Erkki Vuori, and Antti Holopainen. "Abuse Liability of Buprenorphine-Naloxone Tablets in Untreated IV Drug Users." *Drug and Alcohol Dependence* 88, no. 1 (2007): 75–78.

Allen, R.L. "Whiteness and Critical Pedagogy." *Educational Philosophy and Theory* 36, no. 2 (2004): 121–36.

Altilio, T., M. Brennan, J. Dahl, A. Edwards, J. Fouladbakhsh, and F. Keefe. *Treatment Options: A Guide for People Living with Pain.* Baltimore: American Pain Foundation, 2007.

American Academy of Pain Medicine and American Pain Society. "The Use of Opioids for the Treatment of Chronic Pain: A Consensus Statement from the American Academy of Pain Medicine and the American Pain Society." *Clinical Journal of Pain* 13, no. 1 (1997): 6–8.

American Civil Liberties Union. *A Tale of Two Countries: Racially Targeted Arrests in the Era of Marijuana Reform.* New York: American Civil Liberties Union, 2020. www.aclu.org/report/tale-two-countries-racially-targeted-arrests-era-marijuana-reform.

American Pain Foundation. Testimony. In *Senate Health, Education, Labor and Pensions Committee Hearing to Examine the Effects of the Painkiller Oxy-Contin, Focusing on Risks and Benefits,* 107th Cong., 2nd sess., February 12, 2002. www.govinfo.gov/content/pkg/CHRG-107shrg77770/pdf/CHRG-107shrg77770.pdf.

American Society for Addiction Medicine. "ASAM's Commitment to Addressing Racial Injustice and Health Disparities." Letter to members, June 12, 2020. www.asam.org/docs/default-source/membership/asam-letter-on-racial-injustice-and-health-disparities-final.pdf?sfvrsn=aedb55c2_2.

———. "Regulation of Office-Based Opioid Treatment." Public policy statement, January 17, 2018. www.asam.org/advocacy/public-policy-statements/details/public-policy-statements/2021/08/09/regulation-of-office-based-opioid-treatment.

Amutah, C., K. Greenidge, A. Mante, M. Munyikwa, S.L. Surya, E. Higginbotham, D.S. Jones, R. Lavizzo-Mourey, D. Roberts, J. Tsai, and J. Aysola. "Misrepresenting Race: The Role of Medical Schools in Propagating Physician Bias." *New England Journal of Medicine* 384, no. 9 (2021): 872–78.

Anderson, L. "Private Interests in a Public Profession: Teacher Education and Racial Capitalism." *Teachers College Record* 121, no. 6 (2019): 1–38.

Arria, A., and R. DuPont. "Nonmedical Prescription Stimulant Use among College Students: Why We Need to Do Something and What We Need to Do." *Journal of Addictive Diseases* 29 (2010): 417–26.

Auriacombe, Marc, Mélina Fatséas, Jacques Dubernet, Jean-Pierre Daulouède, and Jean Tignol. "French Field Experience with Buprenorphine." *American Journal on Addictions* 13, Suppl. 1 (2004): S17–S28.

Avila, Eric. *Popular Culture in the Age of White Flight.* Berkeley: University of California Press, 2006.

Baca, C.T., and K.J. Grant. "What Heroin Users Tell Us about Overdose." *Journal of Addictive Diseases* 26, no. 4 (2007): 63–68.

Bailey, Zinzi D., Justin M. Feldman, and Mary T. Bassett. "How Structural Racism Works: Racist Policies as a Root Cause of U.S. Racial Health Inequities." *New England Journal of Medicine* 384 (2021): 768–73.

Baker, David W. "History of the Joint Commission's Pain Standards: Lessons for Today's Prescription Opioid Epidemic." *Journal of the American Medical Association* 317, no. 11 (2017): 1117–18.

Baldwin, James. "As Much Truth as One Can Bear: To Speak Out about the World as It Is." *New York Times Book Review*, January 14, 1962, BR1, BR38.

———. "On Being White—and Other Lies." In *The Cross of Redemption: Uncollected Writings*, edited by Randall Kenan, 166–70. New York: Vintage, 2011. Originally published in *Essence*, April 1984.

Baler, Ruben D., and Nora D. Volkow. "Drug Addiction: The Neurobiology of Disrupted Self-Control." *Trends in Molecular Medicine* 12, no. 2 (2006): 559–66.

Baum, Dan. "Legalize It All: How to Win the War on Drugs." *Harper's Magazine*, April 2016. https://harpers.org/archive/2016/04/legalize-it-all/.

Bazazi, Alexander R., Michael Yokell, Jeannia J. Fu, Josiah D. Rich, and Nickolas D. Zaller. "Illicit Use of Buprenorphine/Naloxone among Injecting and Noninjecting Opioid Users." *Journal of Addiction Medicine* 5, no. 3 (2011): 175–80.

Beety, Valena Elizabeth, Alex Kreit, Anne Boustead, Jeremiah Goulka, Caitlin Scott, and Leo Beletsky. "Drug-Induced Homicide Defense Toolkit." Ohio State Public Law Working Paper No. 467, October 4, 2019. http://dx.doi.org/10.2139/ssrn.3265510.

Belgrade, Miles J., Cassandra D. Schamber, and Bruce R. Lindgren. "The DIRE Score: Predicting Outcomes of Opioid Prescribing for Chronic Pain." *Journal of Pain* 7, no. 9 (2006): 671–81.

Bellamy, C.D., M. Costa, J. Wyatt, M. Mathis, A. Sloan, M. Budge, K. Blackman, L. Ocasio, G. Reis, K. Guy, and R.R. Anderson. "A Collaborative Culturally-Centered and Community-Driven Faith-Based Opioid Recovery Initiative: The Imani Breakthrough Project." *Social Work in Mental Health* 19, no. 6 (2021): 1–10.

Benjamin, Ruha. "Catching Our Breath: Critical Race STS and the Carceral Imagination." *Engaging Science, Technology, and Society* 2 (2016): 145–56.

———. *People's Science: Bodies and Rights on the Stem Cell Frontier*. Redwood City, CA: Stanford University Press, 2013.

Berg, Roland. "Drugs: The Mounting Menace of Abuse." *Look*, August 8, 1967, 11–28.

Bertakis, K.D., R. Azari, L.J. Helms, E.J. Callahan, and J.A. Robbins. "Gender Differences in the Utilization of Health Care Services." *Journal of Family Practice* 49, no. 2 (2000): 147–52.

Biehl, João. "Life of the Mind: The Interface of Psychopharmaceuticals, Domestic Economies, and Social Abandonment." *American Ethnologist* 31, no. 4 (2004): 475–96.

Bigg, Matthew. "Report Says U.S. Jails More Blacks Than Whites for Drugs." Reuters, December 4, 2007. www.reuters.com/article/us-usa-drugs-race/report-says-u-s-jails-more-blacks-than-whites-for-drugs-id-USN0453686820071205.

Binswanger, Ingrid A., Marc F. Stern, Richard A. Deyo, Patrick J. Heagerty, Allen Cheadle, Joann G. Elmore, and Thomas D. Koepsell. "Release from Prison—A High Risk of Death for Former Inmates." *New England Journal of Medicine* 356, no. 2 (2007): 157–65.

Bipartisan Policy Center. "Tracking Federal Funding to Combat the Opioid Crisis." March 2019. https://bipartisanpolicy.org/wp-content/uploads/2019/03/Tracking-Federal-Funding-to-Combat-the-Opioid-Crisis.pdf.

Birch, K., and D. Tyfield. "Theorizing the Bioeconomy: Biovalue, Biocapital, Bioeconomics or . . . What?" *Science, Technology, and Human Values* 38, no. 3 (2013): 299–327.

Birken, B., and J. Schmidt. "The Average Net Worth of Americas—by Age, Education and Ethnicity." *Forbes*, April 23, 2021. www.forbes.com/advisor/investing/average-net-worth/.

Black, Edwin. *War against the Weak: Eugenics and America's Campaign to Create a Master Race*. Washington, DC: Dialog Press, 2012.

Bliss, Catherine. *Race Decoded: The Genomic Fight for Social Justice*. Redwood City, CA: Stanford University Press, 2020.

Bonilla-Silva, Eduardo. *Racism without Racists: Color Blind Racism and Persistence of Racial Inequality in the U.S.* Lanham, MD: Rowman and Littlefield, 2003.

———. *The Structure of Racism in Color-Blind, "Post-racial" America*. Los Angeles: Sage Publications, 2015.

Bonilla-Silva, Eduardo, and T. Zuberi. *White Logic, White Methods: Racism and Methodology*. Lanham, MD: Rowman and Littlefield, 2008.

Borrell, L. N., J. R. Elhawary, E. Fuentes-Afflick, J. Witonsky, N. Bhakta, A. H. Wu, K. Bibbins-Domingo, J. R. Rodríguez-Santana, M. A. Lenoir, J. R. Gavin III, and R. A. Kittles. "Race and Genetic Ancestry in Medicine: A Time for Reckoning with Racism." *New England Journal of Medicine* 384, no. 5 (2021): 474–80.

Bourdieu, Pierre. "The Forms of Capital." In *Handbook of Theory and Research for the Sociology of Education*, edited by J. G. Richardson. New York: Greenwood Press, 1986.

Bourke, Joanna. *The Story of Pain: From Prayer to Painkillers*. New York: Oxford University Press, 2014.

Bowen, Elizabeth A., and Andrew Irish. "A Policy Mapping Analysis of Goals, Target Populations, and Punitive Notions in the U.S. Congressional Response to the Opioid Epidemic." *International Journal of Drug Policy* 74 (December 2019): 90–97. https://doi.org/10.1016/j.drugpo.2019.09.014.

Bowser, B. P. *The Black Middle Class: Social Mobility—and Vulnerability*. Boulder, CO: Lynne Rienner, 2007.

Braun, Lundy. *Breathing Race into the Machine: The Surprising Career of the Spirometer from Plantation to Genetics*. Minneapolis: University of Minnesota Press, 2014.

Brenton, Myron. "Women, Drugs, and Alcohol." *Redbook*, May 1979, 27, 190.

Brinkley-Rubinstein, Lauren, Alexandria Macmadu, Brandon D.L. Marshall, Andrew Heise, Shabbar I. Ranapurwala, Josiah D. Rich, and Traci C. Green. "Risk of Fentanyl-Involved Overdose among Those with Past Year Incarceration: Findings from a Recent Outbreak in 2014 and 2015." *Drug and Alcohol Dependence* 185 (2018): 189–91.

Brodkin, Karen. *How Jews Became White Folks and What That Says about Race in America*. New Brunswick, NJ: Rutgers University Press, 1998.

Brown, A., and S. Atske. "Black Americans Have Made Gains in U.S. Political Leadership, but Gaps Remain." Pew Research Center, Fact Tank, January 22, 2021. www.pewresearch.org/fact-tank/2021/01/22/black-americans-have-made-gains-in-u-s-political-leadership-but-gaps-remain/.

Brown, Claude. *Manchild in the Promised Land*. New York: Simon and Schuster, 2011.

Bruce, R. Douglas, Sumathi Govindasamy, Laurie Sylla, Adeeba Kamarulzaman, and Frederick L. Altice. "Lack of Reduction in Buprenorphine Injection after Introduction of Co-formulated Buprenorphine/Naloxone to the Malaysian Market." *American Journal of Drug and Alcohol Abuse* 35, no. 2 (2009): 68–72.

Buckley, Cara. "Young and Suburban, and Falling for Heroin." *New York Times*, September 25, 2009. www.nytimes.com/2009/09/27/nyregion/27heroin.html.

Burchell, G., A. Davidson, and M. Foucault. *The Birth of Biopolitics: Lectures at the Collège de France, 1978–1979*. New York: Springer, 2008.

Bush, George H.W. Presidential Proclamation 6158, July 17, 1990. Library of Congress, Project on the Decade of the Brain. www.loc.gov/loc/brain/proclaim.html.

BusinessWire. "The $11.9 Trillion Global Healthcare Market: Key Opportunities and Strategies (2014–2022)—ReearchAndMarkets.com." June 25, 2019. www.businesswire.com/news/home/20190625005862/en/11.9-Trillion-Global-Healthcare-Market-Key-Opportunities.

Butler, Stephen F., Kathrine Fernandez, Christine Benoit, Simon H. Budman, and Robert N. Jamison. "Validation of the Revised Screener and Opioid Assessment for Patients with Pain (SOAPP-R)." *Journal of Pain* 9, no. 4 (2008): 360–72.

Caldwell, Jacques R., M.E. Hale, R.E. Boyd, J.M. Hague, T. Iwan, M. Shi, and P.G. Lacouture. "Treatment of Osteoarthritis Pain with Controlled Release Oxycodone or Fixed Combination Oxycodone Plus Acetaminophen Added to Nonsteroidal Anti-inflammatory Drugs: A Double Blind, Randomized, Multicenter, Placebo Controlled Trial." *Journal of Rheumatology* 26, no. 4 (1999): 862–69.

Campbell, Nancy D. *Discovering Addiction: The Science and Politics of Substance Abuse Research*. Ann Arbor: University of Michigan Press, 2007.

———. *OD: Naloxone and the Politics of Overdose*. Cambridge, MA: MIT Press, 2020.

———. "'Regulating Maternal Instinct': Governing Mentalities of Late Twentieth-Century US Illicit Drug Policy." *Signs: Journal of Women in Culture and Society* 24, no. 4 (1999): 895–923.

———. "Toward a Critical Neuroscience of 'Addiction.'" *BioSocieties* 5, no. 1 (2010): 89–104. https://doi.org/10.1057/biosoc.2009.2.

———. *Using Women: Gender, Drug Policy, and Social Justice.* New York: Routledge, 2000.

Campbell, Nancy D., and Anne M. Lovell. "The History of the Development of Buprenorphine as an Addiction Therapeutic." *Annals of the New York Academy of Sciences* 1248, no. 1 (2012): 124–39.

Canadian Agency for Drugs and Technologies in Health. "Opioid Formulations with Tamper-Resistant or Abuse-Deterrent Features: Products and Policies." Environmental Scan, March 2017. www.cadth.ca/sites/default/files/pdf/ES0298-EH0034_Abuse_Deterrent_Opioid_Formulations.pdf.

Carpenter, Zoe. "Did the Opioid Epidemic Help Trump Win?" *The Nation,* December 7, 2016. www.thenation.com/article/archive/did-the-opioid-epidemic-help-donald-trump-win/.

Carroll, Linda. "Hooked: A Teacher's Addiction and the New Face of Heroin." *Today,* April 8, 2014. www.today.com/health/hooked-teachers-addiction-new-face-heroin-2D79496263.

Carver, Marina. "NYPD Officers Say They Had Stop and Frisk Quota." CNN, March 26, 2013. www.cnn.com/2013/03/22/justice/new-york-stop-and-frisk-trial/index.html.

Casas, Gloria. "'Heroin Highway' between Kane and Chicago Thriving, Officials Say." *Chicago Tribune,* March 30, 2017. www.chicagotribune.com/suburbs/aurora-beacon-news/ct-abn-aurora-heroin-st-0330-20170329-story.html.

Case, Anne, and Angus Deaton. "Rising Morbidity and Mortality in Midlife among White Non-Hispanic Americans in the 21st Century." *Proceedings of the National Academy of Sciences* 112, no. 49 (2015): 15078–83.

Catholic World. "The Opium Habit." September 1881, 827.

Caton, L., H. Shen, M.T. Assefa, T. Fisher, and M.P. McGovern. "Expanding Access to Medications for Opioid Use Disorder in Primary Care: An Examination of Common Implementation Strategies." *Journal of Addiction Research and Therapy* 11, no. 407 (2020): 2. https://doi.org/10.4172/2155-6105.1000407.

CBS. "Brown: Drug Operation Turned Long Island Expressway into 'Heroin Highway.'" January 13, 2012. https://newyork.cbslocal.com/2012/01/13/brown-drug-ring-turned-long-island-expressway-into-heroin-highway/.

Center for Substance Abuse Research, University of Maryland, College Park. "Suboxone® Sales Estimated to Reach $1.4 Billion in 2012—More Than Viagra® or Adderall®." *CESAR FAX* 21, no. 49 (December 10, 2012). http://db.cesar.umd.edu/cesar/cesarfax/vol21/21-49.pdf.

Centers for Disease Control and Prevention. "Drug Overdose Deaths." Accessed 2018. www.cdc.gov/drugoverdose/data/statedeaths.html.

———. "Leading Causes of Death, 1900–1998." Accessed June 19, 2022. www.cdc.gov/nchs/data/dvs/lead1900_98.pdf.

———. "Products—Vital Statistics Rapid Release—Provisional Drug Overdose Data." August 14, 2019. www.cdc.gov/nchs/nvss/vsrr/drug-overdose-data.htm.

———. "Today's Heroin Infographics." July 7, 2015. www.cdc.gov/vitalsigns/heroin/infographic.html.

Chawarski, Marek C., Mahmud Mazlan, and Richard S. Schottenfeld. "Behavioral Drug and HIV Risk Reduction Counseling (BDRC) with Abstinence-Contingent Take-Home Buprenorphine: A Pilot Randomized Clinical Trial." *Drug and Alcohol Dependence* 94, nos. 1–3 (2008): 281–84.

Chen, Ian, James Kurz, Mark Pasanen, Charles Faselis, Mukta Panda, Lisa J. Staton, Jane O'Rorke, Madhusudan Menon, Inginia Genao, and JoAnn Wood. "Racial Differences in Opioid Use for Chronic Nonmalignant Pain." *Journal of General Internal Medicine* 20, no. 7 (2005): 593–98.

Chidgey, Brooke A., Katharine L. McGinigle, and Peggy P. McNaull. "When a Vital Sign Leads a Country Astray: The Opioid Epidemic." *JAMA Surgery* 154, no. 11 (2019): 987–88.

Chou, I-han, and Kalyani Narasimhan. "Neurobiology of Addiction." *Nature Neuroscience* 8, no. 11 (2005): 1427. https://doi.org/10.1038/nn1105-1427.

Chou, Roger, Gilbert J. Fanciullo, Perry G. Fine, Jeremy A. Adler, Jane C. Ballantyne, Pamela Davies, Marilee I. Donovan, et al. "Clinical Guidelines for the Use of Chronic Opioid Therapy in Chronic Noncancer Pain." *Journal of Pain: Official Journal of the American Pain Society* 10, no. 2 (2009): 113–30. https://doi.org/10.1016/j.jpain.2008.10.008.

Choudhury, Suparna, and Jan Slaby, eds. *Critical Neuroscience: A Handbook of the Social and Cultural Contexts of Neuroscience*. New York: John Wiley and Sons, 2016.

Ciccarone, Daniel. "The Triple Wave Epidemic: Supply and Demand Drivers of the U.S. Opioid Overdose Crisis." *International Journal of Drug Policy* 71 (February 2019): 183–88.

Ciccarone, Daniel, Jeff Ondocsin, and Sarah G. Mars. "Heroin Uncertainties: Exploring Users' Perceptions of Fentanyl-Adulterated-and-Substituted 'Heroin.'" *International Journal of Drug Policy* 46 (2017): 146–55.

Cicero, T.J., M.S. Ellis, H.L. Surratt, and S.P. Kurtz. "The Changing Face of Heroin Use in the United States: A Retrospective Analysis of the Past 50 Years." *Journal of the American Medical Association Psychiatry* 71 (2014): 821–26.

Cicero, T., and H. Surratt. "Effect of Abuse-Deterrent Formulation of OxyContin." *New England Journal of Medicine* 367, no. 2 (2012): 187–89.

Cincinnati Commercial. "Opium Eating." *Daily Union and American,* March 4, 1866, 4.

Clark, Claire D. "'Chemistry Is the New Hope': Therapeutic Communities and Methadone Maintenance." *Social History of Alcohol and Drugs* 26, no. 2 (2012): 192–216.

———. *The Recovery Revolution: The Battle over Addiction Treatment in the United States*. New York: Columbia University Press, 2017.

Clinton, William. *Public Papers of the Presidents of the United States: William Clinton, 1997*. Scottsdale, AZ: Best Books, 1998.

Cockerham, William C., Bryant W. Hamby, and Gabriela R. Oates. "The Social Determinants of Chronic Disease." *American Journal of Preventive Medicine* 52, no. 1-S1 (2017): S5–S12.

Cohen, Emily. "From Phantoms to Prostheses." *Disability Studies Quarterly* 32, no. 3 (2012): 18. https://doi.org/10.18061/dsq.v32i3.3269.

Cohen, Lizabeth. *A Consumers' Republic: The Politics of Mass Consumption in Postwar America*. New York: Alfred A. Knopf, 2003.

Collins, Francis, Walter Koroshetz, and Nora Volkow. "Helping to End Addiction over the Long-Term: The Research Plan for the NIH HEAL Initiative." *Journal of the American Medical Association* 320, no. 2 (2018): 129–30.

Connolly, Vera. "Lethal Lullaby." *Collier's*, October 19, 1946, 95–97.

Council of State Governments. "Jails Have Become the Largest Provider of Mental Health Treatment in Our Nation." CSG Justice Center media clip, June 2, 2017. https://csgjusticecenter.org/mental-health/media-clips/jails-have-become-the-largest-provider-of-mental-health-treatment-in-our-nation/.

Courtwright, David T. "The Controlled Substances Act: How a 'Big Tent' Reform Became a Punitive Drug Law." *Drug and Alcohol Dependence* 76, no. 1 (2004): 9–15. http://dx.doi.org/10.1016/j.drugalcdep.2004.04.012.

———. *Dark Paradise: A History of Opiate Use in America*. Cambridge, MA: Harvard University Press, 1982.

Cousins, Gráinne, Fiona Boland, Brenda Courtney, Joseph Barry, Suzi Lyons, and Tom Fahey. "Risk of Mortality on and off Methadone Substitution Treatment in Primary Care: A National Cohort Study." *Addiction* 111, no. 1 (2016): 73–82.

Cowan, Alan, and John Lewis. *Buprenorphine: Combatting Drug Abuse with a Unique Opioid*. New York: Wiley Liss, 1995.

Crenshaw, Kimberle, Neil Gotanda, Gary Peller, and Kendall Thomas, eds. *Critical Race Theory: The Key Writings That Formed the Movement*. New York: New Press, 1996.

Cummings, Janet R., Hefei Wen, Michelle Ko, and Benjamin G. Druss. "Race/Ethnicity and Geographic Access to Medicaid Substance Use Disorder Treatment Facilities in the United States." *JAMA Psychiatry* 71, no. 2 (2014): 190–96.

Dallas, Kelsey, and Sandy Balazic. "The New Face of Heroin Addiction." *Deseret News*, February 19, 2015. www.deseret.com/2015/2/19/20558592/the-new-face-of-heroin-addiction.

Daniels, Jessie. "*Intervention*: Reality TV, Whiteness, and Narratives of Addiction." In Netherland, *Critical Perspectives on Addiction*, 103–28.

———. *White Lies: Race, Class, Gender and Sexuality in White Supremacist Discourse*. New York: Routledge, 1997.

Daniels, Jessie, and Amy J. Schulz. "Constructing Whiteness in Health Disparities Research." In *Gender, Race, Class, and Health: Intersectional Approaches*, edited by A. J. Schulz and L. Mullings, 89–127. San Francisco: Jossey-Bass, 2006.

Dasgupta, Nabarun, Leo Beletsky, and Daniel Ciccarone. "Opioid Crisis: No Easy Fix to Its Social and Economic Determinants." *American Journal of Public Health* 108, no. 2 (2018): 182–86. https://doi.org/10.2105/ajph.2017.304187.

Davidson, Bill. "The Thrill-Pill Menace." *Saturday Evening Post*, December 4, 1965.

Davidson, Richard J., and Bruce S. McEwen. "Social Influences on Neuroplasticity: Stress and Interventions to Promote Well-Being." *Nature Neuroscience* 15, no. 5 (2012): 689–95.

Dávila, Arlene. *Latinos, Inc.: The Marketing and Making of a People.* Berkeley: University of California Press, 2012.

Day, Bernie. "It Happened to a Bright Kid Like Ian." *Roanoke Times,* October 29, 2011. www.roanoke.com/webmin/opinion/it-happened-to-a-bright-kid-like-ian/article_dbdb0437-c827-525f-9221-8d8f2731d5e3.html.

DeGregory, Lane. "A Young Woman Struggles with Oxy Addiction and Recovery." *Tampa Bay Times,* December 17, 2011. Republished December 28, 2011, at *Psychology of Pain* (blog), http://psychologyofpain.blogspot.com/2011/.

Delgado, Richard, and Jean Stefancic. *Critical Race Theory: An Introduction.* 3rd ed. New York: NYU Press, 2017.

DeLisi, M., B.D. Dooley, and K.M. Beaver. "Super-predators Revisited." In *Criminology Research Focus,* edited by K.T. Froeling, 21–30. New York: Nova, 2007.

DeShazo, Richard D., McKenzie Johnson, Ike Eriator, and Kathryn Rodenmeyer. "Backstories on the US Opioid Epidemic: Good Intentions Gone Bad, an Industry Gone Rogue, and Watch Dogs Gone to Sleep." *American Journal of Medicine* 131, no. 6 (2018): 595–601. https://doi.org/10.1016/j.amjmed.2017.12.045.

DeTora, Lisa M., Michelle A. Carey, Dikran Toroser, and Ellen Z. Baum. "Ghostwriting in Biomedicine: A Review of the Published Literature." *Current Medical Research and Opinion,* May 2019, 1–9. https://doi.org/10.1080/03007995.2019.1608101.

Dikotter, Frank, Lares Laamann, and Zhou Xun. *Narcotic Culture: A History of Drugs in China.* Chicago: University of Chicago Press, 2004.

Doane, Ashley W., and Eduardo Bonilla-Silva. "Rethinking Whiteness Studies." In *White Out: The Continuing Significance of Racism,* edited by Ashley W. Doane and Eduardo Bonilla-Silva, 11–26. New York: Routledge, 2013.

Dole, Vincent P., and Marie E. Nyswander. "A Medical Treatment for Diacetylmorphine (Heroin) Addiction." *Journal of the American Medical Association* 193, no. 8 (1965): 646–50.

Dole, Vincent P., Marie E. Nyswander, and Mary Jeanne Kreek. "Narcotic Blockade." *Archives of Internal Medicine* 118, no. 4 (1966): 304–9.

Donelan, Jennifer. "7 On Your Side Presents 'Heroin Highway.'" ABC/WJLA, February 14, 2016. https://wjla.com/features/hooked-on-heroin/7-on-your-side-presents-heroin-highway.

Drake, R.E., J.S. Skinner, G.T. Bond, and H.H. Goldman. "Reducing Disability." *Health Affairs* 28, no. 3 (2009): 761–70.

Drucker, Ernest. *A Plague of Prisons: The Epidemiology of Mass Incarceration in America.* New York: New Press, 2013.

Drug Enforcement Agency. "National Take Back Initiative." Accessed February 18, 2013. www.deadiversion.usdoj.gov/drug_disposal/takeback/.

Drug Policy Alliance. "A Brief History of the War on Drugs." Accessed June 12, 2022. https://drugpolicy.org/issues/brief-history-drug-war.

———. *An Overdose Death Is Not a Murder: Why Drug-Induced Homicide Laws Are Counterproductive and Inhumane.* Report. New York: Drug Policy Alliance, 2019. https://drugpolicy.org/sites/default/files/dpa_drug_induced_homicide_report_0.pdf.

330 | Bibliography

—. *Uprooting the Drug War*. Report. New York: Drug Policy Alliance, 2021. https://uprootingthedrugwar.org.

Drugs.com. "Quarterly U.S. Sales Data for Suboxone | Drugs.Com Statistics." Last updated February 2014. www.drugs.com/stats/suboxone.

Du Bois, W. E. B. *The Souls of Black Folk*. Chicago: A. C. McClurg, 1903.

—. "The Souls of White Folk." In *Darkwater: Voices from within the Veil*, chap. 2. New York: Harcourt, Brace and Howe, 1920.

Dumit, Joe. *Drugs for Life: How Pharmaceutical Companies Define Our Health*. Raleigh, NC: Duke University Press, 2012.

Dunbar, Robin I. M. "The Social Brain: Mind, Language, and Society in Evolutionary Perspective." *Annual Review of Anthropology* 32, no. 1 (2003): 163–81.

Duster, Troy. *Backdoor to Eugenics*. New York: Routledge, 2003.

Dvorak, Richard. "Cracking the Code: De-coding Colorblind Slurs during the Congressional Crack Cocaine Debates." *Michigan Journal of Race and Law* 5 (1999): 611–63.

Dyer, Richard. *White*. London: Routledge, 1997.

Eban, K. "OxyContin: Purdue Pharma's Painful Medicine." *CNN Money* (blog), November 9, 2011. http://features.blogs.fortune.cnn.com/2011/11/09/OxyContin-purdue-pharma/.

Ecks, Stefan. "Pharmaceutical Citizenship: Antidepressant Marketing and the Promise of Demarginalization in India." *Anthropology and Medicine* 12, no. 3 (2005): 239–54.

Edwards, Jim. "One Nation, on Vicodin: Narcotic Painkillers Are Most-Used U.S. Drugs." CBS News, April 20, 2011. www.cbsnews.com/news/one-nation-on-vicodin-narcotic-painkillers-are-most-used-us-drugs/.

Emmanuelli, J., and J. Desenclos. "Harm Reduction Interventions, Behaviours and Associated Health Outcomes in France, 1996–2003." *Addiction* 100, no. 11 (2005): 1690–1700.

Epstein, Steven. *Inclusion: The Politics of Difference in Medical Research*. Chicago: University of Chicago Press, 2008.

Evers-Hillstrom, K. "Majority of Lawmakers in 116th Congress Are Millionaires." Open Secrets, April 23, 2020. www.opensecrets.org/news/2020/04/majority-of-lawmakers-millionaires/.

Eyre, Eric. "Drug Firms Poured 780M Painkillers into WV amid Rise of Overdoses." *Charleston Gazette-Mail*, December 17, 2016. www.wvgazettemail.com/news-health/20161217/drug-firms-poured-780m-painkillers-into-wv-amid-rise-of-overdoses#sthash.fIRPMoj8.dpuf.

Farley, Reynolds. "Trends in Racial Inequalities: Have the Gains of the 1960s Disappeared in the 1970s?" *American Sociological Review* 42, no. 2 (1977): 189–208.

Faul, Mark, Michael W. Dailey, David E. Sugerman, Scott M. Sasser, Benjamin Levy, and Len J. Paulozzi. "Disparity in Naloxone Administration by Emergency Medical Service Providers and the Burden of Drug Overdose in U.S. Rural Communities." *American Journal of Public Health* 105, no. S3 (2015): e26–e32.

Feagin, J. R. *White Party, White Government: Race, Class, and US Politics*. New York: Routledge, 2012.

————. *The White Racial Frame: Centuries of Racial Framing and Counter-framing*. New York: Routledge, 2020.

Feagin, J. R., and S. Elias. "Rethinking Racial Formation Theory: A Systemic Racism Critique." *Ethnic and Racial Studies* 36, no. 6 (2013): 931–60.

Federal Bureau of Investigation. "Arrests by Race, 2014." In *Crime in the United States, 2014*. https://ucr.fbi.gov/crime-in-the-u.s/2014/crime-in-the-u.s.-2014/tables/table-43.

————. "2018 Crime in the U.S." Uniform Crime Reporting, 2018. https://ucr.fbi.gov/crime-in-the-u.s/2018/crime-in-the-u.s.-2018.

Federal Bureau of Prisons. "Inmate Statistics: Offenses." Accessed 2019. www.bop.gov/about/statistics/statistics_inmate_offenses.jsp.

Fiellin, D. A., D. T. Barry, L. E. Sullivan, C. J. Cutter, B. A. Moore, P. G. O'Connor, and R. S. Schottenfeld. "A Randomized Trial of Cognitive Behavioral Therapy in Primary Care-Based Buprenorphine." *American Journal of Medicine* 126, no. 1 (2013): 74.e11–74.e17.

Fiellin, D. A., M. V. Pantalon, M. C. Chawarski, B. A. Moore, L. E. Sullivan, P. G. O'Connor, and R. S. Schottenfeld. "Counseling Plus Buprenorphine-Naloxone Maintenance Therapy for Opioid Dependence." *New England Journal of Medicine* 355, no. 4 (2006): 365–74.

Fine, M. E., L. E. Weis, L. C. Powell, and L. Wong. *Off White: Readings on Race, Power, and Society*. New York: Taylor and Frances/Routledge, 1997.

Fink, David S., Julia P. Schleimer, Aaron Sarvet, Kiran K. Grover, Chris Delcher, Alvaro Castillo-Carniglia, June H. Kim, et al. "Association between Prescription Drug Monitoring Programs and Nonfatal and Fatal Drug Overdoses: A Systematic Review." *Annals of Internal Medicine* 168, no. 11 (2018): 783–90.

Fishman, Scott. *Responsible Opioid Prescribing: A Physician's Guide*. Washington, DC: Waterford Life Sciences, 2007.

Fletcher, M. "White High School Dropouts Are Wealthier Than Black and Hispanic College Graduates: Can a New Policy Tool Fix That?" *Washington Post*, March 10, 2015. www.washingtonpost.com/news/wonk/wp/2015/03/10/white-high-school-dropouts-are-wealthier-than-black-and-hispanic-college-graduates-can-a-new-policy-tool-fix-that/.

Foley, Kathleen. "Current Issues in the Management of Cancer Pain: Memorial Sloan-Kettering Cancer Center." In *New Approaches to Treatment of Chronic Pain: A Review of Multidisciplinary Pain Clinics and Pain Centers*, edited by Lorenz K. Y. Ng, 169–84. NIDA Research Monograph 36. Washington, DC: Government Printing Office, May 1981.

Food and Drug Administration. "Timeline of Selected FDA Activities and Significant Events Addressing Opioid Misuse and Abuse." Accessed 2018. www.fda.gov/drugs/information-drug-class/timeline-selected-fda-activities-and-significant-events-addressing-opioid-misuse-and-abuse.

————. "Tranquilizers: Use, Abuse, and Dependency." *FDA Consumer*, October 1978, 21.

Foreman, James. *Locking Up Our Own: Crime and Punishment in Black America*. New York: Farrar, Straus and Giroux, 2017.

Fortner, Michael. *Black Silent Majority: The Rockefeller Drug Laws and the Politics of Punishment*. Cambridge, MA: Harvard University Press, 2016.

Foucault, Michel. *The History of Sexuality: An Introduction*. New York: Vintage, 1990.

——. *Security, Territory, Population: Lectures at the Collège de France, 1977–1978*. London: Springer, 2007.

Frankenberg, Ruth. *White Women, Race Matters: The Social Construction of Whiteness:*. New York: Routledge, 1993.

Fraser, Suzanne, David Moore, and Helen Keane. *Habits: Remaking Addiction*. London: Springer, 2014.

Friedman, Joseph, and Helena Hansen. "Evaluation of Increases in Drug Overdose Mortality Rates in the US by Race and Ethnicity before and during the COVID-19 Pandemic." *JAMA Psychiatry* 79, no. 4 (2022): 379–81. doi:10.1001/jamapsychiatry.2022.0004.

Friedman, Joseph, N. Clay Mann, Helena Hansen, Philippe Bourgois, Joel Braslow, Alex A. T. Bui, Leo Beletsky, and David L. Schriger. "Racial/Ethnic, Social, and Geographic Trends in Overdose-Associated Cardiac Arrests Observed by US Emergency Medical Services during the COVID-19 Pandemic." *JAMA Psychiatry* 78, no. 8 (2021): 886–95. https://doi.org/10.1001/jamapsychiatry.2021.0967.

Frydl, Kathleen. *The Drug Wars in America, 1940–1973*. New York: Cambridge University Press, 2013.

Frymer, P. "Acting When Elected Officials Won't: Federal Courts and Civil Rights Enforcement in US Labor Unions, 1935–85." *American Political Science Review* 97, no. 3 (2003): 483–99.

Fullilove, Mindy Thompson. *Root Shock: How Tearing Up City Neighborhoods Hurts America, and What We Can Do about It*. New York: New Village Press, 2004.

——. *Urban Alchemy: Restoring Joy in America's Sorted-Out Cities*. New York: NYU Press, 2013.

Fullwiley, Duana. *The Enculturated Gene: Sickle Cell Health Politics and Biological Difference in West Africa*. Princeton, NJ: Princeton University Press, 2011.

Furr-Holden, D., A. J. Milam L. Wang, and R. Sadler. "African Americans Now Outpace Whites in Opioid-Involved Overdose Deaths: A Comparison of Temporal Trends from 1999–2018." *Addiction*, August 27, 2020. https://doi.org/10.1111/add.15233.

Garner, Steve. *Whiteness: An Introduction*. New York: Routledge, 2007.

Garriott, William. *Policing Methamphetamine: Narcopolitics in Rural America*. New York: New York University Press.

Gibbon, S., and C. Novas, eds. *Biosocialities, Genetics, and the Social Sciences*. New York: Routledge, 2008.

Glaser, Frederick B. "The Origins of the Drug-Free Therapeutic Community." *British Journal of Addiction* 76, no. 1 (1981): 13–25.

Glickman, Lawrence B. *Buying Power: A History of Consumer Activism in America*. Chicago: University of Chicago Press, 2009.

Goode, Erica A. "Incarceration Rates for Blacks Dropped, Report Shows." *New York Times*, February 27, 2013. www.nytimes.com/2013/02/28/us/incarceration-rates-for-blacks-dropped-report-shows.html.

Gordon, Avery. *Ghostly Matters: Haunting and the Sociological Imagination.* Minneapolis: University of Minnesota Press, 2008.

Gravlee, C. C. "How Race Becomes Biology: Embodiment of Social Inequality." *American Journal of Physical Anthropology* 139, no. 1 (2009): 47–57.

Greene, S. "Indigenous People Incorporated? Culture as Politics, Culture as Property in Pharmaceutical Bioprospecting." *Current Anthropology* 45, no. 2 (2004): 211–37.

Greenslit, N. "Depression and Consumption: Psychopharmaceuticals, Branding, and New Identity Practices." *Culture, Medicine and Psychiatry* 29, no. 4 (2005): 477–502.

Guy, Gery P., Jr., Kun Zhang, Michele K. Bohm, Jan Losby, Brian Lewis, Randall Young, Louise B. Murphy, and Deborah Dowell. "Vital Signs: Changes in Opioid Prescribing in the United States, 2006–2015." *Morbidity and Mortality Weekly Report* 66, no. 26 (2017): 697–704.

Haddox, David, David Joranson, Robert T. Angarola, Albert Brady, Daniel B. Carr, Richard Blonsky, Kim Burchiel, et al. "The Use of Opioids for the Treatment of Chronic Pain: A Consensus Statement from the American Academy of Pain Medicine and the American Pain Society." *Clinical Journal of Pain* 13, no. 1 (1997): 6–8. www.jpain.org/article/S1526-5900(08)00831-6/fulltext.

Hadland, Scott E., Ariadne Rivera-Aguirre, Brandon D.L. Marshall, and Magdalena Cerdá. "Association of Pharmaceutical Industry Marketing of Opioid Products with Mortality from Opioid-Related Overdoses." *JAMA Network Open* 2, no. 1 (2019): e186007–e186007.

Haffajee, Rebecca, Anupam B. Jena, and Scott G. Weiner. "Mandatory Use of Prescription Drug Monitoring Programs." *Journal of the American Medical Association* 313, no. 9 (2015): 891–92.

Hale, Martin E., Roy Fleischmann, Robert Salzman, James Wild, Tad Iwan, Ruth E. Swanton, Robert F. Kaiko, and Peter G. Lacouture. "Efficacy and Safety of Controlled-Release versus Immediate-Release Oxycodone: Randomized, Double-Blind Evaluation in Patients with Chronic Back Pain." *Clinical Journal of Pain* 15, no. 3 (1999): 179–83.

Halewood, P. "Citizenship as Accumulated Racial Capital." *Columbia Journal of Race and Law* 1 (2011): 313–25.

Hall, Wayne, Adrian Carter, and Cynthia Forlini. "The Brain Disease Model of Addiction: Is It Supported by the Evidence and Has It Delivered on Its Promises?" *Lancet Psychiatry* 2, no. 1 (2015): 105–10.

Hamid, Ansley, Richard Curtis, Kate McCoy, Judy McGuire, Alix Conde, William Bushell, Rose Lindenmayer, et al. "The Heroin Epidemic in New York City: Current Status and Prognoses." *Journal of Psychoactive Drugs* 29, no. 4 (1997): 375–91.

Hammer, Rachel, Molly Dingel, Jenny Ostergren, Brad Partridge, Jennifer McCormick, and Barbara A. Koenig. "Addiction: Current Criticism of the Brain Disease Paradigm." *AJOB Neuroscience* 4, no. 3 (2013): 27–32.

Hansen, Helena. *Addicted to Christ: Remaking Men in Puerto Rican Pentecostal Drug Ministries.* Berkeley: University of California Press, 2018.

———. "Assisted Technologies of Social Reproduction: Pharmaceutical Prosthesis for Gender, Race, and Class in the White Opioid 'Crisis.'" *Contemporary Drug Problems* 44, no. 4 (2017): 321–38.

Hansen, Helena, Philippe Bourgois, and Ernest Drucker. "Pathologizing Poverty: New Forms of Diagnosis, Disability, and Structural Stigma under Welfare Reform." *Social Science and Medicine* 103 (2014): 76–83.

Hansen, Helena, and Jonathan M. Metzl, eds. *Structural Competency in Mental Health and Medicine: A Case-Based Approach to Treating the Social Determinants of Health.* New York: Springer, 2019.

Hansen, Helena, and Samuel K. Roberts. "Two Tiers of Biomedicalization: Methadone, Buprenorphine, and the Racial Politics of Addiction Treatment." In Netherland, *Critical Perspectives on Addiction*, 79–102.

Hansen, Helena, Carole Siegel, Joseph Wanderling, and Danae DiRocco. "Buprenorphine and Methadone Treatment for Opioid Dependence by Income, Ethnicity and Race of Neighborhoods in New York City." *Drug and Alcohol Dependence* 164 (2016): 14–21.

Hansen, Helena, and Mary E. Skinner. "From White Bullets to Black Markets and Greened Medicine: The Neuroeconomics and Neuroracial Politics of Opioid Pharmaceuticals." *Annals of Anthropological Practice* 36, no. 1 (2012): 167–82. https://doi.org/10.1111/j.2153-9588.2012.01098.x.

Hansen, Randall, and Desmond King. *Sterilized by the State: Eugenics, Race, and the Population Scare in Twentieth-Century North America.* Cambridge: Cambridge University Press, 2013.

Hardon, Anita. *Chemical Youth: Navigating Uncertainty in Search of the Good Life.* London: Palgrave Macmillan, 2020.

Harris, Cheryl. "Whiteness as Property." *Harvard Law Review* 106, no. 8 (1993): 1707–91.

Hart, Carl. *High Price: A Neuroscientist's Journey of Self-Discovery That Challenges Everything You Know about Drugs and Society.* New York: Harper Collins, 2013.

Hartmann, D., J. Gerteis, and P. R. Croll. "An Empirical Assessment of Whiteness Theory: Hidden from How Many?" *Social Problems* 56, no. 3 (2009): 403–24.

Hatch, Anthony Ryan. *Blood Sugar: Racial Pharmacology and Food Justice in Black America.* Minneapolis: University of Minnesota Press, 2016.

Hatcher, A., and H. Hansen. "At the Expense of a Life: Race, Class, and the Meaning of Buprenorphine in Pharmaceuticalized 'Care.'" *Substance Use and Misuse* 53, no. 2 (2018): 301–10.

Hausmann, Leslie R.M., Shasha Gao, Edward S. Lee, and C. Kent Kwoh. "Racial Disparities in the Monitoring of Patients on Chronic Opioid Therapy." *Pain* 154, no. 1 (2013): 46–52.

Hayden, C. "From Market to Market: Bioprospecting's Idioms of Inclusion." *American Ethnologist* 30, no. 3 (2003): 359–71.

Hayhurst, Chris. "Moving Away from Opioid Reliance." *APTA Magazine*, October 1, 2018. www.apta.org/apta-magazine/2018/10/01/moving-away-from-opioid-reliance.

Healy, David. "Good Science or Good Business?" *Hastings Center Report* 30, no. 2 (2000): 19–22.

———. *Let Them Eat Prozac: The Unhealthy Relationship between the Pharmaceutical Industry and Depression.* New York: NYU Press, 2004.

———. "Shaping the Intimate: Influences on the Experience of Everyday Nerves." *Social Studies of Science* 34, no. 2 (2004): 219–45.

Healy, David, and Dinah Cattell. "Interface between Authorship, Industry and Science in the Domain of Therapeutics." *British Journal of Psychiatry* 183, no. 1 (2003): 22–27.

Heath, D., R. Rapp, and K. S. Taussig. "Genetic Citizenship." In *A Companion to the Anthropology of Politics,* edited by David Nugent and Joan Vincent, 152–67. Blackwell, 2007.

Hedegaard, Holly, Margaret Warner, and Arialdi M. Miniño. "Drug Overdose Deaths in the United States, 1999–2015." Centers for Disease Control and Prevention, NCHS Data Brief No. 273, February 2017. https://stacks.cdc.gov/view/cdc/44356?utm_source=miragenews&utm_medium=miragenews&utm_campaign=news.

Helmrich, Stefan. "Species of Biocapital." *Science as Culture* 17, no. 4 (2008): 463–78.

Henderson, Gary L. "Designer Drugs: Past History and Future Prospects." *Journal of Forensic Science* 33, no. 2 (1988): 569–75.

Henry J. Kaiser Family Foundation. "Opioid Overdose Deaths by Race/Ethnicity." State Health Facts. Accessed January 16, 2019. www.kff.org/other/state-indicator/opioid-overdose-deaths-by-raceethnicity/.

Herzberg, David. *Happy Pills in America: From Miltown to Prozac.* Baltimore: Johns Hopkins University Press, 2009.

———. *White Market Drugs: Big Pharma and the Hidden History of Addiction in America.* Chicago: University of Chicago Press, 2020.

Hickman, T. A. *The Secret Leprosy of Modern Days: Narcotic Addiction and Cultural Crisis in the United States, 1870–1920.* Boston: University of Massachusetts Press, 2007.

Hodacs, H. Review of *A Consumers' Republic: The Politics of Mass Consumption in Post-war America,* by Lizabeth Cohen. *Business History Review* 4 (2003): 134–35.

Hoffman, Kelly M., Sophie Trawalter, Jordan R. Axt, and M. Norman Oliver. "Racial Bias in Pain Assessment and Treatment Recommendations, and False Beliefs about Biological Differences between Blacks and Whites." *Proceedings of the National Academy of Sciences* 113, no. 16 (2016): 4296–4301.

Horwitz, Allan V. *Creating Mental Illness.* Chicago: University of Chicago Press, 2002.

Hughes, Richard, and Robert Brewin. *The Tranquilizing of America: Pill Popping and the American Way of Life.* New York: Warner Books, 1979.

Hughey, M. W. "The (Dis) Similarities of White Racial Identities: The Conceptual Framework of 'Hegemonic Whiteness.'" *Ethnic and Racial Studies* 33, no. 8 (2010): 1289–1309.

Hunt, Sharon, and Jim Baumohl. "Drink, Drugs and Disability: An Introduction to the Controversy." *Contemporary Drug Problems* 30 (2003): 9–76.

Huskamp, Haiden A. "Prices, Profits, and Innovation: Examining Criticisms of New Psychotropic Drugs' Value." *Health Affairs* 25, no. 3 (2006): 635–46. https://doi.org/10.1377/hlthaff.25.3.635.

IBIS World. "Biotechnology in the US—Market Size, 2005–2027." Accessed July 31, 2021. www.ibisworld.com/industry-statistics/market-size/biotechnology-united-states/.

Inciardi, J. A., and T. J. Cicero. "Black Beauties, Gorilla Pills, Footballs, and Hillbilly Heroin: Some Reflections on Prescription Drug Abuse and Diversion Research over the Past 40 Years." *Journal of Drug Issues* 39, no. 1 (2009): 101–14.

Inflexxion Inc. "Screener and Opioid Assessment for Patients with Pain (SOAPP)® Version 1.0-SF." 2008. www.mcstap.com/docs/SOAPP-5.pdf.

Ingraham, Christopher. "White People Are More Likely to Deal Drugs, but Black People Are More Likely to Get Arrested for It." *Washington Post,* September 30, 2014. www.washingtonpost.com/news/wonk/wp/2014/09/30/white-people-are-more-likely-to-deal-drugs-but-black-people-are-more-likely-to-get-arrested-for-it/.

Jacobson, Matthew Frye. *Whiteness of a Different Color.* Cambridge, MA: Harvard University Press, 1999.

Jaffe, Jerome H., and Charles O'Keeffe. "From Morphine Clinics to Buprenorphine: Regulating Opioid Agonist Treatment of Addiction in the United States." *Drug and Alcohol Dependence* 70, no. 2 (2003): S3–S11.

Jans, L, S. Stoddard, and L. Kraus. *Chartbook on Mental Health and Disability in the United States.* InfoUse Report. Washington, DC: US Department of Education, National Institute on Disability and Rehabilitation Research, 2004.

Jauffret-Roustide, M., G. Pedrono, and N. Beltzer. "Supervised Consumption Rooms: The French Paradox." *International Journal of Drug Policy* 24 (2013): 628–30.

Jenkins, Janis H. *Pharmaceutical Self: The Global Shaping of Experience in an Age of Psychopharmacology.* Santa Fe, NM: School for Advanced Research Press, 2010.

Joel, Lucille. "The Fifth Vital Sign: Pain." *American Journal of Nursing* 99, no. 2 (1999): 9.

Johanson, Chris-Ellyn, Cynthia L. Arfken, Salvatore di Menza, and Charles Roberts Schuster. "Diversion and Abuse of Buprenorphine: Findings from National Surveys of Treatment Patients and Physicians." *Drug and Alcohol Dependence* 120, nos. 1–3 (2012): 190–95.

Jones, Christopher M., Joseph Logan, R. Matthew Gladden, and Michele K. Bohm. "Vital Signs: Demographic and Substance Use Trends among Heroin Users—United States, 2002–2013." *Morbidity and Mortality Weekly Report* 64, no. 26 (2015): 719–25.

Journal of the American Medical Association Editorial Board. "The United States Opium Commission." *Journal of the American Medical Association* 51, no. 8 (1908): 678–79.

Joynt, Michael, Meghan K. Train, Brett W. Robbins, Jill S. Halterman, Enrico Caiola, and Robert J. Fortuna. "The Impact of Neighborhood Socioeconomic Status and Race on the Prescribing of Opioids in Emergency Departments throughout the United States." *Journal of General Internal Medicine* 28, no. 12 (2013): 1604–10.

Jurecic, Q. "Trump Administration Releases 'Briefing Issues' on Foreign Policy and Security." *Lawfare* (blog), January 20, 2017. www.lawfareblog.com /trump-administration-releases-briefing-issues-foreign-policy-and-security.

Kaba, Mariame. *We Do This 'Til We Free Us: Abolitionist Organizing and Transforming Justice.* Boston: Haymarket Books, 2021.

Kahn, Jonathan. "Exploiting Race in Drug Development: BiDil's Interim Model of Pharmacogenomics." *Social Studies of Science* 38, no. 5 (2008): 737–58.

———. *Race in a Bottle: The Story of BiDil and Racialized Medicine in a Postgenomic Age.* New York: Columbia University Press, 2012.

Kalani, Cozen O'Connor-Lori, and Bernard Nash. "33 Attorneys General, U.S. Department of Justice, FTC Settle with Pharmaceutical Manufacturer over Allegedly Monopolizing Opioid Addiction Treatment Market." *State AG Report Weekly Update,* July 18, 2019. www.lexology.com/library/detail .aspx?g=7f987c51-7d86-434d-bff6-d208090e8642.

Kane, Harry Hubbel. *Drugs That Enslave: The Opium, Morphine, Chloral, and Hashisch Habits.* Philadelphia: Presley Blakiston, 1881.

Katersky, Aaron. "'Blue Fairy' Arrested in New York Drug Bust." ABC News, February 15, 2013. https://abcnews.go.com/Blotter/blue-fairy-arrested-york-drug-bust/story?id=18511865.

Kaye, Kerwin. *Enforcing Freedom: Drug Courts, Therapeutic Communities, and the Intimacies of the State.* New York: Columbia University Press, 2019.

Keefe, Patrick Radden. *Empire of Pain: The Secret History of the Sackler Dynasty.* New York: Doubleday, 2021.

———. "The Family That Built an Empire of Pain: The Sackler Dynasty's Ruthless Marketing of Painkillers Has Generated Billions of Dollars—and Millions of Addicts." *New Yorker,* October 23, 2017. www.newyorker.com /magazine/2017/10/30/the-family-that-built-an-empire-of-pain.

Keel, T. *Divine Variations: How Christian Thought Became Racial Science.* Redwood City, CA: Stanford University Press, 2018.

Kemp, Cathryn. "I Was a Painkiller Addict." *The Guardian,* September 9, 2012. www.theguardian.com/lifeandstyle/2012/sep/09/i-was-a-painkiller-addict.

Kesselheim, Aaron S., Jerry Avorn, and Ameet Sarpatwari. "The High Cost of Prescription Drugs in the United States: Origins and Prospects for Reform." *Journal of the American Medical Association* 316, no. 8 (2016): 858–71.

Kilty, K. M., and A. Joseph. "Institutional Racism and Sentencing Disparities for Cocaine Possession." *Journal of Poverty* 3, no. 4 (1999): 1–17.

Kim, Victoria. "Naltrexone Is Now Being Offered to Inmates in 30 States." *The Fix,* July 14, 2016. www.thefix.com/naltrexone-now-being-offered-inmates-30-states.

Klein, Naomi. *The Shock Doctrine: The Rise of Disaster Capitalism.* New York: Macmillan, 2007.

Kline, Wendy. *Building a Better Race: Gender, Sexuality, and Eugenics from the Turn of the Century to the Baby Boom.* Berkeley: University of California Press, 2001.

Knight, Kelly Ray. *Addicted, Pregnant, Poor.* Durham, NC: Duke University Press, 2015.

Kohler-Hausmann, Julilly. *Getting Tough: Welfare and Imprisonment in 1970s America*. Princeton, NJ: Princeton University Press, 2019.

Kolata, Gina. "Death Rates Rising for White Middle-Aged Americans, Study Says." *New York Times*, November 5, 2015. www.nytimes.com/2015/11/03 /health/death-rates-rising-for-middle-aged-white-americans-study-finds.html.

Kolb, Bryan, and Ian Q. Whishaw. "Brain Plasticity and Behavior." *Annual Review of Psychology* 49, no. 1 (1998): 43–64.

Kolb, Lawrence. "Drug Addiction: A Study of Some Medical Cases." *Archives of Neurology and Psychiatry* 20, no. 1 (1928): 171–88.

Koob, George F., and Eric J. Simon. "The Neurobiology of Addiction: Where We Have Been and Where We Are Going." *Journal of Drug Issues* 39, no. 1 (2009): 115–32. https://doi.org/10.1177/002204260903900110.

Kosten, T. R. "Taking Addiction Research into the Clinic." *Nature Neuroscience* 8, no. 11 (2005): 1413. https://doi.org/10.1038/nn1105-1413.

Kowal, E. "Orphan DNA: Indigenous Samples, Ethical Biovalue and Postcolonial Science." *Social Studies of Science* 43, no. 4 (2013): 577–97.

Krawczyk, Noa, Megan Buresh, Michael S. Gordon, Thomas R. Blue, Michael I. Fingerhood, and Deborah Agus. "Expanding Low-Threshold Buprenorphine to Justice-Involved Individuals through Mobile Treatment: Addressing a Critical Care Gap." *Journal of Substance Abuse Treatment* 103 (2019): 1–8.

Krupar, Shiloh, and Nadine Ehlers. "Target: Biomedicine and Racialized Geo-Body-Politics." *Occasion* 8 (January 2013): 1–25.

Kuhl, Stefan. *The Nazi Connection: Eugenics, American Racism, and German National Socialism*. New York: Oxford University Press, 2002.

Kuzmarov, Jeremy. *The Myth of the Addicted Army: Vietnam and the Modern War on Drugs*. Amherst: University of Massachusetts Press, 2009.

Lagisetty, Pooja A., Ryan Ross, Amy Bohnert, Michael Clay, and Donovan T. Maust. "Buprenorphine Treatment Divide by Race/Ethnicity and Payment." *Journal of the American Medical Association—Psychiatry*, prepublished May 8, 2019. https://jamanetwork.com/journals/jamapsychiatry/article-abstract/2732871.

Lakdawalla, D., J. Bhattacharya, and D. Goldman. "Are the Young Becoming More Disabled?" *Health Affairs* 23, no. 1 (2004): 168–76.

Lakoff, Andrew. *Pharmaceutical Reason: Knowledge and Value in Global Psychiatry*. Cambridge: Cambridge University Press, 2006.

———. "The Right Patients for the Drug: Managing the Placebo Effect in Antidepressant Trials." *BioSocieties* 2, no. 1 (2007): 57–71. https://doi.org/10 .1017/S1745855207005054.

Larochelle, Marc R., Dana Bernson, Thomas Land, Thomas J. Stopka, Na Wang, Ziming Xuan, Sarah M. Bagley, Jane M. Liebschutz, and Alexander Y. Walley. "Medication for Opioid Use Disorder after Nonfatal Opioid Overdose and Association with Mortality: A Cohort Study." *Annals of Internal Medicine* 169, no. 4 (2018): 137–45. https://doi.org/10.7326/m17-3107.

Lassiter, Matthew D. "Impossible Criminals: The Suburban Imperatives of America's War on Drugs." *Journal of American History* 102 (2015): 126–40.

———. *The Silent Majority: Suburban Politics in the Sunbelt South*. Princeton, NJ: Princeton University Press, 2006.

Laws, Chris. *Narcotics in Workers Compensation*. National Council on Compensation Insurance, NCCI Research Brief. May 2012. www.gwca.info /articles/II_narcotics-wc.pdf.

Lee, Jonathan. "The New Face of Drug Addiction," Fox News, July 19, 2013. http://fox40.com/2013/07/19/new-face-of-drug-addiction/.

Lee, Joshua D., Ellie Grossman, Andrea Truncali, John Rotrosen, Andrew Rosenblum, Stephen Magura, and Marc N. Gourevitch. "Buprenorphine-Naloxone Maintenance Following Release from Jail." *Substance Abuse* 33, no. 1 (2012): 40–47.

Lee, Sandra Soo-Jin. "Racializing Drug Design: Implications of Pharmacogenomics for Health Disparities." *American Journal of Public Health* 95, no. 12 (2005): 2133–38.

Leger, Donna. "Police Carry Special Drug to Reverse Overdoses." *USA Today*, February 3, 2014. www.usatoday.com/story/news/nation/2014/01/30/police-use-narcan-to-reverse-heroin-overdoses/5063587/.

Lembke, Anna. *Drug Dealer, MD: How Doctors Were Duped, Patients Got Hooked, and Why It's So Hard to Stop*. Baltimore: Johns Hopkins University Press, 2016.

Leonardo, Zeus. *Race, Whiteness, and Education*. New York: Routledge, 2009.

Leshner, Alan. "Addiction Is a Brain Disease, and It Matters." *Science* 278, no. 5335 (1997): 47–49.

Lin, L.A., M.R. Lofwall, S.L. Walsh, and H.K. Knudsen. "Perceived Need and Availability of Psychosocial Interventions across Buprenorphine Prescriber Specialties." *Addictive Behaviors* 93 (2019): 72–77.

Link, Bruce G., and Jo Phelan. "Social Condition as Fundamental Causes of Disease." *Journal of Health and Social Behavior* 36, extra issue (1995): 80–94.

Linnemann, Travis. *Meth Wars: Police, Media, Power*. New York: New York University Press, 2016.

Linnemann, Travis, and D. Kurtz. "Beyond the Ghetto: Police Power, Methamphetamine and the Rural War on Drugs." *Critical Criminology* 22 (2014): 339–55.

Lipsitz, George. "The Possessive Investment in Whiteness." In *White Privilege: Essential Readings on the Other Side of Racism*, 2nd ed., edited by Paula S. Rothenberg, chap. 12. New York: Worth, 2004.

———. *The Possessive Investment in Whiteness: How White People Profit from Identity Politics*. Philadelphia: Temple University Press, 2006.

Lopez, German. "How America's Prisons Are Fueling the Opioid Epidemic." *Vox*, March 26, 2018. www.vox.com/policy-and-politics/2018/3/13/17020002 /prison-opioid-epidemic-medications-addiction.

Lopez, Ian H. *White by Law: The Legal Construction of Race*. Critical America 21. New York: NYU Press, 1997.

Lovan, Dylan. "Appalachia's Approach to Drugs at Odds with AG's Policy." ABC News, May 15, 2017. www.wtvq.com/2017/05/15/appalachias-approach-drugs-odds-ag-policy/.

Low, S. "Maintaining Whiteness: The Fear of Others and Niceness." *Transforming Anthropology* 17, no. 2 (2009): 79–92.

Mack, Karin A., Christopher M. Jones, and Leonard J. Paulozzi. "Vital Signs: Overdoses of Prescription Opioid Pain Relievers and Other Drugs among Women—United States, 1999–2010." *Morbidity and Mortality Weekly Report* 62, no. 26 (2013): 537–42.

Magura, Stephen, Joshua D. Lee, Jason Hershberger, Herman Joseph, Lisa Marsch, Carol Shropshire, and Andrew Rosenblum. "Buprenorphine and Methadone Maintenance in Jail and Post-release: A Randomized Clinical Trial." *Drug and Alcohol Dependence* 99, nos. 1–3 (2009): 222–30.

Malat, J., S. Mayorga-Gallo, and D. R. Williams. "The Effects of Whiteness on the Health of Whites in the USA." *Social Science and Medicine* 199 (2018): 148–56.

Mann, Brian. "The Sacklers, Who Made Billions from OxyContin, Win Immunity from Opioid Lawsuits." NPR, September 1, 2021. www.npr.org/2021/09/01/1031053251/sackler-family-immunity-purdue-pharma-oxycontin-opioid-epidemic.

Marijuana Arrest Research Project. "Reports, Publications, Testimony." Spring 2020. http://marijuana-arrests.com/reports-publications-testimony.html.

Mark, Tami L., and Rita Vandivort-Warren. "Spending Trends on Substance Abuse Treatment under Private Employer-Sponsored Insurance, 2001–2009." *Drug and Alcohol Dependence* 125, no. 3 (2012): 203–7.

Marks, J., J. Dupre, S. Haslanger, D. Bolnick, M. Feldman, R. Lewontin, S. Tate, D. Goldstein, H. Greely, J. Kahn, and D. Fullwiley, eds. *Revisiting Race in a Genomic Age.* New Brunswick, NJ: Rutgers University Press, 2008.

Mars, Sarah G., Philippe Bourgois, George Karandinos, Fernando Montero, and Daniel Ciccarone. "'Every "Never" I Ever Said Came True': Transitions from Opioid Pills to Heroin Injecting." *International Journal of Drug Policy* 25, no. 2 (2014): 257–66.

Martin, Emily. "The Pharmaceutical Person." *BioSocieties* 1, no. 3 (2006): 273–87.

Martins, Silvia S., William Ponicki, Nathan Smith, Ariadne Rivera-Aguirre, Corey S. Davis, David S. Fink, Alvaro Castillo-Carniglia, et al. "Prescription Drug Monitoring Programs Operational Characteristics and Fatal Heroin Poisoning." *International Journal of Drug Policy* 74 (2019): 174–80.

Maté, Gabor. *In the Realm of Hungry Ghosts: Close Encounters with Addiction.* Mississauga, ON: Knopf Canada, 2008.

Mattick, Richard P., Courtney Breen, Jo Kimber, and Marina Davoli. "Buprenorphine Maintenance versus Placebo or Methadone Maintenance for Opioid Dependence." *Cochrane Database of Systematic Reviews*, no. 2 (2014). www.cochranelibrary.com/cdsr/doi/10.1002/14651858.CD002207.pub4/abstract.

Mattick, Richard P., J. Kimber, C. Breen, and M. Davoli. "Buprenorphine Maintenance versus Placebo or Methadone Maintenance for Opioid Dependence (Cochrane Methodology Review)." *Cochrane Library*, no. 4 (2003). www.dronet.org/lineeguida/ligu_pdf/Oppiacei.pdf.

Mauer, Marc. "Race, Class, and the Development of Criminal Justice Policy 1." *Review of Policy Research* 21, no. 1 (2004): 79–92.

Mauss, Marcel. "Les techniques du corps." *Journal de Psychologie* 32, nos. 3–4 (1934).

Maxwell, Jane Carlisle. "The Pain Reliever and Heroin Epidemic in the United States: Shifting Winds in the Perfect Storm." *Journal of Addictive Diseases* 34, nos. 2–3 (2015): 127–40.

May, Everette, and Arthur Jacobson. "Committee on Problems of Drug Dependence: A Legacy of the National Academy of Sciences. A Historical Account." *Drug and Alcohol Dependence* 23, no. 3 (1989): 183–218.

McCoy, Alfred. *The Politics of Heroin: CIA Complicity in the Global Drug Trade*. Chicago: Lawrence Hill Books, 2003.

McDermott, M., and F. L. Samson. "White Racial and Ethnic Identity in the United States." *Annual Review of Sociology* 31 (2005): 245–61.

McDonald, Douglas C., Kenneth Carlson, and David Izrael. "Geographic Variation in Opioid Prescribing in the U.S." *Journal of Pain* 13, no. 10 (2012): 988–96.

McGinnis, Derek. *Exit Wounds: A Survival Guide to Pain Management for Returning Veterans and Their Families*. With Stephen R. Braun. Washington, DC: Waterford Life Science, 2009.

McGirr, Lisa. *The War on Alcohol: Prohibition and the Rise of the American State*. New York: Norton, 2016.

McLellan, Thomas, David Lewis, Charles O'Brien, and Herbert D. Kleber. "Drug Dependence, a Chronic Medical Illness: Implications for Treatment, Insurance, and Outcomes Evaluation." *Journal of the American Medical Association* 284, no. 13 (2000): 1689–95.

Meier, Barry. *Pain Killer: A "Wonder" Drug's Trail of Addiction and Death*. Emmaus, PA: Rodale, 2003.

Melamed, J. "Racial Capitalism." *Critical Ethnic Studies* 1, no. 1 (2015): 76–85.

Meldrum, Marcia. "A Brief History of the Multidisciplinary Management of Chronic Pain." In *Chronic Pain Management: Guidelines for Multidisciplinary Program Development*, edited by Michael Schatman and Alexandra Campbell, chap. 1. Boca Raton, FL: CRC Press, Taylor and Francis, 2007.

Mendoza, Sonia, Allyssa S. Rivera, and Helena Hansen. "The Prescription Opioid 'Crisis' among Middle Class White Americans." *Transcultural Psychiatry* 53, no. 4 (2016): 465–87.

———. "Re-racialization of Addiction and the Re-distribution of Blame in the White Opioid Epidemic." *Medical Anthropology Quarterly* 33, no. 2 (2018): 242–62.

Mendoza, Sonia, Allyssa S. Rivera-Cabrero, and Helena Hansen. "Shifting Blame: Buprenorphine Prescribers, Addiction Treatment, and Prescription Monitoring in Middle-Class America." *Transcultural Psychiatry* 53, no. 4 (2016): 465–87.

Merrill, Joseph O., Lorna A. Rhodes, Richard A. Deyo, G. Alan Marlatt, and Katharine A. Bradley. "Mutual Mistrust in the Medical Care of Drug Users." *Journal of General Internal Medicine* 17, no. 5 (2002): 327–33.

Metzl, Jonathan M. *Dying of Whiteness: How the Politics of Racial Resentment Is Killing America's Heartland*. New York: Basic Books, 2019.

————. *The Protest Psychosis: How Schizophrenia Became a Black Disease.* Boston: Beacon Press, 2010.

————. *Prozac on the Couch.* Durham, NC: Duke University Press, 2003.

Metzl, Jonathan M., and Helena Hansen. "Structural Competency: Theorizing a New Medical Engagement with Stigma and Inequality." *Social Science and Medicine* 103 (February 2014): 126–33. https://doi.org/10.1016/j.socscimed.2013.06.032.

Metzl, Jonathan M., and Dorothy E. Roberts. "Structural Competency Meets Structural Racism: Race, Politics, and the Structure of Medical Knowledge." *American Medical Association Journal of Ethics* 16, no. 9 (2014): 674–90. https://doi.org/10.1001/virtualmentor.2014.16.9.spec1-1409.

Michels, Scott. "Heroin in Suburbia: The New Face of Addiction." ABC News, September 29, 2008. http://abcnews.go.com/TheLaw/Story?id=5494972&page=1.

Mills, Charles W. *The Racial Contract.* Ithaca, NY: Cornell University Press, 2014.

Minna Stern, Alexandra. *Eugenic Nation: Faults and Frontiers of Better Breeding in Modern America.* 2nd ed. Berkeley: University of California Press, 2015.

Mitra, Sanjana, Jade Boyd, Evan Wood, Cameron Grant, Kora DeBeck, Thomas Kerr, and Kanna Hayashi. "Elevated Prevalence of Self-Reported Unintentional Exposure to Fentanyl among Women who Use Drugs in a Canadian Setting: A Cross-sectional Analysis." *International Journal of Drug Policy* 83 (2020): 102864. https://doi.org/10.1016/j.drugpo.2020.102864.

Mock, Brentin. "California's Race to the Top on Cannabis," Bloomberg, February 5, 2018. www.bloomberg.com/news/articles/2018-02-05/trading-cannabis-for-racial-equity-in-california.

Molina, N. "The Long Arc of Dispossession: Racial Capitalism and Contested Notions of Citizenship in the US-Mexico Borderlands in the Early Twentieth Century." *Western Historical Quarterly* 45, no. 4 (2014): 431–47.

Monnat, Shannon M. "Opioid Crisis in the Rural US." In *Rural Families and Communities in the United States,* edited by Jennifer E. Glick, Susan M. McHale, and Valarie King, 117–43. Cham: Springer, 2020.

Montoya, Iván D., Jennifer R. Schroeder, Kenzie L. Preston, Lino Covi, Annie Umbricht, Carlo Contoreggi, Paul J. Fudala, et al. "Influence of Psychotherapy Attendance on Buprenorphine Treatment Outcome." *Journal of Substance Abuse Treatment* 28, no. 3 (2005): 247–54.

Montoya, Michael. *Making the Mexican Diabetic: Race, Science, and the Genetics of Inequality.* Berkeley: University of California Press, 2011.

Moore, Anna. "Eternal Sunshine." *The Guardian,* May 13, 2007. www.theguardian.com/society/2007/may/13/socialcare.medicineandhealth.

Moore, Kelly E., Walter Roberts, Holly H. Reid, Kathryn M. Z. Smith, Lindsay M. S. Oberleitner, and Sherry A. McKee. "Effectiveness of Medication Assisted Treatment for Opioid Use in Prison and Jail Settings: A Meta-analysis and Systematic Review." *Journal of Substance Abuse Treatment* 99 (2019): 32–43.

Morning, Ann. *The Nature of Race: How Scientists Think and Teach about Human Difference.* Berkeley: University of California Press, 2011.

Motivans, Mark. "Federal Justice Statistics, 2011–2012." *Bureau of Justice Statistics Bulletin*, January 2015. www.bjs.gov/content/pub/pdf/fjs1112.pdf.

Mueller, Benjamin, Robert Gebeloff, and Sahil Chinoy. "Surest Way to Face Marijuana Charges in New York: Be Black or Hispanic." *New York Times*, May 13, 2018. www.nytimes.com/2018/05/13/nyregion/marijuana-arrests-nyc-race.html.

Mueller, J.C. "Producing Colorblindness: Everyday Mechanisms of White Ignorance." *Social Problems* 64, no. 2 (2017): 219–38.

Muhuri, P.K., J.C. Gfroerer, and C. Davies. "Associations of Nonmedical Pain Reliever Use and Initiation of Heroin Use in the United States." *CBHSQ Data Review* (Substance Abuse and Mental Health Services Administration), August 2013. www.samhsa.gov/data/sites/default/files/DR006/DR006/nonmedical-pain-reliever-use-2013.htm.

Murakawa, N. "Toothless." *Du Bois Review: Social Science Research on Race* 8 (2011): 219–28.

Murphy, J., and B. Russell. "Police Officers' Views of Naloxone and Drug Treatment: Does Greater Overdose Response Lead to More Negativity?" *Journal of Drug Issues* 50, no. 4 (2020): 455–71.

Musto, David F. *The American Disease: Origins of Narcotic Control.* New York: Oxford University Press, 1999.

Nadelmann, E., and L. LaSalle. "Two Steps Forward, One Step Back: Current Harm Reduction Policy and Politics in the United States." *Harm Reduction Journal* 14, no. 1 (2017): 1–7.

Nam, Young Hee, Dennis G. Shea, Yunfeng Shi, and John R. Moran. "State Prescription Drug Monitoring Programs and Fatal Drug Overdoses." *American Journal of Managed Care* 23, no. 5 (2017): 297–303.

National Harm Reduction Coalition. "Harm Reduction Resource Center." Accessed 2020. https://harmreduction.org/resource-center/.

National Institute on Drug Abuse. *Prescription Drug Abuse.* Research Report Series, October 2011. www.drugabuse.gov/sites/default/files/rxreportfinal print.pdf.

———. "2016–2020 NIDA Strategic Plan: Translation, Implementation, and Dissemination." February 15, 2015. www.drugabuse.gov/about-nida/strategic-plan/ensuring-effective-translation-implementation-dissemination-scientific-research-findings.

Nelson, Alondra. *The Social Life of DNA: Race, Reparations, and Reconciliation after the Genome.* New York: Beacon Press, 2016.

Nestler, Eric J. "From Neurobiology to Treatment: Progress against Addiction." *Nature Neuroscience* 5, Suppl. (November 2002): 1076–79. https://doi.org/10.1038/nn945.

Netherland, Julie. "Becoming Normal: The Social Construction of Buprenorphine and New Attempts to Medicalize Addiction." PhD diss., City University of New York, 2011.

———, ed. *Critical Perspectives on Addiction.* Bingley, UK: Emerald Group, 2012.

Netherland, Julie, and Helena B. Hansen. "The War on Drugs That Wasn't: Wasted Whiteness, 'Dirty Doctors,' and Race in Media Coverage of

Prescription Opioid Misuse." *Culture, Medicine, and Psychiatry* 40, no. 4 (2016): 664–86.

———. "White Opioids: Pharmaceutical Race and the War on Drugs That Wasn't." *BioSocieties* 12, no. 2 (2017): 217–38.

Newman, Katherine S. *Falling from Grace: The Experience of Downward Mobility in the American Middle Class.* Berkeley: University of California Press, 1999.

News Service of Florida. "Worker's Comp System Hit by Opioid Crisis." April 25, 2018. https://wusfnews.wusf.usf.edu/2018-04-25/workers-comp-system -hit-by-opioid-crisis.

Newsweek. "Tension and the Nerves of the Nation . . . Psychiatry Eyes the Breaking Point." March 5, 1956, 54–58.

New York City Department of Health and Mental Hygiene. "Opioid Misuse in New York City." Paper presented at the New York City Department of Health and Mental Hygiene, May 5, 2014.

New York State Criminal Justice Knowledge Bank. "Heroin Overdose Prevention and Eduction (HOPE) Program." October 2018. https://knowledge-bank.criminaljustice.ny.gov/heroin-overdose-prevention-and-education-hope-program.

New York Times. "Chinese in New York." December 26, 1873, 3.

———. "The Opium Habit's Power." January 6, 1878, 5.

Ngai, Mae M. *Impossible Subjects: Illegal Aliens and the Making of Modern America.* Princeton, NJ: Princeton University Press, 2004.

Nietzsche, Friedrich. *On the Genealogy of Morals.* Translated by Reginald John Hollingdale. New York: Vintage Books, 1989.

Nixon, Richard. Address to the American Medical Association, June 22, 1971, Atlantic City, NJ. In *Advertising of Proprietary Medicines: Hearings before the Subcommittee on Monopoly of the Select Committee on Small Business, US Senate, 92nd Congress, First Session,* 924–30. Washington, DC: Government Printing Office, 1971.

Nixon Foundation. "Public Enemy Number One: A Pragmatic Approach to America's Drug Problem." June 29, 2016. www.nixonfoundation.org/2016 /06/26404/.

North Carolina Harm Reduction Coalition. "US Law Enforcement Who Carry Naloxone." Accessed 2020. www.nchrc.org/law-enforcement/us-law-enforcement-who-carry-naloxone/.

Novas, C. "The Political Economy of Hope: Patients' Organizations, Science and Biovalue." *BioSocieties* 1, no. 3 (2006): 289–305.

Ohio, Andrew. "New Details Revealed about Purdue's Marketing of OxyContin." *STAT,* January 15, 2019. www.statnews.com/2019/01/15/massachusetts-purdue-lawsuit-new-details/.

Okie, Susan. "A Flood of Opioids, a Rising Tide of Deaths." *New England Journal of Medicine* 363, no. 21 (2010): 1981–85. https://doi.org/10.1056 /NEJMp1011512.

Open Society Institute–Baltimore. *Using Buprenorphine to Treat Opioid Addiction.* OSI-Baltimore Brief, May 24, 2016. www.osibaltimore.org/wp -content/uploads/Buprenorphine-Brief.pdf.

Ostrow, Joanne. "Heroin's Harsh Reality." *Denver Post*, January 2, 2001. http://extras.denverpost.com/scene/ost102.htm.

Paone, Denise, Michelle Nolan, Ellenie Tuazon, and J. Blachman-Forshay. *Unintentional Drug Poisoning (Overdose) Deaths in New York City, 2000 to 2016.* New York City Department of Health and Mental Hygiene, Epi Data Brief No. 89, June 2017. www1.nyc.gov/assets/doh/downloads/pdf /epi/databrief89.pdf.

Paone, Denise, Ellenie Tuazon, Daniella Bradley O'Brien, and Michelle Nolan. *Opioid Misuse in New York City.* New York City Department of Health and Mental Hygiene, Epi Data Brief No. 50, August 2014. www1.nyc.gov/assets /doh/downloads/pdf/epi/databrief50.pdf.

Parker, Caroline M., and Helena Hansen. "How Opioids Became 'Safe': Pharmaceutical Splitting and the Racial Politics of Opioid Safety." *BioSocieties*, June 14, 2021, 1–24. https://doi.org/10.1057/s41292-021-00230-y.

Patrick, Stephen W., and Davida M. Schiff. "A Public Health Response to Opioid Use in Pregnancy." *Pediatrics* 139, no. 3 (2017): e20164070.

Pauly, V., V. Pradel, L. Pourcel, S. Nordmann, E. Frauger, M. Lapeyre-Mestre, J. Micallef, and X. Thirion. "Estimated Magnitude of Diversion and Abuse of Opioids Relative to Benzodiazepines in France." *Drug and Alcohol Dependence* 126, nos. 1–2 (2012): 13–20.

Peffley, Mark, Todd Shields, and Bruce Williams. "The Intersection of Race and Crime in Television News Stories: An Experimental Study." *Political Communication* 13, no. 3 (1996): 309–27.

Petryna, Adriana. *Life Exposed: Biological Citizens after Chernobyl.* Princeton, NJ: Princeton University Press, 2013.

Pettey, George E. "The Heroin Habit: Another Curse." *Alabama Medical Journal* 15 (1902–3): 174–80.

Phalen, Peter, Bradley Ray, Dennis P. Watson, Philip Huynh, and Marion S. Greene. "Fentanyl Related Overdose in Indianapolis: Estimating Trends Using Multilevel Bayesian Models." *Addictive Behaviors* 86 (2018): 4–10.

Phillips, John. "Prevalence of the Heroin Habit: Especially the Use of the Drug by 'Snuffing.'" *Journal of the American Medical Association* 59, no. 24 (1912): 2146–47.

Phys.org. "New York's Poorest Area Has 44% Living in Poverty." November 20, 2015. https://phys.org/news/2015-11-york-poorest-area-poverty.html.

Pieters, Toine, and Stephen Snelders. "From King Kong Pills to Mother's Little Helpers—Career Cycles of Two Families of Psychotropic Drugs: The Barbiturates and Benzodiazepines." *Canadian Bulletin of Medical History* 24, no. 1 (2007): 93–112. https://doi.org/10.3138/cbmh.24.1.93.

Pittsburg Post-Gazette. "Addiction's Toll: The Scourge of Heroin Strikes Too Close to Home." July 31, 2011. www.post-gazette.com/opinion/editorials /2011/07/31/Addiction-s-toll-The-scourge-of-heroin-strikes-too-close-to-home/stories/201107310204.

Pitts-Taylor, Victoria. "The Plastic Brain: Neoliberalism and the Neuronal Self." *Health* 14, no. 6 (2010): 635–52.

Pletcher, Mark J., Stefan G. Kertesz, Michael A. Kohn, and Ralph Gonzales. "Trends in Opioid Prescribing by Race/Ethnicity for Patients Seeking Care in

US Emergency Departments." *Journal of the American Medical Association* 299, no. 1 (2008): 70–78.

Poindexter, C.C. "Passage of the Ryan White Comprehensive AIDS Resources Emergency Act as a Case Study for Legislative Action." *Health and Social Work* 24, no. 1 (1999): 35–41.

PolicyAdvice. "The State of the Healthcare Industry: Statistics for 2021." Accessed August 6, 2021.

Pollock, Anne. *Medicating Race: Heart Disease and Durable Preoccupations with Difference.* Durham, NC: Duke University Press, 2012.

Poltilove, Josh. "Julie Schenecker's Attorney: Dad Should Never Have Left Kids with Her." *Tampa Tribune*, December 5, 2011.

Polydorou, Soteri, Stephen Ross, Peter Coleman, Laura Duncan, Nichole Roxas, Anil Thomas, Sonia Mendoza, and Helena Hansen. 2016. "Integrating Buprenorphine into an Opioid Treatment Program: Tailoring Care for Patients with Opioid Use Disorders." *Psychiatric Services* 68, no. 3 (2017): 295–98.

Porter, Jane, and Hershel Jick. "Addiction Rare in Patients Treated with Narcotics." Letter to editor. *New England Journal of Medicine* 302, no. 2 (1980): 123.

Posner, Gerald. *Pharma: Greed, Lies, and the Poisoning of America.* New York: Simon and Schuster, 2020.

Precious, Tom. "Lessons from 1977 Resonate in 2019 Marijuana Debate in Albany." *Buffalo News*, August 3, 2019. https://buffalonews.com/news/local/govt-and-politics/lessons-from-1977-resonate-in-2019-marijuana-debate-in-albany/article_59484c56-4d50-5e55-a057-e36e79116ac6.html.

Preminger, Otto. *The Man with the Golden Arm.* Screenplay by Walter Newman and Lewis Meltzer. United Artists, 1955.

Prescription Drug Abuse Policy System. "Naloxone Overdose Prevention Laws." Accessed 2017. http://pdaps.org/datasets/laws-regulating-administration-of-naloxone-1501695139.

Provine, Doris. *Unequal under Law: Race in the War on Drugs.* Chicago: University of Chicago Press, 2007.

Quadagno, J. "Social Movements and State Transformation: Labor Unions and Racial Conflict in the War on Poverty." *American Sociological Review* 57, no. 5 (1992): 616–34.

Quinones, Sam. *Dreamland: The True Tale of America's Opiate Epidemic.* New York: Bloomsbury, 2015.

Rabinow, Paul. "Artificiality and Enlightenment: From Sociobiology to Biosociality." *Politix*, no. 2 (2010): 21–46.

Rabinow, Paul, and Nikolas Rose. "Biopower Today." *BioSocieties* 1, no. 2 (2006): 195–217.

Radel, Laura, Melinda Baldwin, Gilbert Crouse, Robin Ghertner, and Annette Waters. *Substance Use, the Opioid Epidemic, and the Child Welfare System: Key Findings from a Mixed Methods Study.* Office of the Assistant Secretary for Planning and Evaluation, ASPE Research Brief, March 7, 2018. https://aspe.hhs.gov/sites/default/files/private/pdf/258836/SubstanceUseChildWelfareOverview.pdf.

Raikhel, Eugene, and William Garriott. *Addiction Trajectories*. Durham, NC: Duke University Press, 2013.

Rajan, K. S. *Biocapital*. Durham, NC: Duke University Press, 2006.

Rasmussen, Nicolas. "Goofball Panic: Barbiturates, 'Dangerous' and Addictive Drugs, and the Regulation of Medicine in Postwar America." In *Prescribed: Writing, Filling, Using, and Abusing the Prescription in Modern America*, edited by Jeremy A. Greene and Elizabeth Siegel Watkins, 23–45. Baltimore: Johns Hopkins University Press, 2012.

———. *On Speed: The Many Lives of Amphetamine*. New York: NYU Press, 2008.

Raver, Diane. "Heroin Death: 'She Thought It Would Be Fun.'" *Batesville Herald-Tribune*, March 25, 2011.

Raz, Mical. "Treating Addiction or Reducing Crime? Methadone Maintenance and Drug Policy under the Nixon Administration." *Journal of Policy History* 29, no. 1 (2017): 58–86.

Reflective Democracy Campaign. "Reflective Democracy Research Findings: Summary Report." October 2017. https://wholeads.us/wp-content /uploads/2019/04/2017-report-corrected-4.2019.pdf.

Reinarman, Craig. "Addiction as Accomplishment: The Discursive Construction of Disease." *Addiction Research and Theory* 13, no. 4 (2005): 307–20.

Reinarman, Craig, and Harry G. Levine, eds. *Crack in America: Demon Drugs and Social Justice*. Berkeley: University of California Press, 1997.

———. "Crack in the Rearview Mirror: Deconstructing Drug War Mythology." *Social Justice* 31, nos. 1–2 (2004): 182–99.

Rembis, Michael. *Defining Deviance: Sex, Science, and Delinquent Girls, 1890–1960*. Urbana: University of Illinois Press, 2013.

Rich, Josiah D., Sarah E. Wakeman, and Samuel L. Dickman. "Medicine and the Epidemic of Incarceration in the United States." *New England Journal of Medicine* 364, no. 22 (2011): 2081–83. https://dx.doi.org/10.1056% 2FNEJMp1102385.

Richardson, Diane. "More Funds Needed for Opioid Abuse." New York Assembly video clip, uploaded June 17, 2016. https://nyassembly.gov/mem /Diana-C-Richardson/video/7898/.

Rizzo, Mary. "Embodying Withdrawal: Abjection and the Popularity of Heroin Chic." *Michigan Feminist Studies* 15 (2001). http://hdl.handle.net/2027/spo .ark5583.0015.004.

Roberts, Dorothy E. *Fatal Invention: How Science, Politics, and Big Business Re-create Race in the Twenty-First Century*. New York: New Press, 2011.

———. *Is Race-Based Medicine Good for Us? African American Approaches to Race, Biomedicine, and Equality*. Los Angeles: Sage Publications, 2008.

———. "Punishing Drug Addicts Who Have Babies: Women of Color, Equality, and the Right of Privacy." *Harvard Law Review* 104, no. 7 (1991): 1419–82.

Roberts, Samuel. *Infectious Fear: Politics, Disease, and the Health Effects of Segregation*. Chapel Hill: University of North Carolina Press, 2009.

———. "'Rehabilitation' as Boundary Object: Medicalization, Local Activism, and Narcotics Addiction Policy in New York City, 1951–62." *Social History of Alcohol and Drugs* 26, no. 2 (2012): 147–69.

Robert Wood Johnson Foundation. "Health Care's Blind Side." December 1, 2011. www.rwjf.org/en/library/research/2011/12/health-care-s-blind-side.html.

Robinson, Cedric. *Black Marxism: The Making of the Black Radical Tradition.* London: Zed Books, 1983.

Rodríguez-Muñiz, Michael. "Bridgework: STS, Sociology, and the 'Dark Matters' of Race." *Engaging Science, Technology, and Society* 2 (2016): 214–26.

Roediger, David. *Working towards Whiteness: How America's Immigrants Became White.* New York: Basic Books, 2006.

Rose, Nikolas. *The Politics of Life Itself: Biomedicine, Power, and Subjectivity in the Twenty-First Century.* Princeton, NJ: Princeton University Press, 2006.

Roth, S.H., R.M. Fleischmann, F.X. Burch, F. Dietz, B. Bockow, R.J. Rapoport, J. Rutstein, and P.G. Lacouture. "Around-the-Clock, Controlled-Release Oxycodone Therapy for Osteoarthritis-Related Pain: Placebo-Controlled Trial and Long-Term Evaluation." *Archives of Internal Medicine* 160, no. 6 (2000): 853–60.

Rothman, B.K. *The Book of Life: A Personal and Ethical Guide to Race, Normality, and the Implications of the Human Genome Project.* New York: Beacon Press, 2001.

Rudd, Rose A., Puja Seth, Felicita David, and Lawrence Scholl. "Increases in Drug and Opioid-Involved Overdose Deaths—United States, 2010–2015." *Morbidity and Mortality Weekly Report* 65, nos. 50–51 (2016): 1445–52. https://doi.org/10.15585/mmwr.mm655051e1.

Saloner, Brendan, Rachel Landis, Bradley D. Stein, and Colleen L. Barry. "The Affordable Care Act in the Heart of the Opioid Crisis: Evidence from West Virginia." *Health Affairs* 38, no. 4 (2019): 633–42. https://doi.org/10.1377/hlthaff.2018.05049.

Saucier, R., D. Wolfe, and N. Dasgupta. "Correction to: Review of Case Narratives from Fatal Overdoses Associated with Injectable Naltrexone for Opioid Dependence." *Drug Safety* 41, no. 10 (2018): 989.

Savage, Seddon R., David E. Joranson, Edward C. Covington, Sidney H. Schnoll, Howard A. Heit, and Aaron M. Gilson. "Definitions Related to the Medical Use of Opioids: Evolution towards Universal Agreement." *Journal of Pain and Symptom Management* 26, no. 1 (2003): 655–67. https://doi.org/10.1016/S0885-3924(03)00219-7.

Scheper-Hughes, Nancy. "Parts Unknown: Undercover Ethnography of the Organs-Trafficking Underworld." *Ethnography* 5, no. 1 (2004): 29–73.

Schneider, Eric. *Smack: Heroin and the American City.* Philadelphia: University of Pennsylvania Press, 2011.

Scholl, Lawrence, Puja Seth, Mbabazi Kariisa, Nana Wilson, and Grant Baldwin. "Drug and Opioid-Involved Overdose Deaths—United States, 2013–2017." *Morbidity and Mortality Weekly Report* 67, no. 5152 (2019): 1419–27.

Schulte, Fred. "How America Got Hooked on a Deadly Drug." *Kaiser Health News,* June 13, 2018. https://khn.org/news/how-america-got-hooked-on-a-deadly-drug/.

Schwab, Tim. "US Opioid Prescribing: The Federal Government Advisers with Recent Ties to Big Pharma." *BMJ* 366 (2019): l5167. https://doi.org/10.1136/bmj.l5167.

Schwartz, Yardena. "Painkiller Use Breeds New Face of Heroin Addiction." NBC News, June 19, 2012. http://dailynightly.nbcnews.com/_news/2012 /06/19/12303942-painkiller-use-breeds-new-face-of-heroin-addiction?lite.

ScienceDaily. "Opioids Now Most Prescribed Drug Class in America." April 6, 2011. www.sciencedaily.com/releases/2011/04/110405161906.htm.

Sears, Cornelia, and Jessica Johnson. "Waste." Media/Culture Journal 13, no. 4 (2010). https://doi.org/10.5204/mcj.286.

Seelye, Katherine. "Heroin in New England, More Abundant and More Deadly." New York Times, July 19, 2013, A11.

———. "In Heroin Crisis, White Families Seek Gentler War on Drugs." New York Times, October 30, 2015. www.nytimes.com/2015/10/31/us/heroin-war-on-drugs-parents.html.

Seewer, John, and Geoff Mulvihill. "Deal with OxyContin Maker Leaves Families Angry, Conflicted." Associated Press, September 2, 2021. https://apnews .com/article/business-health-6c2ad3d4164f3711eb5c2d443d23a75e.

Sentencing Project. "Criminal Justice Facts." Accessed 2019. www.sentencing project.org/criminal-justice-facts/.

Sered, Susan Starr. "The Opioid Crisis and the Infrastructure of Social Capital." International Journal of Drug Policy 71 (2019): 47–55.

Shah, Nayan. Contagious Divides: Epidemics and Race in San Francisco's Chinatown. Berkeley: University of California Press, 2001.

Shanafelt, T.D., S. Boone, L. Tan, L.N. Dyrbye, W. Sotile, D. Satele, C.P. West, J. Sloan, and M.R. Oreskovich. "Burnout and Satisfaction with Work-Life Balance among US Physicians Relative to the General US Population." Archives of Internal Medicine 172, no. 18 (2012): 1377–85.

Shavers, Vickie L., Alexis Bakos, and Vanessa B. Sheppard. "Race, Ethnicity, and Pain among the US Adult Population." Journal of Health Care for the Poor and Underserved 21, no. 1 (2010): 177–220.

Sherman, Melina. "Opiates for the Masses: Constructing a Market for Prescription (Pain) Killers." Journal of Cultural Economy 10, no. 6 (2017): 485–97.

Shkolnikova, Svetlana. "On Route 23, or 'Heroin Highway,' a Growing Suburban Demand for Drugs Meets Urban Supply." northjersey.com, March 11, 2019. www.northjersey.com/story/news/crime/2019/03/11/nj-route-23-heroin-highway-demand-drugs-meets-urban-supply/2955089002/.

Silverman, Amy, and Jeremy Voas. "Opiate for the Mrs." Phoenix New Times, September 8, 1994. www.phoenixnewtimes.com/news/opiate-for-the-mrs-6432986.

Singer, Merrill. Drugging the Poor: Legal and Illegal Drugs and Social Inequality. Long Grove, IL: Waveland Press, 2007.

Sismondo, Sergio. "Ghost Management: How Much of the Medical Literature Is Shaped behind the Scenes by the Pharmaceutical Industry?" PLOS Medicine 4, no. 9 (2007): e286. https://doi.org/10.1371/journal.pmed.0040286.

Skelos, Dean G. "Senate Gives Final Legislative Approval to 'Good Samaritan' Law." New York State Senate, press release, June 20, 2011. www.nysenate .gov/newsroom/press-releases/dean-g-skelos/senate-gives-final-legislative-approval-%E2%80%9Cgood-samaritan%E2%80%9D-law.

Skloot, Rebecca. *The Immortal Life of Henrietta Lacks*. New York: Broadway Paperbacks, 2017.

Sommerfeldt, Chris, and Reuven Blau. "New Website Shows Crotona Park East and Morrisania in the Bronx Have City's Highest Rate of Jailed Residents." *New York Daily News,* January 19, 2016. www.nydailynews.com/new-york/people-city-jails-bronx-neighborhoods-article-1.2501101.

Spade, Dean. *Mutual Aid: Building Solidarity during This Crisis (and the Next)*. London: Verso Books, 2020.

Spencer, Merianne, Margaret Warner, Brigham A. Bastian, James P. Trinidad, and Holly Hedegaard. *Drug Overdose Deaths Involving Fentanyl, 2011–2016*. Centers for Disease Control National Vital Statistics Reports, March 21, 2019. https://stacks.cdc.gov/view/cdc/77832.

Spies, Mike, Dave Gutt, and James Peterson. "Welcome to Heroin Island." *Vocativ,* August 21, 2014. www.vocativ.com/underworld/drugs/heroin-staten-island/index.html.

Spillane, Joseph F. "Debating the Controlled Substances Act." *Drug and Alcohol Dependence* 76, no. 1 (2004): 17–29. https://doi.org/10.1016/j.drugalcdep.2004.04.011.

Spindler, Amy. "The 90's Version of the Decadent Look." *New York Times,* May 7, 1996. www.nytimes.com/1996/05/07/style/the-90-s-version-of-the-decadent-look.html.

Stanton, A., C. McLeod, B. Luckey, W. Kissin, and L. J. Sonnefeld. "Expanding Treatment of Opioid Dependence: Initial Physician and Patient Experiences with the Adoption of Buprenorphine." American Society of Addiction Medicine, May 5, 2006.

Steiner, Benjamin D., and Victor Argothy. "White Addiction: Racial Inequality, Racial Ideology, and the War on Drugs." *Temple Political and Civil Rights Law Review* 10 (2001): 443–75.

Stohr, Greg, and Susan Decker. "Supreme Court Justice Refuses to Block Generic Suboxone Film." Bloomberg, February 19, 2019. www.bloomberg.com/news/articles/2019-02-19/supreme-court-justice-refuses-to-block-generic-suboxone-film.

Stopthedrugwar.com. "New York Mayor Giuliani Reverses Himself on Methadone." *Drug War Chronicle,* January 22, 1999. http://stopthedrugwar.org/chronicle-old/075/giuliani.shtml.

Substance Abuse and Mental Health Services Administration. "Buprenorphine Waiver Management." Accessed June 22, 2015. www.samhsa.gov/medication-assisted-treatment/training-materials-resources/buprenorphine-waiver.

———. *Expanding the Use of Medications to Treat Individuals with Substance Use Disorders in Safety Net Settings*. September 2014. www.thenationalcouncil.org/wp-content/uploads/2020/01/Expanding_the_Use_of_Medications_to_Treat_Individuals_with_SU_Disorders_in_Safety_Net_Settings.pdf.

———. "National Survey Shows Continued Reduced Levels of Prescription Drug Use among Young Adults." News release, September 2013.

———. *Results from the 2009 National Survey on Drug Use and Health*. Vol. 1, *Summary of National Findings*. Rockville, MD: Office of Applied Studies, 2010.

Substance Abuse and Mental Health Services Administration, Center for Substance Abuse Treatment. *Clinical Guidelines for the Use of Buprenorphine in the Treatment of Opioid Addiction.* Treatment Improvement Protocol (TIP) Series, No. 40. Rockville, MD: Substance Abuse and Mental Health Services Administration, 2004. www.ncbi.nlm.nih.gov/books /NBK64234/.

Sugrue, Thomas. *The Origins of the Urban Crisis: Race and Inequality in Postwar Detroit.* Princeton, NJ: Princeton University Press, 2005.

Sullivan, Caryn. "Prescription Drugs: Lock Your Cabinets, and Know the Risks." *St. Paul Pioneer Press,* May 27, 2011. www.carynsullivanscribe .com/prescription-drugs-lock-your-cabinets-and-know-the-risks/.

Sutter, M.E., R.R. Gerona, M.T. Davis, B.M. Roche, D.K. Colby, J.A. Chenoweth, A.J. Adams, et al. "Fatal Fentanyl: One Pill Can Kill." *Academic Emergency Medicine* 24, no. 1 (2017): 106–13.

Szalavitz, Maia. "Opioid Addiction Is a Huge Problem, but Pain Prescriptions Are Not the Cause." *Scientific American, MIND* guest blog, May 10, 2016. https://blogs.scientificamerican.com/mind-guest-blog/opioid-addiction-is-a-huge-problem-but-pain-prescriptions-are-not-the-cause/.

Talbot, M. "Brain Gain: The Underground World of 'Neuroenhancing' Drugs." *New Yorker,* April 27, 2009. www.newyorker.com/magazine/2009/04/27 /brain-gain.

Temple, John. *American Pain: How a Young Felon and His Ring of Doctors Unleashed America's Deadliest Drug Epidemic.* Guilford, CT: Rowman and Littlefield, 2015.

Thistle, Scott. "LePage: Over 90 Percent of Drug Dealers Busted in Maine Are Black or Hispanic." *Press Herald,* August 24, 2016. www.pressherald .com/2016/08/24/gov-lepage-says-most-drug-traffickers-arrested-in-maine-are-Black-or-hispanic/.

Tompkins, D.A., J.G. Hobelmann, and P. Compton. "Providing Chronic Pain Management in The 'Fifth Vital Sign' Era: Historical and Treatment Perspectives on a Modern-Day Medical Dilemma." *Drug and Alcohol Dependence* 173 (2017): S11–S21.

Trocki, Carl. *Opium, Empire and the Global Political Economy: A Study of the Asian Opium Trade, 1750–1950.* London: Routledge, 1999.

Tunnell, Kenneth D. "Cultural Constructions of the Hillbilly Heroin and Crime Problem." In *Cultural Criminology Unleashed,* edited by J. Ferrell, K. Hayward, W. Morrison, and M. Presdee, 147–56. 2004. Reprint, London: Routledge, 2016.

Twine, F.W., and C. Gallagher. "The Future of Whiteness: A Map of the 'Third Wave.'" *Ethnic and Racial Studies* 31, no. 1 (2008): 4–24.

Twohey, Megan. "Mike Pence's Response to HIV Outbreak: Prayer, Then a Change of Heart." *New York Times,* August 7, 2016. www.nytimes.com/2016 /08/08/us/politics/mike-pence-needle-exchanges-indiana.html.

Unick, George, Daniel Rosenblum, Sarah Mars, and Daniel Ciccarone. "The Relationship between US Heroin Market Dynamics and Heroin-Related Overdose, 1992–2008." *Addiction* 109, no. 11 (2008): 1889–98.

University of Pennsylvania School of Medicine. "Opioids Now Most Prescribed Class of Medications in America." ScienceDaily, April 6, 2011. www .sciencedaily.com/releases/2011/04/110405161906.htm.

USA Today. "War on Drugs Requires New Tactics: Our View." May 16, 2016. www.usatoday.com/story/opinion/2016/05/16/heroin-safe-injections-van-couver-opioids-overdose-editorials-debates/84421772/.

US Census Bureau. "Law Enforcement, Courts, and Prisons: Arrests, 2009." Section 5 of the Statistical Abstract of the United States: 2012. www.census .gov/compendia/statab/cats/law_enforcement_courts_prisons/arrests.html.

———. "Quick Facts: New York County, New York (Manhattan Borough)." Accessed 2014. www.census.gov/quickfacts/table/HSD410214/36061.

———. "Quick Facts: Richmond County (Staten Island Borough)." Accessed 2014. www.census.gov/quickfacts/table/PST045215/36085.

US Council of Economic Advisors. "The Full Cost of the Opioid Crisis: $2.5 Trillion over Four Years." October 28, 2019. https://trumpwhitehouse .archives.gov/articles/full-cost-opioid-crisis-2-5-trillion-four-years/.

US Food and Drug Administration. "21st Century Cures Act." FDA, January 31, 2020. www.fda.gov/regulatory-information/selected-amendments-fdc-act /21st-century-cures-act.

US Office of National Drug Control Policy. "Office of National Drug Control Policy: President's Commission on Opioids." 2017. https://trumpwhitehouse .archives.gov/ondcp/the-administrations-approach/presidents-commission-opioids/.

US Senate Finance Committee. Findings from the Investigation of Opioid Manufacturers' Financial Relationships with Patient Advocacy Groups and Other Tax-Exempt Entities. Report, December 16, 2020. www.finance .senate.gov/imo/media/doc/2020-12-16%20Finance%20Committee%20 Bipartisan%20Opioids%20Report.pdf.

US Senate Homeland Security and Governmental Affairs Committee. Fueling an Epidemic: Exposing the Financial Ties between Opioid Manufacturers and Third Party Advocacy Groups. HSGAC Minority Staff Report, 2018. www .hsgac.senate.gov/imo/media/doc/REPORT-Fueling%20an%20Epidemic-Exposing%20the%20Financial%20Ties%20Between%20Opioid%20 Manufacturers%20and%20Third%20Party%20Advocacy%20Groups.pdf.

Van Zee, Art. "The Promotion and Marketing of Oxycontin: Commercial Triumph, Public Health Tragedy." American Journal of Public Health 99, no. 2 (2009): 221–27.

Vicknasingam, B., M. Mazlan, R. S. Schottenfeld, and M. C. Chawarski. "Injection of Buprenorphine and Buprenorphine/Naloxone Tablets in Malaysia." Drug and Alcohol Dependence 111, nos. 1–2 (2010): 44–49.

Virginia Attorney General's Office. "Herring Sues Sackler Family for Role in Opioid Crisis, Trying to Illegally Enrich Themselves and Shield Company Money." Press release, September 11, 2019. www.oag.state.va.us/consumer-protection/index.php/news/359-september-11-2019-herring-sues-sackler-family-for-role-in-opioid-crisis-trying-to-illegally-enrich-themselves-and-shield-company-money.

Vocci, Frank, Jane Acri, and Ahmed Elkashef. "Medication Development for Addictive Disorders: The State of the Science." *American Journal of Psychiatry* 162, no. 8 (2005): 1432–40.

Volkow, Nora. "Addiction Is a Disease of Free Will." National Institute on Drug Abuse, June 12, 2015. www.drugabuse.gov/about-nida/noras-blog /2015/06/addiction-disease-free-will.

———. "America's Addiction to Opioids: Heroin and Prescription Drug Abuse." National Institute on Drug Abuse Archives, May 14, 2014. https:// archives.drugabuse.gov/testimonies/2014/americas-addiction-to-opioids-heroin-prescription-drug-abuse.

Volkow, Nora D., and Francis S. Collins. "The Role of Science in Addressing the Opioid Crisis." *New England Journal of Medicine* 377, no. 4 (2017): 391–94. https://doi.org/10.1056/nejmsr1706626.

Volkow, Nora, and Ting-Kai Li. "The Neuroscience of Addiction." *Nature Neuroscience* 8, no. 11 (2005): 1429–30.

Wacquant, Loïc. *Punishing the Poor: The Neoliberal Government of Social Insecurity*. Durham, NC: Duke University Press, 2009.

Wailoo, Keith. *Pain: A Political History*. Baltimore: Johns Hopkins University Press, 2014.

Wailoo, Keith, A. Nelson, and C. Lee, eds. *Genetics and the Unsettled Past: The Collision of DNA, Race, and History*. New Brunswick, NJ: Rutgers University Press, 2012.

Wallace, Rodrick. "Urban Desertification, Public Health and Public Order: 'Planned Shrinkage,' Violent Death, Substance Abuse and AIDS in the Bronx." *Social Science and Medicine* 31, no. 7 (1990): 801–13.

Warren, Katie, and Rogers, Taylor Nicole. "The Family behind Purdue Pharma: Meet the Sacklers, Who Built Their $13 Billion Fortune Off the Controversial Opioid." *Business Insider*, March 23, 2020. www.businessinsider.com /who-are-the-sacklers-wealth-philanthropy-oxycontin-photos-2019-1.

Washington, Harriet A. *Medical Apartheid: The Dark History of Medical Experimentation on Black Americans from Colonial Times to the Present*. New York: Doubleday, 2006.

———. *Deadly Monopolies: The Shocking Corporate Takeover of Life Itself— and the Consequences for Your Health and Our Medical Future*. New York: Anchor Books, 2012.

Webster, Lynn R., and Rebecca M. Webster. "Predicting Aberrant Behaviors in Opioid-Treated Patients: Preliminary Validation of the Opioid Risk Tool." *Pain Medicine* 6, no. 6 (2005): 432–42.

Weicker, N.P., J. Owczarzak, G. Urquhart, J.N. Park, S. Rouhani, R. Ling, M. Morris, and S.G. Sherman. "Agency in the Fentanyl Era: Exploring the Utility of Fentanyl Test Strips in an Opaque Drug Market." *International Journal of Drug Policy* 1, no. 84 (2020): 102900.

Weissman, David E., and J. David Haddox. "Opioid Pseudoaddiction: An Iatrogenic Syndrome." *Pain* 36, no. 3 (1989): 363–66.

Wentzell, Emily. "Marketing Silence, Public Health Stigma and the Discourse of Risky Gay Viagra Use in the US." *Body and Society* 17, no. 4 (2011):

105–25. https://doi-org.manchester.idm.oclc.org/10.1177%2F1357034X 11410449.

White Trash Clan. "My World Is Blue." Music video, July 16, 2012. www .youtube.com/watch?v=1kOoyWVDNZc.

Whyte, Susan Reynolds, Sjaak Van der Geest, and Anita Hardon. *Social Lives of Medicines.* New York: Cambridge University Press, 2002.

Willard-Grace, Rachel, Margae Knox, Beatrice Huang, Hali Hammer, Coleen Kivlahan, and Kevin Grumbach. "Burnout and Health Care Workforce Turnover." *Annals of Family Medicine* 17, no. 1 (2019): 36–41.

Williams, Edward Huntington. "Negro Cocaine 'Fiends' Are a New Southern Menace." *New York Times,* February 8, 1914, SM12.

Wiltz, Teresa. "The Changing Face of Heroin Addiction." *Buffalo News,* February 8, 2015. https://buffalonews.com/news/national/the-changing-face-of-heroin-addiction/article_7de1e471-13cc-5ff2-baa9-837cf8068b95.html.

Wininger, Phillip. "Pharmaceutical Overpromotion Liability: The Legal Battle over Rural Prescription Drug Abuse." *Kentucky Law Journal* 93, no. 1 (2004): 269–94.

Wiseman, M., and S. Wamhoff. "The TANF/SSI Connection." *Social Security Bulletin* 66, no. 4 (2005–6): 21–23.

WKRC Local 12 News. "Fort Thomas Police Launch Heroin Highway Interdiction; Arrests Made." February 19, 2016. https://local12.com/news/local /fort-thomas-police-launch-heroin-highway-interdiction-arrest-made.

Woolf, Steven H., and Laudan Aron, eds. *US Health in International Perspective: Shorter Lives, Poorer Health.* Washington, DC: National Academies Press, 2013.

Wray, Matt. *Not Quite White: White Trash and the Boundaries of Whiteness.* Durham, NC: Duke University Press, 2006.

Wright, Ty. "A Small Indiana County Sends More People to Prison Than San Francisco and Durham, NC, Combined. Why?" *New York Times,* September 2, 2016. www.nytimes.com/2016/09/02/upshot/new-geography-of-prisons.html.

Yensi, Amy. "Bronx Continues to See Highest Number of Opioid Overdose Deaths." NY1 News, November 23, 2019. www.ny1.com/nyc/all-boroughs /news/2019/11/23/the-bronx-continues-to-see-highest-number-of-opioid-overdose-deaths.

Zatkulak, Karen. "News 13 Investigates: Heroin Highway." ABC 13 News, November 20, 2017. https://wlos.com/news/news-13-investigates/news-13-investigates-heroin-highway.

Zoorob, Michael J., and Jason L. Salemi. "Bowling Alone, Dying Together: The Role of Social Capital in Mitigating the Drug Overdose Epidemic in the United States." *Drug and Alcohol Dependence* 173 (2017): 1–9.

Index

Founded in 1893,
UNIVERSITY OF CALIFORNIA PRESS
publishes bold, progressive books and journals
on topics in the arts, humanities, social sciences,
and natural sciences—with a focus on social
justice issues—that inspire thought and action
among readers worldwide.

The UC PRESS FOUNDATION
raises funds to uphold the press's vital role
as an independent, nonprofit publisher, and
receives philanthropic support from a wide
range of individuals and institutions—and from
committed readers like you. To learn more, visit
ucpress.edu/supportus.